# Community Counseling

# *Related Titles of Interest*

**Group Design and Leadership: Strategies for Creating Successful Common Theme Groups**
Henry B. Andrews
ISBN: 0-205-16197-9

**Psychological Interventions and Cultural Diversity**
Joseph F. Aponte, Robin Young Rivers, and Julian Wohl
ISBN: 0-205-14668-6

**Fundamentals of Clinical Supervision**
Janine M. Bernard and Rodney K. Goodyear
ISBN: 0-205-12869-6

**Multicultural Assessment Perspectives for Professional Psychology**
Richard H. Dana
ISBN: 0-205-14092-0

**Counseling for Diversity: A Guide for School Counselors and Related Professionals**
Courtland C. Lee (Editor)
ISBN: 0-205-15321-6

**Small Groups: Process and Leadership, Second Edition**
Barbara W. Posthuma
ISBN: 0-205-16169-3

# Community Counseling
## Contemporary Theory and Practice

**DAVID B. HERSHENSON**
University of Maryland

**PAUL W. POWER**
University of Maryland

**MICHAEL WALDO**
New Mexico State University

**ALLYN AND BACON**

Boston • London • Toronto • Sydney • Tokyo • Singapore

**Library of Congress Cataloging-in-Publication Data**

Hershenson, David B. (date)
    Community counseling: contemporary theory and practice / David B. Hershenson, Paul W. Power, Michael Waldo.
       p.     cm.
    Includes bibliographical references and index.
    ISBN 0-205-17274-1
    1. Community psychology.   2. Mental health counseling.
3. Community mental health services.    I. Power, Paul W.    II. Waldo,
Michael (date)  .  III. Title.
RA790.55.H47   1996
362.2'2—dc20                       95-37945
                                           CIP

Printed in the United States of America

10  9  8  7  6  5  4  3  2  1     00  99  98  97  96

*To Marian, Barbara, and Susan*

# Contents

# *Preface*

Since 1987, when our book *Mental Health Counseling: Theory and Practice* was published, new directions and priorities have emerged to guide the delivery of counseling services. The emphasis on short-term interventions; consumer involvement in the development of counseling plans; the expanded range of populations needing counseling services, such as the elderly; the continued attention to community treatment of those with chronic mental illness problems; the suggested redefinition of physical and mental disability to underline the influence of the environment on one's limitations; the increased number of states that have passed counselor certification and licensure legislation; the revision of accreditation standards for professional preparation programs—all have provided an impetus to reexamine the philosophy and practice of community counseling. This book has evolved from this impetus, as well as from the realization that effective delivery of services to all clients represents a current challenge for counselors. New priorities and directions have reformulated the goals of counseling and have created new opportunities for counseling professionals.

As will be evident to those familiar with our 1987 book, this book draws on material presented in that volume. The obvious question is why we did not entitle this book as the second edition of the original title. Our reason is that because the field has shifted over the past eight years, the original title no longer fits the content we are presenting. Despite our pleas to

the contrary (Hershenson, 1992a, 1992b, 1993; Hershenson, Power, & Seligman, 1989; Hershenson & Strein, 1991), mental health counseling has sought to redefine itself as a clinical field. Thus, the professional specialty certification for mental health counselors is now titled Certified Clinical Mental Health Counselor, and the required specialty training emphasizes psychopathology, psychodiagnosis using DSM, psychotherapy, and psychopharmacology. This clinical focus represents, in our view, an attempt to identify mental health counseling with the medical model fields (for example, clinical psychology or clinical social work) that currently receive third-party payment for services (that is, from government or insurance companies), in the hopes of thereby also qualifying for such payments. This identification with the medical model is, however, in direct opposition to the view of mental health counseling presented in our 1987 book. It now appears that many of the fundamental concepts that we emphasized in that book are more consistent with counseling as generally practiced in community settings than with the redefined clinical mental health counseling specialty.

These basic premises include: (1) that healthy human development, not psychopathology, provides the scientific basis for counseling; (2) that the counseling process aims to assist the client to learn to identify, develop, and use personal and environmental resources to achieve stated goals; it does not aim to diagnose and treat psychopathology; (3) that the desired outcome of counseling is to have developed the ability to choose, to cope, and to grow; not to be cured. Thus, we were faced with the choice of either keeping the old title and adding significant quantities of material on psychopathology, clinical psychodiagnosis, and psychotherapy that are not compatible with our viewpoint or changing the title in order to maintain and build upon our original thrust. As there are dozens of books that adequately do the former and very few that do the latter (indeed, none with our particular viewpoint), there seemed to us to be only one reasonable choice.

There are currently more than 85 CACREP accredited community counseling programs in the country, but there is substantial lack of consensus among these programs in defining exactly what community counseling means. With this book, we are trying to provide a basis for discussion within the field toward arriving at agreement on our professional identity. We hope that educators, students, and practitioners of community counseling will involve themselves in this process. In our effort, we are guided by the Talmudic principle that knowing that one will never achieve full understanding does not release one from the obligation to pursue it.

We have, of course, changed much more than the title. We have revised our conceptual models, updated our research base, placed much greater emphasis on career and multicultural counseling, and added illustrative case studies. Each chapter is followed by a case example and/or discussion questions, and the increased use of case illustrations make this book particularly well suited for classroom use by students.

The book is comprised of two major parts: I. The Context of Community Counseling and II. Community Counseling Practices. Each part and the content of the respective chapters have been organized, developed, and written to address the topics called for by the national accreditation standards (CACREP) for community counselor education. Each chapter is also a current reflection of our thoughts based on our professional experience and interpretations of the work of others. The vast amount of literature existing in many topical areas of the book challenged us to select the material that was most relevant to the professional needs of community counselors.

While the intended primary audience for this book is counselors in training or who are employed in a variety of settings, such as career centers, colleges, government agencies, and community mental health facilities, the book can also be helpful to those who are well versed in counseling practice, but who wish to update their knowledge and discover how their skills may be expanded to different settings or population groups. The book is also written for those counselors who are in private practice, since many of the chapters provide information on dealing with such issues as the family, assessment, and client advocacy. Of benefit to all counselors is the realization that much of the book's content can be applied not only to client populations representing age groups from late adolescence to the elderly, but also to members of different minority groups.

The actualization of this book is a result not only of the authors, but of those who helped us in typing or reviewing the manuscript. In particular, we would like to acknowledge the assistance of Claire Ward, Pamela Sikowitz, and Barbara Power, who typed and reviewed many of the chapters. We would also like to acknowledge the editorial reviewing and the suggestions made by Dennis M. Beaufait, Western Michigan University; Terry Bordan, Long Island University; and John D. West, Kent State University.

## REFERENCES

Hershenson, D. B. (1992a). The operation was a success, but the patient died: Theoretical orthodoxy versus empirical validation. *Journal of Mental Health Counseling, 14*,180–186.

Hershenson, D. B. (1992b). A genuine copy of a fake Dior: Mental health counseling's pursuit of pathology. *Journal of Mental Health Counseling, 14*, 419–421.

Hershenson, D. B. (1993). Healthy development as the basis for mental health counseling theory. *Journal of Mental Health Counseling, 15*, 430–437.

Hershenson, D. B., & Power, P. W. (1987). *Mental health counseling: Theory and practice.* Elmsford, NY: Pergamon.

Hershenson, D. B., Power, P. W., & Seligman, L. (1989). Mental health counseling theory: Present status and future prospects. *Journal of Mental Health Counseling, 11*, 44–69.

Hershenson, D. B., & Strein, W. (1991). Toward a mentally healthy curriculum for mental health counselor education. *Journal of Mental Health Counseling, 13*, 247–252.

# About the Authors

**David B. Hershenson**, Ph.D., is currently a professor and director of the masters program in community/career counseling and the doctoral program in counselor education in the Department of Counseling and Personnel Services at the University of Maryland, College Park. Previously, he was chairperson of the Department of Psychology at Illinois Institute of Technology and dean of the College of Allied Health at Boston University. He has served on the editorial boards of the *Journal of Vocational Behavior*, the *Journal of Counseling Psychology*, the *Rehabilitation Counseling Bulletin*, and the *Australian Journal of Rehabilitation Counselling*.

He has authored more than 60 book chapters, journal articles, and monographs in the field of counseling as well as co-authoring *Mental Health Counseling: Theory and Practice* and co-editing *The Psychology of Vocational Development: Readings in Theory and Research*.

He has received the research award of the American Mental Health Counselors Association and the distinguished professional award of the American Rehabilitation Counseling Association. He is a National Certified Counselor, National Certified Career Counselor, and Certified Rehabilitation Counselor.

**Paul W. Power**, Sc.D., is a professor and director of the Rehabilitation Counseling Program, University of Maryland. Dr. Power is the author of numerous articles, books, and book chapters on the topic of family counseling and counseling those with physical or mental disabilities. His speeches and work-shops on both national and international levels have focused on counseling issues with different populations. Dr. Power serves as a member of the editorial advisory board of the *Journal of Rehabilitation Education*, and has also served on the advisory boards of the *Journal of Mental Health Counseling* and the *Journal of Allied Health and Behavioral Sciences*. Dr. Power is a certified counselor in the state of Maryland and a National Certified Counselor, as well as a Certified Rehabitation Counselor.

**Michael Waldo** is currently the head of the Counseling and Educational Psychology Department at New Mexico State University. He received a bachelor's degree in psychology from the University of California, Berkeley; a doctoral degree in counseling psychology from the University of Utah; and completed internships at the University of Utah's Counseling Center and the Veteran's Administration Medical Center in New Orleans. He has held faculty positions at the University of Maryland and Montana State University. He has authored 25 articles in professional journals, offered 57 presentations at professional conferences, served on the editorial boards of the *Journal of Mental Health Counseling* and the *Journal for Specialists in Group Work*, and is currently president of the Rocky Mountain Association for Counselor Education and Supervision. His research interests include evaluation of efforts to improve interpersonal relations, group counseling, and prevention/treatment of spouse abuse. He is licensed as a psychologist and as a professional counselor.

# PART I

# THE CONTEXT OF COMMUNITY COUNSELING

It is the main theme of this book that community counseling is provided by professionals trained to assist clients to work on developmental tasks or major life transitions, such as disability adjustment, career changes, divorce, or caregiving responsibilities. These words convey a challenge for counselors, for they imply that practitioners will have a unique body of knowledge and skills to assist clients who may present varied, complex problems. Community counselors carry out different professional activities with clients, and all of these tasks demand that counselors understand the historical development of counseling; the professional identity of community counseling; the different practice settings in which the community counselor may assist clients to achieve life adjustment goals; the many ethical, legal, and economic issues that affect professional practice; and the developmental foundations that underlie the work of the community counselor.

Chapter 1 provides a definition of counseling that has emerged from different viewpoints maintained by helping professionals on how to make a difference in the lives of many individuals. The definition emphasizes the promotion of healthy development, effective coping with problems of living, and the empowerment of clients to achieve healthy growth. The chapter concludes with a discussion of both the evolution of the mental health movement and counseling. The identification of these historical developments suggests themes that influence the current practice of community counseling.

Chapter 2 focuses on the specific history of community counseling and offers important information on the CACREP standards and specialty requirements. A definition of community counseling, which includes concepts that were explained in Chapter 1 relevant to an understanding of counseling in general, is also presented. This definition provides a framework for explaining a conceptual model for community counseling. Following the explanation of the model, which highlights a focus of intervention for counseling practice as well as a set of counseling skills, the topics of current professional issues, relevant literature, and education and training are discussed.

In Chapter 3 the many, varied practice settings for the community counselor are identified and explained. Each public or independent setting may offer different counseling opportunities for the complex variety of problems that are presented today to counselors. A description of the many sites for community counseling practice pinpoints the reality that different counseling skills are needed for special populations, such as those with physical or mental disabilities or those representing historically underserved minority groups.

Chapter 4 is written from the premise that certain criteria need to be met in order for community counselors to attain the status of being members of a profession. These criteria include following an explicit code of ethics and understanding the legal issues that affect counseling practice. The most up-to-date code of counseling ethics is explained, and case examples are provided to illustrate selected ethical standards.

Chapter 5 presents two important themes that contribute to the knowledge base for community counselors, namely, developmental theories and taxonomic approaches to problems of living. Several developmental perspectives are explained, namely, Erikson's stages, Havighurst's developmental tasks, Maslow's need hierarchy, and Piaget's theory of cognitive development. Following this overview of models of human development, systems for categorizing the problems of living are discussed. Counseling disciplines have evolved a number of ways of conceptualizing these problems. In this chapter information about the DSM-IV classification system is also presented, since for many counseling practitioners this system provides a useful framework for evaluating a client's problems. The reader will discover, moreover, after understanding the material in this chapter, that a counselor's views of the nature of development and problems of living are inevitably interrelated. The way in which one conceptualizes individual development determines how one conceptualizes problems of living.

# 1

# THE EVOLUTION OF COUNSELING

The subject of this book is community counseling, an area of specialization within the profession of counseling. While there has been a great deal of debate about the nature and organizational structure of community counseling, which we shall review in Chapter 2, there is almost no debate about the fact that community counseling is an aspect of professional counseling. Therefore, in order to understand any view of community counseling one may choose, one must first understand counseling. Thus, the task of this chapter is to define counseling and to provide some insight into how it arose and developed as a profession.

## DEFINING COUNSELING

Tyler (1969) observed that while most people agree that counseling is beneficial and should be made more widely available, there is considerably less agreement on what they mean by counseling. She attributed this lack of a generally agreed-upon meaning to the fact that the word *counseling* was in common usage before it was adopted by the profession as its designation. The choice of the term *counseling* was an unfortunate decision for the profession on two scores: first, as Tyler noted,

because it carried multiple prior meanings; and second, in our view, because it identified the entire profession by a single activity from among a broad repertoire of activities regularly practiced by members of the profession (e.g., appraisal, counseling, educating, coordinating services, programming, consulting, advocacy), and moreover, an activity that is not unique to the profession but is also performed by practitioners of a wide range of other professions, such as clergy, lawyers, and physicians.

Tyler went on to point out that lack of agreement on the definition of counseling was not limited to those outside the profession.

*Among professional counselors two main interpretations of the essential function of counseling can be distinguished, growing out of the two main lines of historical development that have coalesced in the counseling profession. According to the first of these kinds of definition, the central purpose of counseling is to facilitate wise choices and decisions; according to the second, its central purpose is to promote adjustment or mental health. It is recognized that the working counselor finds it*

3

*necessary to concern himself with both of these objectives, but which he considers to be the focal one makes some difference in the way he handles his responsibilities.* (Tyler, 1969, p. 10)

Another aspect of the definition of counseling on which there are divergent views within the field is whether counseling is synonymous with psychotherapy. Throughout the history of counseling, many authors have treated the two terms as a single phrase, "counseling and psychotherapy" (e.g., Corey, 1991; Ivey & Simek-Downing, 1980; Rogers, 1942). We, however, place ourselves among those who distinguish between the two processes (for example, Gladding, 1992; Hansen, Stevic, & Warner, 1986; Pietrofesa, Hoffman, & Splete, 1984). In our view, psychotherapy implies adherence to a medical model, which views the person seeking help (the patient) as ill and the goal of intervention as curing that illness. Counseling, while it can have therapeutic effects, focuses instead on promoting healthy development by assisting the person seeking help (the client) to learn to cope effectively with problems of living. Thus, the goal of psychotherapy is the elimination of psychopathology, whereas the goal of counseling is to empower the client to achieve healthy growth. The psychotherapist takes the roles of healer and of treatment provider, that is, an expert who works on a patient to remove or to cure the pathology that is blocking the patient's reaching his or her goal. The counselor takes the roles of cultivator and of coach, that is, a partner who works with a client to help that client develop and use the skills and conditions needed to reach his or her goal (Hershenson, 1993; Pietrofesa et al., 1984). It may, incidentally, be noted that a similar distinction can be drawn between counseling and guidance, in which guidance implies an expert who directs (guides) the person seeking help toward a predetermined goal.

Given these complexities and the resulting array of differing definitions of counseling (and the equally frequent failure to provide a definition) in textbooks in the field, we may somewhat arbitrarily take as our point of departure the definition approved by the Maryland legislature in its counselor certification law. This definition focuses on the activities performed in counseling.

*"Counseling" means assisting an individual, family, or group through the client-counselor relationship:*

1. *To develop understanding of intrapersonal and interpersonal problems;*
2. *To define goals;*
3. *To make decisions;*
4. *To plan a course of action reflecting the needs, interests, and abilities of the individual, family, or group; and*
5. *To use informational and community resources, as these procedures are related to personal, social, emotional, educational, and vocational development and adjustment.* [Maryland Annotated Code, Health Occupations, Sec. 15.5–101(f)]

To this definition, we would add two additional steps [(6) To implement their plan, and (7) To evaluate the effectiveness of their action] and three additional sets of defining attributes, one philosophical, one empirical, and one educational. Philosophically, counseling may be identified by its adherence to the following principles (the evolution of which will be discussed later in this chapter) in carrying out the tasks specified in the preceding definition:

**1.** A belief that behavior is a function of the interaction between an individual and that individual's environment at a particular point in time (that is, within the individual's personal development and the conditions prevailing in the environment). As Rounds and Tracey (1990) have noted, this interaction is one of dynamic reciprocity, that is, an ongoing process in which individuals shape the environment and the environment influences individuals. Hence, behavior must be viewed in the context in which it occurs. Moreover, depending on the problem, resolution of it may be attained by changing the person, changing the environment, or changing their interaction.

**2.** A belief that human development naturally tends toward healthy growth, and consequently the study of normal human development provides the basis for counseling intervention.

**3.** A belief that the aim of intervention is to assist a client to learn: (a) to select a feasible goal, and (b) to identify, develop, and use personal and environmental resources to achieve that goal. Thus, counseling is essentially an educational process.

**4.** A belief that the process of intervention should utilize only techniques and methods that have been empirically demonstrated to be effective and that the counselor should be able to account for each intervention used on this basis.

**5.** A belief that the outcome of counseling is to be evaluated by how well the client has learned to assess situations realistically, to make feasible choices, to mobilize personal and environmental resources to implement those choices, to cope with problems, and to grow from life experiences.

Additionally, Remley (1992, August) added that counseling can be identified by:

**6.** A focus on prevention and early intervention as ways of forestalling more serious problems that would develop if not attended to early on;

**7.** A focus on the active promotion of wellness and healthy lifestyles; and

**8.** A focus on empowering clients to participate in the counseling process in an active and informed manner and to make their own decisions.

Turning from the philosophical to the empirical, Loesch and Vaac (1993) recently conducted a work behavior analysis of professional counselors under the auspices of the professional certifying agency in the field, the National Board for Certified Counselors. This consisted of surveying a 10 percent random sample of National Certified Counselors (1500 surveys sent out, of which 722 usable responses were returned) on the frequency with which they performed and the importance they attributed to each of 151 activities that had been identified as counselor work behaviors through a search of the literature and through self-reports by counselors. Factor analysis of both the frequency and the importance ratings yielded essentially the same five factors: (1) fundamental counseling practices (such items as counsel clients concerning personal change, establish counseling goals); (2) counseling for career development (such items as use test results for client decision making, use occupational information in counseling); (3) counseling groups (such items as identify harmful group-member behaviors, evaluate progress toward group goals); (4) counseling families (such items as counsel concerning family member interaction, counsel concerning divorce); and (5) professional practice (such items as provide consultation services for human resource needs evaluation, supervise counselor trainees, engage in counseling process research). While some differences in frequency and in importance were found in clusters (2) and (5) between counselors working in academic/educational settings and counselors working in community settings, the fact that stable, consistent clusters could be identified across respondents from the whole range of the profession indicates that counseling is a realm of professional activity that is well defined and consensually perceived by its practitioners. There are certain evident risks in defining a profession by the common agreement of some of its practitioners (that is, by what it is rather than by what it should be and by the perception of those within it rather than by the perception of the general public), but this study provides at least some evidence that counseling has attained structure, coherence, and recognized meaning.

Finally, a counselor is defined educationally by the professional certifying and program accrediting bodies in counseling as having earned a master's (minimum of 48 semester hours credit) or doctoral degree in counseling from an accredited university, including coursework in the following areas along with supervised practicum and internship experience:

1. *human growth and development*
2. *social and cultural foundations of counseling*
3. *theory and methods of counseling and consultation*
4. *group procedures*
5. *assessment and appraisal*
6. *career and lifestyle development*
7. *professional orientation and ethics*
8. *research and evaluation* (Council for Accreditation of Counseling and Related Educational Programs [CACREP] 1994, January; National Board for Certified Counselors [NBCC], 1994)

Putting all these considerations together, we may arrive at the following definition: Counseling is a proactive, holistically oriented process for helping persons learn to cope with problems of living and for promoting healthy development. It is an interpersonal process involving a professional with the requisite graduate education and experience in counseling (the counselor), using scientifi-

cally validated methods, working with an individual, family, group, organization, or segment of a community that is seeking assistance (the client). This process involves empowering the client to decide on feasible goals and to identify, develop, and use personal and environmental resources to attain these goals. Depending on the nature of the client's situation, the process may be: (a) facilitative (that is, assisting healthy growth to occur in an unimpeded manner), (b) preventive (that is, preventing a difficulty from arising), (c) remedial (that is, redirecting a maladaptive pattern of development to a healthy course), (d) rehabilitative (that is, assisting the client to compensate for existing limitations in ability to cope by promoting the use of other strengths that the client possesses), and/or (e) enhancing (that is, improving the client's quality of life above its present level).

Having arrived at a working definition of counseling, we shall examine how the field evolved.

## THE EVOLUTION OF THE MENTAL HEALTH MOVEMENT

In considering the historical evolution of counseling, we shall apply a counseling principle mentioned earlier, that behavior must be viewed in context. Hence, to understand the evolution of counseling, we must first understand the evolution of the broader mental health movement within which counseling arose. This will provide the context necessary for understanding the emergence of counseling as a field of study and as a profession.

The history of mental health has been closely linked with changing client needs, cyclic government interest and funding, and the social concerns in a given historical period. As social conditions change, so do our views about mental health care. Zilboorg (1941) suggested that the development of mental health services consists of a series of revolutions. The first revolution took place in the period immediately following the French Revolution, around 1800. In this period, treatment came to replace confinement and punishment as the basis for dealing with the mentally disturbed. "The second revolution centered on the work of Sigmund Freud and occurred in the culture emerging from the Victorian era" (Hollander, 1980, p. 561), that is, a century later. There is no general agreement on the time and place of the third revolution, though Hollander (1980) believed that a change has been taking place in the mental health field since 1950. This change is characterized by a rejection of professional domination in the mental health sphere, accompanied by a more equal relationship between professional and consumer.

We will first present a brief overview of the history of the mental health movement in premodern times (prior to the late nineteenth century), followed by a more detailed review of the period since 1875.

## Premodern History

From the days of ancient Greece and Rome through the Middle Ages, the prevalent conception of mental illness in Western culture was that it represented divine or demonic punishment for transgressions. Thus, treatment generally consisted of brutal measures such as beating, chaining, torture, or ostracism, in order either to purge or to punish sins. At the same time, the Greek physician Hippocrates (ca. 460–370 B.C.) proposed that mental illness was caused by natural medical causes and should be treated with benevolence. This approach was followed in a few sanatoria in the classical Greek and Roman period, but was available only to the wealthy. It was not until the Renaissance (sixteenth century) that the view represented by Hippocrates reemerged; nonetheless, throughout the next several centuries, treatment generally remained more punitive than therapeutic. In both Europe and

America in the 1700s and early 1800s, the treatment approach was again largely determined by socioeconomic status. Philippe Pinel (1745–1826) in France, William Tuke (1732–1822) in England, and Benjamin Rush (1745–1813) in America pioneered the routine practice of humane treatment for persons with mental illness. This approach was popularized during the mid-nineteenth century by Hack Tuke (1827–1895), the great-grandson of William Tuke, in England and by Dorothea Dix (1802–1887) in America. While Pinel, Rush, and Hack Tuke were physicians, William Tuke and Dorothea Dix were not members of that profession but acted largely out of their liberal religious beliefs (McKown, 1961; Rubin & Roessler, 1987).

Because the current practice of mental health care is the product of so many historical trends, varied federal and state laws and policies, and diverse social problems, the authors believe that it would be helpful to divide the modern history of mental health care into five periods: 1875–1940: The Beginnings; 1941–1950: The Awakening Period; 1951–1965: Growth Period; 1966–1980: Consolidation and Reassessment; and 1981 on: Current and Emerging Issues.

## 1875–1940: The Beginnings

The modern approach to mental health problems originated in the late nineteenth and early twentieth centuries. Prior to this time, there was the widespread belief that heredity had irrevocably stamped each individual. It was assumed that there was little to be gained in attempting to improve those who were mentally disturbed. The professions of social work, clinical psychology, and psychiatry working in the community were almost unknown until the 1900s (Musto, 1975). Rarely were new approaches developed to deal with emotional disability or to explore the functional or social causes of abnormal behavior.

At the turn of the twentieth century, the social milieu came to be viewed as an important factor in maladjustment (Musto, 1975). Effective treatment evolved, then, from a fundamental change in the environment. Beginning efforts were made to change "disorders" in society, such as slums. Also, as the person with a mental problem was viewed holistically, it became recognized that to understand the individual, one must be familiar with the whole social context in which the person lives. Paradoxically, however, during this period the practice of therapy was mainly aimed at the individual and directed to individual adjustment.

Such a holistic belief generated new professions, such as social psychologists and psychiatric social workers (Ewalt, 1975; Musto, 1975). Outpatient clinics were developed that, in turn, promoted the rise of the treatment team in mental health. Each member of the team would utilize a distinct professional perspective to meet the needs of the individual. Resources were to be quickly available through this team approach. Moreover, with the development of this community orientation and outpatient resources, there was a focus on the prevention and treatment of juvenile delinquency. In the late 1930s, child guidance clinics and the child guidance movement emerged. The movement stressed the early detection of emotional disorders, and treatment was directed both to the child and to the immediate environment.

Even though the role of the environment was emphasized in mental health care, psychoanalysis entered the treatment scene in the 1900s. It claimed its usefulness as an approach to change individual personalities (Musto, 1975; Saccuzzo, 1977). Leading Americans who followed the practice of psychoanalysis were A. A. Brill, Ernest Jones, Adolph Meyer, and Harry Stack Sullivan. Sullivan was among those who sought to integrate psychoanalytic theory with the social sciences; and Meyer was an early proponent of the need to study the person in his or her environmental setting, a principle he termed "psychobiology" (McKown, 1961).

It was during this period that popular concern with the issue of mental health greatly expanded. In 1908, Clifford W. Beers (1876–1943), a Yale graduate who had been institutionalized for serious mental illness, published *A Mind That Found Itself,* an autobiographical account of his illness and treatment. This book became the most widely read autobiography of its time and stimulated the formation, in 1909, of the National Committee for Mental Hygiene, of which Beers served as executive secretary for life and which included the psychiatrist Adolph Meyer and the psychologist William James among the charter members. In 1917, the committee initiated the journal *Mental Hygiene.* The work of the committee was expanded internationally, with the first International Congress on Mental Hygiene held in Washington, D.C., in 1930 and the second in Paris in 1937 (McKown, 1961).

Despite the surge of popular concern with mental health and the new directions of treatment during this beginning period, massive sums of federal monies were not available. Mental health leadership resided in the states and in voluntary agencies and private foundations, such as Russell Sage, Carnegie, and Rockefeller. They were the funding resources for many years. The small federal role began to change as the Depression of the 1930s prompted the initiation and then support by government of social welfare programs. Though direct federal aid to health services (including mental services) was limited, federal support for research on mental health was being increased (Ewalt, 1975).

Also during this period self-help groups began to be established. Initially, in the period of 1880–1920, these groups were established to assist immigrants to adjust to American culture. In 1935, Alcoholics Anonymous was established, applying the self-help approach to the treatment of alcohol addiction. Two years later, in 1937, Recovery, Incorporated was founded as a self-help group for persons recovering from mental illness (Lewis & Lewis, 1989).

## 1941–1950: The Awakening Period

The Second World War brought a new awakening to the mental health field. Many people believe that mental health policy as we know it today is largely a post–World War II development. The rejection of over a million men during World War II for psychiatric reasons and the development of psychiatric evaluation and mental hygiene clinics at recruitment and training centers alerted America to the extent and seriousness of mental health problems. Also, by utilizing intensive treatment techniques, mental health professionals were able to return to active duty a large number of military personnel who suffered sudden emotional breakdowns. Both the techniques and recovery rates impressed many clinicians who were more traditional in their mental health treatment approaches. During this war, legislation was developed to establish the National Institute of Mental Health.

From these war experiences, both government and informed laypersons became aware of the necessity to learn more about the causes of mental health problems and the means of preventing them. In 1946, the National Mental Health Act was adopted by the federal government. This legislation authorized funds for research, demonstration, training, and assistance to states in the use of the most effective methods of prevention, diagnosis, and treatment of mental health disorders. In the late 1940s, state budgets began to show larger financial commitments for mental health concerns than at any time in the past; but considering the mental health needs, these budgets were still quite low.

Another effect of mental health practices during World War II was the stimulus the war provided to devise new treatment techniques that were feasible in dealing with relatively large groups of patients (Mechanic, 1980). Group techniques were seriously studied. Drug therapies began to be developed. Unfortunately, however, these advances had very little impact on practices in mental hospitals. Most states still lacked the facilities, personnel, and financial resources to implement the many new ideas that had been developed in the mental health field (Mechanic, 1980).

## 1951–1965: Growth Period

This was a time of optimism, a period that saw an increase in expenditures for training mental health professionals, mental health services, the construction and staffing of new community mental health centers, and a broad increase in the boundaries of mental health concepts. It was the beginning of a postwar generation that became the catalyst for an extraordinary period both of ferment and of searching for new ways to understand a broad range of issues (Hollander, 1980). In the early 1950s, continued research and developing theories concerning the possible link between the environment and individual mental health prompted the renewed or enhanced development of outpatient clinics that could postpone or prevent hospitalization. Early detection of emotional problems was again emphasized by mental health practitioners. The concept of crisis intervention was introduced, which implied that "in emotional crisis an individual's behavior patterns were much more easily directed to new and ideally healthier forms than in periods of better adjustment" (Musto, 1975, p. 8). Also, new estimates of the number of citizens needing evaluation and treatment were made known, stimulating a perceived need for many more mental health workers to work at all levels in each community.

Many of these advances were the result of a report that was a product of the Joint Commission on Mental Illness and Health. In the late

1950s, the Mental Health Study Act authorized an appropriation to the Joint Commission to study and make recommendations concerning various aspects of mental health policy. On December 31, 1960, the commission submitted its final report to Congress, "Action for Mental Health" (Bloom, 1977; Mechanic, 1980). Though basically an ideological document, it strongly emphasized the necessity of an increased program of services and of more funds for basic, long-term mental health research. It also recommended that expenditures in the mental health field be doubled in the next five years and tripled in ten years. The report argued for new and better recruitment and training programs for mental health workers, and it suggested the expansion of treatment programs for acutely ill patients in all facilities, including community mental health clinics, general hospitals, and mental hospitals (Mechanic, 1980).

This report generated a vigorous battle at the federal level between those mental health workers who wanted to develop new approaches for patient care in the community and those workers who believed, within the traditional medical model, that more federal assistance should be invested in improving the quality of mental hospitals. After all the arguments, pro and con, the final decision was to give the greatest impetus to community mental health centers (Mechanic, 1980).

Also coming out of the Joint Commission was a new emphasis on positive mental health, rather than focusing solely on mental illness. Thus, as part of the work of the commission, Jahoda (1958) published *Current Concepts of Positive Mental Health,* which specified positive criteria, rather than the mere absence of disease, as the basis for defining mental health (see Chapter 5).

The National Institute of Mental Health budget also expanded during the late 1950s, and the Kennedy administration gave special attention to mental retardation and dramatically increased support for the delivery of

mental health services. Such funding was facilitated by the Community Mental Health Centers Act of 1963, which also encouraged a national network of mental health centers (Musto, 1975; Ewalt, 1975). The Community Mental Health Centers (CMHCs) Act of 1963 (Title II, Public Law 88-164) authorized funds for federal assistance to states in the construction of community mental health centers, which were defined in the act as "providing services for the prevention or diagnosis of mental illness, or the care and treatment of mentally ill patients, or rehabilitation of such persons…residing in a particular community or communities in or near where the facility is situated" (Title IV, Sec. 401 [c], Public Law 88–164). The regulations accompanying Title II specified that to qualify for funds, states had to develop a state plan for comprehensive mental health services that included:

1. *Inpatient services;*
2. *Outpatient services;*
3. *Partial hospitalization services, such as day care, night care, weekend care;*
4. *Emergency services 24 hours per day must be available within at least one of the first three services listed above;*
5. *Consultation and education services available to community agencies and professional personnel;*
6. *Diagnostic services;*
7. *Rehabilitative services, including vocational and educational programs;*
8. *Pre- and after-care services in the community, including foster home placement, home visiting, and halfway houses;*
9. *Training; and*
10. *Research and evaluation.* (Sec. 54.203)

The federal budget, which provided for growth and development of new approaches and additional manpower in mental health, resulted not only from the commission's report, but also because abundant funds were available in the American economy for meeting domestic needs. Also, in part because of an awareness heightened by his family history, President Kennedy was strongly committed to programs in mental health and mental retardation. Further, the development and widespread use of psychiatric drugs changed the climate of mental health care as well as administrative attitudes (Mechanic, 1980).

As the number of mental health professionals grew, these practitioners actively sought greater recognition and pressed for more and better training in clinical practice (Caddy, 1981). The 1965 Chicago Conference on the Professional Preparation of Clinical Psychologists brought the issues of professional training in psychology into greater prominence, and various models of doctoral training were discussed. The conference finally reaffirmed the scientist-professional educational approach that utilizes the traditional academic-university setting for training.

## 1966–1980: Consolidation and Reassessment

During the early years of this period, the number of both care settings and mental health care specialists continued to increase. For example, there was considerable expansion in the numbers of psychologists, psychiatric social workers, psychiatric nurses, counselors, and individuals in other fields (such as the ministry) who worked part- or full-time in mental health service delivery. Between 1955 and 1977, moreover, out-patient care episodes rose 282 percent (Beigel & Sharfstein, 1984).

During this period, the federal government continued to support and to expand the scope of community mental health centers by passing laws that: (a) authorized funding of start-up costs for staffing these centers (Public Law 889-105, 1965); (b) continued support for the earlier acts (Public Law 90-31, 1967); (c)

specified the addition of preventive and treatment services for alcoholism and narcotics addiction (Public Law 90-574, 1968); (d) specified that child mental health services be provided (Public Law 91-211, 1970); (e) expanded the category of narcotics addiction to include all drug abuse or dependency problems (Public Law 91-513, 1970); and (f) extended the earlier acts (Public Laws 93-45, 1973 and 94-63, 1975).

The shift away from public mental hospitals accelerated, with more acute psychiatric illness being treated in general hospitals and outpatient clinics. Behavioral techniques for treating many types of mental health problems were commonly adopted, and treatment of disorders became more focused and diversified (Mechanic, 1980). The institutional setting was no longer depended upon as a vehicle for change, and many patients in need were recognized and treated more quickly in the community. An understanding of new psychoactive drugs and their adverse effects increased. Private and nonprofit insurance companies providing medical coverage substantially increased outpatient coverage for mental health services.

Hollander (1980) believed that the third revolution in the history of mental health care, mentioned earlier in this account, began taking place from the early 1960s. This revolution has resulted in some of the most important contemporary trends in mental health. Community mental health centers, for example, began to move in the direction of a real sharing of power between the consumer and the agency. Implications of this involvement were that consumers or citizens could push for services that they identified as relevant to their needs. No longer were they passive recipients of services, but consumers now had a responsible share in the decision-making process of a particular agency. Another implication of this "third revolution" was the therapeutic community concept. It implies that both patients and paraprofessionals are genuine partners in the helping process. Consequently, more attention was given to increasing social interaction, group involvement, informal patient status and living arrangements, and creating expectations for "normal" responsible living (Sprafkin, 1977).

Contributing to the growth of mental health care systems during this period were the so-called "boom areas." These are areas of rapidly shifting population, with communities experiencing above-average growth. This is particularly true in the southwestern rim of the United States (Moffic, Adams, Rosenburg, Blattstein, & Chacko, 1983). What occurred and continues to occur is an increase in certain populations at particular risk for mental problems. Minority groups, migrants and refugees, people in communities with inadequate health services or who are subject to rapid urbanization, and people at sensitive periods in the life cycle all are included as "at risk" for mental problems. Boom areas involve crowding, people who have been uprooted and who lack their accustomed extended family and communal support systems, and people who suffer from depression and substance abuse. Such problems generate an urgent need for mental health services.

The Vietnam War and the years immediately following brought a curtailment of the funds for mental health programs. During the Nixon years, the administration phased out or allowed only minimal funds for such existing programs as mental health centers, research, training, and professional manpower development. Massive deinstitutionalization revealed the poor planning for release of patients into the community and the inadequacy of continuing supervision and treatment (Mechanic, 1980). Deinstitutionalization began in the 1950s in response to several converging factors. The cost of keeping individuals in institutions began to exceed acceptable levels. At the same time, legal decisions that individuals must be maintained and treated in the "least restrictive environment" required that individuals with emotional problems remain in or return to society. Finally, advances in medication made noninstitutional care not only possible, but permissible.

In the early 1970s, moreover, Congress became increasingly concerned about alcoholism and drug abuse. With the limitation of funds, traditional mental health monies were used to develop new national efforts in these areas. The Alcohol, Drug Abuse, and Mental Health Administration was formed by merger to oversee a variety of service programs, research efforts, and professional training programs.

During this consolidation period, previously little-known treatment methods such as Gestalt, transactional analysis, and reality therapies began to grow at a rapid pace. Mental health workers were also taking a broader view of their helping role in the context of social responsibility. There was a willingness to train new professionals and to extend service to low-income persons. There appeared to be a renewed movement away from the one-to-one model of treatment to exploring and implementing again varied methods of group treatment of mental problems. Family techniques also grew.

In reviewing this period, it becomes apparent that the issues of core concern were deinstitutionalization, the development of community service programs, the prevention and treatment of alcohol and drug problems, and how to survive with reduced funding. Many of these issues received a new, more encouraging focus when President Carter, in large part because of his wife's interest in mental health, revived presidential support for mental health services. In February 1977, soon after his inauguration, President Carter created the President's Commission on Mental Health to determine the current and projected needs for service and research and to suggest the role of the federal government and other agencies in meeting those needs. The commission's report was completed in 1978, the same year that PL 95-622 was signed, extending support for community mental health centers until September 1980. The commission looked at such issues as the organization of community services, community supports, financing, personnel, legal rights, research, prevention, and public understanding. The report recommended a greater investment in mental health services. Though mental health problems were one of the largest in terms of the number of persons involved (Mechanic, 1980; "Mental Disorders," 1984), mental health services received only 12 percent of general health expenditures. The report cited the need to develop community-based services; to make them financially, geographically, and socially accessible; and to make them flexible so as to serve the needs of varying social and racial groups. Suggestions made in the commission's report for a network of coordinated community-oriented services led to the immediate development of a number of new programs, including the community support programs initiated and supported by the National Institute of Mental Health (Turner & TenHoor, 1978). In October 1980, PL 96-398 was signed into law by President Carter. This act authorized continued support for community mental health services created under earlier laws and added a number of provisions suggested by the presidential commission report of 1978. A month later, however, President Carter was defeated for reelection by Ronald Reagan, who instead of implementing this act, instituted a program of block grants to the states.

## 1981–Present: Current and Emerging Issues

During the 1980s, inflation in the American economy was a prime concern, and health care costs increased much more rapidly than the economy as a whole. Government expenditures on health care were high and even uncontrollable, in part due to the structure of

the Medicare and Medicaid programs (Mechanic, 1980). Policymakers were reluctant to make large new investments in health care initiatives. A central piece of legislation that has affected the continued growth of the mental health services was the Omnibus Budget Reconciliation Act of 1981, known as the block grant legislation. The central features of this legislation were the amalgamation of the funds for alcohol, drug abuse, and mental health into a single block grant, and the transfer of authority for planning, priority-setting, and administration, distribution, and monitoring of the block grant funds from the federal government to the states (Okin, 1984). Under this policy, there was less money in toto and even less assurance that the available money would be used for mental health. With the reduction in other federal programs on which the mentally disabled depend, many community mental health centers have had to decrease their overall level of services and staffing when, at the same time, they are experiencing increased demands for services.

Thus, categorical federal funding for mental health care has been decreased, and progress with regard to reimbursement practices has been limited (Beigel & Sharfstein, 1984). Despite intensive efforts, the mental health professions have been unsuccessful in getting Congress to expand mental health benefits under either Medicare or Medicaid (Beigel & Sharfstein, 1984). With fewer opportunities for employment in the public sector as a result of reduced categorical funding, more mental health professionals have entered private practice and/or become involved with emerging health care settings, such as health maintenance organizations. Currently, the issue of national health insurance and the place of mental health services within it are principal concerns of all the mental health professions.

There are other related legislative, social, and economic trends that have received sharper identification during this period. One trend is related to the broadened consumer movement and its concomitant reliance on self-help and distrust of professional help. This movement spawned self-help groups emphasizing reliance on personal resources and, accordingly, rejecting the unequal doctor-patient relationship in every area of health care (Gottlieb, 1979).

Avoidance of professionals has led to a demystification of the helping process. No longer is what occurs in therapy attributable to inscrutable unconscious or preconscious forces. No longer are unobservable, subjective phenomena acceptable benchmarks for progress in therapy. The counseling process must rely on skills that are observable, clearly understood, empirically based, and amenable to evaluation (Anderson, 1975).

As the helping process has become demystified, the stigma attached to seeking help has been reduced. As client and counselor are seen as active, equal partners in the change process, a greater acceptance of services has occurred. As services become specific and time-limited, clients can obtain help at savings of both time and money. Short-term treatment is receiving a renewed emphasis, because this form of care can be more economical and provides the opportunity for many more people to receive mental health services. This is related to ethical concerns about the relative effectiveness of long-term treatment and to the emerging associated issues of professional and social accountability.

Another trend is the wider range of professionals to provide mental health services. As treatment moved into the community and as individuals became more sophisticated in their understanding of how change occurs, mental health needs were responded to by an increased number of established disciplines. The counseling profession, for example, had traditionally involved some specialties that focused on vocational-educational functioning and others that focused on personal-social functioning. Over the past decade, all areas within the counseling profession have to come to recognize the interrelatedness of these aspects of life. Thus, it has become recognized that social and emotional problems affect one's performance at school or work (absenteeism, inattention to tasks, etc.) and that, conversely, problems at school or work affect one's social and emotional functioning in other arenas, such as family life. Thus, the executive director of the American Counseling Association declared that all counselors are mental health counselors (Remley, 1993, November).

A final trend is a greater awareness of the role of prevention in promoting positive mental health. This includes promoting positive lifestyles, restructuring the environment to reduce stress, and building personal competencies in such areas as decision making, problem solving, and coping with transient crises. This reflects a broadening of the concept of mental health from its original connotation of getting rid of psychopathology to include assisting persons with normal life transitions that present problems of living, and finally, to include proactively promoting holistic health and wellness (Herr & Cramer, 1987). This broadened conception of mental health has contributed to the more active entry of counseling into the mental health field, since from its earliest formulations counseling saw its role as helping people to cope with problems of living and promoting healthy development.

The current field of mental health is the result of many and varied emerging issues and social trends in the history of mental health care. Advances in treatment, the cyclical nature of government funding, and changing societal conditions have contributed to the directions in which the field has evolved. It is a field that will continue to show diversity as social and government priorities and the needs of the population change, and as newer treatment approaches are developed.

# THE EVOLUTION OF COUNSELING

As with the history of mental health, some writers have traced the origins of counseling to the ancient Greeks, specifically the philosopher Plato (ca. 427–347 B.C.) because of his speculations on individual development and on how behavior could be influenced (Brown & Srebalus, 1988; Gibson & Mitchell, 1990). Actually, however, the process of advising others on how to cope with problems of living probably goes back at least to the dawn of language, and may even have provided a stimulus for the development of language in the first place. Fortunately, it is easier, and more relevant for our present purposes, to establish when this sort of human activity became the basis for a profession.

Jaques and Hershenson (1970) suggested that two basic conditions were necessary for the eventual emergence of helping professions: (1) the division of labor so that differentiated work roles could be identified, and (2) sufficient affluence so that not every member of the group had to engage full-time in providing food and shelter for survival, but some members could be supported to perform other functions. Given these preconditions, formal counseling probably began as a priestly or shamanistic function, reflecting the ancient and medieval view that problems were caused by divine or demonic powers, as was discussed in the prior section. It was not until after the Enlightenment at the end of the eighteenth century and the Industrial Revolution at the beginning of the nineteenth century that empirical science replaced faith as the dominant cultural value in Western society (Hershenson, 1983). In the mid-nineteenth century, the social sciences emerged, and with them, the popular preference for a counseling process that was based on empirical evidence rather than on transmitted dogma. The shift, however, was an evolutionary process, rather than a revolutionary one. Thus, the pioneers in developing an empirically based counseling process, such as Freud and Jung, generally mixed a liberal dose of revealed wisdom into their formulations (for example, Bakan, 1958; or the Jungean idea of collective unconscious).

It was not until the beginning of the twentieth century that a solid foundation appeared on which a scientific profession of counseling could be built. It is more than coincidental that within a single decade three separate events occurred in different places in the United States that led to the establishment of the counseling profession. In 1898, at Central High School in Detroit, Jesse B. Davis became the first person appointed as a school counselor, thus establishing the educational aspect of counseling. In 1908, Frank Parsons opened the Vocation Bureau of Boston, the first career counseling agency, thus establishing the vocational aspect of counseling. Significantly, Parson's job title at the Vocation Bureau was Director and Vocational Counselor. Although Parsons died in that same year, his book, *Choosing a Vocation,* published posthumously the following year, clearly established the field of career counseling (Borow, 1964). Also in 1908, as discussed earlier, Clifford Beers, in New Haven, Connecticut, published *A Mind That Found Itself,* leading to the mental hygiene movement and providing a basis for the personal-social/mental health aspect of counseling. None of these three pioneers was trained in counseling. Davis was a school administrator; Parsons, a lawyer; and Beers, an executive. However, all three were ardent adherents of the social reform movement that dominated the intellectual life of the United States in the quarter century before World War I.

The concatenation of these events in the first decade of the twentieth century, with their common theme of counseling (in schools, on careers, and on mental health) led rapidly to the emergence of a profession based on that common theme. Thus, in 1911, the first university-level course in vocational guidance was offered at Harvard University. In 1912, the first city-wide school counseling program was established in Grand Rapids, Michigan (followed within three years by permanent systems in Cincinnati; Minneapolis; Lincoln, NE; Oakland, CA; Boston; and Philadelphia). In 1913, the first national professional organization in a counseling field, the National Vocational Guidance Association, was founded. In World War I, standardized tests were used effectively for the selection of soldiers. The adoption of these tests by the field of counseling in the 1920s and 1930s, spearheaded by faculty at the University of Minnesota, provided the field with a mantle of scientific respectability that led to increased public acceptance. During these two decades, national organizations related to a number of other areas of counseling (school counseling, college student personnel, counselor supervision and training) were established.

In 1952, four of these organizations merged to form the American Personnel and Guidance Association (APGA), which within a year of its formation included school counselors, career counselors, college student personnel workers, counselor supervisors, and counselor educators. As a result of the 1954 amendments to the federal Vocational Rehabilitation Act (Public Law 83-565), the specialty of rehabilitation counseling was established; and in 1958, a division representing rehabilitation counselors was formed in APGA. In half a century, counseling had grown to be a nationally recognized field that incorporated those concerned with its practice in schools, institutions of higher education, career counseling agencies, and medical and psychiatric rehabilitation settings (Borow, 1964; Romano, 1992). During the 1960s, 1970s, and 1980s, various other specialty groups joined the organization, including mental health counselors in 1978 and gerontological counselors in 1986 (Romano, 1992). Thus, counseling established itself as a lifespan, broad-ranging field.

In 1983, APGA changed its name to the American Association for Counseling and Development and again, in 1992, to the American Counseling Association (ACA). These name changes reflected the changing conception of the nature of counseling within the profession, from offering directive guidance toward a socially approved goal (the model initially proposed by Jesse Davis, 1914, with a moral thrust and later presented by Paterson, Schneidler, & Williamson, 1938, with a scientific thrust) to providing a nondirective counseling relationship, with no predetermined moral agenda, in which the client could arrive at and pursue his or her own goals. The latter position primarily derived from the writings of Carl Rogers (1942, 1951). Today, because of its wide array of specializations, counseling has become more eclectic in its practices. At the same time, the field has maintained a set of core principles that define the counseling orientation, which is basic to all specializations. These principles include:

**1.** Respect for the individual (present in Davis, Parsons, Beers, and codified by Rogers).

**2.** That given the opportunity, normal human growth and development will naturally take place (also implicit in the founders of counseling and codified by Rogers). This principle underlies counseling's distinctive emphases on prevention and on early intervention noted by Remley (1992, August), and the extension of this principle led to counseling's distinctive emphasis on promoting wellness, which he also noted.

**3.** That the goal of counseling is to promote healthy growth and development by helping the client learn to define and achieve realistic goals and to cope with problems of living (present in Davis, Parsons, Beers, and all their successors).

**4.** That counseling is an educational process (fundamental to Davis and Parsons); and that since it involves client learning, it requires the active participation of the client in the counseling process. This principle underlies the fourth distinctive characteristic that Remley (1992, August) noted, that counseling empowers its clients. By its very nature, counseling is not a process in which the client can take a passive role (like a patient being treated by a physician or surgeon).

**5.** That counseling works primarily by building on strengths, rather than by attacking weaknesses (again, fundamental to Davis and Parsons).

**6.** That since behavior is a function of the person and the environment, the counseling process must focus equally on the person and on the person's environment (codified by Lewin, 1936, but clearly present in Parson's [1909] assertion that vocational counseling required clear understanding of both the person and the world of work).

**7.** That counseling uses empirically validated procedures (derived from counseling's historical identification with scientific method as a basis for legitimizing the field).

Based on these seven principles, the essential orientation of counseling, underlying all counseling specializations, is now seen as using empirically validated methods to empower clients to set and achieve feasible goals, to cope with problems of living, and to grow by a process of identifying and mobilizing their personal and environmental resources. In the next chapter, we shall examine how this orientation is implemented in the specialization of community counseling.

## EXERCISE

Before proceeding, however, consider how the field of counseling would have been different if it had developed in: (a) a totalitarian country that rejected the notion of personal freedom, (b) an impoverished country where all that people could concern themselves about was their survival needs, (c) a democratic country in which contributing to the goals of one's social and work groups was highly valued but seeking individual self-actualization was considered inappropriate, and (d) a country in which one was expected

to follow without questioning the advice of authority figures, such as elders or counselors.

## REFERENCES

Anderson, T. P. (1975). An alternative frame of reference for rehabilitation:The helping process versus the medical model. *Archives of Physical Medicine and Rehabilitation, 56,* 101–104.

Bakan, D. (1958). *Sigmund Freud and the Jewish mystical tradition.* Princeton, NJ: Van Nostrand.

Beers, C. W. (1908). *A mind that found itself.* New York: Doubleday.

Beigel, A., & Sharfstein, S. (1984). Mental health care providers: Not the only cause or only cure for rising costs. *American Journal of Psychiatry, 141,* 668–671.

Bloom, B. L. (1977). *Community mental health: A general introduction* (2nd ed.). Monterey, CA: Brooks/Cole.

Borow, H. (1964). Milestones: A chronology of notable events in the history of vocational guidance. In H. Borow (Ed.), *Man in a world at work* (pp. 45–64). Boston: Houghton Mifflin.

Brown, D., & Srebalus, D. J. (1988). *An introduction to the counseling profession.* Englewood Cliffs, NJ: Prentice Hall.

Caddy, R. G. (1981). The development and current status of professional psychology. *Professional Psychology, 12,* 377–384.

Corey, G. (1991). *Theory and practice of counseling and psychotherapy* (4th ed.). Pacific Grove, CA: Brooks/Cole.

Council for Accreditation of Counseling and Related Education *Programs.* (1994, January). *CACREP accreditation standards and procedures manual.* Alexandria, VA: Author.

Davis, J. B. (1914). *Moral and vocational guidance.* Boston: Ginn.

Ewalt, J. R. (1975). The birth of the community mental health movement. In W. E. Barton & C. J. Sanborn (Eds.), *An assessment of the community mental health movement* (pp. 13–20). Lexington, MA: D.C. Heath.

Gibson, R. L., & Mitchell, M. H. (1990). *Introduction to counseling and guidance* (3rd ed.). New York: Macmillan.

Gladding, S. T. (1992). *Counseling: A comprehensive profession (2nd ed.).* New York: Merrill.

Gottlieb, B. H. (1979). The primary group as supportive milieu: Applications to community psychology. *American Journal of Community Psychology, 7,* 469–480.

Hansen, J. C., Stevic, R. R., & Warner, R. W., Jr. (1986). *Counseling: Theory and process* (4th ed.). Boston: Allyn and Bacon.

Herr, E. L., & Cramer, S. H. (1987). *Controversies in the mental health professions.* Muncie, IN: Accelerated Development.

Hershenson, D. B. (1983). A viconian interpretation of psychological counseling. *Personnel and Guidance Journal, 62,* 3–9.

Hershenson, D. B. (1993) Healthy development as the basis for mental health counseling theory. *Journal of Mental Health Counseling, 15,* 430–437.

Hollander, R. (1980). A new service ideology: The third mental health revolution. *Professional Psychology, 11,* 561–566.

Ivey, A. E., & Simek-Downing, L. (1980). *Counseling and psychotherapy: Skills, theories, and practice.* Englewood Cliffs, NJ: Prentice-Hall.

Jahoda, M. (1958). *Current concepts of positive mental health.* New York: Basic Books.

Jaques, M., & Hershenson, D. B. (1970). Culture, work and deviance: Implications for rehabilitation counseling. *Rehabilitation Counseling Bulletin, 14,* 49–56.

Lewin, K. (1936). *Principles of topological psychology.* New York: McGraw-Hill.

Lewis, J. A., & Lewis, M. D. (1989). *Community counseling.* Pacific Grove, CA: Brooks/Cole.

Loesch, L. C., & Vaac, N. A. (1993). *A work behavior analysis of professional counselors.* Greensboro, NC: National Board for Certified Counselors and Muncie, IN: Accelerated Development.

Maryland, State of. Health occupations, Title 15.5. Professional counselors. *Annotated code of Maryland.* Annapolis, MD: Author.

McKown, R. (1961). *Pioneers in mental health.* New York: Dodd, Mead.

Mechanic, D. (1980). *Mental health and social policy* (2nd ed.). Englewood Cliffs, NJ: Prentice-Hall.

Mental disorders may afflict 1 in 5. (1984, October 3). *Washington Post,* p. A1.

Moffic, H. S., Adams, G. L., Rosenburg, S., Blattstein, A., & Chacko, R. (1983). *Boom areas: Implications for mental health care systems.* Amherst, MA: Human Science Press.

Musto, D. (1975). The community mental health center movement in historical perspective. In W.

E. Barton & C. J. Sanborn (Eds.), *An assessment of the community mental health movement* (pp. 1–11). Lexington, MA: D.C. Heath.

National Board for Certified Counselors. (1994). *General practice counselor certification 1994.* Greensboro, NC: Author.

Okin, R. L. (1984). How community mental health centers are coping. *Hospital and Community Psychiatry, 35,* 1118–1125.

Parsons, F. (1909). *Choosing a vocation.* Boston: Houghton Mifflin.

Paterson, D. G., Schneidler, G., & Williamson, E. G. (1938). *Student guidance techniques: A handbook for counselors in high schools and colleges.* New York: McGraw-Hill.

Pietrofesa, J. J., Hoffman, A., & Splete, H. H. (1984). *Counseling: An introduction.* Boston: Houghton Mifflin.

Remley, T. P., Jr. (1992, August). Perspectives from the executive director: Are counselors unique? *ACA Guidepost,* p. 4.

Remley, T. P., Jr. (1993, November). Perspectives from the executive director: We are all mental health counselors. *ACA Guidepost,* p.4.

Rogers, C. R. (1942). *Counseling and psychotherapy: Newer concepts in practice.* Boston: Houghton Mifflin.

Rogers, C. R. (1951). *Client-centered therapy.* Boston: Houghton Mifflin.

Romano, G. (1992). AACD's 40th anniversary. *American Counselor, 1*(2), 18–26.

Rounds, J. B., & Tracey, T. J. (1990). From trait-and-factor to person-environment fit counseling: Theory and process. In W. B. Walsh & S. H. Osipow (Eds.), *Career counseling* (pp. 1–44). Hillsdale, NJ: Erlbaum.

Rubin, S. E., & Roessler, R. T. (1987). *Foundations of the vocational rehabilitation process* (3rd ed.). Austin, TX: Pro-ed.

Saccuzzo, D. P. (1977). The practice of psychotherapy in America: Issues and trends. *Professional Psychology, 8,* 297-303.

Sprafkin, R. (1977). The rebirth of the moral movement. *Professional Psychology, 8,* 161–168.

Turner, J. C., & TenHoor, W. J. (1978). The NIMH community support program: Pilot approach to a needed social reform. *Schizophrenia Bulletin, 4,* 319–344.

Tyler, L. E. (1969). *The work of the counselor* (3rd ed.). New York: Appleton-Century-Crofts.

Zilboorg, G.A. (1941). *History of medical psychology.* New York: Norton.

# 2

# PROFESSIONAL IDENTITY OF COMMUNITY COUNSELING

Having gained some perspective on how its parent discipline of counseling evolved, we may turn to the specific topic of this book, community counseling. On February 7, 1993, the Governing Council of the American Counseling Association (ACA) officially recognized the following counseling specializations: career counseling, college counseling, community counseling, counselor education, gerontological counseling, marriage and family counseling, mental health counseling, rehabilitation counseling, and school counseling (Richmond & Robinson, 1993, April). Additionally mentioned elsewhere in ACA publications as areas of specialization are addictions counseling, employment counseling, and counseling legal offenders (O'Bryant, 1993, August). Among all of these specializations, community counseling is unquestionably the most problematic to define. In order to understand the problems that arise in trying to arrive at a definition, we must review the history of community counseling. After we have done that, we shall attempt to formulate a definition and a model for community counseling. We shall then indicate how the contents of this book relate to

that model, and finally, we shall discuss a number of major professional issues that affect the identity of community counseling.

## HISTORY OF COMMUNITY COUNSELING

Recalling the history of counseling presented in Chapter 1, it is worthy of note that the first professional counseling specialization to become organized, career counseling, was established in a community agency setting when Frank Parsons opened the Vocation Bureau of Boston in 1908. For the following five decades, however, schools and colleges dominated the field in terms of the number of settings in which counselors were employed. As a result of the Great Depression and of World War II, however, the balance began to shift. In 1933, the Wagner-Peyser Act established the United States Employment Service, with its system of state employment offices to assist persons seeking jobs. These offices grew to provide vocational testing and counseling services, as well as job placement. In the mid-1940s, as World War II was drawing to a close, the Veterans Administration was greatly expanded to provide services, including vocational, educational, and personal counseling, for the flood of discharged and disabled veterans resulting from the war. Both of these programs, which continue to the present time, would come to provide employment for significant numbers of counselors in community (that is, nonschool) settings (Rockwell, 1991). The range of nonschool settings for counselors was further expanded a decade later when the federal vocational rehabilitation legislation was amended to specifically provide for the training of counselors and other personnel to work in this area.

In 1952, William V. Lockwood, a counselor for adults with the Baltimore public school system, published an article in the *Personnel and Guidance Journal* (the national journal of APGA, now ACA) entitled, "Adult Guidance: A Community Responsibility," in which he stated that: "Confronting today's adults are adjustments in the realms of family living, job change or advancement, education, citizenship, worthy use of leisure time, occupational choice, intercultural understanding, better use of community resources, self-understanding, and the gamut of interpersonal relationships.... By offering educational, vocational, marriage, and personal counseling to so-called 'normal' persons at least a large part of this public responsibility could be met, and many serious maladjustments prevented by early attention" (pp. 31–32). He noted that the Baltimore public school system had begun such a service in 1945, providing "information, counseling, referral, and related services to individuals who desire assistance in adjusting their problems" (Lockwood, 1952, p. 32). He went on to recommend that more such services should be established around the country.

This trend toward the expansion of counseling into community settings was abetted by an accident of history. In 1956, the Soviet Union launched the first successful space satellite. Given the political tensions of the time, the United States government reacted by passing the National Defense Education Act (NDEA) to increase the nation's supply of scientists in order to catch up with our potential adversary. Title V of this act provided federal funds for institutes to train school counselors. This legislation was in force from 1958 through 1965. Responding to this incentive, a number of universities expanded or started programs to train school counselors; more than 14,000 counselors were trained through this initiative (Borow, 1964). The end of NDEA funding coincided with the end of the post–World War II baby boom (the 76 million persons born in this country between 1946 and 1964 [Lewis, 1993, November]). By the early 1970s, schools were being closed as the school age population shrank. Consequently, the demand for school counselors dropped precipitously, and fewer students entered the counselor preparation programs that had been built up. The colleges (usually, colleges of education) were left with more counselor education programs and faculty than were needed to train rehabilitation counselors, for whom demand still existed in the state/federal vocational rehabilitation system and related agencies, and the greatly diminished number of school counseling students.

As was noted in the discussion of the evolution of the concept of mental health, the Community Mental Health Centers Act of 1963 led to the establishment of a nationwide network of community mental health centers. In order to utilize their resources, many counselor education programs shifted their focus from preparing counselors for work in the contracting area of the schools to preparing counselors for work in the expanding area of community agencies. (Parenthetically, it may be noted that since the late 1980s, as counselors have been more widely placed in elementary schools and as the NDEA-trained school counselors have started to reach retirement, the demand for school counselors has once again risen.)

Another trend that supported the movement of counseling into the area of community mental health was the broadening of the concept of mental health from its original, medical model meaning of the absence of mental illness (as health was the absence of disease) to a conception that involved being able to cope successfully with problems of living, and then on to a conception of high-level wellness (Herr & Cramer, 1987). From the time of Jesse B. Davis and Frank Parsons, counseling had defined its role as helping people learn to cope with problems of living (school, work, social adjustment) and as promoting healthy development. It was, therefore, only natural that counseling should see itself as having evolved an approach that was particularly applicable to the emerging reconceptualization of mental health.

In the early 1970s, the Association for Counselor Education and Supervision (ACES), a division of ACA that was one of the four groups that founded that organization in 1952, undertook the task of developing profession-wide standards for counselor education programs. In 1973, ACES published "Standards for Entry Preparation of Counselor and Other Personnel Services Specialists" and in the late 1970s began a process of voluntary review of counselor education programs using these standards.

In 1976, Stadler and Stahl (1979) surveyed the 420 known counselor education programs in the country concerning their community/agency counselor training activities as related to the 1973 ACES standards. Of the 210 responses, they found that even though most community/agency programs had been started in the prior six years, there were faculty with appropriate experience and high student interest in these programs. They also found that respondents were "interested in the development of standards for community counselor preparation" (Stadler & Stahl, 1979, p. 48). Interestingly, two years later, in 1978, Conyne (1980) surveyed the 450 counselor education

programs then listed as to their current and ideal theoretical base and specific trainee competencies for masters-level community counselor preparation. The 308 responses showed strong consensus already existed on what constituted the community counseling orientation (active rather than passive, multifaceted, developmental-preventive rather than remedial, based on person-environment interaction) and skills (helping, consultation, social change, program development and evaluation, education and training).

In 1981, the profession as a whole responded to the perceived need for profession-wide standards and review procedures for training programs, and so the Council for Accreditation of Counseling and Related Educational Programs (CACREP) was established and took over the ACES initiative. Initially, CACREP recognized three categories of educational programs: those that prepared school counselors, those that prepared college student personnel workers, and those that prepared counselors for settings other than educational institutions or rehabilitation agencies (since a separate accrediting agency for rehabilitation counselor education programs was already in existence). This third category was called Counseling in Community and Other Agency Settings. In 1982, Stickle and Schnacke (1984) surveyed the 16 counselor education programs that had been accredited by CACREP during the first two years of its existence. The 13 programs that responded indicated that over the past two years, they had graduated a combined total of 450 students in agency counseling, 224 in school counseling, and 82 in college student personnel.

While there has never been a division of Community Agency Counseling or Community Counseling in ACA, a Committee on Community Counseling was formed within ACES in 1983 (Hayes, 1984, March) and has continued in existence as the ACES Community Agency Interest Network (Cowger, 1991,

Winter). In 1984, the ACES Committee on Community Counseling proposed their view of community counseling as a "generic counselor preparation program of 30 hours into which a preventative and developmental model should be infused" (Hayes, 1984, March, p. 15) and onto which an additional 30 credit hours of training in an area of specialization should be added. This viewpoint saw community counseling as

> *an approach to helping that is a process and an orientation rather than a work setting. It emphasizes preventative interventions and favors using a multi-faceted approach that is developmental and educative rather than remedial. Community counselors take into account the effects of the community environment on individuals and seek to empower individuals through serving as client advocates in affecting the community as a whole.* (Hayes, 1984, March, p. 15)

Community counseling was thus defined as an orientation to the counseling process, rather than as a specific specialization. If a school counselor subscribed to the prescribed orientation, he or she could be considered a community counselor, although a counselor who worked in a community agency but who did not subscribe to this orientation would not qualify as a community counselor.

It may be noted that this interpretation of the meaning of community counseling was consistent with the approach taken in the two books then in print that were entitled *Community Counseling* (Amos & Williams, 1972; Lewis & Lewis, 1977, 1983). Amos and Williams (1972) were specifically concerned with establishing multidisciplinary teams of mental health, social welfare, employment, and education specialists and indigenous coaches to work with disadvantaged, multiproblem urban youth in their home communities. Lewis and Lewis (1977, 1983) presented a model for

community-oriented counseling that emphasized the role of the environment, prevention, and a multifaceted approach to service delivery. They indicated that their conception of community counseling was applicable to counselors in any setting, including schools and colleges.

In 1986, Richardson and Bradley published the results of a national survey of counselor education programs on their community agency counselor preparation activities. This survey was conducted in fall, 1983, under the sponsorship of ACES, ACA, and another of its divisions, the American Mental Health Counselors Association (AMHCA). This project stemmed from a charge by the president of ACES to its Resources and Research Committee "to conduct a study on the status of community agency counseling" (Richardson & Bradley, 1986, p. 1). They found, as had Stickle and Schnacke (1984), that community agency counseling constituted the largest and fastest growing segment of counselor preparation programs. The greatest growth in these programs occurred between 1973 and 1980. There was considerable diversity among these programs, and the factor that appeared to differentiate community agency preparation programs most consistently from other counselor preparation programs was the use of community agencies as practicum and internship placement sites. They concluded that, "Community agency counseling graduates are employed in positions in a broad range of agencies emphasizing the delivery of prevention and rehabilitation services to a diversity of clientele" (Richardson & Bradley, 1986, p. 136).

Thus, while the ACES Committee on Community Counseling was promulgating the position that "community" was to be defined as a particular orientation to the practice of counseling regardless of setting (Hayes, 1984, March), the ACES Resources and Research Committee was pursuing a study based on the premise that "community" referred to the location of the agency in which the counseling was carried out (Richardson & Bradley, 1986). This typifies the conflict in defining the area that has dogged community counseling up to the present time.

In 1988, CACREP issued a major revision of its accreditation standards. Under these standards, the title of the Counseling in Community and Other Agency Settings category was changed to Community Counseling (CACREP, 1988, July). This change, however, added a further dimension of ambiguity to the one Tyler (1969) noted was already present in the word *counseling*. It now was unclear whether Community Counseling meant "counseling in community settings" (that the name change was merely intended to shorten a cumbersome title) or that it indicated a change in the nature of the field, possibly to a counseling analogue of the then burgeoning psychology specialty of community psychology (Levine & Perkins, 1987; Mann, 1978; Orford, 1992; Rappaport, 1977). No clue to the intent behind this name change is evident in the wording of the revised CACREP standards for community counseling programs, which merely stated, in their entirety:

> *CC-A. Provide a list of and syllabi for courses or curricular experiences related to the general environment or system in which students intend to practice.*
>
> *CC-B. Provide a list of and syllabi for courses or curricular experiences related to the specific and unique knowledge and skills needed for the particular setting in which, or client population with which the students intend to work.* (CACREP, 1988, July, p. 59)

To add to the definitional problems for community counseling in the 1988 CACREP Standards, these standards also contained a new category of program accreditation, Mental Health Counseling (60 credits in length), as well as the renamed 48-credit Community Counseling category. Wilcoxon (1990) responded to this situation by suggesting that these two categories be merged into a unified 60-credit category of Community Mental Health Counseling as a way of resolving potential overlap between the two categories. He further proposed that there could then be different emphases within this unified program, one of which would be mental health counseling and another essentially community counseling. This proposal, which would have had the effect of increasing the community counseling program to 60 credits in length, was not adopted.

This set of standards was not improved upon by a 1991 revision of the 1988 standards, which stated, "Community Counseling is a generic term which includes specialized areas of counselor training other than those for which specialty standards have been developed" (CACREP, 1991, October, p. 67), and left it up to each counselor education program to designate its own area(s) of specialization under the community label.

As the profession looked ahead to the new CACREP standards that were to come out in 1994, the ACES Community Agency Interest Network continued to press for essentially the same position that was set forth by its predecessor group, the ACES Committee on Community Counseling (Hayes, 1984, March). In its report to an ACA task force that was set up to examine training standards for community agency counseling, the Community Agency Interest Network proposed the establishment of a program accreditation category of "community mental health counseling program" that "would contain those skills and competencies common to the community setting" (Cowger, 1991, Winter, p. 2). This would be a common 48-hour program, to which additional 12-credit specializations in clinical mental health, marriage and family, gerontology, or other areas could be added.

The acceptability of a definition of this sort was dealt a major blow by ACA's decision in

February, 1993, to identify community counseling as an officially recognized counseling specialization in its own right (Richmond & Robinson, 1993, April). Interestingly, community counseling was the only one of the specializations recognized that was not represented by a specific division in ACA (and consequently, the only one that did not have a specialty journal). It was also one of only a few of the specializations recognized that lacked a specialized certification process for its practitioners. Further, in the summer of 1993, the ACA Governing Council asked each division to provide a definition of its area, so that persons outside the field would understand its place within counseling. Community counseling, lacking a division to represent it, was again the only area that emerged without a defining statement (O'Bryant, 1993, August). Nonetheless, having been officially recognized as a specialization, community counseling could not remain as a catch-all or as an extended core program for other specializations. Consequently, it is not surprising that the 1994 CACREP standards for community counseling programs were much more specific than previous ones. The perennial problem of defining community counseling was considerably ameliorated by these standards, which explicitly spell out specialized requirements for community counseling programs, above and beyond the core educational requirements for all counselors (indicated in Chapter 1).

These specialized requirements include, but are not limited to, study of the following topics:

**A.** *Foundations Of Community Counseling*

   *1. historical, philosophical, societal, cultural, economic, and political dimensions of the mental health movement;*

   *2. roles, functions, and professional identity of community counselors;*

   *3. structures and operations of professional organizations, training standards, credentialing bodies, and ethical codes pertaining to the practice of community counseling;*

   *4. implications of professional issues unique to community counseling including, but not limited to recognition, reimbursement, and right to practice; and*

   *5. implications of sociocultural, demographic, and lifestyle diversity relevant to community counseling.*

**B.** *Contextual Dimensions Of Community Counseling*

   *1. roles of community counselors in a variety of practice settings and the relationships between counselors and other professionals in these settings;*

   *2. organizational, fiscal, and legal dimensions of the institutions and settings in which community counselors practice;*

   *3. theories and techniques of community needs assessment to design, implement, and evaluate community counseling interventions, programs, and systems; and*

   *4. general principles of community intervention, consultation, education, and outreach; characteristics of human services programs and networks, public, private, and volunteer, in local communities.*

**C.** *Knowledge And Skills For The Practice Of Community Counseling*

   *1. client characteristics of individuals served by institutions and agencies offering community counseling services, including, but not limited to the effects of socioeconomic status, unemployment, aging, gender, culture, race, ethnicity, chronic illness, developmen-*

*tal transitions, and interpersonal, family, and community violence;*

2. *principles of program development and service delivery for a clientele based on assumptions of normal development, including, but not limited to prevention, implementation of support groups, peer facilitation training, parent education, career information and counseling, and encouragement of self-help;*

3. *effective strategies for promoting client understanding of and access to community resources;*

4. *principles of conducting an intake interview and mental health history for planning counseling interventions; and*

5. *effective strategies for client advocacy in public policy and government relations issues.* (CACREP, 1994, January, pp. 66–67)[*]

Moreover, the supervised internship (required of all CACREP accredited programs) must be carried out in a community setting and must include "preventive, developmental, and remedial interventions with appropriate clientele and community interventions" (CACREP, 1994, January, p. 67).

While this set of standards for community counseling is clearly a quantum leap ahead of the earlier ones in terms of its specificity, it still leaves a number of essential questions unanswered, the most central of which is embodied in item A.2. What are the distinguishing roles, functions, and professional identity of community counselors? That is the principal question that this book will attempt to answer.

To summarize the position of community counseling at the end of 1995, it lacked a division in ACA to represent it, a specialized professional journal, and an officially sanctioned

or generally agreed-upon definition. Nonetheless, it had been officially recognized as a specialization by the major professional organization in counseling; it had almost twice as many accredited counselor preparation programs as any other category of program within CACREP except school counseling, with which it was tied; and its practitioners had been shown to differ systematically from counselors who work in educational and academic settings in terms of their degree of involvement with various work activities (Loesch & Vaac, 1993). One must therefore conclude that community counseling clearly exists. All we have to do is define it.

## DEFINITION OF COMMUNITY COUNSELING

One may approach the task of defining community counseling by looking at how other counseling specializations have been named. At least six different parameters have been used to designate specializations within the field of counseling. These parameters include: (1) particular practice setting (for example, school counseling), (2) particular segment of the population served (for example, gerontological counseling), (3) particular issue addressed (for example, career counseling), (4) particular focus of intervention (for example, marriage and family counseling), (5) particular orientation (for example, clinical mental health counseling, by its addition of the word "clinical"), and (6) particular set of skills used (for example, specialists in group work). Naturally, none of these labels fully defines the specialization it designates; but taken together, they suggest a set of parameters by which a specialization can be defined.

As we have seen in the history of community counseling, various approaches to defining the specialization have been proposed. One approach has sought to define community counseling by the setting in which counseling is practiced, a community agency (as differentiated from a school or a college). Another approach has sought to define community counseling by its particular focus of intervention, the community (as distinct from focusing solely on the individual or the family). A third approach has been to try to define community counseling as a particular orientation toward counseling (proactive, multifaceted, environmentally sensitive, empowering) that can be held by counselors who work with any population of clients in any setting. A fourth approach has attempted to define community counseling as possessing a particular set of skills in community mental health, skills that derive from social sciences such as anthropology and sociology and from applied social engineering fields such as community organization and human resources development. These approaches have continued to vie with each other for acceptance as the one true basis for defining community counseling.

We believe that these approaches are not mutually exclusive and that they all represent necessary aspects of a definition of community counseling. No one of these aspects taken alone, however, is sufficient to define community counseling. Thus, we would define community counseling as the application of counseling principles and practices in agency, organizational, or individual practice settings that are located in and interact with their surrounding community. In general, if one creates a continuum of practice settings from schools to colleges to agencies and organizations to individual practice, the modal setting for community counseling is agencies and organizations. Community counseling is directly applicable to the adjacent category of individual practice, may be applied with some modifications in college settings (particularly those that see themselves as communities), and is generally perceived as furthest in direct applicability from the school setting (grades K–12). While one might argue that greater cross-fertilization between counseling as practiced in school settings and counseling as

practiced in agency settings would benefit both, these two settings remain the perceived poles of the distribution of settings in which counseling is practiced. The practice of counseling in community settings involves a particular orientation, focus of intervention, and set of skills, without which the goals of counseling cannot be effectively achieved. The community counseling orientation is based on the general counseling principles, presented at the end of Chapter 1, (1) that the natural human condition is one of healthy growth and development and (2) that human behavior is a function of the person and that person's environment (community). Consequently, community counseling maintains that to promote healthy development, the focus of appraisal and intervention must be as much on the community as on the client. This intervention follows a proactive, health-promoting approach, is educative and empowering, and is based on the principle of building on strengths, that is, it concentrates on the identification and mobilization of client and community resources as the basis for goal attainment, coping, and growth. Implementation of this orientation in this setting requires specialized knowledge and skills drawn from such fields as anthropology, sociology, community organization, organizational development, human resources development, and management, as well as from the study of individual and group behavior change. That specialized body of knowledge will be presented in this book.

It may be noted that in defining community counseling we have not focused on a particular segment of the population served or a particular set of issues addressed in counseling, since these are widely variable, depending on the specific community setting involved. A community counselor working with clients from a particular segment of the the population or assisting clients with a particular issue may have to use skills developed by other counseling specialties (for example, gerontological counseling or career counseling) within a community counseling framework. By the same token, it would be equally appropriate for a counselor in any other specialty, working in any setting, to focus the intervention process on the client's community environment, to follow a community counseling orientation, and/or to use specialized community counseling skills. Identity as a community counselor, however, requires that one's professional center of interest is the body of knowledge that involves the integration of all four aspects of community counseling: practice setting, orientation, focus of intervention, and specialized skills. We shall next provide a model that integrates these aspects.

## A CONCEPTUAL MODEL FOR COMMUNITY COUNSELING

By our definition, there are four components to community counseling: practice setting, orientation, focus of intervention, and specialized skills. The following model integrates the last three of these components. This model is applicable across the range of community counseling practice settings, which will be discussed in Chapter 3. The model presented here draws on three principal sources, one for each component. These sources are Lewis and Lewis's (1989) model of the four facets of community counseling services for the focus of intervention component, the model for analyzing client and community strengths and deficits developed by Anthony and his colleagues (Anthony, Cohen, & Farkas, 1990; Anthony, Pierce, & Cohen, 1979) for the orientation component, and Brown and Srebalus's (1972) model of principal counselor functions for the specialized skills component.

Lewis and Lewis (1989) proposed a two-by-two cell model for community counseling in which the targets of service are the community and the client and the service modes are direct and indirect. Thus, their four facets are: "1. Direct community services (preventive education)... 2. Direct client services (outreach)... 3. Indirect community services (influencing public policy).. 4. Indirect client services (advocacy)" (Lewis & Lewis, 1989, p. 11). From this model, we have taken the categories of client and community as the focus of intervention. In our terminology, as indicated in Chapter 1, the client may be an individual, family, group, organization, or segment of a community seeking assistance. The community is the larger set of social systems in which the client exists and which directly affect the client's functioning. Thus, for an individual, the family is part of the community, as are the neighborhood, cultural group, and possibly city within which the family is located. When the client is a family, the community would include the extended family, the neighborhood, the cultural group, and so on. For a department in a company, the company and its physical and economic setting (city, state, marketing region) constitute the community. Generally, the more inclusive the client (for example, a segment of a community or a part of a multinational corporation), the broader will be the community that has a direct impact on the client's functioning. Of course, at some levels of breadth, counseling cannot do much more with communities than assist the client to develop ways of coping with their effects.

Anthony and his colleagues developed a model for rehabilitation intervention with persons with psychiatric difficulties. This model follows a counseling orientation and provides methods and techniques that are applicable to working with other sorts of clients as well. One aspect of this model is a two-dimensional grid for client appraisal in terms of what is needed to achieve a particular goal. One dimension of this grid is the areas of physical, emotional, and intellectual functioning; the other dimension is strengths and deficits. This latter dimension provides a basis for planning the intervention so that strengths are built on and deficits are overcome or compensated for to the extent necessary to achieve the specific goal in question. As should be evident from the prior discussion of the history and definition of community counseling, this approach is fully consistent with a community counseling orientation and so has been adopted here. We have, however, modified the terminology from "strengths" and "deficits" (Anthony, Pierce, & Cohen, 1979, p. 93) to "resources" and "barriers," as we believe that these words are more applicable across both the categories of client and of community that constitute the other dimension of our grid. Anthony et al.'s original underlying concept of identifying and mobilizing strengths is, however, retained without modification.

The third component incorporated into our model is Brown and Srebalus's (1972) "C-C-C" formulation of counselor functioning, which was developed for school counselors but is equally applicable to counselors in other settings (for example, Hershenson, 1990). Brown and Srebalus proposed that the three equally important functions of the counselor are counseling, coordinating, and consulting. We fully concur with this formulation, but would include three additional central functions for community counselors: educating, programming, and advocacy. As indicated in Chapter 1, an educational function of counseling has been recognized throughout the history of the field. As used here, however, education refers specifically to teaching clients new knowledge and skills needed for coping. Programming involves the development and delivery of programs that are designed to meet specific, empirically identified needs of clients and/or of the community. Actually, as Herr and Cramer (1992) pointed out, "such programs must be designed to achieve the purposes of the organization within which they are located as well as to facilitate the...development of those who are directly served" (p. 285). Advocacy involves the process of influencing the community, on behalf of the client, to provide needed resources. This differs from consultation, which involves working with an established community resource to improve its effectiveness in working with the client. In advocacy, the target of the intervention is the community, particularly its power structure, and the aim is to create or to make available a resource that the client needs. In consultation, the target of intervention is a particular community resource that is already providing services, and the aim is to assist that resource to better meet the client's needs. Essentially, counseling, coordination, and consultation involve working with existing resources; education, programming, and advocacy involve the development of new resources where they are lacking.

Our model for community counseling practice is presented in Figure 2–1. By this model, when a specific counseling goal has been established, relevant client and community resources (factors that can help achieve or support that goal) and barriers (factors that can impede the achievement or maintenance of that goal) should be entered into their respective cells. For example, if the goal is for the client to develop social contacts, client resources might include verbal fluency, intellectual competence, and physical attractiveness; and client barriers might be shyness or hostility. Community resources might be the presence of social clubs, churches, or other meeting places; and community barriers might be that the social class composition of the neighborhood is different from the client's, local prejudice against the client's race or religion, or the distance of potential meeting places from the client's home. Recalling the points made by Remley (1992, August), discussed at the end of Chapter 1, the goals of community counseling, reflecting the orientation of the broader field of counseling, will emphasize early intervention, prevention, and promoting wellness, rather than treatment of long-standing, well-entrenched problems.

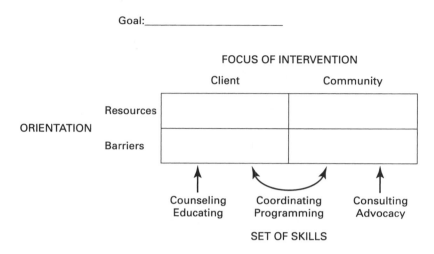

Goal:_____

FIGURE 2–1    Model for Community Counseling Practice

In terms of counselor functioning in relation to this grid, the counselor counsels the client as to the selection and specification of the goal and as to the identification and mobilization of resources (personal skills and abilities, environmental supports) and the overcoming of barriers necessary to attaining that goal. When the client lacks the skills needed to identify or mobilize resources or to overcome barriers, the counselor educates the client in these skills. The counselor consults with existing community resources or advocates with the community to create or help bring resources to bear and to lower barriers to the attainment of the client's goal (for instance, in the example used above, to advocate with the community to reduce their prejudice or to provide transportation for the client to be able to reach the places where social contacts can be made). Additionally, the counselor coordinates, connecting the client with the community resources that can assist in the attainment of the goal. This frequently involves a number of different community resources that have to be orchestrated in terms of the specific contribution that each can make to the attainment of the goal. The counselor also organizes programs that meet the needs of clients and the

particular settings in which they are experiencing problems. Generally, to be both effective and cost effective, programs must meet the needs of a number of individuals and of the setting in which the program is to be carried out. These counselor functions are all interrelated; for example, the counselor must counsel the client in terms of the client's attitudes toward and use of the resources being programmed, coordinated, or advocated for. One must know what resources exist and can be coordinated in order to determine what needs to be programmed or advocated for, and so on.

In terms of the definition of community counseling presented earlier in this chapter, the client-community dimension of this model represents the focus of intervention. The relationship between the stated goal and the resources identified and used (including the barriers identified and removed) to achieve that goal (that is, the left margin of Figure 2–1) represents the counseling orientation. Counseling, educating, coordinating, programming, consulting, and advocacy represent the set of skills that are employed to implement this orientation. In the model in Figure 2–1, these skills are arranged in terms of their specific focus of intervention. Counseling and education are focused on the client; consulting and advocacy are focused on the community; and coordinating and programming are focused on both the client and the community, since they involve linking the two foci. As noted earlier, counseling, coordinating, and consulting deal with existing resources, while educating, programming, and advocacy deal with the creation of new resources.

## ORGANIZATION OF THIS BOOK

This book has been organized in accordance with the conception of community counseling just presented. Within this framework, we shall address each of the items in the 1994 CACREP standards for community counseling programs, given in the prior section. The coverage of items indicated in the CACREP specialty standards, by chapter in this book, are indicated in Table 2–1.

In terms of the foregoing definition and model of community counseling, Chapters 1,

2, and 16 address community counseling orientation; Chapters 3 and 4 address practice setting; Chapters 5, 6, and 7 address focus of intervention; and Chapters 8 through 15 address specialized skills (other than assessment methods, which were covered in Chapters 6 and 7).

This book will not cover the general literature on client assessment or on individual, family, or group counseling, since these topics are covered in detail in numerous books on each of these topics and are the subject matter of specifically mandated courses in the core counseling curriculum. Therefore, Chapters 6, 8, 9 and 10 will focus on the specific application of these areas of counseling within the specialty of community counseling. Similarly, this book will address only the specific applications to community counseling of other topics that are broadly covered in the core counseling curriculum: human development, career development, multicultural counseling, consultation process, and research and evaluation methods. Here again, numerous text-

**TABLE 2–1**   Coverage of Community Counseling Specialty Standards

| Chapter | 1994 CACREP Standard |
| --- | --- |
| 1. The Evolution of Counseling | A.1 |
| 2. Professional Identity of Community Counseling | A.2, 3 |
| 3. Practice Settings | B.1, 2 |
| 4. Ethical and Legal Issues | A.3, 4 |
| 5. Developmental Foundations | C.1, A.5 |
| 6. Client Assessment | C.4 |
| 7. Environmental and Needs Assessment | B.3 |
| 8. Community Counseling with Individuals | A.2, C.2 |
| 9. Community Counseling with Families | A.2, C.2 |
| 10. Community Counseling with Groups | A.2, C.2 |
| 11. Educating and Programming | C.2, B.4 |
| 12. Consultation and Supervision | B.4 |
| 13. Case Management and Coordination of Resources | C.3, B.1 |
| 14. Policy Formation and Advocacy | C.5 |
| 15. Evaluation of Services | B.3 |
| 16. Future Directions for Community Counseling | A.2 |

books on each of these topics are available, and specific coverage of these topics is mandated by the CACREP core program accreditation standards. To keep this book to manageable length, it will be assumed that the reader has general familiarity with (or access to) the literature in these core areas of counseling. We shall focus on their specific applications in community counseling. We shall now turn to current professional issues confronting community counseling.

## CURRENT PROFESSIONAL ISSUES

Several topics that qualify as professional issues will be addressed in the following two chapters: scope of practice roles and settings in Chapter 3, and ethical and legal issues, including licensure, in Chapter 4. In this chapter, we shall look at the issues of professional organization, professional credentials, relevant literature, and education and training.

### Professional Organization

Unquestionably, as an area of professional counseling, community counseling must find its organizational home within the American Counseling Association. As was noted earlier, community counseling is the only counseling specialization officially recognized by ACA (Richmond & Robinson, 1993, April) that is not represented by a division in ACA. Without a divisional structure, community counseling will be hard put to develop a specialized journal (since these are all published by ACA divisions) or a specialized certification procedure. This lack of specific representation is rendered particularly difficult to understand when one recalls that more people graduate from counselor preparation programs in community counseling than from programs in any other specialty in which CACREP accredits programs.

By our observation, at the present time graduates of community counseling programs tend to join the ACA division or divisions that represent the particular segment of the population or client issue on which they primarily practice (for example, gerontological counseling, career counseling, mental health counseling). While these divisional affiliations are undoubtedly valuable for community counselors, their primary field of community counseling remains without a body to advocate for it and to promote research and development in its areas of specific concern. Consequently, the improvement of methods in areas that are focal to community counseling, such as preventive interventions, needs assessment, programming, using support systems, and resource development, does not receive its appropriate share of attention (Hershenson & Strein, 1991). Clearly, the establishment of an ACA division to promote the development of the community counseling specialization is sorely needed.

### Professional Credentials

We shall focus here on credentials conferred by the profession, rather than on those conferred by the state, which will be discussed in Chapter 4. Professions typically engage in two types of credentialing: (1) certifying individuals as qualified to practice the profession ethically and at an acceptable level of competence, and (2) accrediting training programs as qualified to train these practitioners. States are concerned with licensing (who may legally perform the activities that the state defines as within the scope of practice of that profession) or certification (who may legally present themselves to the public by a particular job title). Professional certification, program accreditation, and legal licensure or certification all are intended for one principal purpose: to notify the public as to who is qualified to practice a given profession and thereby to protect the public from charlatans. Coincidentally, some professions have been accused of using these credentialing processes to limit the supply of qualified practitioners, in order to keep the incomes of those within the profession high. This accusation has, however, frequently come from those excluded from the field and has lost even more of its credibility as economic and population shifts have produced surpluses of professionals in the very professions most often accused of using this tactic to control their numbers (Herr & Cramer, 1987).

### Professional Certification

The National Board for Certified Counselors (NBCC), established by the American Counseling Association, offers a certification procedure for all counselors, including those in community counseling. This procedure leads to the designation of National Certified Counselor (NCC). The procedure involves a review of academic credentials and of references by already qualified professionals and the passing of an examination covering the areas of (a) human growth and development; (b) social and cultural foundations of counseling; (c) the helping relationship (counseling and consultation theory and practices); (d) group dynamics, processes, and counseling; (e) lifestyles and career development; (f) appraisal of individuals; (g) research and evaluation; and (h) professional orientation (ethics, roles, practices). Graduates of programs accredited by the Council for Accreditation of Counseling and Related Educational Programs (CACREP, to be discussed later under accreditation) may take the examination immediately upon graduation. Persons with graduate degrees in counseling from nonaccredited programs must have two years of supervised professional counseling experience (3,000 hours) following their degree in order to be qualified to sit for the examination. Moreover, their academic program must have included a course in counseling theory, a supervised counseling practicum, and courses in the eight areas covered on the examination. Although the NCC certification process certifies an individual as having the knowledge and experience required of a professional counselor, it is a general practice credential that does not distinguish among types of counselors (community counselors, school counselors, career counselors, etc.).

Once certified as an NCC, the counselor must maintain this certification by taking continuing professional education and documenting the required number of hours of approved training to the certifying agency. This assures clients that certified counselors will remain up to date as to the knowledge base, techniques, and practices within their profession.

Finally, the NBCC periodically publishes a register listing the names and addresses of those who have been certified, so that the public and third-party payers can be aware of who is considered qualified by the profession. This practice is followed by most professional certifying groups. As of September, 1995, more than 21,700 counselors held the NCC credential (NBCC, personal communication, September 1, 1995).

A number of counseling specializations (for example, career counseling, school counseling, clinical mental health counseling) have established specialized examinations that may be taken by those who have passed the NCC examination and who wish recognition for their specific education and supervised experience in that specialization. To this point, no such specialized recognition has been available to the practitioners of community counseling, and so many obtain only the general counseling credential of NCC. This lack of specialized credential is not surprising when one recalls the ambiguous definition of community counseling in the past. With the increasing clarification of its definition, however, there is a reasonable basis on which a specialized examination can be constructed. As suggested earlier, the other element necessary for the creation of a specialized examination, an ACA division of community counseling to advocate for it, has yet to be established.

### Academic Program Accreditation

One area in which community counseling clearly excels is in the number of professionally accredited academic programs in the specialization. Established at the beginning of the 1980s under the auspices of the American Counseling Association, the Council for Accreditation of Counseling and Related Educational Programs (CACREP) is an independent body that accredits (that is, approves as meeting the standards set by the profession) counselor education programs in colleges and universities. Currently, only master's degree professional entry-level programs in school counseling, college counseling, career counseling, gerontological counseling, marriage and family counseling, clinical mental health counseling, and community counseling and doctoral programs in counselor education are evaluated for accreditation. To qualify for accreditation, an academic program must submit an extensive self-study (frequently running several hundred pages) documenting that it meets all of the standards of the accrediting body. Then a team of site visitors comes to the campus to speak with program faculty, students, alumni, field supervisors, employers of graduates, and university administrators about their views of the program. The site visitors prepare a written report, to which the program may respond. The self-study, the site visitors' report, and the program's response to that report are evaluated by the CACREP board. The board may vote to give a full or limited term of accreditation or to deny accreditation to the program. Full accreditation means that the program has substantially met all of the standards. A limited term accreditation means that the program has met most of the standards, including all major ones, and can be expected to meet the remaining ones within several years. Denial of accreditation means that the program has failed to meet one or more major standards and/or so many minor standards that it is improbable that it could remedy its deficiencies within several years.

Although there are a large number of explicit standards, some central ones are that a master's program must be at least two years (48 semester hours or 72 quarter hours) in length and include a supervised practicum and a supervised internship of specified length. The academic program must include courses in the eight core areas of human growth and development, social and cultural foundations, helping relationships (counseling and consultation theory and practice), group work, career and lifestyle development, appraisal, research and program evaluation, and professional orientation (ethics and professional practices). Standards relating to faculty size, student-faculty ratios, admissions and student evaluation procedures, program resources and support staff, and so on, must also be met.

In addition to meeting these core standards, a program must meet a set of standards in an area of specialization. The current standards for community counseling were given earlier in this chapter.

As of Summer, 1995, there were over 85 CACREP accredited programs in community counseling in the United States and Canada, which was more than the number of programs in any other category except school counseling, with which it was tied (CACREP Fact Sheet, 1995, Summer).

## Relevant Literature

To be recognized as a professional area of specialization, a field must have an identifiable body of literature, usually including one or more specialized journals in which current research and practices in the field are reported. Within the profession of counseling, as has been noted, specialized journals traditionally have been created and maintained by individual divisions of ACA. Lacking a division of community counseling, there has been no group to take responsibility for establishing a journal of community counseling. As a recognized counseling specialization, the field has a compelling need for such a journal.

At the present time, articles of specialized interest to community counselors can be found in the general scholarly journal of the ACA, the *Journal of Counseling and Development*, and in the journals put out by its divisions, listed in Table 2–2. Also listed in Table 2–2 are other journals in which articles of immediate relevance to community counseling are frequently found.

Surveys of journal articles published on a topic of interest may be carried out by using *Psychological Abstracts*, which is published by the American Psychological Association and is available at research libraries, or by purchasing a computerized search of the topic from any of several services, also generally available through research libraries. These sources provide the titles, reference citations, and frequently abstracts to all articles on a particular topic of interest that were published in journals indexed by the service. Usually, these journals account for most of what one would hope to find on a topic, although some important articles (for example, those in certain foreign journals, state counseling association journals, special interest group newsletters, or marginally related journals) may be missed by these searches.

In addition to journals, community counselors should keep up with books and other published sources of information of relevance to their profession. Many new publications are reviewed in the professional journals (such as the *Journal of Counseling and Development*). The American Counseling Association also publishes a catalog of books, films, and videotapes on counseling, which may be obtained from the organization. Finally, a good way to keep up with newly published books is to check *Books in Print*, which is available at most libraries or bookstores. By looking under the topics of "counseling," "mental health," and the other topics to which these two topics refer the reader, one can rapidly learn the authors, titles, publishers, and prices of new or unread books of relevance to community counseling.

## Education and Training

For a specialization to exist over time, it must have a mechanism for transmitting its specialized body of knowledge and skills to persons wishing to enter into the practice of that field. Until about a century ago, most professionals (for example, lawyers) were trained by apprenticing to someone already recognized as a practitioner of that profession. Today, however, in counseling and most other professions, the primary (and often exclusive) accepted mechanism for professional preparation is through accredited academic programs located in institutions of higher education.

Having determined that community counselor preparation programs are to be located in academic settings, the next issue to be addressed is how to design the curriculum for these programs so that a graduate of any given community counselor preparation program can be expected to possess the same basic set of competencies as a community counselor educated in any other program bearing the same designation. Two approaches to curriculum development have appeared in the literature, one based on a theoretical premise of what should constitute community counseling, and the other based on empirical surveys of what actually exists in training programs or what employers of community counselors are looking for in graduates of training programs. The former, prescriptive approach underlies the current CACREP (1994, January) standards for community counseling programs, discussed in detail earlier in this chapter. This approach also appears to be represented in Wilcoxon and Cecil's (1985) proposed model program for community agency counselor preparation, since the authors do not indicate that they had as yet put this model into operation (for example, "[A]11 students would

**TABLE 2–2**  Journals Containing Relevant Articles for Community Counselors

| Journal Category | Journals |
|---|---|
| Journals published by the American Counseling Association and its divisions | Journal of Counseling and Development<br>Counseling and Values<br>Counselor Education and Supervision<br>Elementary School Guidance and Counseling<br>Journal for Specialists in Group Work<br>Journal of Addictions and Offender Counseling<br>Journal of College Student Development<br>Journal of Employment Counseling<br>Journal of Mental Health Counseling<br>Journal of Multicultural Counseling & Development<br>Measurement and Evaluation of Counseling & Development<br>Rehabilitation Counseling Bulletin<br>The Career Development Quarterly<br>The Family Journal: Counseling & Therapy for Couples and Families<br>The Journal of Humanistic Education & Development<br>The School Counselor |
| Counseling journals published by other groups | International Journal for the Advancement of Counseling<br>Journal of Applied Rehabilitation Counseling |
| Journals published by the American Psychological Association and its divisions | American Journal of Community Psychology<br>Journal of Abnormal Psychology<br>Journal of Consulting and Clinical Psychology<br>Journal of Counseling Psychology<br>Professional Psychology: Research and Practice<br>Psychotherapy: Theory, Research, and Practice<br>The Counseling Psychologist<br>Psychology of Women Quarterly |
| Journals published in related fields | American Journal of Family Therapy<br>American Journal of Orthopsychiatry<br>Behavioural Psychotherapy<br>Community Mental Health Journal<br>Crisis Intervention<br>Family Therapy<br>Hospital and Community Psychiatry<br>International Journal of Family Therapy<br>International Journal of Group Psychotherapy<br>Journal of Community Psychology<br>Journal of Health and Social Behavior<br>Journal of Marital and Family Therapy<br>Journal of Primary Prevention<br>Journal of Psychosocial Nursing and Mental Health Services<br>Journal of Rehabilitation<br>Mental Retardation<br>Prevention in Human Services<br>Psychosocial Rehabilitation Journal<br>Schizophrenia Bulletin<br>Social Work |

complete a required core curriculum in addition to elective coursework," Wilcoxon & Cecil, 1985, p. 104). Their proposed 60-credit program included 45 semester hours of required coursework covering the CACREP core areas, a two-semester course sequence on community-agency counseling that would cover "an array of information concerning service, management, supervision, and programming in a community-agency setting" (Wilcoxon & Cecil, 1985, p. 102), practicum, and an internship in a community agency. Additionally, their proposed program would include 15 semester hours of elective coursework in an area of the student's interest "such as marital and family counseling, gerontological counseling, substance-abuse counseling, correctional counseling (adult or juvenile), agency administration, counseling of special population (e.g., hearing-impaired clients, mentally retarded clients), psychometrics and assessment, and health care counseling" (Wilcoxon & Cecil, 1985, p. 103).

A third example of a prescriptive approach is provided by Lewis and Lewis's (1983) suggestion of a number of principles that should be employed in training community counselors. These include: training counselors to be open to working with paraprofessionals and volunteers; developing skills in needs assessment and in program development and evaluation; developing knowledge of the full range of service delivery systems; developing skills in working as a member of a team; having student counselors learn about social systems and the principles of social change; having students learn to be trainers, consultants, and mental health educators, as well as direct service providers; and having students examine how their values, attitudes, and goals affect their practice of their profession.

Examples of the descriptive approach to community counseling program development include DeRidder, Stephens, English, and Watkins (1983); Richardson and Bradley (1986); Cowger, Hinkle, DeRidder, and Erk

(1991); and Hershenson and Strein (1991). Instead of starting from theoretical premises, DeRidder et al. (1983) surveyed the directors of a wide range of agencies that employ community counseling graduates (aged, alcohol and drug, children and youth, community action, employment, mental health, mental retardation, probation, public health, public welfare, and vocational rehabilitation agencies). A total of 345 agency administrators, spread across these 11 types of agencies, ranked 13 skill areas that they wished new counselors they hired to possess. These skills were derived from state certification criteria. Skills were rated as essential (3), of possible value (2), or of little value (1). Somewhat surprisingly, all agency directors across all settings agreed that four competencies from the list were essential. These were: (a) an understanding of human growth and development and of the barriers to learning and adjustment; (b) skills in individual, group, and family counseling across diverse socioeconomic and cultural groups for varied personal, educational, and career issues; (c) knowledge of ethics; and (d) ability to write clear, coherent, usable reports. All also agreed that statistics and research was the least essential skill from among those listed for the entry-level counselor. The other eight skills on the list included: knowledge of personality theory; knowledge of substance and child abuse; client assessment; group counseling; career development and job placement; consulting; knowledge of and ability to use resources; and applying knowledge gained from supervised experiences (practicum and internship). These skills varied in ranking depending on the work setting of the respondents. Thus, career development and job placement, ranked next to last by the mental health agency directors, was ranked at the top by the employment agency directors and by the vocational rehabilitation agency directors. Through studies of this sort, counselor educators can determine what content to include and to emphasize in preparing community counselors for work in various types of settings. This assumes, of course, that the samples of agency directors polled were representative and that other factors, such as future directions in which the profession will probably move, are also taken into consideration.

As noted earlier in this chapter, Richardson and Bradley (1986) conducted a national survey of all 425 known counselor education programs for ACA and two of its divisions (ACES and AMHCA). This survey sought to determine the then-current status of preparation programs for community agency counselors. Of the 309 usable responses, they found that 90 percent of the programs were offering training in community agency counseling. Typically, these programs utilized faculty who had appropriate training, credentials, and experience in community agency settings. There was considerable diversity across programs in curriculum, practicum, and internship requirements. At the time of the survey, only 55 percent of the responding programs offered an introductory course in community agency counseling; only 29 percent required a course covering ethical, legal, and professional issues relevant to community agency counseling; and only 25 percent required that their students in community agency counseling take both a practicum and an internship in an agency setting. An increasing number of programs appeared to be developing specialization areas within community agency counseling. At the same time, the content areas of these programs appeared to be significantly influenced by two forces: state licensure/certification laws and professional accreditation standards (primarily CACREP). The resulting trend was toward greater professionalization of the specialty. At the time of the survey (1983), 22 of the responding programs had CACREP accreditation in Counseling in Community and Other Agency Settings, and a larger number of other programs indicated that they were preparing to apply for it.

In 1988, Cowger, Hinkle, DeRidder, and Erk (1991) surveyed all 45 CACREP-accredited community counseling programs concerning the content of their curriculum in the CACREP core areas and in their community counseling specialization. Among the 32 departments responding, they found considerable diversity in their community counseling specializations, including a lack of consistency in the title of the program, the number of courses required, the required coursework in community counseling, and the specialized elective courses that were offered as part of the community counseling program. On the basis of their findings, the authors concluded that a number of fundamental issues need to be resolved before one can determine what a community counselor education program should look like. These issues include the nature and scope of community counseling programs, the need for greater clarity and consistency in core and specialty requirements across programs (as to both topics covered and number of credits required), the nature and role of specialized areas within a community counseling program curriculum, and the place of courses in psychopathology, clinical diagonis, and psychopharmacology in community counselor education.

In 1989, Hershenson and Strein (1991) contacted all 51 CACREP-accredited community counseling programs for a copy of their curriculum. Of the 23 responses received, they found that programs tended to focus more on the treatment of psychopathology (as is characteristic of master's programs in clinical psychology) than on the approaches that are uniquely identified with counseling, such as prevention, resource utilization, attention to the client's environment, the use of support systems, and the area of work behavior.

Thus, we have reviewed examples of the two principal approaches to community counseling program development. The prescriptive approach provides a theory-based ideal, and the descriptive approach provides a picture of what exists in reality. The greatest advantage of the prescriptive approach is that it begins with an idealized conception of the field and thus creates a program "as it should exist." Conversely, the greatest disadvantage of the prescriptive approach is that ideal conceptions rarely are capable of being perfectly realized, and one has little control over exactly where and how the reality will fall short. Thus, what might appear to be a minor compromise to facilitate implementation may significantly affect the intended end product. On the other hand, the alternative descriptive approach of seeing what exists as the basis for defining a proper training program has its own advantages and disadvantages. The principal advantage is that one has an empirically proven example to follow. One can be reasonably sure that if one does a certain thing, one will get a predictable outcome. The principal disadvantage is that what currently exists may not be that good or that indicative of what will be needed in the future. Therefore, in constructing a curriculum for community counseling, one must utilize insights derived from both approaches. A program that neglects the theory base of the field in its design will produce technicians who possess only a specific set of skills that may rapidly become outdated, rather than professionals who will move the field forward. At the same time, a program that neglects current practices in the field and the wishes of employers will produce sophisticated but unemployable graduates.

In the next chapter, we shall examine the range of settings in which community counseling graduates are employed.

## EXERCISE

Before proceeding, prepare your response to the following situation:

You have been asked to testify before the health and welfare committee of your state legislature, which is developing legislation designating which fields should be recognized as service providers by the state. Your task is to give a 15- to 20-minute presentation explaining what community counseling is, what is unique about the field, and why it should be recognized as a service provider. Outline your presentation, using the information you gained from reading this chapter.

## REFERENCES

Amos, W. E., & Williams, D. E. (1972). *Community counseling: A comprehensive team model for developmental services.* St. Louis: Warren H. Green.

Anthony, W., Cohen, M., & Farkas, M. (1990). *Psychiatric rehabilitation.* Boston, MA: Center for Psychiatric Rehabilitation.

Anthony, W. A., Pierce, R. M., & Cohen, M. R. (1979) *The skills of diagnostic planning. Psychiatric rehabilitation practice series: Book 1.* Amherst, MA: Carkhuff Institute of Human Technology.

Borow, H. (1964). Milestones: A chronology of notable events in the history of vocational guidance. In H. Borow (Ed.), *Man in a world at work* (pp. 45–64). Boston: Houghton Mifflin.

Brown, D., & Srebalus, D. J. (1972). *Contemporary guidance concepts and practices: An introduction.* Dubuque, IA: Wm. C. Brown.

CACREP Fact Sheet. (1995, Summer). *CACREP Connection*, p. 8.

Conyne, R. K. (1980). The "community" in community counseling: Results of a national survey. *Counselor Education and Supervision, 20,* 22–28.

Council for Accreditation of Counseling and Related Educational Programs. (1988, July). *Accreditation procedures manual and application.* Alexandria, VA: Author.

Council for Accreditation of Counseling and Related Educational Programs. (1991, October). *Accreditation procedures manual and application: July, 1988, revised.* Alexandria, VA: Author.

Council for Accreditation of Counseling and Related Educational Programs. (1994, January). *CACREP accreditation standards and procedures manual*. Alexandria, VA: Author.

Cowger, E. (1991, Winter). Community agency interest network update. *ACES Spectrum*, p. 2.

Cowger, E. L., Jr., Hinkle, J. S., DeRidder, L. M., & Erk, R. R. (1991). CACREP community counseling programs: Present status and implications for the future. *Journal of Mental Health Counseling, 13*, 172–186.

DeRidder, L. M., Stephens, T. A., English, J. T., & Watkins, C. E., Jr. (1983). The development of graduate programs in community counseling: One approach. *AMHCA Journal, 5*, 61–68.

Hayes, R. L. (1984, March). Report on community counseling. *ACES Newsletter*, p. 15.

Herr, E. L., & Cramer, S. H. (1987). *Controversies in the mental health professions*. Muncie, IN: Accelerated Development.

Herr, E. L., & Cramer, S. H. (1992). *Career guidance and counseling through the lifespan: Systematic approaches* (4th ed.). New York: Harper Collins.

Hershenson, D. B. (1990). A theoretical model for rehabilitation counseling. *Rehabilitation Counseling Bulletin, 33*, 268–278.

Hershenson, D. B., & Strein, W. (1991). Toward a mentally healthy curriculum for mental health counselor education. *Journal of Mental Health Counseling, 13*, 247–252.

Levine, M., & Perkins, D. V. (1987). *Principles of community psychology: Perspectives and applications*. New York: Oxford Univ. Press.

Lewis, J. A., & Lewis, M. D. (1977). *Community counseling: A human services approach*. New York: Wiley.

Lewis, J. A., & Lewis, M. D. (1983). *Community counseling: A human services approach* (2nd ed.). New York: Wiley.

Lewis, J. A., & Lewis, M. D. (1989). *Community counseling*. Pacific Grove, CA: Brooks/Cole.

Lewis, R. (1993, November). Boomers may have rosier retirement than predicted. *AARP Bulletin*, p. 14.

Lockwood, W. V. (1952). Adult guidance: A community responsibility. *Personnel and Guidance Journal, 31*, 31–34.

Loesch, L. C., & Vaac, N. A. (1993). *A work behavior analysis of professional counselors*. Greensboro, NC: National Board for Certified Counselors and Muncie, IN: Accelerated Development.

Mann, P. A. (1978). *Community psychology: Concepts and applications*. New York: Free Press.

O'Bryant, B. J. (1993, August). Presidential perspectives: The quest. *ACA Guidepost*, pp. 3, 18.

Orford, J. (1992). *Community psychology: Theory and practice*. Chichester, UK: Wiley.

Rappaport, J. (1977). *Community psychology: Values, research, action*. New York: Holt, Rinehart, & Winston.

Remley, T. P., Jr. (1992, August). Perspectives from the executive director: Are counselors unique? *ACA Guidepost*, p. 4.

Richardson, B. K., & Bradley, L. J. (1986). *Community agency counseling: An emerging specialty in counselor preparation programs*. Alexandria, VA: American Association for Counseling and Development Foundation.

Richmond, L., & Robinson, G. (1993, April). ACA and AMHCA confer on professional identity. *AMHCA Advocate*, p. 16.

Rockwell, P. J., Jr. (1991). The counseling profession: A historical perspective. In D. Capuzzi & D. R. Gross (Eds.), *Introduction to counseling: Perspectives for the 1990s* (pp. 5–24). Boston: Allyn and Bacon.

Stadler, H. A., & Stahl, E. (1979). Trends in community counselor training. *Counselor Education and Supervision, 19*, 42–48.

Stickle, F. E., & Schnacke, S. B. (1984). A survey of accredited counselor education programs. *Counselor Education and Supervision, 23*, 187–196.

Tyler, L. E. (1969). *The work of the counselor* (3rd ed.). New York: Appleton-Century-Crofts.

Wilcoxon, S. A. (1990). Community mental health counseling: An option for the CACREP dichotomy. *Counselor Education and Supervision, 30*, 26–36.

Wilcoxon, S. A., & Cecil, J. H. (1985). Community-agency counseling: A model for counselor preparation. *Counselor Education and Supervision, 25*, 99–106.

# 3

# PRACTICE SETTINGS

In this chapter, we shall survey the principal settings in which community counselors work. As we have stated, community counselors typically practice in agency or organizational settings rather than in elementary and secondary schools. At the same time, as was noted in Chapter 2, in 1945 the Baltimore Public School System began providing community counseling as "a free public service where [adults and out-of-school youth] can obtain guidance in making educational, vocational, and other plans. The Information and Counseling Service for Adults...offer[ed] information, counseling, referral, and related services to individuals who desire assistance in adjusting their problems" (Lockwood, 1952, p. 32). The location of community counseling programs in public school systems, while never common, did not end with this program. In 1978, Lazes and Feldberg reported on a community counseling program that was offered through the Adult Consumer Homemaking Project of the Great Neck, New York, public schools. Like the Baltimore program, this service was free. In this case, however, the clientele was limited to "the disadvantaged, defined as those who have special needs that are not being satisfied by a community service or agency. The list

includes: low income, foreign born, senior citizens, mentally and physically handicapped, unemployed, school dropouts, teenage and single parents, socially isolated" (Lazes & Feldberg, 1978, p. 60). This program included courses, workshops, and up to six 45-minute sessions of individual counseling that provided support, information, and/or referral. Clients evaluated the community counseling program favorably.

When, however, in 1983 Richardson and Bradley (1986) surveyed counselor preparation programs as to the types of community settings that employed their graduates, all of the 219 respondents listed community mental health centers, just over half listed juvenile and adult probation agencies, and between 40 percent and 13 percent listed, in descending order of frequency: family and children's services, alcohol and drug abuse programs, rehabilitation services, hospitals, educational agencies, and broad-based community services. Such settings as churches, services for the elderly, business and industry, employee services, government programs, and private practice were listed by fewer respondents; but at the time of the survey, most of these settings represented relatively new employment options for counselors. In a separate study of agencies in a single state (Tennessee) that employed counselors, conducted at about the same time, DeRidder et al. (1983) also identified employment security and mental retardation agencies as settings in which community counselors were employed. Moreover, in the decade after these two surveys, new settings that employ community counselors have come into existence, including shelters for victims of domestic violence and abuse, health maintenance organizations, psychosocial rehabilitation programs, counseling programs for military personnel and their dependents, and programs for the homeless. In this chapter we shall review a variety of these settings, beginning with the more prevalent ones.

## COMMUNITY MENTAL HEALTH CENTERS

The development of community mental health centers (CMHCs) over the past 30 years was discussed in Chapter 1. One of the objectives for the development of CMHCs was to change rapidly the balance of community versus mental hospital resources (Gruenberg, 1972). Since the legislation was enacted in 1963, more than 760 catchment areas have received federal support for the development of a local, population-based, prevention-oriented system of services that was intended to be accessible and available to all who needed it irrespective of their ability to pay (Pardes, 1982). The federal commitment to community mental health, fueled by the steady infusion of millions of dollars of federal funds, was reaffirmed regularly for almost two decades (Winslow, 1982).

Since their inception, these centers have attempted to maintain an emphasis on:

1. Primary prevention, namely, a service designed to assist groups of individuals identified as high risks for the development of behavior disorders (Gibson et al., 1983).

2. Crisis intervention, a major service of most CMHCs.

3. Consultation, an indirect service that may take the form of consulting with other institutions or agencies, such as schools, welfare agencies, law enforcement personnel, substance abuse centers, and hospitals.

4. Remediation and rehabilitation services, including the diagnosis and treatment of mental disorders. The clients of CMHCs may range in severity from those who require intensive psychiatric-medical treatment to those who need only routine adjustment counseling. The treatment approaches might include a broad spectrum from intensive, long-term psychotherapy to a skill building orientation in which the individual is helped to acquire the social and other skills that are necessary for adjustment to everyday-life tasks and roles.

5. Educational programs, which include programs concerning the nature of mental health and those that encourage community involvement in planning and evaluating services.

Also, many CMHCs offer advocacy services on behalf of individual clients, assistance in organizing the local community to bring about needed environmental change, and linkage with support systems and helping networks (Lewis & Lewis, 1977). Further, partial hospitalization and home services have been offered by many centers, but these opportunities have decreased as federal funds have been reduced (Okin, 1984). Moreover, CMHCs have played a significant role in the education and training of mental health professionals (Winslow, 1982).

Though the main target population in the CMHC was intended to be the severely and chronically mentally ill, during the period from 1971 to 1975 there was a significant decrease in the percentage of new patients diagnosed as having a depressive disorder or schizophrenia, and an increase in the percentage classified as socially maladjusted, no mental disorder, deferred diagnosis, or nonspecific condition (DHEW, 1978). Over the years, centers have been widely criticized for inadequate attention to this population, for evidence is cited demonstrating that patients with schizophrenia and affective illness constituted only 16 percent and 18 percent, respectively, of total admissions in 1971 and declined further to 10 percent and 13 percent in 1978 (Goldman, Regier, & Taub, 1980; Langeley, 1980). Considering this information, the reader should note two factors of particular importance: the inability of hospital-affiliated centers to gain access to general and private hospital inpatient beds for their acutely disturbed patients; and the fact that the entire financing and reimbursement system appears to conspire against the noninstitutional care of the chronically ill client (Talbott, 1978). But there is evidence that the block grant mechanism has resulted in greater attention to the chronically mentally disabled population (Okin, 1984). Additionally, a population of young, adult, chronically mentally disabled clients who have spent relatively little time in mental hospitals has emerged in the community (Green & Koprowski, 1981). In order to serve this population and at the same time survive in an era of increasing budget cuts, CMHCs must begin, according to Winslow (1982), "to develop closer relationships with community health centers, clinics, hospitals, and medical centers" (p. 276). The real question for the future of CMHCs may not be whether they will survive, but in what form, responding to which funding sources, caring for which patients, with what manpower, and through what services (Okin, 1984).

The staffing patterns have changed significantly since the initial development of CMHCs. There has been a decline in psychiatrists, and administratively the percentage of centers directed by psychiatrists decreased from more than 60 percent in 1971 to 16.4 percent in 1980 (Winslow, 1982). Large gains have been made, however, by psychologists and social workers, whose positions in the average center increased by 55 percent and 32 percent, respectively, between 1973 and 1979 (Okin, 1984). The involvement of registered nurses has also grown considerably in CMHCs. CMHC leadership has been increasingly entrusted to nondoctoral-level professionals. More centers are being directed by master's- and bachelor's-level staff who often are not mental health professionals but who have a wide variety of human service–related skills.

In 1969 Randolph investigated CMHC employers' perceptions of desirable skills and characteristics of master's-level counselors. Using a 76-item questionnaire and with 117 completed instruments that were returned to the author, Randolph (1979) reported that highly ranked skills included intake interviewing; individual, family, and group counseling; crisis intervention; consultation; psychodiagnostic and educational assessment; knowledge of community referral resources; and good oral and written communication skills.

In late 1985 and early 1986, West, Hosie, and Mackey (1987) surveyed the 250 CMHCs that were identified by the National Institute of Mental Health (NIMH) as multiservice mental health agencies concerning their use of employees with master's degrees in counseling. Of the 213 centers responding, 80 percent employed master's-level counselors. In over 90 percent of the agencies that employed counselors, counselors conducted intake interviews, participated in treatment decisions, and conducted individual, family, and group counseling for outpatients. In over 80 percent of these agencies, counselors provided consultation and educational services; and in 25 percent to 45 percent of the agencies, counselors did various types of testing. In late 1986, West, Hosie, and Mackey (1988) sent a second survey to the 170 CMHCs that employed counselors as identified by their first survey. This second survey focused on the center directors' evaluation of the knowledge, service delivery skills, and administrative skills of the counselors whom they employed. These evaluations were made on a 7-point scale, with 4 being "adequate" and 7 being "very high. " On the 150 responses, the average rating for counselors was above 4.4 on all 20 items included in the survey except knowledge of psychotropic medication (the only item that averaged below 4.0), personality testing, knowledge of DSM III, and assisting in evaluating services. The four highest rated items, all averaging above 5.0, were outpatient individual counseling, crisis intervention, intake interviews, and client staffings. The authors concluded that community counselors preparing to work in CMHCs should gain additional knowledge of psychotropic medication, abnormal behavior and the DSM classification system, and the administration and use of tests.

## CORRECTIONS AND PROBATIONS

Prisons serve both to help rehabilitate criminals and to control and isolate persons viewed as hazards to the general public. Although programs to rehabilitate offenders through prison counseling and vocational education classes have recently been deemphasized (Geis, 1983), these efforts have resulted in counselors performing multiple roles such as assessment, treatment, training consultation, and research (Whiteley & Hosford, 1983). Yet the need for counseling services in prisons and jails is substantial (Scott, 1985). Widespread prison overcrowding and the process of incarceration induce high levels of stress (Masuda, Cutler, Hein, & Holmes, 1978).

Scott (1985) explained that "because of the diversity and magnitude of problems encountered in prison environments, counselors often function in inter-related roles, assessing and treating prisoners, training prison staff, and serving as human relations or research consultants to prison administrators" (p. 272). Such role diversity, however, may lead to ethical and therapeutic dilemmas (Scott, 1985). Counselors who function in a prison and who attempt to maintain awareness of their professional values or ethical codes that emphasize the value, worth, and dignity of the individual often find themselves enmeshed in at least two roles—individual counselor and environmental consultant or potential environmental change agent. These two roles and their competing ethical responsibilities may pose serious ethical dilemmas (Scott, 1985).

Though many public offenders—those who have broken the law and who have problems living within the confines of society—are located in prisons or jails, these persons can also be found in corrections facilities, divisions of youth services, rehabilitation settings, schools, mental health settings, and private practice settings (Page, 1985). Community counselors who have an interest in this client population may be employed, consequently, in a variety of settings, including probation/parole agencies and local/state governments. Similar to counselors in prisons, however, the role of counselors in correctional agencies can be a conflicted one. Though they perform assessment, consultation, and short-term counseling functions, it is difficult to form effective relationships with clients (Page, 1985). The counselor is often expected to act as a custodial officer, namely, to police the deviant behavior of clients and to punish clients when necessary (Page, 1985).

The role of the community counselor working in correctional settings is, therefore, a challenging one. The future of programs to assist in the vocational education and life adjustment of public offenders is uncertain. Ethical dilemmas are ever present and are a pervasive problem related to the fact that the average citizen of the United States probably has, as Page (1985) stated,

> *a great deal of ambivalence about whether or not public offenders should receive counseling. The average American often thinks that public offenders have broken the law, are manipulators, and should be punished for what they have done. The hardening of people's attitudes in society and within the criminal justice system toward criminals has been a problem for the Public Offender Counselor Association because there has been a tendency within the criminal justice system to eliminate rehabilitation programs.* (p. 455)

## FAMILY COUNSELING SERVICES

The ever-increasing divorce rate, children living in single-parent households, and the stress often created by dual-career marriages have all led to a significant increase in marriage and family counseling. Much of this increase is reflected in the caseloads of counseling professionals in community counseling centers or in private practice. Additionally, private and tax-supported marriage and family counseling centers have been growing in large metropolitan areas (Gibson et al., 1983).

A variety of counseling approaches are used in these settings, including:

1. Conjoint marital counseling, perhaps the most popular approach among marital counselors today, which emphasizes the counseling of both spouses together during all the therapeutic sessions (Gibson et al., 1983).

2. Concurrent marital counseling, when both partners undergo concurrent but separate counseling directed at providing each partner with insights that may lead ultimately to change.

3. Family counseling, which involves the whole family.

4. Group counseling, which consists of groups of couples seeking marital assistance.

5. Enrichment groups, or programs that focus on enhancement of the marital and family relationship by emphasizing, for example, educational skill-building techniques in the areas of communication, cooperation, and problem solving.

6. Sex therapy or counseling.

In addition to providing counseling to troubled couples and families, counselors also perform assessment and community education functions. An accurate diagnosis of marital and family problems is essential if intervention is to be successful. Community education may take the form of developing programs that alert families to existing resources for help.

## DOMESTIC VIOLENCE AND CHILD ABUSE SHELTERS

Domestic violence and child abuse is rampant in the United States and the personal, social, and economic costs are inestimable. Abramson (1977) reported that one third of all married people engage in spouse assault. The National Center on Child Abuse and Neglect estimates that every year approximately 1 million children are maltreated by their parents; of these, 100,000 to 200,000 are physically abused, 60,000 to 100,000 are sexually abused, and the remainder are neglected (Barnett, Pittman, Ragan, & Salus, 1980). To respond to these serious problems, agencies and programs have been established to assist helping professionals, including community counselors, to aid these victimized individuals.

Safe houses, refuges, or shelters have become the cornerstone of treatment for battered women who do not wish to return home (Walker, 1979). Erin Pizzey founded the first known refuge in England in 1971; since then, approximately 400 have been established in the United States (Alessi & Hearn, 1984). These shelters may provide medical help, vocational training, counseling, and rehousing, as well as impart information on women's legal rights, welfare, and court advocacy. Many shelters also offer a self-development program for the women that will encourage their self-determination, facilitate increased public awareness of the problem of household violence and the need for the support of the public and private sectors, and attempt to induce change within the existing public agencies that are in a position to respond effectively to the victims of household violence (Roberts, 1984). Many shelters further provide a 24-hour crisis telephone line. The importance of the shelter movement is that it provides a sense of community and a support system. The amount of time that women spend in a shelter varies. Most shelters in this country find between four and six weeks to be the optimum stay (Walker, 1979).

Another treatment population has also emerged within the area of domestic violence. This population is the children who find themselves in shelters for victims of domestic violence (Alessi & Hearn, 1984). They are usually in crisis and are experiencing acute feelings of separation and loss (experienced as anger, fear, and emotional pain), and they have difficulty coping with these feelings in a healthy fashion (Fleming, 1979). A crisis model and educational components have been developed within the shelters to alleviate these problems (Alessi & Hearn, 1984).

Programs for abused and neglected children may include day care, foster care, physical health care, mental health services, companion advocacy, or group residential treatment. There are very few settings that deal exclusively with the delivery of counseling services for abused children, because assistance opportunities can be found in community mental health centers and many marriage and family counseling resources. Many programs have been initiated, however, for abusive parents,

and they are frequently offered by municipal and county governments (Benjamin & Walz, 1983). Community-based volunteer groups have also been successful in providing multidisciplinary consultation for developing a comprehensive management plan in cases of child abuse and neglect (LeBlang, 1979). Also, primary prevention programs are vitally important to remedy this widespread problem, and they are offered in school, family counseling, and community centers.

The predominant staffing pattern for the shelters for battered women includes paraprofessionals and volunteer workers (Roberts, 1984). Almost half of existing programs report having a former battered woman on staff, and self-help or peer counseling groups are generally an important component of programs for abused women (Roberts, 1984). Roberts (1984) has also explained that survey research conducted in 1980 among shelters for abused women indicated that 44 percent of the reporting agencies had professional counselors, social workers, and/or psychologists on staff. Because many different kinds of agencies deliver services to abused children and their families, the job functions of the counselor will vary. To function effectively in these settings, community counselors need an extensive background not only in crisis, short-term, and group counseling approaches, but also in marriage and family dynamics. Community counselors should also be prepared to act as consultants. In this capacity they conduct training for paraprofessionals and/or assist the staff in improving their group counseling techniques, intervention approaches with the abusive partner, and methods of influencing local community agencies (i.e., police, courts) about the necessity for early identification of family violence. Roberts (1984) indicated, "that battered women's programs should recruit counselors with advanced training who, in addition, possess the following attributes: nonjudgmental attitude; good listening ability, supportive and caring attitude; and an overriding concern for the welfare of the client" (p. 74).

## SUBSTANCE ABUSE PROGRAMS

Over the past 25 years there has been a substantial increase in the number of counseling centers that specialize in working with persons who have problems with alcohol and drug abuse (Gibson et al., 1983). Many of these centers are located in large metropolitan areas and medium-sized communities. They tend to provide three categories of services: (1) education/prevention, (2) treatment and rehabilitation, and (3) consultation. Some of the programs have residential treatment centers, and staffing is often comparable to other community mental health agencies.

Client assessment is an important function for counselors working in these facilities, for most substance abuse centers do extensive "workups" on their clients. Family, education, and career information are gathered, as well as the history of substance abuse and personal traits. From this assessment an intervention plan is developed. Gibson et al. (1983) explained that in the formulation of this plan, the staff should be aware of the legal guidelines and implications in the treatment of drug use and of federal regulations governing client records and information exchange.

Other job duties for counselors in these agencies are short-term individual and group counseling; family counseling, when necessary; and liaison with the community. Many substance abuse centers also assume a preventive role in the community. Early detection and intervention of youthful abusers is a particularly essential element of a prevention program.

These centers may be located in hospitals as part of the outpatient services, in a community mental health setting, or as a separate agency not attached to a larger institution. Within these settings various intervention approaches may be followed. Many agencies assist the client by utilizing a medical model approach, whereas others, once the substance abuse is under control, follow a more psychoeducational model that emphasizes the client's development of needed skills to function effectively in the community.

With the incidence of substance abuse increasing in the United States, communities are reaffirming the need to respond to this growing problem. Substance abuse centers are a vital part of the delivery of counseling services. For a community counselor to work effectively in these settings, however, requires special training in the dynamics of substance abuse and the use of direct, tough, and often radical approaches to break through the client's gamesmanship (Forman, 1979).

Hosie, West, and Mackey (1988) surveyed 435 substance abuse centers, a 60 percent sample of all such centers accredited by the Joint Commission on Accreditation of Hospitals. On the 287 questionnaires returned, more reported that their program directors (30 percent) held master's degrees in counseling than held degrees in any other category (social work, psychology, other degrees, or nondegreed), while more programs employed master's degree counselors (73 percent) and master's degree social workers (73 percent) as staff members than any other category of professional. Duties performed by master's-level counselors included individual, group, and family therapy and vocational counseling with inpatient, outpatient, and aftercare clients; substance abuse education and consultation to the community; supervision; community needs assessment; program evaluation; and budget planning for the agency.

In a subsequent survey of 206 substance abuse centers (157 usable questionnaires returned), Hosie, West, and Mackey (1990) found that over 80 percent of the respondents rated master's-level counselors as adequate or above on 14 of 17 knowledge areas and 8 of 10 skills. The three knowledge areas in which counselors were rated as adequately prepared by less than 80 percent of the respondents were measures of personality, methadone maintenance programs, and measures of neurological impairment. The two deficient skill areas were testing and evaluating neurological impairment and (by just one percentage point below 80 percent) vocational counseling. In all other areas of knowledge of substance abuse treatment and in all other relevant therapeutic and administrative skills, master's-level counselors were seen as adequately prepared to provide professional services in substance abuse centers.

## SERVICES FOR THE AGING

The number of persons over 60 years of age (and proportionately more so, those over 85 years of age) continues to grow rapidly, concomitant with the social and economic problems inherent to their age group. Shanks (1983) reported that consequently there is a pressing demand to expand counseling services to the elderly. The very nature of the aging process strongly implies a need for intensified and additional support, yet older people are underserved by all forms of mental health service (Redick & Taube, 1980). Myers (1983) reported "that it has been well established that although over 12% of the nation's population is elderly, only 2% to 4% of persons seen in outpatient mental health clinics are in the over-60 age group" (p. 69). Well over half of all nursing home patients have symptoms of mental health problems, yet mental health services for this group are, in general, nonexistent (Edinberg, 1985). Puterski (1982) stated that programs that successfully reach the elderly are usually ones that bring in the least amount of fees, are costly in terms of outreach and coordination, and are therefore the first to be cut back when budgets become tight. As a result, however, of a trend in the late 1960s to "return" older schizophrenics and persons with senile dementia to

their communities, which often meant a nursing home ill-prepared to cope with behavioral problems presented by these persons, custodial care of the elderly has risen proportionately. Older persons have left or never entered the formal mental health system, and settings such as nursing homes have frequently become the agencies to provide mental health care (Kahn, 1975). Edinberg (1985) also asserted that agencies that fall under the auspices of the Older Americans Act of 1965, including meal programs, certain social service programs, and programs funded by discretionary grants do not, as a rule, have close working relationships with mental health system services.

Even with all these obstacles to effectively serving the elderly, community agencies to serve this population have increased since 1978, and many employ community counselors. The delivery of services to the elderly usually takes place within organizations of two general types, namely, institutions and community settings. Ordinarily, institutional facilities include nursing homes and mental hospitals, both of which are designed to care for persons from a few weeks to an indefinite period of time. The number of elderly patients in public facilities, however, has been decreasing substantially, suggesting that in the future, nursing homes and community services will need to provide better follow-up and active treatment for the growing number of older persons with diagnosed and identified chronic mental health problems (Edinberg, 1985). At any time, 5 percent of the elderly population is institutionalized, primarily in nursing homes (Butler & Lewis, 1982).

Concerning community settings, a wide variety of agencies providing mental health services may be available to the elderly in a given community. These include community mental health centers; adult day care; and geriatric day hospitals, one of the most rapidly growing services for the elderly (Edinberg, 1985). Agencies generally fall under two types: a medical-rehabilitative model and a psychosocial model. The former emphasizes recovery and rehabilitation from strokes or surgery; the latter emphasizes adaptation and coping with losses, including cognitive impairment (Weiler & Rathbone-McCuen, 1978). Community agencies also include senior centers, which emphasize recreation and leisure activities, though some have active and ongoing programs for health, legal, or housing benefits, and mental health intervention. These senior centers are located in a variety of settings, ranging from newly built senior centers in the middle of towns to church basements, and with adult day care provide excellent opportunities for the delivery of mental health services (Edinberg, 1985). There are private, nonprofit social service agencies that offer such programs as home health aides, outreach, family support groups, and counseling; congregate meal sites established in churches, housing for the elderly, and so on. Although social services and outreach are supposed to be provided in each of these settings, the meals and transportation are usually a higher priority. There are also state and municipal programs, developed to provide mental health assistance, and hospitals and visiting nurse associations.

Community counselors working in these different settings may perform a variety of functions, such as short-term counseling, crisis intervention, consultation, program development, and education. The principal duties, of course, depend on the main goals of the agency and its particular intervention approach, namely, a medical model or a psychosocial model. Importantly, there are several trends in mental health services to the elderly that can be considered extensions of traditional direct service: outreach, peer counseling, and working with support systems (Edinberg, 1985). Outreach services locate older persons and inform them of available services (Harbert & Ginsberg, 1979), and Edinberg (1985) believes that "the major mental health service offered

through outreach is creating a trusting relationship that becomes the basis for other services" (p. 273). Peer counselors are older individuals who are trained by professionals and offer counseling to their peers under the auspices of a service agency (Bratter & Tuvman, 1980). Working with support systems usually refers to family, friends, or neighbors who help maintain the older person in his or her home. The family is usually the focus of most professional interest, though other, unrelated older persons can be utilized as volunteers for the source of support.

From their research to identify the essential goals and appropriate roles of counselors engaged in assisting older persons, Johnson and Riker (1982) reported that a preventive, developmental, positive growth approach to counseling older persons is preferred among gerontological counselors. Instead of a reactive or crisis-oriented approach, counselors recognized the need for both preventive and remedial services for older persons. Yet the concerns of older persons are multidimensional and thus demand counseling services that are equally comprehensive in scope (Johnson & Riker, 1982). Barry (1980) reported that the counselor who deals with aging clients must be aware that health needs and financial support are likely to be among their most prevalent and pressing problems. These problems interact with other psychological problems that the aging client may bring to the counselor. Other important problems may include loneliness, low self-esteem, a lack of independence, feelings of uselessness, and dissatisfaction (Barry, 1980).

Counselors, along with other helping groups, are becoming more and more interested in understanding the aging and their needs. This commitment, along with demographic changes and the increased appreciation of nontraditional approaches, strongly suggest that the professional community may change its focus to better serve the elderly. Some of the approaches specifically suggested for use by counselors in working with older persons include life review (Waters, 1990), bibliotherapy (Hynes & Wedl, 1990), genograms (Erlanger, 1990), and cognitive screening (Agresti, 1990).

## PSYCHOSOCIAL REHABILITATION PROGRAMS

Over the past three decades, models of psychosocial rehabilitation have evolved in the community to provide services to persons with long-term mental illness. Leitner (1986) explained that throughout the 1950s and 1960s, several agencies emerged providing community psychosocial rehabilitation services. Following accumulation of 25 years of community experience, the International Association of Psychosocial Rehabilitation Services (IAPSRS) was established in 1975, based on the belief that psychosocial rehabilitation is the core of community support programs. The organization suggested a comprehensive definition of psychosocial rehabilitation:

*A goal oriented program for the mentally ill which provides coping experiences toward improved living in the community. The program emphasizes common sense and practical needs and usually includes services of vocational, residential, social, educational and personal adjustment, and the prevention of unnecessary hospitalization. The psychosocial rehabilitation setting is purposely informal to reduce the psychological distance between staff and members and consciously engages the member as an active participant in program planning, development, policy making, implementation and evaluation.* (Tanaka, 1983, p. 7)

Lanoil (1982) summarized the common elements and goals of many psychosocial centers. These centers provide a type of rehabilitation that emphasizes social, vocational, educational, residential, and evaluation services. In addition, they play an advocacy role in the community while providing emotional support through fostering warm relationships between staff and clients. Clients are called members and are highly involved in the daily running of the "clubhouse. " Basic guidelines include: (a) profound respect for individual differences; (b) belief in mutual self-help; (c) no time limits on participation; (d) basic acceptance of members; (e) emphasis on short-range, realistic goals; (f) social climate of warmth and action; and (g) active participation of members working toward obtaining optimal level of functioning in the community.

Smith, Brown, Gibbs, Sanders, and Cramer (1984) discussed key ingredients that facilitate implementing these principles: an open and clear structure, supportive staff who provide clear limits while fostering client responsibility, and an informal agency atmosphere. These elements encourage clients to make their own plans as well as to gain a sense of belonging and pride that contribute to improving functional abilities. "Significant client involvement makes empowerment of clients possible. Client empowerment means a better mental health system for consumers, families and friends, and that, in turn, means a better community" (Smith et al., 1984, p. 42).

Around the country, many individual programs exist. Each has its unique features resulting from its specific target population and cultural, environmental setting. The initiator of each innovative program takes the responsibility not only to implement the specific program, but also to evaluate it, report outcome measures, and seek improvements (Leitner, 1986).

Community counselors working in these psychosocial centers not only should have an understanding of mental disability and varied counseling approaches, but should also possess diagnostic planning skills. These include extensive interviewing and assessment skills in order to explore the client's strengths and deficits and how they affect one's abilities to function in a particular environment; programming skills, namely, the ability to teach new skills through systematic programming and outlining a series of behavioral goals; career counseling skills; career placement skills; and community coordinating skills, namely, the ability to develop and implement an appropriate program and aid in overcoming client and/or environmental barriers in using available resources (Anthony, Cohen, & Cohen, 1983).

Counselors can also serve as consultants, especially in the training of paraprofessionals, who are frequently utilized in psychosocial centers (Anthony, Cohen, & Farkas, 1990).

## CAREER COUNSELING AGENCIES

Work (including homemaking) occupies about half of most adults' waking hours, at least five days a week. Therefore, issues of career choice, career preparation, job finding, work adjustment, career change, and retirement loom large among the concerns for which people seek counseling. These issues may arise and be dealt with in the course of personal adjustment counseling, such as might be provided at a community mental health center or counseling agency. Frequently, however, career issues may be the identified problem for which counseling is sought. Agencies that focus on providing career counseling (and sometimes along with it, job placement) exist on many college campuses and in the community. Community career counseling services may be supported by government funds, supported by philanthropy (for example, the Jewish Vocational Services), or operated on a private for-profit basis. These agencies are staffed primarily by career counselors and community counselors.

DeRidder et al. (1983) found that in addition to the four competencies reported as essential for counselors across all settings (learning and adjustment, counseling, ethics, and report writing), employers of counselors for positions in employment-related services also indicated that competencies in career development and in consulting were essential. More recently, the National Career Development Association (NCDA Professional Standards Committee, 1992) published a specific list of the competencies required by career counselors. This list includes: (1) individual and group counseling skills, (2) individual and group assessment, (3) program management and implementation, (4) consultation, (5) information and resources, (6) career development theory, (7) special populations, (8) supervision, (9) ethical and legal issues, and (10) research and evaluation. Each of these competencies is spelled out in detail.

## EMPLOYEE ASSISTANCE PROGRAMS

Employee Assistance Programs (EAPs) are providing an increasing number of employment opportunities for community counselors (Hayes, 1990). Associated with business and industry, these programs are intended to assist employees who have job performance problems or who are likely to as a result of personal problems or substance abuse. Twenty percent of United States employees have problems that adversely affect their jobs and personal lives (Myers, 1984). Causes include alcoholism, marital discord, legal and financial difficulties, and excessive stress.

Employee assistance programs incorporate a set of company policies and procedures for identifying (or responding to self-identified) employees experiencing personal or emotional problems that may interfere, directly or indirectly, with acceptable job performance (Walsh, 1982). Yet within those guidelines there remains wide scope for variation from one program to another. Policies and procedures may vary widely in their specific content, and the identification process of employee problems differs from program to program. Also, EAPs vary in the functional units of the company to which they report (medical, personnel, industrial relations), and in the specific arrangements they make with outside referral resources for diagnostic, treatment, and follow-up services (Walsh, 1982).

It is out of the background of occupational alcoholism efforts that the basic ideas on which the EAP concept is based were conceived (Wrich, 1980). In the early 1940s, Alcoholics Anonymous (AA) was beginning to gain recognition as an effective means of helping people to recover from alcoholism and live successful lives without the use of alcohol. A few companies allowed alcoholic employees to return to work after having been terminated when they were able to demonstrate they could maintain sobriety with the help of AA. The idea emerged that perhaps employers could be effective as a source for alleviating the alcoholism problem (Wrich, 1980). In addition to helping in the recovery process by employing recovering alcoholics, perhaps they could participate in the identification process by recognizing employees' problems and then encouraging them to get help before poor job performance resulted in termination. Wrich (1980) explained that "as this concept evolved, the idea emerged that supervisors could be trained in alcoholism symptomatology enabling them to look for these symptoms among subordinates" (p. 11).

In the 1960s, however, programs began to shift their focus from symptomatology of alcoholism to impaired job performance caused by alcoholism. Contributing to this change were such factors as: (a) it would be less stigmatizing to focus on job performance rather than alcoholism symptoms, and (b) supervisors simply were not very good diagnosticians (Wrich, 1980).

Consequently, the underlying theory behind the development of EAPs has been that business and private industry can benefit from providing counseling and related support services to employees and their families. Talagrand (1982) estimated that the behavioral and medical problems of employees represent an annual expense of $1,500 to $4,000 per worker in terms of reduced productivity and absenteeism. These programs are normally designed to provide a range of early intervention services to troubled employees and their families in order to improve the employee's on-the-job performance and productivity. EAPs operate on the premise that both employees and employers can benefit from early detection and treatment of a wide range of employee problems (NCCMH, 1984).

Many EAPs provide: (a) supervisor training in the identification and referral of troubled employees, (b) employee education and orientation to the program, (c) personnel policy development, (d) short-term counseling or referral for all of the previously described problems, and (e) periodic program evaluations. In addition, programs may offer a variety of other services, such as 24-hour emergency treatment, one or more telephone hotlines, on-site workshops, and extensive consultation services for management. When an EAP includes the availability of direct treatment for employees and their families, the service setting may be at the work location or at the offices of a community mental health facility.

The traditional EAP is designed as a "top-down" program. McClellan (1982) explained that

> *It starts with top management support and utilizes a pyramid-shaped, supervisory structure to identify and confront employees with impaired work performance. It works best when superiors are dealing with subordinates; there are clear lines of authority; and there are job descriptions with specific, measurable work performance criteria.* (p. 25)

Yet many modern professional and technical work settings are not structured with pyramid-shaped lines of authority. Work teams sometimes replace authoritarian supervisory structures, and when such an organization does exist, it often has little practical application for many white-collar workers (McClellan, 1982). Also, the nature of a professional's work makes it difficult to document impaired work performance objectively. Consequently, because the pyramid model does not appear to function well for professional, technical, managerial, and clerical workers, other EAP models have developed, such as: (a) the peer group confrontation model as a means of motivating fellow company members into appropriate treatment; or (b) the EAP Service Center model, namely, contracting with an outside agent for EAP services. McClellan (1982) believes that professional and technical workers are more willing than other workers to use EAP services that are located off work premises than to use services located at their place of work. External programs also have the advantage that they can simultaneously use supervisory, personnel department, peer group, family, and voluntary referral systems, whereas an internal program is severely limited in how it can link to peer groups, family members, and self-awareness models as methods of helping the impaired worker.

The backgrounds of service providers and internal EAPs vary. To explore the backgrounds of EAP staff, questionnaires were mailed to member centers of the National Council of Community Mental Health Centers (1984). Of the 614 centers that were mailed the survey questions, a response rate of 74 percent was obtained. The EAPs reported that social workers, psychologists, and counselors comprised 47 percent, 38 percent, and 36 percent, respectively, of the staff. In a survey of 275 EAPs that were members of the Employee Assistance Professionals Association, Hosie, West, and Mackey (1993) received 203 responses. These indicated that persons with master's degrees in counseling were hired by more internal EAPs and more external EAPs than any other type of helping professional, although somewhat more social workers comprised the staff of the respondents and were hired by more external/affiliated EAPS.

The EAP staff have many duties, which include the assessment of each client's presenting problem; crisis intervention; brief counseling; referral, when necessary, to selected community resources most capable of addressing the situation; following the intervention plan, developed in conjunction with the community resource; serving as consultant to physicians, insurance companies, worker's compensation resources, unions and management, and others concerned with the client's well-being; providing professional supervision of employees who volunteer to provide peer support and follow-up services; programming and workshops; performing related administrative duties such as budget; maintaining timely, accurate, and concise case records; outcome evaluation; and marketing of services.

## COUNSELING IN MILITARY SETTINGS

A special type of work setting in which community counselors are employed is the military services. Within this structure, counselors work in a variety of settings, such as family service centers, hospitals, outpatient clinics, and educational programs. These counselors encourage the delivery of guidance, counseling, and educational programs for all members of the armed services, their dependents, veterans, and civilian employees of the armed services. Educational counseling represents a large part of the counseling services offered in the military, because personnel and manpower policies of the military are moving education to a more central role (Cox, 1985). These policies are taking the form of increased opportunities and new programs for men and women in uniform. Every major military installation in the United States and overseas has an on-base education program.

A major component of mental health services delivery for those in the armed forces overseas is the family service center. Usually staffed by counselors and related professional personnel whose main job function is prevention and remediation, these centers are responding to a growing mental health need. Willis and Power (1985) reported that mobility (families in the military are usually moved every few years, causing disruption in family life), separation from the extended family, cross-cultural parentage, a fortress mentality (in which families reside, work, and attend school in a tightly organized, closely observant community that demands conformity to conservative and relatively inflexible behavioral demands), the single-parent military family caused by extended temporary duty, and cross-cultural divorce are all problems for military personnel and their dependents while living overseas. These concerns often cause severe life adjustment problems, and the military, recognizing these difficulties, has established resources to assist in their prevention and remediation. Whether located in a family service/support center or the outpatient department of a military clinic or hospital, social workers, psychologists, and/or community counselors act as consultants to on-base elementary and secondary schools and provide individual and group counseling and psychotherapy. Counselors are also called upon to provide counseling to members of the military who are incarcerated in stockades or brigs for infractions of rules or for legal offenses. Importantly, with a stronger emphasis on the family of military personnel, prevention is being highlighted in many mental health programs on overseas bases. The role of consultant to different military units in order to address potential problems is becoming a large part of the counselor's job duties.

The importance of counseling to the military may be inferred from the fact that for over 25 years, the military has supported graduate counselor training programs for military personnel and their dependents at locations in Japan and Europe where large numbers of service personnel are stationed.

## PRIVATE PRACTICE

Over the past several decades, there has been a significant increase in the number of community counselors who are engaged in individual or group private practice. Much of this growth is due to the increasing number of states that have passed counselor licensure laws. Licensure requirements for counselors vary from state to state, but they have generally facilitated opportunities for counselors to deliver services for independent financial gain. The attainment of licensure or certification, depending on the state in which one seeks to practice, is essential to one's credibility as a private practitioner.

The reasons for referral to these counselors include a wide range of problems, such as emotional, marital, family, job-related, and substance abuse. The intervention approaches vary, of course, according to the philosophy of the counselor and the specific problem. But the process of helping usually involves an initial interview, an information analysis, assessment, the development of counseling objectives, and the implementation of the counseling plan. This implementation may embrace such approaches as individual short-term or long-term counseling, group counseling, marriage and family counseling, and resource mobilization.

Most private practice settings are in an office-like environment. The practice is usually developed by referrals, which are generally created by contacts made in the community by the counselor. Networking is most important for a continuous flow of referrals.

An interesting phenomenon in the private practice sector is the increased number of community counselors who receive referrals from insurance companies to assist claimants with work-related injuries. Of the approximately 4,150 professionals who are employed in private rehabilitation (Workman, 1983), many are counselors. A large number of these serve clients who have back injuries, while persons with other physically disabling conditions (i.e., knee, hand, head, neck, and leg injuries) comprise the rest of this clientele. The ultimate goal of the insurer is the client's return to work, a function that is within the particular expertise of the rehabilitation counselor. Community counselors, however, may provide counseling to assist the client to come to terms with the disability and to regain the motivation to work.

## HEALTH MAINTENANCE ORGANIZATIONS

A major change toward prepaid group health practices is occurring today in the United States. Skyrocketing medical costs and increasing inflation since 1975 have made necessary the search for innovative, more cost-effective ways of providing health care to consumers (Forrest & Affemann, 1986). This trend is best exemplified by a 10 percent annual growth rate of health maintenance organizations (HMOs) (Mayer & Mayer, 1985). Although HMOs have been in existence since the turn of the century, their real period of growth has been since the passage of the Health Maintenance Organization Act of 1973 (PL 93-222), which provided a mechanism to qualify HMOs federally. All employers offering health benefits with more than 25 employees are required to offer their employees access to a federally qualified HMO (Deleon, Vyeda, & Welch, 1985).

The philosophy underlying HMOs is essentially prevention or primary care, and this philosophy is expressed through a contractual arrangement to provide a range of specified health services to subscribers in return for prepaid enrollment. The incentive, therefore, from the HMO standpoint is to maintain health by providing programs or strategies that contribute to healthy behaviors or to increased personal control over medical conditions.

The attractiveness of HMOs comes from their documented cost-effectiveness relative to fee-for-service health care systems. The emphasis on prevention also reduces the long-term financial, physical, and emotional costs associated with unhealthy behaviors. Conversely, HMOs have been criticized as impersonal and lacking in "quality" care because the user purchases services from a system rather than from an individual.

When considering practice settings, it is important to understand that HMOs are essentially controlled by medical systems and service providers. This is always the case, despite the fact that they do not ostensibly espouse the traditional medical model of remediation. There are three typical HMO models with various service plan emphases:

1. The individual practice association (IPA) model, which most nearly approximates the traditional medical care model. Under this model, fee-for-service practitioners function as separate legal entities and submit claims to HMOs for services provided to members of that HMO. The IPA model is the one most frequently used by HMOs, particularly ones that have been established since the 1973 Health Maintenance Organization Act.

2. The group practice model, in which professional staff are salaried employees of the HMO.

3. A combination of the IPA and staff models, in which a group of providers who are separately incorporated receive payments of services on a per member/per month basis.

Mental health services must be offered by federally qualified HMOs. Forrest and Affemann (1986) have identified several reasons for including a mental health department in HMOs. For example, the HMO's stress on secondary (developmental) problems and tertiary (crisis) issues necessitates the use of varied counseling approaches, and this utilization can assist primary physicians in evaluating the contribution of psychological and social factors to the development, course, and outcome of physical and psychiatric disorders. Also, clients would receive counseling in settings with which they were already familiar and comfortable and that often were near their workplaces. Moreover, financial barriers would be kept at a minimum and follow-up could be encouraged because clients would maintain an affiliation with the plan (Forrest & Affemann, 1986).

The patterns of mental health services offered by HMOs have been documented by Chafetz and Salloway (1984). Services include short-term (up to 20) outpatient visits for evaluation and crisis intervention and "as needed" inpatient services. The prevention focus and nature of intervention strategies provided by HMOs are consistent with current community counseling philosophies, particularly Conyne's (1985) "counseling ecology" model, Egan's (1982) developmental model, and the orientation of this book.

The types of services utilized by enrollees of federally qualified HMOs in the survey of Chafetz and Salloway (1984) were in descending order of frequency: diagnostic interviews, individual psychotherapy, group psychotherapy, marital therapy, behavior therapy/modification, alcoholism and drug abuse programs, school problem counseling, psychological testing, biofeedback, psychiatric day-hospital, and vocational counseling. Additional health education approaches utilized include weight control, stress adaptation, and smoking control programs.

Among the workers employed by HMOs are psychiatrists, psychologists, psychiatric nurses, counselors, and social workers. Sank and Shapiro (1979) identified the various roles that mental health workers have performed in HMOs, including:

1. Organizational consultant to the unit on an as-needed basis.

2. Administrator or liaison between full-time administrative staff and clinical providers, particularly when the well-being of patients must be weighted against the limited availability of services and funds.

3. Patient ombudsman, particularly with chronic patients whose needs may be beyond the scope of routine treatment.

4. Clinical consultant as a resource to health care providers in dealing with behavioral and emotional problems of patients.

5. Teacher to outside groups, such as medical students.

6. Supervisor as part of internship programs at the HMO.

These roles are familiar to community counselors. Furthermore, Resnick (1982) stressed the importance of developmental theory and life-span work as part of the preventive philosophy of HMOs. Forrest and Affemann (1986) stated that "according to Resnick (1982), the largest, most prevalent, and most appropriate role of mental health providers in HMOs is offering short-term counseling" (p. 67). The provision of short-term intervention severely limits, of course, the opportunity to deliver consultation, education, and other primary preventive services (Forrest & Affemann, 1986).

With national health insurance policy now being formulated, the role of HMOs and the place of counselors within them remains unresolved.

## OTHER SETTINGS

Other settings in which DeRidder et al. (1983), Richardson and Bradley (1986), and/or Collison and Garfield (1990) reported that community counselors were employed included: (1) hospitals (where they have been used to counsel patients about understanding and adjusting to their illness and about maintaining treatment regimens, to counsel families about family planning and posthospital care of their ill family members, and to consult with medical personnel about interpersonal communications issues; Kim, 1993), (2) residential treatment centers (providing personal adjustment counseling), (3) churches (as pastoral counselors), (4) community college counseling centers, (5) independent living programs for persons with mental retardation, (6) community services such as women's centers and job training programs, (7) public and private employment agencies, and (8) a broad range of local, state, and federal government programs set up to address specific societal needs (for example, the homeless, persons with AIDS, new immigrants, and victims of catastrophic disasters such as floods, fires, and earthquakes).

## CONCLUSION

We have seen that community counselors currently work in a wide array of agencies and programs. Each agency or program may have distinctive expectations for how their services will be delivered. Together with these expectations are the particular needs of major segments of the population for assistance. The community counseling field has demonstrated flexibility in the way these needs receive attention. This range of services, as well as the variety of agencies in which community counselors are called on to provide services, will continue to increase if counselors remain responsive to the changing environment and open to the development of new intervention approaches. In the next chapter, we shall review the ethical and legal aspects of the practice of community counseling across the range of settings in which this field is practiced.

## EXERCISE

As a concluding exercise for this chapter, visit two or three different types of agencies in your geographic area in which community counselors are employed. Speak to one or more community counselors who work there and find out what their job involves, what professional skills they primarily utilize, and how they fit into the overall scope of service of the agency. If you are in a course on community counseling, share your findings with the other members of the class to gain the broadest possible first-hand perspective of the practice settings in which community counselors function.

### REFERENCES

Abramson, C. (1977). *Spouse abuse—An annotated bibliography*. Washington, DC: Center for Women's Policy Studies.

Agresti, A. A. (1990). Cognitive screening of the older client. *Journal of Mental Health Counseling, 12*, 384–392.

Alessi, J. J., & Hearn, K. (1984). Group treatment of children in shelters for battered women. In A. R. Roberts (Ed.), *Battered women and their families* (pp. 49–61). New York: Springer.

Anthony, W., Cohen, M. R., & Cohen, B. F. (1983). Philosophy, treatment process, and principles of the psychiatric rehabilitation approach. *New Directions in Mental Health, 17*, 67–69.

Anthony, W., Cohen, M., & Farkas, M. (1990). *Psychiatric rehabilitation*. Boston, MA: Center for Psychiatric Rehabilitation.

Barnett, E. R., Pittman, C. B., Ragan. C. K., & Salus, M. K. (1980). *Family violence: Intervention strategies*. Washington, DC: U. S. Department of Health and Human Services, Office of Human Development Services, U. S. Government Printing Office.

Barry, J. R. (1980). Counseling the aging. *Personnel and Guidance Journal, 57,* 122–124.

Benjamin, L., & Walz, G. R. (1983). *Violence in the family: Child and spouse abuse.* Ann Arbor: University of Michigan.

Bratter, B., & Tuvman, E. (1980). A peer counseling program in action. In S. S. Sargent (Ed.), *Nontraditional therapy and counseling with the aging.* New York: Springer.

Butler, R. N., & Lewis, M. I. (1982). *Aging and mental health: Positive psychosocial approaches* (3rd ed.). St. Louis: C. V. Mosby.

Chafetz, D. I., & Salloway, J. C. (1984). Patterns of mental health services provided by HMOs. *American Psychologist, 39,* 495–502.

Collison, B. B., & Garfield, N. J. (1990). *Careers in counseling and human development.* Alexandria, VA: American Association for Counseling and Development.

Conyne, R. K. (1985). The counseling ecologist: Helping people and environments. *Counseling and Human Development, 18,* 1–12.

Cox, W. E. (1985). Military educators and counselors association. *Journal of Counseling and Development, 63,* 461–463.

Deleon, P. H., Vyeda, M. K., & Welch, B. L. (1985). Psychology and HMOs: New partnership or new adversary? *American Psychologist, 40,* 1122–1124.

Department of Health, Education, and Welfare. (1978). *The president's commission on mental health. Report to the president* (Vol. 1). Washington, DC: U. S. Government Printing Office.

DeRidder, L. M., Stephens, T. A., English, J. T., & Watkins, C. E., Jr. (1983). The development of graduate programs in community counseling: One approach. *AMHCA Journal, 5,* 61–68.

Edinberg, M. A. (1985). *Mental health practice with the elderly.* Englewood Cliffs, NJ: Prentice-Hall.

Egan, G. (1982). *The skilled helper: Model, skills, and methods for effective helping.* Monterey, CA: Brooks/Cole.

Erlanger, M. A. (1990). Using the genogram with the older client. *Journal of Mental Health Counseling, 12,* 321–331.

Fleming, J. B. (1979). *Stopping wife abuse.* New York: Anchor Press.

Forman, S. I. (1979). Pitfalls in counseling alcoholic clients. *Personnel and Guidance Journal, 57,* 546.

Forrest, D. V., & Affemann, M. (1986, April). The future for mental health counselors in health maintenance organizations. *American Mental Health Counselors Association Journal, 8,* 65–72.

Geis, G. (1983). Criminal justice and adult offenders: An overview. *The Counseling Psychologist, 11,* 11–16.

Gibson, R. L., Mitchell, M. H., & Higgins, R. E. (1983). *Development and management of counseling programs and guidance services.* New York: Macmillan.

Goldman, H., Regier, D., & Taub, C. (1980). Community mental health centers and the treatment of severe mental disorders. *American Journal of Psychiatry, 137,* 83–86.

Green, R. S., & Koprowski, P. F. (1981). The chronic patient with a nonpsychotic diagnosis. *Hospital and Community Psychiatry, 32,* 479–481.

Gruenberg, E. M. (1972). Obstacles to optimal psychiatric service delivery systems. *Psychiatric Quarterly, 46,* 483–496.

Harbert, A. S., & Ginsberg, L. H. (1979). *Human services for older adults: Concepts and skills.* Belmont, CA: Wadsworth.

Hayes, B. (1990). Careers in business and industry. In B. B. Collison & N. J. Garfield (Eds.), *Careers in counseling and human development* (pp. 61–70). Alexandria, VA: American Association for Counseling and Development.

Hosie, T. W., West, J. D., & Mackey, J. A. (1988). Employment and roles of mental health counselors in substance abuse centers. *Journal of Mental Health Counseling, 10,* 188–198.

Hosie, T. W., West, J. D., & Mackey, J. A. (1990). Perceptions of counselor performance in substance abuse centers. *Journal of Mental Health Counseling, 12,* 199–207.

Hosie, T. W., West, J. D., & Mackey, J. A. (1993). Employment and roles of counselors in employee assistance programs. *Journal of Counseling & Development, 71,* 355–359.

Hynes, A. M., & Wedl, L. C. (1990). Bibliotherapy: An interactive process in counseling older persons. *Journal of Mental Health Counseling, 12,* 288–302.

Johnson, R. P., & Riker, H. C. (1982). Counselor's goals and roles in assisting older persons. *American Mental Health Counselors Association Journal, 4,* 30–37.

Kahn, R. L. (1975). The mental health system and the future aged. *The Gerontologist, 15,* 24–31.

Kim, Y. M. (1993). Helping health professionals with the human factor. *American Counselor, 2*(3), 22–24.

Langeley, D. G. (1980). The community mental health center: Does it treat patients? *Hospital and Community Psychiatry, 31,* 815–819.

Lanoil, J. C. (1982). An analysis of the psychiatric psychosocial rehabilitation. *Psychosocial Rehabilitation Journal, 5,* 55–59.

Lazes, R. S., & Feldberg, M. (1978). Community counseling in an adult education setting. *Personnel and Guidance Journal, 57,* 60–61.

LeBlang, T. R. (1979). The family stress consultation team: An Illinois approach to protective services. *Child Welfare, 58,* 597–604.

Leitner, R. (1986). *Deinstitutionalization and community alternatives for the chronically mentally ill.* Seminar paper submitted for the MEd degree, University of Maryland, College Park, MD.

Lewis, M. D., & Lewis, J. A. (1977). The counselor's impact on community environments. *Personnel and Guidance Journal, 55,* 356–358.

Lockwood, W. V. (1952). Adult guidance: A community responsibility. *Personnel and Guidance Journal, 31,* 31–34.

Masuda, M., Cutler, D. L., Hein, L., & Holmes, T. H. (1978). Life events and prisoners. *Archives of General Psychiatry, 35,* 197–203.

Mayer, T. R., & Mayer, G. G. (1985). HMO's: Origins and development. *The New England Journal of Medicine, 312,* 594.

McClellan, K. (1982, September/October). Changing EAP services. *EAP Digest,* pp. 25–29.

Myers, D. W. (1984, March/April). Measuring EAP cost effectiveness: Results and recommendations. *EAP Digest,* pp. 22–25, 44.

Myers, J. E. (1983). A national survey of geriatric mental health services. *American Mental Health Counselors Association Journal, 5,* 69–74.

National Council of Community Mental Health Centers. (1984). Community-based employee assistance programs: A providers' overview. Rockville, MD: Author.

NCDA Professional Standards Committee (1992). Career counseling competencies. *Career Development Quarterly, 40,* 378–386.

Okin, R. L. (1984). How community mental health centers are coping. *Hospital and Community Psychiatry, 35,* 1118–1125.

Page, R. C. (1985). The unique role of the public offender counselor association. *Journal of Counseling and Development, 63,* 455–456.

Pardes, H. C. (1982). Budget, policy changes: NIMH in transition. *Hospital and Community Psychiatry, 33,* 525–526.

Puterski, D. (1982, August). The role of the community mental health center: A case study. In M. Edinberg (Chair), *Aging and mental health: A continuum of care?* Symposium at the annual meeting of the American Psychological Association, Washington, DC.

Randolph, D. L. (1979). CMHC requisites for employment of master's level psychologists/counselors. *American Mental Health Counselors Association Journal, 1,* 64–68.

Redick, R. W., & Taube, C. A. (1980). Demography and mental health care of the aged. In J. E. Birren & R. B. Sloane (Eds.), *Handbook of mental health and aging.* Englewood Cliffs, NJ: Prentice-Hall.

Resnick, H. (1982). The counseling psychologist in community mental health centers and health maintenance organizations—Do we belong? *Counseling Psychologist, 10,* 53–59.

Richardson, B. K., & Bradley, L. J. (1986). *Community agency counseling: An emerging specialty in counselor preparation programs.* Alexandria, VA: American Association for Counseling and Development Foundation.

Roberts, A. R. (1984). *Battered women and their families* (Vol. 1, Springer Series on Social Work). New York: Springer.

Sank, L. I., & Shapiro, J. R. (1979). Case examples of the broadened role of psychology in health maintenance organizations. *Professional Psychology, 10,* 402–406.

Scott, N. A. (1985). Counseling prisoners: Ethical issues, dilemmas, and cautions. *Journal of Counseling and Development, 64*, 272–273.

Shanks, J. L. (1983). Expanding treatment for the elderly: Counseling in a private medical practice. *Personnel and Guidance Journal, 61*, 553–555.

Smith, M., Brown, D., Gibbs, L., Sanders, H., & Cramer, K. (1984). Client involvement in psychosocial rehabilitation. *Psychosocial Rehabilitation Journal, 8*, 35–42.

Talagrand, P. C. (1982, March/April). Implementation of an employee assistance program in a local government setting. *EAP Digest*, pp. 12–25.

Talbott, J. A. (Ed.). (1978). *The chronic mental patient: Problems, solutions and recommendations for a public policy.* Washington, DC: American Psychiatric Association.

Tanaka, H. (1983). Psychosocial rehabilitation: Future trends and directions. *Psychosocial Rehabilitation Journal, 6*, 7–12.

Walker, L. E. (1979). *The battered woman.* New York: Harper & Row.

Walsh, D. C. (1982). Employee assistance programs and untested assumptions. *Milbank Memorial Fund Quarterly/Health and Society, 60*, 493–517.

Waters, E. B. (1990). The life review: Strategies for working with individuals and groups. *Journal of Mental Health Counseling, 12*, 270–278.

Weiler, P. E., & Rathbone-McCuen, E. (1978). *Adult day care: Community work with the elderly.* New York: Springer.

West, J. D., Hosie, T. W., & Mackey, J. A. (1987). Employment and roles of counselors in mental health agencies. *Journal of Counseling and Development, 66*, 135–138.

West, J. D., Hosie, T. W., & Mackey, J. A. (1988). The counselor's role in mental health: An evaluation. *Counselor Education and Supervision, 27*, 233–239.

Whiteley, S. M., & Hosford, R. E. (1983). Counseling in prisons. *The Counseling Psychologist, 11*, 27–34.

Willis, B., & Power, P. W. (1985). Counselors as a resource for teachers in overseas schools. *Elementary School Guidance and Counseling, 19*, 291–299.

Winslow, W. W. (1982). Changing trends in CMHCs: Keys to survival in the eighties. *Hospital and Community Psychiatry, 33*, 273–277.

Workman, E. L. (1983). Vocational rehabilitation in the private, profit-making sector. In E. L. Pan, T. E. Banker, & C. L. Vash (Eds.), *Annual review of rehabilitation* (Vol. 3). New York: Springer.

Wrich, J. T. (1980). *The employee assistance program.* Center City, MN: The Hazelden Foundation.

# 4

# ETHICAL AND LEGAL ISSUES

Certain criteria need to be met for community counselors to attain the status of being members of a profession. Community counselors must: provide specific services; possess specialized knowledge and skills; be competent to utilize their specialized skills in service to their clients; follow an explicit code of ethics; be regulated by legal standards; and assess and upgrade their professional practice (Nugent, 1990). The areas of services, knowledge, skills, competencies, and evaluation of community counseling professionals are addressed specifically in other chapters in this book. This chapter will concentrate on ethical standards related to community counseling and how the profession is regulated by laws. Ethical standards will be addressed first, followed by legal issues related to community counseling.

## ETHICAL STANDARDS

Ethical standards are in essence a code of rules that govern the behavior of members of a profession. They clarify professionals' responsibilities to clients and society, and protect clients and members of the profession from unethical or incompetent practice (Nugent, 1990). Ultimately they serve to develop public trust in the profession (Blocher, 1987). By specifying a code of ethics, professionals proclaim to the public that members of the profession can be expected to follow the rules in the code. If members of a profession fail to adhere to ethical standards they can be publicly sanctioned by the profession's ethics board (Bennett, Bryant, VandenBos, & Greenwood, 1990). This protects the public by informing potential clients about individuals who cannot be trusted to act ethically. It also protects other members of the profession from being associated with those who act unethically and having the public view their profession as untrustworthy.

Codes of ethics serve functions beyond public trust building and ensuring the integrity of a profession's membership. When a profession establishes a code of ethics it consolidates the accepted truths about the profession's goals and how it should function (Smith, McGuire, Abbott, & Blau, 1991). These truths are distilled from a collective history of professional experience, including many painful mistakes. Ideally, codes of ethics offer, in abbreviated form, the most sound wisdom possessed by a profession. This wisdom is an essential foundation for practitioners. It guides them toward greater effectiveness and away from potential disasters. It empowers them to oppose forces outside the profession that may promote unwise practice.

As an example of how the cumulative professional wisdom represented in an ethical standard can guide and empower, consider the case of a community counselor newly employed in a domestic abuse crisis center. The counselor was told by the center's administrator to immediately admit all clients referred to him into a group for anger management. The counselor recognized that this directive violated an ethical standard. Failure to prepare and screen potential group members prior to their entering groups during the boom period of the encounter group movement in the 1960s had resulted in a number of people being hurt by group participation (Yalom, 1985). Cumulative professional experience with this problem resulted in the current American Counseling Association ethical standard that group counselors screen potential group members to ensure they are compatible with the group before admitting them to group counseling. The ethical standard offered the community counselor clear guidance on how to proceed regarding admitting members to the group. The standard also proved persuasive to the administrator of the crisis center, who was not as likely to be persuaded by the opinions of a newly hired community counselor.

## Ethics of Community Counseling

As was noted in Chapter 2, community counseling as a specialty area is disadvantaged by not having a division within the American Counseling Association specifically dedicated to community counseling. One probable result of there being no Community Counseling Division is that unlike other counseling specialties (for example, Mental Health Counseling and Group Work), there are no ethical standards designed specifically for community counseling. Fortunately, the Code of Ethics and Standards of Practice of the American

Counseling Association (1995) are sufficiently broad that they provide a foundation of ethical guidance for community counselors. There are eight sections of the ACA Code of Ethics, as follows: A. The Counseling Relationship; B. Confidentiality; C. Professional Responsibility; D. Relationships with Other Professionals; E. Evaluation, Assessment, and Interpretation; F. Teaching, Training, and Supervision; G. Research and Publication; H. Resolving Ethical Issues. Each area offers descriptions of community counselors' ethical responsibilities within that area. The American Counseling Association also provides 54 Standards of Practice. The Standards of Practice represent minimal behavioral statements of appropriate professional conduct regarding each area in the Ethical Code. The Ethical Code constitutes guidelines for professional behavior; the Standards of Practice are rules governing professional behavior which have been derived from the Ethical Code. The complete American Counseling Association Code of Ethics and Standards of Practice (ACA, 1995) is presented at the end of this chapter.

Effective application of the ACA Code and Standards to community counseling requires applying it to the goals and values inherent in community counseling practice. The community counseling orientation directs counselors to look continually at the function of community in fostering clients' well-being and preventing dysfunction. Community counselors are committed to preventive education, influencing social policy, outreach, and client advocacy (Lewis & Lewis, 1989). They face the challenge of pursuing these values within the general guidelines for ethical practice provided by ACA. As Corey, Corey, and Callanan (1993) point out, this is not always easily done. For example, a community could be sensitized to and educated about mental illness if it became public information that a successful and well-respected business person in the community suffered from depression. Community counselors might welcome public disclosure by this person about his or her struggle with depression as a way of enlightening the community and destigmatizing mental illness. At the same time, it is the community counselors' ethical responsibility to protect their clients' confidentiality. Should a community counselor encourage or discourage disclosure on the part of such a person? The ACA Code and Standards offer guidance by pointing out both that counselors respect clients' right to privacy, *and* that the right to waive privacy belongs to the client. Clearly, the decision to disclose or not rests with the client.

The eight sections of the ACA Code and Standards are summarized below, highlighting how they apply to community counseling and with examples of ethical problems community counselors face related to each of the sections.

## Section A:
## The Counseling Relationship

Ethical standards in this section focus on the goals of counseling (promotion of client development), who is being counseled (individuals, families, and groups, and how they interface during counseling), the process of counseling (plans, clients' rights, coordination of counseling services, fees), respecting diversity (nondiscrimination, understanding clients' cultures, not imposing values), safeguards in counseling (avoidance of dual relationships, prohibition on sex with clients), use of computers (ensuring computer use is appropriate and understandable to clients), and termination (not engaging in or continuing unhelpful counseling, arranging appropriate referral).

Ethical standards governing the counseling relationship are at the heart of the community counseling profession. Protecting clients from harm and promoting their welfare is of central importance. For community counseling the term "client" is expanded to include not only those persons who present themselves for counseling, but their community as well. What follows are two examples of how stan-

dards regarding the counseling relationship could guide community counseling.

A sixteen-year-old Hispanic American high school student seeks counseling regarding her recent discovery that she is pregnant. Following ethical standards the counselor plans, with the client, counseling procedures to promote her development. The counselor suggests involvement of her family and the father, respects her cultural background, and does not impose personal values regarding teen motherhood on the client. The counselor, with the client's permission, coordinates counseling services with a clergy member the client has been seeing. The counselor arranges for the client to be involved in parent effectiveness workshops and a single parent support group prior to termination of counseling. To affect the community, the counselor also works to increase the visibility of planned parenthood services and to influence the high school's policies to make them conducive to the adjustment and development of pregnant students.

As part of their outreach efforts, community counselors are often responsible for providing services to clients whose participation in counseling is not entirely voluntary. Examples include prisoners, patients in hospitals, adolescents in group homes, and court-referred clients. Offering counseling in a way that respects clients' rights to refuse recommended services under these circumstances is particularly challenging. The following steps are helpful:

1. Fully acknowledge the client's perspective on the situation that has brought him or her to counseling and the consequences the client faces if he or she chooses not to engage in counseling.

2. Carefully explain the goals and process of counseling.

3. Provide the client impartial assistance in deciding if he or she will agree to cooperatively engage in counseling. The client's

rights are respected in that it remains his or her decision whether to engage in counseling.

4. If the client decides not to cooperatively engage in counseling, then the counselor is unlikely to be of assistance to the client and should refrain from beginning counseling. An appropriate referral should be offered for the client's consideration.

5. If the client decides to engage in counseling, then an expectation of cooperation has been established. This is conducive to the development of a respectful, productive counseling relationship.

In some settings with some clients, these steps need to be repeated periodically during the course of the counseling relationship.

Community counselors, particularly those working in small communities, often are faced with dual relationship dilemmas. Is it unethical to provide counseling to your third grader's teacher, to your landlord, or to your spouse's best friend? In each case the counselor must assess whether the relationship outside of counseling will compromise the client's integrity, promotion of the client's welfare in counseling, or confidentiality. Community counselors must also recognize that initiation of a counseling relationship will necessarily alter, and usually diminish, the previously established relationship outside of counseling. This can be a high price to pay. In potential dual relationship situations the ethical standard requiring consultation with other professionals when a community counselor has questions about the proper course for ethical behavior is a welcome recommendation.

## Section B: Confidentiality

Confidentiality is considered an essential component of community counseling relationships because it permits clients to disclose material they would be reluctant to share publicly. Confidentiality permits these disclo-sures and establishes counseling relationships as uniquely safe and intimate. Ethical standards address clients' rights to privacy and to be informed about limits to their privacy. The standards cover the confidentiality of counseling sessions (including group and family counseling), records of counseling (written notes, tapes, computer files), when and how confidentiality might not be maintained (client waiver, danger to self or others, contagious fatal disease, court order, minors or incompetent clients), and not revealing the identity of clients when data from the counseling session are used for research or educational purposes.

The standards regarding exceptions to confidentiality are among the most important and difficult for community counselors. For example, confidentiality may need to be broken against the client's wishes if the client is in danger or dangerous. Promoting clients' welfare may involve their being forcibly placed in physical restraints so that they cannot harm themselves, a practice that is safe, but hardly confidential. Informing possible victims that dangerous clients might attack them is an important step toward preventing harm, but a significant step away from confidentiality. Clearly, a counselor telling a client's sexual partner that the client has the HIV virus breaks the client's confidentiality. Is this more or less ethical than maintaining the client's confidentiality and allowing his or her partner to become infected? Given the gravity of acting on exceptions to confidentiality against a client's wishes, ethical standards recommend that counselors consult with other professionals when in doubt as to the validity of an exception.

Maintenance of client confidentiality can be particularly challenging for community counselors. In their effort to make maximum use of community resources to serve their clients, they need to communicate about their clients and their needs to a wide variety of individuals and agencies in their communities. Doing so without revealing their clients' identities can make this process cumbersome and result in inaccuracies. In smaller communities it may be almost impossible to talk in detail about clients without others discerning their identities because of the high degree of familiarity community members have with each other. Also, many referrals to community counselors come from individuals or agencies that strongly desire or insist on feedback concerning the clients' engagement and progress in counseling. Under these circumstances community counselors should discuss with clients the advantages and disadvantages of sharing confidential information with appropriate individuals and agencies within the community and request each client's written consent to share information. This request conveys respect for the client's confidentiality. If the client agrees, then the community counselor has been both respectful of the client's confidentiality and is able to promote his or her welfare. If the client disagrees, the counselor must decide if he or she can be of assistance to the client without sharing confidential information; and if not, then not begin counseling with the client.

### Section C: Professional Responsibilty

This section of the standards addresses counselors' responsibilities to know and follow ethical standards, to be active in professional associations, to not exceed their competence (not practice in areas in which they have not been trained or accept positions for which they are not qualified, not misrepresent their qualifications or credentials, not practice if personal problems impair their effectiveness), to continually learn and develop their competence (monitor their own effectiveness, engage in consultation and continuing education), practice integrity in advertising and soliciting clients, and be respectful and responsible in their interactions with the public and other professionals (be nondiscriminatory, not engage in sexual harassment, give

accurate media presentations). Because community counselors focus on use of community resources, preventive education within communities, and influencing public policy, these ethical standards are particularly relevant to community counseling practice. Following are examples of community counselor adherence to ethical guidelines related to professional responsibility.

***Not Provide Services or Accept Positions the Counselor Is Not Qualified for.*** A community counselor who has been asked to provide counseling for sexually abused children and who has not had training or supervised experience in this area should decline.

***Accurate Representation of Qualifications.*** If a community counselor holding a master's degree discovered that his or her agency had published a brochure listing the counselor as "Dr.", the counselor is responsible for correcting this misrepresentation.

***Continual Effort to Improve.*** Community counselors should not only be constantly learning about their profession through reading, workshop participation, and formal courses, but also learning through direct evaluation of their work. For example, a community counselor who is offering group sessions for adolescents exploring career options should be assessing the overall effectiveness of the group as well as the extent to which specific components of the group experience contribute to the group's goals.

***Not Recruit Private Clients from the Counselor's Place of Employment.*** Community counselors should not promote their private practice by indicating they are affiliated with a community mental health center or transfer community mental health center clients into their private practice.

***Not Engage in or Condone Sexual Harassment.*** A community counselor should not offer casual comment on the sexual attractiveness of his or her clients. Furthermore, community counselors are responsible for working to reduce sexual harassment in their communities. For example, community counselors could offer workshops on respectful cross-gender relationships for community teenagers.

**Adhere to Ethical Standards in Professional Communication Outside as Well as Within Counseling Sessions.**  A community counselor who is a guest on a radio talk show or is making a presentation to a class of graduate students should ensure that his or her comments are accurate, unbiased, and protect clients' confidentiality and dignity. Presenting a distorted assessment of clients' success in counseling to increase public support for counseling services is not ethical.

### Section D:
### Relationships with Other Professionals

This section addresses employer/employee relationships, consultation, and rules regarding referrals and subcontracting. It holds community counselors accountable for their contribution to the functioning of the institution or agency within which they work. Community counselors are responsible for helping to communicate and coordinate agency and employee goals, procedures and abilities; identifying and helping to resolve problems that limit effectiveness; and participating in the fair recruitment, placement, evaluation, and development of staff.

Community counselors employed in agencies may not view the functioning of the agency as their responsibility. This set of ethical standards clearly indicates that it is. If a community counselor discovers that his or her agency has placed staff members in positions they are not competent to fulfill, or that noise from the staff lounge is so persistently loud that it disrupts counseling sessions in adjacent rooms, they are ethically responsible for acting to correct the problems.

Ethical standards related to consulting focus on clarifying the consultant's role. The consultant's tasks should be clearly defined and agreed on at the outset of consultation. The consultant is endeavoring to resolve issues as opposed to personal problems. The consultant encourages self-direction from clients rather than dependency. Consultants must be careful not to misrepresent the services they can provide, and be careful that they are not charging private fees for services they should be providing as part of their employment with an agency.

As will be discussed in Chapter 12, consultation provides community counselors with tremendous opportunities to enhance the quality of services available in their community. To do so, however, they must avoid the potential pitfalls pointed out in these ethical standards, including overselling their expertise, transforming consultation into personal counseling, making themselves indispensable to those to whom they consult, and "double dipping" (e.g., a community counselor employed in a college counseling center charging the college's residence halls for consultation with the residence halls staff).

### Section E:  Evaluation,
### Assessment, and Interpretation

Chapter 6 of this book deals extensively with the potential usefulness of testing in provision of community counseling service. Test results (because they are quantified, allowing comparisons between individuals and comparison of individuals to population norms) can have a powerful impact on clients' perceptions of themselves, others' beliefs about them, and the opportunities available to them. For these reasons community counselors must exercise judicious caution in their use of tests and other assessment procedures with their clients. Ethical standards in this section address the proper selection, administration, scoring, interpretation, and protection of tests. Each area will be summarized below.

**Test Selection.** Community counselors have an ethical obligation to select tests that are appropriate to clients' needs and accurate for them (particularly with regard to the influence of culture). A community counselor who used an objective measure of personality pathology, which was normed on majority-culture-Veterans-Administration-Hospital-inpatient-adults, to provide career information to a female-Asian-American-high-school-student, would be in gross violation of ethical standards. While this example is extreme, community counselors who select tests because of their accessibility and/or their familiarity with the test, rather than the quality of the test and its appropriateness for their clients, are in danger of making the same mistake.

**Administration and Scoring.** Respect for clients' integrity is maintained by informing clients of the purpose of testing and how results will be reported prior to test administration. As with all counseling procedures, counselors should not exceed their level of competence by administering tests they are not qualified to use. They are responsible for promoting proper administration, scoring, and interpretation of tests, including computer-based and self-administered/scored tests and other assessment/diagnostic procedures. Community counselors often find themselves in settings where testing is conducted as a routine part of client intake and/or counseling procedures. For example, community counselors may find that computer-based testing for psychopathology is a standard part of the intake procedure in a substance abuse clinic where they become employed. It is the community counselor's ethical responsibility to ensure that the tests are being properly administered, scored, and interpreted in the clinic.

**Reporting Results.** Test results should be reported only with clients' consent and only to address the specific concerns for which testing was requested. Test results should be accompanied by an interpretation to promote their appropriate use, and should not be reported if there is reason to believe they are no longer accurate. Counselors are responsible for promoting accuracy and appropriate use when making statements to the public about tests in general, as well as when reporting results for specific clients. In compliance with these ethical standards, a community counselor would not report the scores a client received on an aptitude test taken at the beginning of a vocational rehabilitation program to an employer who is requesting the scores five years after the client completed the program.

**Protection.** Because the validity of the results of many tests is dependent on the client not being familiar with the test prior to taking it, counselors are responsible for protecting test security. Protecting test security includes respecting copyright laws with regard to reproducing published tests. Community counselors may find themselves working in agencies where test security is lax and/or economic pressures encourage the agency to copy, rather than purchase, tests. It is the ethical responsibility of community counselors to assist agencies in correcting these practices.

### Section F:
### Teaching, Training, and Supervision

This section outlines the unique ethical responsibilities incumbent on counselors who assume training functions. The standards focus both on the qualities counselor educators should possess and the content and process of the training they provide. Community counselor educators should have counseling expertise in practice and teaching, maintain professional relationships with students (avoiding dual, in particular sexual, relationships), appropriately share credit for publications with students, and retain responsibility for services delivered to clients by the students they supervise. Standards for programs include recruitment of a diverse student body, appropriate student orientation, guidance and evaluation, exposure to a variety of theories and research, involvement in the development of values and self-understanding without entering into counseling relationships with faculty, and provision of supervised counseling practice.

It is an impressive list. Assuming that the majority of readers of this book are community counselors who are in training, have completed training, and/or are offering training, it may be interesting to compare these ethical standards regarding counselor preparation to your personal experience. Because the majority of community counseling training programs involve students in practicum or internships in community settings, the guidelines regarding supervised counseling practice are especially germane to community counseling. Supervision in community settings can vary widely, from outstanding to practically nonexistent. Community counselor educators are responsible for ensuring that students receive high-quality supervision in community placements.

## Section G: Research and Publication

Because community counseling is a relatively young profession, research and publication is a particularly important responsibility for community counselors. ACA offers ethical standards guiding this important activity. In essence, the ethical standards pertaining to the counseling relationship are reapplied in this section of the code to research subjects. Similarly, standards pertaining to evaluation, assessment, and interpretation are reapplied to conducting and reporting research. Respect for research subjects' integrity, promotion of their welfare, and maintenance of their confidentiality are addressed. Community counselors must take care in conducting and reporting research to avoid inaccurate interpretation of the results. In contrast to ethical standards for evaluation, assessment, and interpretation, standards related to research

dictate the widest possible dissemination of results (even if they do not support the researchers' biases), and providing enough information for other professionals to draw their own conclusions. The research standards also offer guidance with regard to crediting other researchers' contributions, following through on publication commitments, and protocols for manuscript submission.

To remain in compliance with ethical standards regarding research, a community counselor would publish the results of a careful study he or she did on the effectiveness of a community counseling approach, even if the results suggested the approach was not effective.

## Section H: Resolving Ethical Issues

This section requires community counselors to be knowledgeable about ethical standards and to address breaches of ethics when they become aware of them. It offers guidelines for appropriate action in response to ethical violations including consultation, working to bring organizations in line with ethical standards, informal resolution of ethical concerns between professionals, and reporting unresolved ethical violations to state licensing boards and/or state or national ethics committees. It also indicates that frivolous complaints are unethical.

An example of a community counselor addressing an ethics violation in a domestic abuse crisis center was offered at the beginning of this section on ethics. Two more examples of community counselors dealing with ethical violations are offered below.

**Influence the Agency or Institution in Which the Counselor Is Employed to Offer the Highest Caliber Service.** A community counselor working in a shelter that provides counseling for battered spouses could identify assertion training as an essential component of counseling for the spouses. It is the counselor's responsibility to convince the shelter to initiate assertion training if possible. Furthermore, if the counselor believed substandard services were being provided and could not influence the shelter to improve services, the counselor should terminate employment with the shelter.

***Take Action to Correct Unethical Behavior on the Part of Other Professionals.*** A community counselor who is aware that a colleague is sexually involved with clients is responsible for pursuing avenues to correct this behavior, including confronting the colleague and informing the colleague's supervisor, professional association ethics committee, and the state licensure board.

Dealing with ethical violations is among the most difficult of the professional responsibilities assumed by community counselors. Because community counselors are concerned with the mental health of the entire community, they may find themselves dealing with ethical dilemmas that counselors working in more circumscribed arenas are not subjected to. For example, Corey, Corey, and Callanan (1993) presented a situation in which a public policy maker tries to affect the nature of services offered by a community counselor by covertly threatening to cut off funding to the counselor's agency. Would it be more ethical to continue the service and risk losing funding, or stop the service to protect funding of other services? Another community counseling ethical dilemma offered by Corey, Corey, and Callanan (1993) is related to provision of services by paraprofessionals. Is it more ethical to provide services to poor clients in a community through use of paraprofessionals who have limited training, or make the clients wait until more well-trained professionals are available to work with them? The following section is offered to assist community counselors in making ethical decisions and following through with ethical behavior.

## Adherence to Ethical Standards

Functioning as a community counselor entails adherence to the Code of Ethics and Standards of Practice of the American Counseling Association. To do so, community counselors must know the ethical standards, make decisions congruent with those standards in response to specific situations, and follow through on their decisions. Given that ethics may at times appear to be in conflict with laws (Mappes, Robb, & Engels, 1985), or two or more ethical standards may appear to offer contradictory direction when applied to some specific situations (Austin, Moline, & Williams, 1990) (for example, promoting client integrity, and taking reasonable personal action to prevent harm, when applied to involuntary hospitalization of a potentially dangerous client), ethical decision making can be difficult. A number of authors have offered guidelines for making ethical decisions (Jordan & Meara, 1990; Keith-Spiegel & Koocher, 1985; Kitchener, 1984; and Loewenberg & Dolgoff, 1988). There is also a casebook available that offers practice in making ethics decisions (Herlihy & Golden, 1990). This book presents ethical dilemmas and rulings on proper ethical behavior according to ACA Ethical Standards in response to the dilemmas. Readers can make a decision about ethics regarding each dilemma and then check their decision against the ruling. However, in practice community counselors are continually faced with ethical dilemmas that have not been precisely described and ruled on in a casebook. To assist counselors in arriving at ethical decisions in response to dilemmas that arise in practice, Corey, Corey, and Callanan (1993, p. 11) suggested the following steps:

1. Identify the problem or dilemma.
2. Identify the potential issues involved.
3. Review the relevant ethical guidelines.
4. Obtain consultation.
5. Consider possible and probable courses of action.
6. Enumerate the consequences of various decisions.

**7.** Decide on what appears to be the best course of action.

As is the case with all important and potentially contentious professional actions, it is advisable to carefully document steps taken in making an ethics decision.

Having examined ethics, this chapter will now briefly address legal issues related to community counseling.

## LEGAL ISSUES IN COMMUNITY COUNSELING

As was indicated at the beginning of this chapter, one criteria for designation of an occupation as a profession is that it be regulated by legal standards. Legal standards regulating community counseling are a relatively recent phenomenon. The first licensure law for master's-level counselors was passed in 1975. Since that time, counselor licensure laws have been passed in forty-two states (Glosoff, 1994). Clearly, there is a trend toward increased legal regulation and thus professionalization of community counseling. Legal regulation has not been confined to licensure. Since the 1960s, there has been ever increasing legal activity that clarifies and limits the power of professionals (Bednar, Bednar, Lambert, & Waite, 1991; Rinas & Clyne-Jackson, 1988). Counselor licensure laws will be addressed first, followed by examination of legal action that affects community counseling.

Counselor licensure laws are passed and regulated by state governments. They mandate minimum standards of training. They provide legal recourse when professionals violate ethical standards; and they offer legal definitions of counselors' roles, who can perform counseling services, and/or who can refer to themselves as a counselor (Gerstein & Brooks, 1990). In a state with a licensing law, counselors are given exclusive rights, or rights along with certain other professions, to perform certain specified activities (for example,

individual and group counseling, client appraisal) (Fretz & Mills, 1980). Anyone not licensed under a profession that is authorized to perform a particular activity, but who engages in that activity, is subject to prosecution by the state for practicing a profession without a license. It is generally the profession that defines what activities are within its domain, although in developing laws, legislatures must consider the claims of other groups to perform some of these activities. Similarly, the profession ordinarily provides the legislature with the standards for training and the appropriate methods of evaluating those seeking to become licensed under the law. Such laws set up licensing boards, consisting of both members of the profession and members of the public, to carry out the law. Licensing boards serve to admit or retain only those who meet the standards established by the law and to remove those with licensure who violate those standards. The aim of these boards is to protect the public, who are presumed to lack the specialized knowledge to be able to distinguish between qualified and unqualified practitioners on their own.

Similarly, certification laws establish educational, experience, and examination criteria (generally dictated by the profession). Those who qualify under these criteria may use a certain title (for example, professional counselor) to designate their expertise to the public; and anyone not so qualified who uses that title is subject to legal prosecution for misrepresentation. The structure of the licensing boards in states with certification laws and in states with licensure laws are generally similar.

Obviously, most professions prefer licensure to certification laws, because the former gives the profession exclusive rights to engage in certain activities and thus to control the accepted practice and the marketplace for those services. As more and more professions claiming overlapping expertise develop, it becomes harder to define exclusive domains of activity. For example, physicians and nurses, clergy, lawyers, clinical and counseling psychologists, social workers, and a wide variety of other occupations all do some counseling in the course of their work. Thus, it would be practically impossible to establish a law giving any one profession exclusive rights to engage in this activity. Consequently, many state legislatures prefer to pass certification laws than to get into the interprofessional territorial disputes that almost inevitably come up in seeking to define what activities should be reserved exclusively for a given profession.

The American Counseling Association (ACA) and, in particular, the American Mental Health Counseling Association division of ACA have been actively promoting passage of counselor licensure laws throughout the United States. Beginning with Virginia in 1975, there are now forty-two states that have laws certifying, registering, or licensing counselors (Glosoff, 1994). Titles employed in the laws include "Licensed Professional Counselor," "Certified Professional Counselor," and "Registered Practicing Counselor." A list of titles used for counselor licensure laws is available from the American Counseling Association.

Community counselors are eligible for licensure, certification, or registration in the states that have counselor licensure laws, if the community counselors have the requisite education and experience and have passed required examinations. Each state has unique stipulations about the nature of the graduate training counselors should receive. The requirements for each state are also available from the American Counseling Association. While the stipulations vary by state, for the most part they have been based on the ACA training standard, which are followed in CACREP-accredited community counseling programs. For this reason, community counselors who graduated from CACREP-accredited programs typically are well prepared for licensure. It is important to note, however, that a number of states have educational requirements that exceed the minimum standards for community counseling programs established by CACREP. Commonly these states require 60 semester credits of graduate study, whereas CACREP requires 48 semester credits in community counseling programs. Because licensure and certification laws vary by state, and because the laws are subject to periodic modification, community counselors are advised to seek current information from the American Counseling Association and directly from the state in which they plan to become licensed.

## Legal Action Related to Community Counseling

It could be argued that attainment of licensure is a mixed blessing for community counselors, because the existence of laws defining what appropriate professional practice should be increases the likelihood of malpractice suits (Hopkins & Anderson, 1990). In the last twenty years, court decisions have played an increasing role in determining counselors' obligations and duties. For example, in the case of *Tarasoff v. Regents of the University of California* (1976), the principle of reasonable care was established (Fulero, 1988). That is, if during a client's discussion with a counselor the client threatens to harm someone and the counselor determines (or the standards of the profession indicate) that there is a serious danger of violence to that person, then the counselor is obliged to use reasonable care to protect the intended victim from danger. Generally, this is taken to mean warning the intended victim, but in at least one case *(Hedlund v. Superior Court)* it has been extended to warning persons who may be near the intended victim (Corey, Corey, & Callanan, 1993). Mental health professionals have also been held liable for negligently releasing a client from inpatient care who subsequently committed murder (Corey, Corey, & Callanan, 1993). Obligations to prevent harm place a limit on the confidentiality of the counselor-client relationship. Even when there is no evidence of danger, confidentiality of the counselor-client relationship (privileged communication) is only fully protected by law if specifically recognized by the laws of the state (Corey, Corey, & Callanan, 1993). Also, the right to privileged communication belongs to the client, not the counselor. If the client waives this privilege, then the community counselor has no legal grounds for refusing to disclose information (Hopkins & Anderson, 1990). If a community counselor is uncertain about the extent to which clients' confidentiality is protected by law, it would be wise to seek advice from a lawyer (for example, a counselor who is called to testify in a law case involving a client, such as a child custody battle) (Remley, 1991).

Other legal issues that affect community counseling practice include informed consent (Did the counselor explain to the client what procedures and risks were entailed in all parts of the counseling process and get the client's agreement to participate?)(Bray, Shepherd & Hays, 1985) and malpractice (Did the counselor deviate from accepted professional practice in a way that caused harm or injury to the client?) (Austin, Moline, & Williams, 1990). These are issues on which a counselor is most liable to be sued as a consequence of practicing the profession.

In their efforts to expand the impact of counseling, community counselors train and/ or consult with paraprofessionals, endeavor to influence policymakers, and engage in client advocacy (Corey, Corey & Callanan, 1993). These activities can have legal implications. Community counselors could be held liable for inappropriate behavior on the part of paraprofessionals with whom they've been working. On the other hand, community counselors may employ legal means to influence policymakers or advocate for clients' rights. An example would be community counselors lobbying for laws, and potentially filing a lawsuit against health insurance companies to ensure that victims of spouse abuse are not discriminated against by health insurance policies.

For a comprehensive discussion of the legal issue relating to the practice of counseling, see Austin, Moline and Williams, 1990; Bednar, Bednar, Lambert and Waite, 1991; Hopkins and Anderson, 1990; Rinas and Clyne-Jackson, 1988; or Van Hoose and Kottler, 1985. An excellent overview, including a chapter devoted to the counselor in the community is offered by Corey, Corey, and Callanan (1993).

Adherence to ethical standards and legal regulations are two critical components of the professionalization of community counseling. By entering the profession, community counselors assume responsibility for knowledge of, and compliance with, the guidelines provided by ethics and laws.

## EXERCISE

### Case Study

Harold, a 26-year-old, single, employed, college graduate, is seeking career counseling because he would like to change his employment and possibly his career from being a manager of a food catering business to a field that provides medical services. During the second counseling visit Harold mentions that seven months ago he was diagnosed as H.I.V. positive, and he further states to the counselor that he has been dating one woman and they have engaged in sexual relations many times during the past four months. Yet the client states that he has not told anyone about this diagnosis, and not even his parents with whom he has been living for many, many years. He claims that he feels guilty about this complete non-disclosure, especially since he cares very much for his girl friend and is in daily contact with food because of his job demands.

Considering this information, what is the responsibility of the counselor from the perspective of what was discussed in this chapter?

Please identify all the ethical issues involved, and outline a strategy that the counselor could pursue to resolve the ethical situation.

## REFERENCES

American Counseling Association. (1995). *Code of ethics and standards of practice*. Alexandria, VA.

Austin, K. M., Moline, M. M., & Williams, G. T. (1990). *Confronting malpractice: Legal and ethical dilemmas in psychotherapy*. Newbury Park, CA: Sage.

Bednar, R. L., Bednar, S. C., Lambert, M. J., & Waite, D. R. (1991). *Psychotherapy with high-risk clients*. Pacific Grove, CA: Brooks/Cole.

Bennett, B. E., Bryant, B. K., VandenBos, G. R., & Greenwood, A. (1990). *Professional liability and risk management*. Washington, D. C.: American Psychological Association.

Blocher, D. H. (1987). *The professional counselor*. New York: Macmillan.

Bray, J. H., Shepherd, J. N., & Hays, J. R. (1985). Legal and ethical issues in informed consent to psychotherapy. *American Journal of Family Therapy, 13*, 50–60.

Corey, G., Corey, M. S., & Callanan, P. (1993). *Issues and ethics in the helping professions*. Pacific Grove, CA: Brooks/Cole.

Fretz, B. R., & Mills, D. H. (1980). *Licensing and certification of psychologists and counselors*. San Francisco: Jossey-Bass.

Fulero, S. M. (1988). Tarasoff: 10 years later. *Professional Psychology: Research and Practice, 19,* 184–190.

Gerstein, L. H., & Brooks, D. K. (1990). Introduction for a special feature. The helping professions' challenge: Credentialing and interdisciplinary collaboration. *Journal of Counseling and Development, 68*, 475–476.

Glosoff, H. L. (1994). Education, experience, and examination requirements of credentialed counselors as dictated by state statutes. Alexandria, VA. American Counseling Association.

Herlihy, B., & Golden, L. B. (1990). *AACD ethical standards casebook* (4th ed.). Alexandria, VA: American Association for Counseling and Development.

Hopkins, B. R., & Anderson, B. S. (1990). *The counselor and the law* (3rd ed.). Alexandria, VA: AACD Press.

Jordan, A. E., & Meara, N. M. (1990). Ethics and the professional practice of psychologists: The role of virtues and principles. *Professional Psychology: Research and Practice, 21*, 107–114.

Keith-Spiegel, P., & Koocher, G. (1985). *Ethics in psychology: Professional standards and cases*. New York: Random House.

Kitchener, K. S. (1984). Intuition, critical evaluation and ethical principles: The foundation for ethical decisions in counseling psychology. *The Counseling Psychologist, 12*, 43–55.

Lewis, J. A., & Lewis, M. D. (1989). *Community counseling*. Pacific Grove, CA: Brooks/Cole.

Loewenberg, F., & Dolgoff, R. (1988). *Ethical decisions for social work practice* (3rd ed.). Itasca, IL: F. E. Peacock.

Mappes, D. C., Robb, G. P., & Engels, D. W. (1985). Conflicts between ethics and law in counseling and psychotherapy. *Journal of Counseling and Development, 65*, 246–252.

Nugent, F. A. (1990). *An introduction to the profession of counseling*. Columbus, OH: Merrill.

Remley, T. P. (1991). *Preparing for court appearances*. Alexandria, VA: AACD.

Rinas, J., & Clyne-Jackson, S. (1988). *Professional conduct and legal concerns in mental health practice*. Norwalk, CT: Appleton & Lange.

Smith, T. S., McGuire, J. M., Abbott, D. W., & Blau, B. I. (1991). Clinical ethical decision making: An investigation of the rationales used to justify doing less than one believes one should. *Professional Psychology: Research and Practice, 22*, 235–239.

Van Hoose, W. H., & Kottler, J. A. (1985). *Ethical and legal issues in counseling and psychotherapy* (2nd ed.). San Francisco: Jossey-Bass.

Yalom, I. D. (1985). *The theory and practice of group psychotherapy* (3rd ed.). New York: Basic Books.

# APPENDIX

## AMERICAN COUNSELING ASSOCIATION CODE OF ETHICS AND STANDARDS OF PRACTICE*

### (Approved by the Governing Council, April 1995)

## PREAMBLE

The American Counseling Association is an educational, scientific and professional organization whose members are dedicated to the enhancement of human development throughout the life span. Association members recognize diversity in our society and embrace a cross-cultural approach in support of the worth, dignity, potential and uniqueness of each individual.

The specification of a code of ethics enables the association to clarify to current and future members, and to those served by members, the nature of the ethical responsibilities held in common by its members. As the code of ethics of the association, this document establishes principles that define the ethical behavior of association members. All members of the American Counseling Association are required to adhere to the *Code of Ethics* and the *Standards of Practice*. The Code of Ethics will serve as the basis for processing ethical complaints initiated against members of the association.

## CODE OF ETHICS

### Section A: The Counseling Relationship

#### A.1. CLIENT WELFARE

**a.** *Primary Responsibility.* The primary responsibility of counselors is to respect the dignity and to promote the welfare of clients.

**b.** *Positive Growth and Development.* Counselors encourage client growth and development in ways that foster the clients' interest and welfare; counselors avoid fostering dependent counseling relationships.

**c.** *Counseling Plans.* Counselors and their clients work jointly in devising integrated, individual counseling plans that offer reasonable promise of success and are consistent with abilities and circumstances of clients. Counselors and clients regularly review counseling plans to ensure their continued viability and effectiveness, respecting clients' freedom of choice. (See A.3.b.)

**d.** *Family Involvement.* Counselors recognize that families are usually important in clients' lives and strive to enlist family understanding and involvement as a positive resource, when appropriate.

**e.** *Career and Employment Needs.* Counselors work with their clients in considering employment in jobs and circumstances that are consistent with the clients' overall abilities, vocational limitations, physical restrictions, general temperament, interest and aptitude patterns, social skills, education, general qualifications, and other relevant characteristics and needs. Counselors neither place nor participate in placing clients in positions that will result in damaging the interest and the welfare of clients, employers, or the public.

## A.2. RESPECTING DIVERSITY

**a.** *Nondiscrimination.* Counselors do not condone or engage in discrimination based on age, color, culture, disability, ethnic group, gender, race, religion, sexual orientation, marital status, or socioeconomic status. (See C.5.a., C.5.b., and D.l.i.)

**b.** *Respecting Differences.* Counselors will actively attempt to understand the diverse cultural backgrounds of the clients with whom they work. This includes, but is not limited to, learning how the counselor's own cultural/ethnic/racial identity impacts her/his values and beliefs about the counseling process (See E.8. and F.2.i.)

## A.3. CLIENT RIGHTS

**a.** *Disclosure to Clients.* When counseling is initiated, and throughout the counseling process as necessary, counselors inform clients of the purposes, goals, techniques, procedures, limitations, potential risks and benefits of services to be performed, and other pertinent information. Counselors take steps to ensure that clients understand the implications of diagnosis, the intended use of tests and reports, fees, and billing arrangements. Clients have the right to expect confidentiality and to be provided with an explanation of its limitations, including supervision and/or treatment team professionals; to obtain clear information about their case records; to participate in the ongoing counseling plans; and to refuse any recommended services

and be advised of the consequences of such refusal. (See E.5.a. and G.2.)

**b.** *Freedom of Choice.* Counselors offer clients the freedom to choose whether to enter into a counseling relationship and to determine which professional(s) will provide counseling. Restrictions that limit choices of clients are fully explained. (See A.l.c.)

**c.** *Inability to Give Consent.* When counseling minors or persons unable to give voluntary informed consent, counselors act in these clients' best interests. (See B.3.)

## A.4. CLIENTS SERVED BY OTHERS

If a client is receiving services from another mental health professional, counselors, with client consent, inform the professional persons already involved and develop clear agreements to avoid confusion and conflict for the client. (See C.6.c.)

## A.5. PERSONAL NEEDS AND VALUES

**a.** *Personal Needs.* In the counseling relationship, counselors are aware of the intimacy and responsibilities inherent in the counseling relationship, maintain respect for clients, and avoid actions that seek to meet their personal needs at the expense of clients.

**b.** *Personal Values.* Counselors are aware of their own values, attitudes, beliefs, and behaviors and how these apply in a diverse society, and avoid imposing their values on clients. (See C.5.a.)

## A.6. DUAL RELATIONSHIPS

**a.** *Avoid When Possible.* Counselors are aware of their influential positions with respect to clients, and they avoid exploiting the trust and dependency of clients. Counselors make every effort to avoid dual relationships with clients that could impair professional judgment or increase the risk of harm to clients. (Examples of such relationships include, but are not limited to, familial, social, financial, business, or close personal relationships with clients.) When a dual relationship cannot be avoided, counselors take appropriate professional precautions such as informed consent, consultation, supervision, and documentation to ensure that judgment is not impaired and no exploitation occurs. (See F.1.b.)

**b.** *Superior/Subordinate Relationships.* Counselors do not accept as clients superiors or subordinates with whom they have administrative, supervisory, or evaluative relationships.

### A.7. SEXUAL INTIMACIES WITH CLIENTS

**a.** *Current Clients.* Counselors do not have any type of sexual intimacies with clients and do not counsel persons with whom they have had a sexual relationship.

**b.** *Former Clients.* Counselors do not engage in sexual intimacies with former clients within a minimum of two years after terminating the counseling relationship. Counselors who engage in such relationship after two years following termination have the responsibility to thoroughly examine and document that such relations did not have an exploitative nature, based on factors such as duration of counseling, amount of time since counseling, termination circumstances, client's personal history and mental status, adverse impact on the client, and actions by the counselor suggesting a plan to initiate a sexual relationship with the client after termination.

### A.8. MULTIPLE CLIENTS

When counselors agree to provide counseling services to two or more persons who have a relationship (such as husband and wife, or parents and children), counselors clarify at the outset which person or persons are clients and the nature of the relationships they will have with each involved person. If it becomes apparent that counselors may be called upon to perform potentially conflicting roles, they clarify, adjust, or withdraw from roles appropriately. (See B.2. and B.4.d.)

### A.9. GROUP WORK

**a.** *Screening.* Counselors screen prospective group counseling/therapy participants. To the extent possible, counselors select members whose needs and goals are compatible with goals of the group, who will not impede the group process, and whose well-being will not be jeopardized by the group experience.

**b.** *Protecting Clients.* In a group setting, counselors take reasonable precautions to protect clients from physical or psychological trauma.

### A.10. FEES AND BARTERING
### (See D.3.a. and D.3.b.)

**a.** *Advance Understanding.* Counselors clearly explain to clients, prior to entering the counseling relationship, all financial arrangements related to professional services including the use of collection agencies or legal measures for nonpayment. (A.11.c.)

**b.** *Establishing Fees.* In establishing fees for professional counseling services, counselors consider the financial status of clients and locality. In the event that the established fee structure is inappropriate for a client, assistance is provided in attempting to find comparable services of acceptable cost. (See A. 10.d., D.3.a., and D.3.b.)

**c.** *Bartering Discouraged.* Counselors ordinarily refrain from accepting goods or services from clients in return for counseling services because such arrangements create inherent potential for conflicts, exploitation, and distortion of the professional relationship. Counselors may participate in bartering only if the relationship is not exploitive, if the client requests it, if a clear written contract is established, and if such arrangements are an accepted practice among professionals in the community. (See A.6.a.)

**d.** *Pro Bono Service.* Counselors contribute to society by devoting a portion of their professional activity to services for which there is little or no financial return (pro bono).

### A.11. TERMINATION AND REFERRAL

**a.** *Abandonment Prohibited.* Counselors do not abandon or neglect clients in counseling. Counselors assist in making appropriate arrangements for the continuation of treatment, when necessary, during interruptions such as vacations, and following termination.

**b.** *Inability to Assist Clients.* If counselors determine an inability to be of professional assistance to clients, they avoid entering or immediately terminate a counseling relationship. Counselors are knowledgeable about referral resources and suggest appropriate alternatives. If clients decline the suggested referral, counselors should discontinue the relationship.

**c.** *Appropriate Termination.* Counselors terminate a counseling relationship, securing client agreement when possible, when it is reasonably clear that the client is no longer benefiting, when services are no longer required, when counseling no longer serves the client's needs or interests, when clients do not pay fees charged, or when agency or institution limits do not allow provision of further counseling services. (See A.10.b. and C.2.g.)

### A.12. COMPUTER TECHNOLOGY

**a.** *Use of Computers.* When computer applications are used in counseling services, counselors ensure that: (1) the client is intellectually, emotionally, and physically capable of using the computer application; (2) the computer application is appropriate for the needs of the client; (3) the client understands the purpose and operation of the computer applications; and (4) a follow-up of client use of a computer application is provided to correct possible misconceptions, discover inappropriate use, and assess subsequent needs.

**b.** *Exlanation of Limitations.* Counselors ensure that clients are provided information as a part of the counseling relationship that adequately explains the limitations of computer technology.

**c.** *Access to Computer Applications.* Counselors provide for equal access to computer applications in counseling services. (See A.2.a.)

### SECTION B: CONFIDENTIALITY

#### B.1. RIGHT TO PRIVACY

**a.** *Respect for Privacy.* Counselors respect their clients' right to privacy and avoid illegal and unwarranted disclosures of confidential information. (See A.3.a. and B.6.a.)

**b.** *Client Waiver.* The right to privacy may be waived by the client or their legally recognized representative.

**c.** *Exceptions.* The general requirement that counselors keep information confidential does not apply when disclosure is required to prevent clear and imminent danger to the client or others or when legal requirements demand that confidential information be revealed. Counselors consult with other professionals when in doubt as to the validity of an exception.

**d.** *Contagious Fatal Diseases.* A counselor who receives information confirming that a client has a disease commonly known to be both communicable and fatal is justified in disclosing information to an identifiable third party, who by his or her relationship with the client is at a high risk of contracting the disease. Prior to making a disclosure the counselor should ascertain that the client has not already informed the third party about his or her disease and that the client is not intending to inform the third party in the immediate future. (See B.1.c and B. 1.f)

**e.** *Court Ordered Disclosure.* When court ordered to release confidential information without a client's permission, counselors request to the court that the disclosure not be required due to potential harm to the client or counseling relationship. (See B. 1.c.)

**f.** *Minimal Disclosure.* When circumstances require the disclosure of confidential information, only essential information is revealed. To the extent possible, clients are informed before confidential information is disclosed.

**g.** *Explanation of Limitations.* When counseling is initiated and throughout the counseling process as necessary, counselors inform clients of the limitations of confidentiality and identify foreseeable situations in which confidentiality must be breached. (See G.2.a.)

**h.** *Subordinates.* Counselors make every effort to ensure that privacy and confidentiality of clients are maintained by subordinates including employees, supervisees, clerical assistants, and volunteers. (See B.1.a.)

**i.** *Treatment Teams.* If client treatment will involve a continued review by a treatment team, the client will be informed of the team's existence and composition.

#### B.2. GROUPS AND FAMILIES

**a.** *Group Work.* In group work, counselors clearly define confidentiality and the parameters for the specific group being entered, explain its importance, and discuss the difficulties related to confidentiality involved in group work. The fact that confidentiality cannot be guaranteed is clearly communicated to group members.

**b.** *Family Counseling.* In family counseling, information about one family member cannot be disclosed to another member without permission. Counselors protect the privacy rights of each family member. (See A.8., B.3., and B.4.d.)

## B.3. MINOR OR INCOMPETENT CLIENTS

When counseling clients who are minors or individuals who are unable to give voluntary, informed consent, parents or guardians may be included in the counseling process as appropriate. Counselors act in the best interests of clients and take measures to safeguard confidentiality. (See A.3.c.)

## B.4. RECORDS

**a.** *Requirement of Records.* Counselors maintain records necessary for rendering professional services to their clients and as required by laws, regulations, or agency or institution procedures.

**b.** *Confidentiality of Records.* Counselors are responsible for securing the safety and confidentiality of any counseling records they create, maintain, transfer, or destroy whether the records are written, taped, computerized, or stored in any other medium. (See B.1.a.)

**c.** *Permission to Record or Observe.* Counselors obtain permission from clients prior to electronically recording or observing sessions. (See A.3.a.)

**d.** *Client Access.* Counselors recognize that counseling records are kept for the benefit of clients, and therefore provide access to records and copies of records when requested by competent clients, unless the records contain information that may be misleading and detrimental to the client. In situations involving multiple clients, access to records is limited to those parts of records that do not include confidential information related to another client. (See A.8.B.1.a., and B.2.b.)

**e.** *Disclosure or Transfer.* Counselors obtain written permission from clients to disclose or transfer records to legitimate third parties unless exceptions to confidentiality exist as listed in Section B. 1. Steps are taken to ensure that receivers of counseling records are sensitive to their confidential nature.

## B.5. RESEARCH AND TRAINING

**a.** *Data Disguise Required.* Use of data derived from counseling relationships for purposes of training, research, or publication is confined to content that is disguised to ensure the anonymity of the individuals involved. (See B.1.g. and G.3.d.)

**b.** *Agreement for Identification.* Identification of a client in a presentation or publication is permissible only when the client has reviewed the material and has agreed to its presentation or publication. (See G.3.d).

## B.6. CONSULTATION

**a.** *Respect for Privacy.* Information obtained in a consulting relationship is discussed for professional purposes only with persons clearly concerned with the case. Written and oral reports present data germane to the purposes of the consultation, and every effort is made to protect client identity and avoid undue invasion of privacy

**b.** *Cooperating Agencies.* Before sharing information, counselors make efforts to ensure that there are defined policies in other agencies serving the counselor's clients that effectively protect the confidentiality of information.

## SECTION C: PROFESSIONAL RESPONSIBILITY

### C.1. STANDARDS KNOWLEDGE

Counselors have a responsibility to read, understand, and follow the *Code of Ethics* and the *Standards of Practice.*

### C.2. PROFESSIONAL COMPETENCE

**a.** *Boundaries of Competence.* Counselors practice only within the boundaries of their competence, based on their education, training, supervised experience, state and national professional credentials, and appropriate professional experience. Counselors will demonstrate a commitment to gain knowledge, personal awareness, sensitivity, and skills pertinent to working with a diverse client population.

**b.** *New Speciality Areas of Practice.* Counselors practice in specialty areas new to them only after appropriate education, training, and supervised experience. While developing skills in new specialty areas, counselors take steps to ensure the competence of their work and to protect others from possible harm.

**c.** *Qualified for Employment*. Counselors accept employment only for positions for which they are qualified by education, training, supervised experience, state and national professional credentials, and appropriate professional experience. Counselors hire for professional counseling positions only individuals who are qualified and competent.

**d.** *Monitor Effectiveness*. Counselors continually monitor their effectiveness as professionals and take steps to improve when necessary. Counselors in private practice take reasonable steps to seek out peer supervision to evaluate their efficacy as counselors.

**e.** *Ethical Issues Consultation*. Counselors take reasonable steps to consult with other counselors or related professionals when they have questions regarding their ethical obligations or professional practice. (See H.1)

**f.** *Continuing Education*. Counselors recognize the need for continuing education to maintain a reasonable level of awareness of current scientific and professional information in their fields of activity. They take steps to maintain competence in the skills they use, are open to new procedures, and keep current with the diverse and/or special populations with whom they work.

**g.** *Impairment*. Counselors refrain from offering or accepting professional services when their physical, mental or emotional problems are likely to harm a client or others. They are alert to the signs of impairment, seek assistance for problems, and, if necessary, limit, suspend, or terminate their professional responsibilities. (See A.11.c.)

## C.3. ADVERTISING AND SOLICITING CLIENTS

**a.** *Accurate Advertising*. There are no restrictions on advertising by counselors except those that can be specifically justified to protect the public from deceptive practices. Counselors advertise or represent their services to the public by identifying their credentials in an accurate manner that is not false, misleading, deceptive, or fraudulent. Counselors may only advertise the highest degree earned which is in counseling or a closely related field

from a college or university that was accredited when the degree was awarded by one of the regional accrediting bodies recognized by the Council on Postsecondary Accreditation.

**b.** *Testimonials*. Counselors who use testimonials do not solicit them from clients or other persons who, because of their particular circumstances, may be vulnerable to undue influence.

**c.** *Statements by Others*. Counselors make reasonable efforts to ensure that statements made by others about them or the profession of counseling are accurate.

**d.** *Recruiting Through Employment*. Counselors do not use their places of employment or institutional affiliation to recruit or gain clients, supervisees, or consultees for their private practices. (See C.5.e.)

**e.** *Products and Training Advertisements*. Counselors who develop products related to their profession or conduct workshops or training events ensure that the advertisements concerning these products or events are accurate and disclose adequate information for consumers to make informed choices.

**f.** *Promoting to Those Served*. Counselors do not use counseling, teaching, training, or supervisory relationships to promote their products or training events in a manner that is deceptive or would exert undue influence on individuals who may be vulnerable. Counselors may adopt textbooks they have authored for instruction purposes.

**g.** *Professional Association Involvement*. Counselors actively participate in local, state, and national associations that foster the development and improvement of counseling.'

## C.4. CREDENTIALS

**a.** *Credentials Claimed*. Counselors claim or imply only professional credentials possessed and are responsible for correcting any known misrepresentations of their credentials by others. Professional credentials include graduate degrees in counseling or closely related mental health fields, accreditation of graduate programs, national voluntary certifications, government issued certifications or licenses, ACA professional membership, or any other credential that might indicate to the public specialized knowledge or expertise in counseling.

**b.** *ACA Professional Membership.* ACA professional members may announce to the public their membership status. Regular members may not announce their ACA membership in a manner that might imply they are credentialed counselors.

**c.** *Credential Guidelines.* Counselors follow the guidelines for use of credentials that have been established by the entities that issue the credentials.

**d.** *Misrepresentation of Credentials.* Counselors do not attribute more to their credentials than the credentials represent, and do not imply that other counselors are not qualified because they do not possess certain credentials.

**e.** *Doctoral Degrees From Other Fields.* Counselors who hold a master's degree in counseling or a closely related mental health field, but hold a doctoral degree from other than counseling or a closely related field do not use the title, "Dr." in their practices and do not announce to the public in relation to their practice or status as a counselor that they hold a doctorate.

### C.5. PUBLIC RESPONSIBILITY

**a.** *Nondiscrimination.* Counselors do not discriminate against clients, students, or supervisees in a manner that has a negative impact based on their age, color, culture, disability, ethnic group, gender, race, religion, sexual orientation, or socioeconomic status, or for any other reason. (See A.2.a.)

**b.** *Sexual Harassment.* Counselors do not engage in sexual harassment. Sexual harassment is defined as sexual solicitation, physical advances, or verbal or nonverbal conduct that is sexual in nature, that occurs in connection with professional activities or roles, and that either (1) is unwelcome, is offensive, or creates a hostile workplace environment, and counselors know or are told this; or (2) is sufficiently severe or intense to be perceived as harassment to a reasonable person in the context. Sexual harassment can consist of a single intense or severe act or multiple persistent or pervasive acts.

**c.** *Reports to Third Parties.* Counselors are accurate, honest, and unbiased in reporting their professional activities and judgments to appropriate third parties including courts, health insurance companies, those who are the recipients of evaluation reports, and others. (See B.1.g.)

**d.** *Media Presentations.* When counselors provide advice or comment by means of public lectures, demonstrations, radio or television programs, prerecorded tapes, printed articles, mailed material, or other media, they take reasonable precautions to ensure that (1) the statements are based on appropriate professional counseling literature and practice; (2) the statements are otherwise consistent with the *Code of Ethics* and the *Standards of Practice*; and (3) the recipients of the information are not encouraged to infer that a professional counseling relationship has been established. (See C.6.b.)

**e.** *Unjustified Gains.* Counselors do not use their professional positions to seek or receive unjustified personal gains, sexual favors, unfair advantage, or unearned goods or services. (See C.3.d.)

### C.6. RESPONSIBILITY TO OTHER PROFESSIONALS

**a.** *Different Approaches.* Counselors are respectful of approaches to professional counseling that differ from their own. Counselors know and take into account the traditions and practices of other professional groups with which they work.

**b.** *Personal Public Statements.* When making personal statements in a public context, counselors clarify that they are speaking from their personal perspectives and that they are not speaking on behalf of all counselors or the profession. (See C.5.d.)

**c.** *Clients Served by Others.* When counselors learn that their clients are in a professional relationship with another mental health professional, they request release from clients to inform the other professionals and strive to establish positive and collaborative professional relationships. (See A.4.)

## SECTION D: RELATIONSHIPS WITH OTHER PROFESSIONALS

### D.1. RELATIONSHIPS WITH EMPLOYERS AND EMPLOYEES

**a.** *Role Definition.* Counselors define and describe for their employers and employees the parameters and levels of their professional roles.

**b.** *Agreements.* Counselors establish working agreements with supervisors, colleagues, and subordinates regarding counseling or clinical relationships, confidentiality, adherence to professional standards; distinction between public and private material, maintenance and dissemination of recorded information, workload, and accountability. Working agreements in each instance are specified and made known to those concerned.

**c.** *Negative Conditions.* Counselors alert their employers to conditions that may be potentially disruptive or damaging to the counselor's professional responsibilities or that may limit their effectiveness.

**d.** *Evaluation.* Counselors submit regularly to professional review and evaluation by their supervisor or the appropriate representative of the employer.

**e.** *In-Service.* Counselors are responsible for in-service development of self and staff.

**f.** *Goals.* Counselors inform their staff of goals and programs.

**g.** *Practices.* Counselors provide personnel and agency practices that respect and enhance the rights and welfare of each employee and recipient of agency services. Counselors strive to maintain the highest levels of professional services.

**h.** *Personnel Selection and Assignment.* Counselors select competent staff and assign responsibilities compatible with their skills and experiences.

**i.** *Discrimination.* Counselors, as either employers or employees, do not engage in or condone practices that are inhumane, illegal, or unjustifiable (such as considerations based on age, color, culture, disability, ethnic group, gender, race, religion, sexual orientation, or socioeconomic status) in hiring, promotion, or training. (See A.2.a. and C.5.b.)

**j.** *Professional Conduct.* Counselors have a responsibility both to clients and to the agency or institution within which services are performed to maintain high standards of professional conduct.

**k.** *Exploitive Relationships.* Counselors do not engage in exploitive relationships with individuals over whom they have supervisory, evaluative, or instructional control or authority.

**l.** *Employer Policies.* The acceptance of employment in an agency or institution implies that counselors are in agreement with its general policies and principles. Counselors strive to reach agreement with employers as to acceptable standards of conduct that allow for changes in institu-

tional policy conducive to the growth and development of clients.

## D.2. CONSULTATION (See B.6.)

**a.** *Consultation as an Option.* Counselors may choose to consult with any other professionally competent persons about their clients. In choosing consultants, counselors avoid placing the consultant in a conflict of interest situation that would preclude the consultant being a proper party to the counselor's efforts to help the client. Should counselors be engaged in a work setting that compromises this consultation standard, they consult with other professionals whenever possible to consider justifiable alternatives.

**b.** *Consultant Comptency.* Counselors are reasonably certain that they have or the organization represented has the necessary competencies and resources for giving the kind of consulting services needed and that appropriate referral resources are available.

**c.** *Understanding with Clients.* When providing consultation, counselors attempt to develop with their clients a clear understanding of problem definition, goals for change, and predicted consequences of interventions selected.

**d.** *Consultant Goals.* The consulting relationship is one in which client adaptability and growth toward self-direction are consistently encouraged and cultivated. (See A.1.b.)

## D.3. FEES FOR REFERRAL

**a.** *Accepting Fees from Agency Clients.* Counselors refuse a private fee or other remuneration for rendering services to persons who are entitled to such services through the counselor's employing agency or institution The policies of a particular agency may make explicit provisions for agency clients to receive counseling services from members of its staff in private practice. In such instances, the clients must be informed of other options open to them should they seek private counseling services. (See A.1O.a., A. 11.b., and C.3.d.)

**b.** *Referral Fees.* Counselors do not accept a referral fee from other professionals.

## D.4. SUBCONTRACTOR ARRANGEMENTS

When counselors work as subcontractors for counseling services for a third party, they have a duty to inform clients of the limitations of confidentiality that the organization may place on counselors in providing counseling services to clients. The limits of such confidentiality ordinarily are discussed as part of the intake session. (See B.1.e. and B.1.f.)

## SECTION E: EVALUATION, ASSESSMENT, AND INTERPRETATION

### E.1. GENERAL

**a.** *Appraisal Techniques.* The primary purpose of educational and psychological assessment is to provide measures that are objective and interpretable in either comparative or absolute terms. Counselors recognize the need to interpret the statements in this section as applying to the whole range of appraisal techniques, including test and nontest data.

**b.** *Client Welfare.* Counselors promote the welfare and best interests of the client in the development, publication, and utilization of educational and psychological assessment techniques. They do not misuse assessment results and interpretations and take reasonable steps to prevent others from misusing the information these techniques provide. They respect the client's right to know the results, the interpretations made, and the bases for their conclusions and recommendations.

### E.2. COMPETENCE TO USE AND INTERPRET TESTS

**a.** *Limits of Competence.* Counselors recognize the limits of their competence and perform only those testing and assessment services for which they have been trained. They are familiar with reliability, validity, related standardization, error of measurement, and proper application of any technique utilized. Counselors using computer-based test interpretations are trained in the construct being measured and the specific instrument being used prior to using this type of computer application. Counselors take reasonable measures to ensure the proper use of psychological assessment techniques by persons under their supervision.

**b.** *Appropriate Use.* Counselors are responsible for the appropriate application, scoring, interpretation, and use of assessment instruments, whether they score and interpret such tests themselves or use computerized or other services.

**c.** *Decisions Based on Results.* Counselors responsible for decisions involving individuals or policies that are based on assessment results have a thorough understanding of educational and psychological measurement, including validation criteria, test research, and guidelines for test development and use.

**d.** *Accurate Information.* Counselors provide accurate information and avoid false claims or misconceptions when making statements about assessment instruments or techniques. Special efforts are made to avoid unwarranted connotations of such terms as IQ and grade equivalent scores. (See C.5.c.)

### E.3. INFORMED CONSENT

**a.** *Explanation to Clients.* Prior to assessment, counselors explain the nature and purposes of assessment and the specific use of results in language the client (or other legally authorized person on behalf of the client) can understand, unless an explicit exception to this right has been agreed upon in advance. Regardless of whether scoring and interpretation are completed by counselors, by assistants, or by computer or other outside services, counselors take reasonable steps to ensure that appropriate explanations are given to the client.

**b.** *Recipients of Results.* The examinee's welfare, explicit understanding, and prior agreement determine the recipients of test results. Counselors include accurate and appropriate interpretations with any release of individual or group test results. (See B.1.a. and C.5.c.)

### E.4. RELEASE OF INFORMATION TO COMPETENT PROFESSIONALS

**a.** *Misuse of Results.* Counselors do not misuse assessment results, including test results, and interpretations, and take reasonable steps to prevent the misuse of such by others. (See C.5.c.)

**b.** *Release of Raw Data.* Counselors ordinarily release data (e.g. protocols, counseling or interview notes, or questionnaires) in which the client is identified only with the consent of the client or the client's legal representative. Such data are usually released only to persons recognized by counselors as competent to interpret the data. (See B.1.a.)

## E.5. PROPER DIAGNOSIS OF MENTAL DISORDERS

**a.** *Proper Diagnosis.* Counselors take special care to provide proper diagnosis of mental disorders. Assessment techniques (including personal interview) used to determine client care (e.g., locus of treatment, type of treatment, or recommended follow-up) are carefully selected and appropriately used. (See A.3.a. and C.5.c.)

**b.** *Cultural Sensitivity.* Counselors recognize that culture affects the manner in which clients' problems are defined. Clients' socioeconomic and cultural experience is considered when diagnosing mental disorders.

## E.6. TEST SELECTION

**a.** *Appropriateness of Instruments.* Counselors carefully consider the validity, reliability, psychometric limitations, and appropriateness of instruments when selecting tests for use in a given situation or with a particular client.

**b.** *Culturally Diverse Populations.* Counselors are cautious when selecting tests for culturally diverse populations to avoid inappropriateness of testing that may be outside of socialized behavioral or cognitive patterns.

## E.7. CONDITIONS OF TEST ADMINISTRATION

**a.** *Administration Conditions.* Counselors administer tests under the same conditions that were established in their standardization. When tests are not administered under standard conditions or when unusual behavior or irregularities occur during the testing session, those conditions are noted in interpretation, and the results may be designated as invalid or of questionable validity.

**b.** *Computer Administration.* Counselors are responsible for ensuring that administration programs function properly to provide clients with accurate results when a computer or other electronic methods are used for test administration. (See A.12.b.)

**c.** *Unsupervised Test Taking.* Counselors do not permit unsupervised or inadequately supervised use of tests or assessments unless the tests or assessments are designed, intended, and validated for self-administration and/or scoring.

**d.** *Disclosure of Favorable Conditions.* Prior to test administration, conditions that produce most favorable test results are made known to the examinee.

## E.8. DIVERSITY IN TESTING

Counselors are cautious in using assessment techniques, making evaluations, and interpreting the performance of populations not represented in the norm group on which an instrument was standardized. They recognize the effects of age, color, culture, disability, ethnic group, gender, race, religion, sexual orientation, and socioeconomic status on test administration and interpretation and place test results in proper perspective with other relevant factors. (See A.2.a.)

## E.9. TEST SCORING AND INTERPRETATION

**a.** *Reporting Reservations.* In reporting assessment results, counselors indicate any reservations that exist regarding validity or reliability because of the circumstances of the assessment or the inappropriateness of the norms for the person tested.

**b.** *Research Instruments.* Counselors exercise caution when interpreting the results of research instruments possessing insufficient technical data to support respondent results. The specific purposes for the use of such instruments are stated explicitly to the examinee.

**c.** *Testing Services.* Counselors who provide test scoring and test interpretation services to support the assessment process confirm the validity of such interpretations. They accurately describe the purpose, norms, validity, reliability, and applications of the procedures and any special qualifications applicable to their use. The public offering of an automated test interpretations service is considered a professional-to-professional consultation. The formal responsibility of the consultant is to the consultee, but the ultimate and overriding responsibility is to the client.

### E.10. TEST SECURITY

Counselors maintain the integrity and security of tests and other assessment techniques consistent with legal and contractual obligations. Counselors do not appropriate, reproduce, or modify published tests or parts thereof without acknowledgment and permission from the publisher.

### E.11. OBSOLETE TESTS AND OUTDATED TEST RESULTS

Counselors do not use data or test results that are obsolete or outdated for the current purpose. Counselor make every effort to prevent the misuse of obsolete measures and test data by others.

### E.12. TEST CONSTRUCTION

Counselors use established scientific procedures, relevant standards, and current professional knowledge for test design in the development, publication, and utilization of educational and psychological assessment techniques.

## SECTION F: TEACHING, TRAINING, AND SUPERVISION

### F.I. COUNSELOR EDUCATORS AND TRAINERS

**a.** *Educators as Teachers and Practitioners.* Counselors who are responsible for developing, implementing, and supervising educational programs are skilled as teachers and practitioners. They are knowledgeable regarding the ethical, legal, and regulatory aspects of the profession, are skilled in applying that knowledge, and make students and supervisees aware of their responsibilities. Counselors conduct counselor education and training programs in an ethical manner and serve as role models for professional behavior. Counselor educators should make an effort to infuse material related to human diversity into all courses and/or workshops that are designed to promote the development of professional counselors.

**b.** *Relationship Boundaries with Students and Supervisees.* Counselors clearly define and maintain ethical, professional, and social relationship boundaries with their students and supervisees. They we aware of the differential in power that exists and the student's or supervisee's possible incomprehension of that power differential. Counselors explain to students and supervisees the potential for the relationship to become exploitive.

**c.** *Sexual Relationships.* Counselors do not engage in sexual relationships with students or supervisees and do not subject them to sexual harassment. (See A.6. and C.5.b)

**d.** *Contributions to Research.* Counselors give credit to students or supervisees for their contributions to research and scholarly projects. Credit is given through coauthorship, acknowledgment, footnote statement, or other appropriate means, in accordance with such contributions. (See G.4.b. and G.4.c.)

**e.** *Close Relatives.* Counselors do not accept close relatives as students or supervisees.

**f.** *Supervision Preparation.* Counselors who offer clinical supervision services are adequately prepared in supervision methods and techniques. Counselors who are doctoral students serving as practicum or internship supervisors to master's level students are adequately prepared and supervised by the training program.

**g.** *Responsibility for Services to Clients.* Counselors who supervise the counseling services of others take reasonable measures to ensure that counseling services provided to clients are professional.

**h.** *Endorsement.* Counselors do not endorse students or supervisees for certification, licensure, employment, or completion of an academic or training program if they believe students or supervisees are not qualified for the endorsement. Counselors take reasonable steps to assist students or supervisees who are not qualified for endorsement to become qualified.

### F.2. COUNSELOR EDUCATION AND TRAINING PROGRAMS

**a.** *Orientation.* Prior to admission, counselors orient prospective students to the counselor education or training program's expectations, including but not limited to the following: (1) the type and level of skill acquisition required for successful completion of the training, (2) subject matter to be covered, (3) basis for evaluation, (4) training components that encourage self-growth or self-disclosure as part of the training process, (5) the type of supervision settings and requirements of the sites for required clinical field experiences, (6) student and supervisee evaluation and dismissal policies and procedures, and (7) up-to-date employment prospects for graduates.

**b.** *Integration of Study and Practice.* Counselors establish counselor education and training programs that integrate academic study and supervised practice.

**c.** *Evaluation.* Counselors clearly state to students and supervisees, in advance of training, the levels of competency expected, appraisal methods, and timing of evaluations for both didactic and experiential components. Counselors provide students and supervisees with periodic performance appraisal and evaluation feedback throughout the training program.

**d.** *Teaching Ethics.* Counselors make students and supervisees aware of the ethical responsibilities and standards of the profession and the students' and supervisees' ethical responsibilities to the profession. (See C.1. and F.3.e.)

**e.** *Peer Relationships.* When students or supervisees are assigned to lead counseling groups or provide clinical supervision for their peers, counselors take steps to ensure that students and supervisees placed in these roles do not have personal or adverse relationships with peers and that they understand they have the same ethical obligations as counselor educators, trainers, and supervisors. Counselors make every effort to ensure that the rights of peers are not compromised when students or supervisees are assigned to lead counseling groups or provide clinical supervision.

**f.** *Varied Theoretical Positions.* Counselors present varied theoretical positions so that students and supervisees may make comparisons and have opportunities to develop their own positions. Counselors provide information concerning the scientific bases of professional practice. (See C.6.a.)

**g.** *Field Placements.* Counselors develop clear policies within their training program regarding field placement and other clinical experiences.

Counselors provide clearly stated roles and responsibilities for the student or supervisee, the site supervisor, and the program supervisor. They confirm that site supervisors are qualified to provide supervision and are informed of their professional and ethical responsibilities in this role.

**h.** *Dual Relationships as Supervisors.* Counselors avoid dual relationships such as performing the role of site supervisor and training program supervisor in the student's or supervisee's training program. Counselors do not accept any form of professional services, fees, commissions, reimbursement, or remuneration from a site for student or supervisee placement.

**i.** *Diversity in Programs.* Counselors are responsive to their institution's and program's recruitment and retention needs for training program administrators, faculty, and students with diverse backgrounds and special needs. (See A.2.a.)

### F.3. STUDENTS AND SUPERVISEES

**a.** *Limitations.* Counselors, through ongoing evaluation and appraisal, are aware of the academic and personal limitations of students and supervisees that might impede performance. Counselors assist students and supervisees in securing remedial assistance when needed, and dismiss from the training program supervisees who are unable to provide competent service due to academic or personal limitations. Counselors seek professional consultation and document their decision to dismiss or refer students or supervisees for assistance. Counselors assure that students and supervisees have recourse to address decisions made, to require them to seek assistance, or to dismiss them.

**b.** *Self-Growth Experiences.* Counselors use professional judgment when designing training experiences conducted by the counselors themselves that require student and supervisee self-growth or self-disclosure. Safeguards are provided so that students and supervisees are aware of the ramifications their self-disclosure may have, on counselors whose primary role as teacher, trainer, or supervisor requires acting on ethical obligations to the profession. Evaluative components of experiential training experiences explicitly delineate predetermined academic standards that are separate and not dependent on the student's level of self-disclosure. (See A.6.)

**c.** *Counseling for Students and Supervisees.* If students or supervisees request counseling, supervisors or counselor educators provide them with acceptable referrals. Supervisors or counselor educators do not serve as counselor to students or supervisees over whom they hold administrative, teaching, or evaluative roles unless this is a brief role associated with a training experience. (See A.6.b.)

**d.** *Clients of Students and Supervisees.* Counselors make every effort to ensure that the clients at field placements are aware of the services rendered and the qualifications of the students and supervisees rendering those services. Clients receive professional disclosure information and are informed of the limits of confidentiality. Client permission is obtained in order for the students and supervisees to use any information concerning the counseling relationship in the training process. (See B.1.e.)

**e.** *Standards for Students and Supervisees.* Students and supervisees preparing to become counselors adhere to the *Code of Ethics* and the *Standards of Practice.* Students and supervisees have the same obligations to clients as those required of counselors. (See H.1.)

# SECTION G:
# RESEARCH AND PUBLICATION
## G.1. RESEARCH RESPONSIBILITIES

**a.** *Use of Human Subjects.* Counselors plan, design, conduct, and report research in a manner consistent with pertinent ethical principles, federal and state laws, host institutional regulations, and scientific standards governing research with human subjects. Counselors design and conduct research that reflects cultural sensitivity appropriateness.

**b.** *Deviation from Standard Practices.* Counselors seek consultation and observe stringent safeguards to protect the rights of research participants when a research problem suggests a deviation from standard acceptable practices. (See B.6.)

**c.** *Precautions to Avoid Injury.* Counselors who conduct research with human subjects are responsible for the subjects' welfare throughout the experiment and take reasonable precautions to avoid causing injurious psychological, physical, or social effects to their subjects.

**d.** *Principal Researcher Responsibility.* The ultimate responsibility for ethical research practice lies with the principal researcher. All others involved in the research activities share ethical obligations and full responsibility for their own actions.

**e.** *Minimal Interference.* Counselors take reasonable precautions to avoid causing disruptions in subjects' lives due to participation in research.

**f.** *Diversity.* Counselors are sensitive to diversity and research issues with special populations. They seek consultation when appropriate. (See A.2.a. and B.6.)

## G.2. INFORMED CONSENT

**a.** *Topics Disclosed.* In obtaining informed consent for research, counselors use language that is understandable to research participants and that: (1) accurately explains the purpose and procedures to be followed; (2) identifies any procedures that are experimental or relatively untried; (3) describes the attendant discomforts and risks; (4) describes the benefits or changes in individuals or organizations that might be reasonably expected; (5) discloses appropriate alternative procedures that would be advantageous for subjects; (6) offers to answer any inquiries concerning the procedures; (7) describes any limitations on confidentiality, and (8) instructs that subjects are free to withdraw their consent and to discontinue participation in the project at any time. (See B.1.f.)

**b.** *Deception.* Counselors do not conduct research involving deception unless alternative procedures are not feasible and the prospective value of the research justifies the deception. When the methodological requirements of a study necessitate concealment or deception, the investigator is required to explain clearly the reasons for this action as soon as possible.

**c.** *Voluntary Participation.* Participation in research is typically voluntary and without any penalty for refusal to participate. Involuntary participation is appropriate only when it can be demonstrated that participation will have no harmful effects on subjects and is essential to the investigation.

**d.** *Confidentiality of Information.* Information obtained about research participants during the course of an investigation is confidential. When the possibility exists that others may obtain access to such information, ethical research practice requires that the possibility, together with the plans for protecting confidentiality, be explained to participants as a part of the procedure for obtaining informed consent. (See B.1.e.)

**e.** *Persons Incapable of Giving Informed Consent.* When a person is incapable of giving informed consent, counselors provide an appropriate explanation, obtain agreement for participation and obtain appropriate consent from a legally authorized person.

**f.** *Commitments to Participants.* Counselors take reasonable measures to honor all commitments to research participants.

**g.** *Explanations After Data Collection.* After data are collected, counselors provide participants with full clarification of the nature of the study to remove any misconceptions. Where scientific or human values justify delaying or withholding information, counselors take reasonable measures to avoid causing harm.

**h.** *Agreements to Cooperate.* Counselors who agree to cooperate with another individual in research or publication incur an obligation to cooperate as promised in terms of punctuality of performance and with regard to the completeness and accuracy of the information required.

**i.** *Informed Consent for Sponsors.* In the pursuit of research, counselors give sponsors, institutions, and publication channels the same respect and opportunity for giving informed consent that they accord to individual research participants. Counselors are aware of their obligation to future research workers and ensure that host institutions are given feedback information and proper acknowledgment.

## G.3. REPORTING RESULTS

**a.** *Information Affecting Outcome.* When reporting research results, counselors explicitly mention all variables and conditions known to the investigator that may have affected the outcome of a study or the interpretation of data.

**b.** *Accurate Results.* Counselors plan, conduct, and report research accurately and in a manner that minimizes the possibility that results will be misleading. They provide thorough discussions of the limitations of their data and alternative hypotheses.

Counselors do not engage in fraudulent research, distort data, misrepresent data, or deliberately bias their results.

**c.** *Obigation to Report Unfavorable Results.* Counselors communicate to other counselors the results of any research judged to be of professional value. Results that reflect unfavorably on institutions, programs, services, prevailing opinions, or vested interests are not withheld.

**d.** *Identity of Subjects.* Counselors who supply data, aid in the research of another person, report research results, or make original data available take due care to disguise the identity of respective subjects in the absence of specific authorization from the subjects to do otherwise. (See B.1.g. and B.5.a.)

**e.** *Replication Studies.* Counselors are obligated to make available sufficient original research data to qualified professionals who may wish to replicate the study.

## G.4. PUBLICATION

**a.** *Recognition of Others.* When conducting and reporting research, counselors are familiar with and give recognition to previous work on the topic, observe copyright laws, and give full credit to those to whom credit is due. (See F.1.d. and G.4.c.)

**b.** *Contributors.* Counselors give credit through joint authorship, acknowledgment, footnote statements, or other appropriate means to those who have contributed significantly to research or concept development, in accordance with such contributions. The principal contributor is listed first and minor technical or professional contributions are acknowledged in notes or introductory statements.

**c.** *Student Research.* For an article that is substantially based on a student's dissertation or thesis, the student is listed as the principal author. (See F.1.d. and G.4.a.)

**d.** *Duplicate Submission.* Counselors submit manuscripts for consideration to only one journal at a time. Manuscripts that are published in whole or in substantial part in another journal or published work are not submitted for publication without acknowledgment and permission from the previous publication.

**e.** *Professional Review.* Counselors who review material submitted for publication, research, or other scholarly purposes respect the confidentiality and proprietary rights of those who submitted it.

# SECTION H:
# RESOLVING ETHICAL ISSUES

## H.1. KNOWLEDGE OF STANDARDS

Counselors are familiar with the *Code of Ethics* and the *Standards of Practice* and other applicable ethics codes from other professional organizations of which they are member, or from certification and licensure bodies. Lack of knowledge or misunderstanding of an ethical responsibility is not a defense against a charge of unethical conduct. (See F.3.e.)

## H.2. SUSPECTED VIOLATIONS

**a.** *Ethical Behavior Expected.* Counselors expect professional associates to adhere to Code of Ethics. When counselors possess reasonable cause that raises doubts as to whether a counselor is acting in an ethical mariner, they take appropriate action. (See H.2.d. and H.2.e.)

**b.** *Consultation.* When uncertain as to whether a particular situation or course of action may be in violation of Code of Ethics, counselors consult with other counselors who are knowledgeable about ethics, with colleagues, or with appropriate authorities.

**c.** *Organization Conflicts.* If the demands of an organization with which counselors are affiliated pose a conflict with Code of Ethics, counselors specify the nature of such conflicts and express to their supervisors or other responsible officials their commitment to Code of Ethics. When possible, counselors work toward change within the organization to allow full adherence to Code of Ethics.

**d.** *Informal Resolution.* When counselors have reasonable cause to believe that another counselor is violating an ethical standard, they attempt to first resolve the issue informally with the other counselor if feasible, providing that such action does not violate confidentiality rights that may be involved.

**e.** *Reporting Suspected Violations.* When an informal resolution is not appropriate or feasible, counselors, upon reasonable cause, take action such as reporting the suspected ethical violation to state or national ethics committees, unless this action

conflicts with confidentiality rights that cannot be resolved.

**f.** *Unwarranted Complaints.* Counselors do not initiate, participate in, or encourage the filing of ethics complaints that are unwarranted or intend to harm a counselor rather than to protect clients or the public.

## H.3. COOPERATION WITH ETHICS COMMITTEES

Counselors assist in the process of enforcing Code of Ethics. Counselors cooperate with investigations, proceedings, and requirements of the ACA Ethics Committee or ethics committees of other duly constituted associations or boards having jurisdiction over those charged with a violation. Counselors are familiar with the ACA Policies and Procedures and use it as a reference in assisting the enforcement of the Code of Ethics.

# STANDARDS OF PRACTICE

All members of the American Counseling Association (ACA) are required to adhere to the *Standards of Practice* and the *Code of Ethics*. The *Standards of Practice* represent minimal behavioral statements of the *Code of Ethics*. Members should refer to the applicable section of *the Code of Ethics* for further interpretation and amplification of the applicable Standard of Practice.

## SECTION A: THE COUNSELING RELATIONSHIP

### Standard of Practice One (SP-1)
### Nondiscrimination

Counselors respect diversity and must not discriminate against clients because of age, color, culture, disability, ethnic group, gender, race, religion, sexual orientation, marital status, or socioeconomic status. (See A.2.a.)

### Standard of Practice Two (SP-2)
### Disclosure to Clients

Counselors must adequately inform clients, preferably in writing, regarding the counseling process and counseling relationship at or before the time it begins and throughout the relationship. (See A.3.a.)

### Standard of Practice Three (SP-3)
### Dual Relationships

Counselors must make every effort to avoid dual relationships with clients that could impair their professional judgment or increase the risk of harm to clients. When a dual relationship cannot be avoided, counselors must take appropriate steps to ensure that judgment is not impaired and that no exploitation occurs. (See A.6.a. and A.6.b.)

### Standard of Practice Four (SP-4)
### Sexual Intimacies with Clients

Counselors must not engage in any type of sexual intimacies with current clients and must not engage in sexual intimacies with former clients within a minimum of two years after terminating the counseling relationship. Counselors who engage in such relationship after two years following termination have the responsibility to thoroughly examine and document that such relations did not have an exploitative nature.

### Standard of Practice Five (SP-5) Protecting
### Clients During Group Work

Counselors must take steps to protect clients from physical or psychological trauma resulting from interactions during group work. (See A.9.b.)

### Standard of Practice Six (SP-6)
### Advance Understanding of Fees

Counselors must explain to clients, prior to their entering the counseling relationship, financial arrangements related to professional services. (See A.10.a–d. and A.11.c.)

### Standard of Practice Seven (SP-7)
### Termination

Counselors must assist in making appropriate arrangements for the continuation of treatment of clients, when necessary, following termination of counseling relationships. (See A.11.a.)

### Standard of Practice Eight (SP-8)
### Inability to Assist Clients

Counselors must avoid entering or immediately terminate a counseling relationship if it is determined that they are unable to be of professional assistance to a client. The counselor may assist in making an appropriate referral for the client. (See A. I Lb.)

## SECTION B: CONFIDENTIALITY

### Standard of Practice Nine (SP-9)
### Confidentiality Requirement

Counselors must keep information related to counseling services confidential unless disclosure is in the best interest of clients, is required for the welfare of others, or is required by law. When disclosure is required, only information that is essential is revealed and the client is informed of such disclosure. (See B.1. a.–f.)

### Standard of Practice Ten (SP-10)
### Confidentiality Requirements
### for Subordinates

Counselors must take measures to ensure that privacy and confidentiality of clients are maintained by subordinates. (See B.1.h.)

### Standard of Practice Eleven (SP-11)
### Confidentiality In Group Work

Counselors must clearly communicate to group members that confidentiality cannot be guaranteed in group work. (See B.2.a.)

### Standard of Practice Twelve (SP-12)
### Confidentiality In Family Counseling

Counselors must not disclose information about one family member in counseling to another family member without prior consent. (See B.2.b.)

### Standard of Practice Thirteen (SP-13)
### Confidentiality of Records

Counselors must maintain appropriate confidentiality in creating, storing, accessing, transferring, and disposing of counseling records. (See B.4.b.)

### Standard of Practice Fourteen (SP-14)
### Permission to Record or Observe

Counselors must obtain prior consent from clients in order to electronically record or observe sessions. (See B.4.c.)

### Standard of Practice Fifteen (SP-15)
### Disclosure or Transfer of Records

Counselors must obtain client consent to disclose or transfer records to third parties, unless exceptions listed in SP-9 exist. (See B.4.e.)

### Standard of Practice Sixteen (SP-16)
### Data Disguise Required

Counselors must disguise the identity of the client when using data for training, research, or publication. (See B.5.a.)

## SECTION C:
## PROFESSIONAL RESPONSIBILITY

### Standard of Practice Seventeen (SP-17)
### Boundaries of Competence

Counselors must practice only within the boundaries of their competence. (See C.2.a.)

### Standard of Practice Eighteen (SP-18)
### Continuing Education

Counselors must engage in continuing education to maintain their professional competence. (See C.2.f.)

### Standard of Practice Nineteen (SP-19)
### Impairment of Professionals

Counselors must refrain from offering professional services when their personal problems or conflicts may cause harm to a client or others. (See C.2.g.)

### Standard of Practice Twenty (SP-20)
### Accurate Advertising

Counselors must accurately represent their credentials and services when advertising. (See C.3.a.)

### Standard of Practice Twenty-one (SP-21)
### Recruiting Through Employment

Counselors must not use their place of employment or institutional affiliation to recruit clients for their private practices. (See C.3.d.)

### Standard of Practice Twenty-two (SP-22)
### Credentials Claimed

Counselors must claim or imply only professional credentials possessed and must correct any known misrepresentations of their credentials by others. (See C.4.a.)

### Standard of Practice Twenty-three (SP-23)
### Sexual Harassment

Counselors must not engage in sexual harassment. (See C.5.b.)

### Standard of Practice Twenty-four (SP-24)
### Unjustified Gains

Counselors must not use their professional positions to seek or receive unjustified personal gains, sexual favors, unfair advantage, or unearned goods or services. (See C.5.e.)

### Standard of Practice Twenty-five (SP-25)
### Clients Served by Others

With the consent of the client, counselors must inform other mental health professionals serving the same client that a counseling relationship between the counselor and client exists. (See C.6.c.)

### Standard of Practice Twenty-six (SP-26)
### Negative Employment Conditions

Counselors must alert their employers to institutional policy or conditions that may be potentially disruptive or damaging to the counselor's professional responsibilities, or that may limit their effectiveness or deny clients' rights. (See D.l.c.)

### Standard of Practice Twenty-seven (SP-27)
### Personnel Selection and Assignment

Counselors must select competent staff and must assign responsibilities compatible with staff skills and experiences. (See D.1.h.)

### Standard of Practice Twenty-eight (SP-28)
### Exploitive Relationships with Subordinates

Counselors must not engage in exploitive relationships with individuals over whom they have supervisory, evaluative, or instructional control or authority. (See D.1.k.)

# SECTION D: RELATIONSHIP WITH OTHER PROFESSIONALS

### Standard of Practice Twenty-nine (SP-29)
### Accepting Fees from Agency Clients

Counselors must not accept fees or other remuneration for consultation with persons entitled to such services through the counselor's employing agency or institution. (See D.3.a.)

### Standard of Practice Thirty (SP-30)
### Referral Fees

Counselors must not accept referral fees. (See D.3.b.)

# SECTION E: EVALUATION, ASSESSMENT, AND INTERPRETATION

### Standard of Practice Thirty-one (SP-31)
### Limits of Competence

Counselors must perform only testing and assessment services for which they are competent. Counselors must not allow the use of psychological assessment techniques by unqualified persons under their supervision. (See E.2.a.)

### Standard of Practice Thirty-two (SP-32)
### Appropriate Use of Assessment Instruments

Counselors must use assessment instruments in the manner for which they were intended. (See E.2.b.)

### Standard of Practice Thirty-three (SP-33)
### Assessment Explanations to Clients

Counselors must provide explanations to clients prior to assessment about the nature and purposes of assessment and the specific uses of results. (See E.3.a.)

### Standard of Practice Thirty-four (SP-34)
### Recipients of Test Results

Counselors must ensure that accurate and appropriate interpretations accompany any release of testing and assessment information. (See E.3.b.)

### Standard of Practice Thirty-five (SP-35)
### Obsolete Tests and Outdated Test Results

Counselors must not base their assessment or intervention decisions or recommendations on data or test results that are obsolete or outdated for the current purpose. (See E.11.)

# SECTION F: TEACHING, TRAINING, AND SUPERVISION

### Standard of Practice Thirty-six (SP-36)
### Sexual Relationships with students or Supervisees

Counselors must not engage in sexual relationships with their students and supervisees. (See F.1.c.)

### Standard of Practice Thirty-seven (SP-37)
### Credit for Contributions to Research

Counselors must give credit to students or supervisees for their contributions to research and scholarly projects. (See F.1.d.)

### Standard of Practice Thirty-eight (SP-38)
### Supervision Preparation

Counselors who offer clinical supervision services must be trained and prepared in supervision methods and techniques. (See F.1.f.)

### Standard of Practice Thirty-nine (SP-39)
### Evaluation Information

Counselors must clearly state to students and supervisees in advance of training, the levels of competency expected, appraisal methods, and timing of evaluations. Counselors must provide students and supervisees with periodic performance appraisal and evaluation feedback throughout the training program. (See F.2.c.)

### Standard of Practice Forty (SP-40)
### Peer Relationships in Training

Counselors must make every effort to ensure that the rights of peers are not violated when students and supervisees are assigned to lead counseling groups or provide clinical supervision. (See F.2.e.)

### Standard of Practice Forty-one (SP-41)
### Limitations of Students and Supervisees

Counselors must assist students and supervisees in securing remedial assistance, when needed, and must dismiss from the training program students and supervisees who are unable to provide competent service due to academic or personal limitations. (See F.3.a.)

### Standard of Practice Forty-two (SP-42)
### Self-Growth Experiences

Counselors who conduct experiences for students or supervisees that include self-growth or self disclosure must inform participants of counselors' ethical obligations to the profession and must not grade participants based on their nonacademic performance. (See F.3.b.)

### Standard of Practice Forty-three (SP-43)
### Standards for Students and Supervisees

Students and supervisees preparing to become counselors must adhere to the *Code of Ethics* and the *Standards of Practice* of counselors. (See F.3.e.)

## SECTION G: RESEARCH AND PUBLICATION

### Standard of Practice Forty-four (SP-44)
### Precautions to Avoid Injury In Research

Counselors must avoid causing physical, social, or psychological harm or injury to subjects in research. (See G.l.c.)

### Standard of Practice Forty-five (SP-45)
### Confidentiality of Research Information

Counselors must keep confidential information obtained about research participants. (See G.2.d.)

### Standard of Practice Forty-six (SP-46)
### Infomation Affecting Research Outcome

Counselors must report all variables and conditions known to the investigator that may have affected research data or outcomes. (See G.3.a.)

### Standard of Practice Forty-seven (SP-47)
### Accurate Research Results

Counselors must not distort or misrepresent research data, nor fabricate or intentionally bias research results. (See G.3.b.)

### Standard of Practice Forty-eight (SP-48)
### Publication Contributors

Counselors must give appropriate credit to those who have contributed to research. (See G.4.a. and G.4.b.)

## SECTION H: RESOLVING ETHICAL ISSUES

### Standard of Practice Forty-nine (SP-49)
### Ethical Behavior Expected

Counselors must take appropriate action when they possess reasonable cause that raises doubts as to whether counselors or other mental health professionals are acting in an ethical manner. (See H.2.a.)

### Standard of Practice Fifty (SP-50)
### Unwarranted Complaints

Counselors must not initiate, participate in, or encourage the filing of ethics complaints that are unwarranted or intended to harm a mental health professional rather than to protect clients or the public. (See H.2.f.)

### Standard of Practice Fifty-one (SP-51)
### Cooperation with Ethics Committees

Counselors must cooperate with investigations, proceedings, and requirements of the ACA Ethics Committee or ethics committees of other duly constituted associations or boards having jurisdiction over those charged with a violation. (See H.3.)

## REFERENCES

The following documents are available to counselors as resources to guide them in their practices. These resources are not a part of the *Code of Ethics* and the *Standards of Practice*.

American Association for Counseling and Development/Association for Measurement and Evaluation in Counseling and Development. (1989). *The responsibilities of users of standardized tests (revised).* Washington, DC: Author.

American Counseling Association. (1988). American Counseling Association Ethical Standards Alexandria, VA: Author.

American Psychological Association. (1985). Standards for educational and psychological testing (revised). Washington, DC: Author.

American Rehabilitation Counseling Association, Commission on Rehabilitation Counselor Certification, and National Rehabilitation Counseling Association. (1995). Code of professional ethics for rehabilitation counselors. Chicago, IL. Author.

American School Counselor Association. (1992). Ethical standards for school counselors. Alexandria, VA: Author.

Joint Committee on Testing Practices (1988). Code for fair testing practices in education. Washington, DC: Author.

National Board for Certified Counselors. (1989). National Board for Certified Counselors Code of Ethics. Alexandria, VA: Author.

Prediger, D.J. (Ed.). (1993, March). Multicultural assessment standards. Alexandria, VA: Association for Assessment in Counseling.

# 5

# DEVELOPMENTAL FOUNDATIONS

Community counseling is based on the premise that human development naturally (that is, under unimpeded conditions) tends toward healthy growth. Consequently, the role of the counselor is to assist the client to establish the conditions under which this natural tendency will occur. This premise, however, raises several basic questions: What do we mean by human development? What is healthy growth? Conversely, how does one conceptualize problems with this process in ways that will be useful in the practice of community counseling?

Explicitly or implicitly, each community counselor must develop a working theory of human development by which clients can be understood, their problems put into a context, and solutions to those problems suggested. Moreover, this theory must be flexible enough to allow the counselor to try other alternatives systematically, if the one first suggested by the theory does not work. Without such a framework, based on a model of human development, counseling becomes a haphazard activity, without validity or chance for improvement (Marx, 1976). This chapter will suggest a number of different approaches to conceptualizing human development, healthy growth and functioning, and problems of living that can be of use to community counselors in formulating their own working theory.

## HUMAN DEVELOPMENT

Human development is a wide-ranging field of study in its own right, with an extensive body of theory and research. Given the focus of this book, we cannot survey this literature in any depth here, particularly since the NBCC counselor certification standards and the CACREP program accreditation standards call for the inclusion of a separate, full course on human growth and development in the core standards for counselor preparation. Suffice it to say here that some theories of human development have been formulated that focus on cognitive development, others that focus on affective development, still others on behavioral development, and yet others on the development of social or environmental transactions. Moreover, theories have been formulated to account for development in a specific area of human functioning, such as one's career (Super, 1990) or work adjustment (Hershenson & Szymanski, 1992); or during a specific time of life, such as adolescence (Muuss, 1975) or adulthood (Levinson, Darrow, Klein, Levinson, & McKee, 1978).

A classic example of a cognitive theory is that of Jean Piaget, which focuses on the development of the individual's capacities to accommodate to external reality, to incorporate information about that process into intellectual structures, and to organize those structures into schema that will permit the person to solve problems. Based on longitudinal observation of a sample of children, Piaget concluded that the development of this process occurs in four stages: (1) the period of sensory-motor intelligence, during the first two years of life, when the individual learns to make adaptive responses to environmental stimuli (such as drawing a hand back from a flame); (2) the period of preoperational thought, from ages two to six, in which the individual develops the ability to conceptualize the environment, albeit in ways that are not yet realistic, inclusive, logical, or critical; (3) the period of concrete operations, from ages six to eleven, in which the individual develops an organized system of logical categories to use in conceptualizing and dealing with the present environment; and (4) the period of formal operations, from ages eleven to fifteen, in which the individual develops the capacity to formulate hypotheses and to test predictions about future situations (Flavell, 1963).

An example of an affective approach is classical psychoanalytic theory, in which Sigmund Freud proposed three hypothetical structures: the id (innate, biologically based drives and impulses), the superego (socially imposed constraints and values), and the ego (the mechanism that tries to reconcile the competing demands of id impulses, superego constraints, and external reality). While the individual is born with an id, the ego and superego develop over a series of stages, each of which is identified by the part of the body that becomes, in sequence, the focus of pleasurable, impulse-gratifying activity. These foci are the oral zone (during the first year of life), the anal zone (during the second year), and the phallic zone (during the next several

years). Upon the resolution of the Oedipal complex (that is, the phallic wish to replace the parent of the same sex in the affections of the parent of the opposite sex), the impulses go into a quiescent period called latency, until they are reactivated by the bodily changes of adolescence into a renewed focus on the genital zone. One problem with this theory for our purposes is that Freud deduced it from the observation of persons with mental health problems whom he saw in his clinical practice as a psychiatrist. As community counseling is premised on healthy development, the applicability of a theory derived from pathological development is questionable.

An example of a behavioral approach to development is Dollard and Miller (1950), who explained the stages that Freud had defined on the basis of learned responses to stimuli, rather than on Freud's basis of innate, affective developmental processes. Other behavioral approaches to development focus on social learning (Bandura & Walters, 1963; Rotter, 1954) or on cognitive-behavioral (Beck, 1976; Ellis, 1962) approaches. In essence, social learning theory posits that human behavior is learned (as does all learning theory), but it goes on to posit that complex social behaviors may be learned through such processes as imitation, modeling, or identification with the teacher of the behavior, rather than only through simple, direct, immediate reward or punishment for trying out a particular behavior (the classical learning theory position). Social learning theory also goes beyond classical learning theory in the social learning assertion that many behaviors are acquired but not exhibited until later. Reinforcement for a behavior may be self-reinforcement or vicarious (observing the consequences to others when they exhibit the behavior), rather than only the classically defined, externally administered kind.

Cognitive-behavioral approaches (e.g., Beck, 1976; Ellis, 1962) generally share most of the ideas and premises of social learning theory, but add a distinction between internal mental process (thoughts and emotions) and overt behaviors (actions). Thoughts, emotions, and actions interact. What people think affects how they feel and how they act; how they act affects their thoughts and feelings, and so on. In this view, people learn in all three domains as they develop over their lives. Problems occur when incorrect learning takes place in one or more of these three domains, which then may go on to affect behavior in the other two domains. These incorrect learnings may involve erroneous ideas, faulty associations, distorted perceptions, and so on, which may be remedied by having the client recognize the faulty learning and learn to replace it with an appropriate thought, feeling, or action. Both logical (getting the client to recognize the error) and behavioral (role playing, skill training, modeling, self-reinforcement, etc.) techniques may be used to correct the error.

Learning theory is of relevance to community counselors not only in offering one consistent explanation of a client's behavior (how it developed, became problematic, and can be changed), but also as a basis for helping a client to learn new skills.

Finally, some developmental theories, such as family systems theory, focus on development as a product of the individual's history of transactions with their social or environmental context. Thus, the person is viewed as a subsystem within a larger system and develops interactively with other subsystems (parent, sibling, peer) within that system. This approach is widely used in family counseling.

Given the huge diversity of approaches to conceptualizing development, it is not surprising that Ivey and Goncalves (1988) concluded that "development" was "a very fashionable adjective, noun, and verb, meaning almost anything" (p. 406). Consequently, Hershenson (1993) proposed that counseling focus its attention on those formulations of development that are consistent with its premises (presented in Chapter 1), that is, (a) formulations that are based on the observation of normal, healthy development and (b) formulations that take into account the interaction between the person and the environment. Hershenson's second criterion for selecting theories of development was that they should be directly applicable to the practice of counseling. Applying these selection criteria, we shall here focus on the developmental theories of Havighurst (1972), Erikson (1963, 1968), and Maslow (1954, 1962). We shall also briefly look at Super's (1990) theory of career development and Hershenson's (Hershenson & Szymanski, 1992) theory of the development of work behavior, as they meet the criteria specified above.

## Havighurst's Compendium of Developmental Tasks

Havighurst (1972) believed that certain life skills are best taught at a particular time of life; and if that "teachable moment" is missed, it becomes much more difficult for an individual to learn that life skill. Therefore, as a guide for educators, Havighurst compiled a list of the tasks that, through his research, he believed were the major learnings for each stage of life. In that way, parents and/or teachers could teach each life skill at the teachable moment, rather than too early or too late. This list of life skills provides an excellent reference point for the counselor to use in assessing a client's assets and age-appropriate competencies.

Havighurst's (1972) compendium of developmental tasks, by stage of life, is as follows:*

I. Infancy and early childhood
   1. Learning to walk
   2. Learning to take solid foods
   3. Learning to talk

*From *Developmental Tasks and Education* by Robert J. Havighurst, Third Edition. Copyright © 1972 by Longman Publishers. Reprinted with permission.

4. Learning to control the elimination of body wastes

5. Learning sex differences and sexual modesty

6. Forming concepts and learning language to describe social and physical reality

7. Getting ready to read

8. Learning to distinguish right and wrong and beginning to develop a conscience

II. Middle childhood (about ages 6–12)

1. Learning physical skills necessary for ordinary games

2. Building wholesome attitudes toward oneself as a growing organism

3. Learning to get along with age-mates

4. Learning an appropriate masculine or feminine social role

5. Developing fundamental skills in reading, writing, and calculating

6. Developing concepts necessary for everyday living

7. Developing conscience, morality, and a scale of values

8. Achieving personal independence

9. Developing attitudes toward social groups and institutions

III. Adolescence (about ages 12–18)

1. Achieving new and more mature relations with age-mates of both sexes

2. Achieving a masculine or feminine social role

3. Accepting one's physique and using the body effectively

4. Achieving emotional independence of parents and other adults

5. Preparing for marriage and family life

6. Preparing for an economic career

7. Acquiring a set of values and an ethical system as a guide to behavior—developing an ideology

8. Desiring and achieving socially responsible behavior

IV. Early adulthood (about ages 18–30)

1. Selecting a mate

2. Learning to live with a marriage partner

3. Starting a family

4. Rearing children

5. Managing a home

6. Getting started in an occupation

7. Taking on civic responsibility

8. Finding a congenial social group

V. Middle age (about 30–60)

1. Assisting teenage children to become responsible and happy adults

2. Achieving adult social and civic responsibility

3. Reaching and maintaining satisfactory performance in one's occupational career

4. Developing adult leisure-time activities

5. Relating to one's spouse as a person

6. Accepting and adjusting to the physiological changes of middle age

7. Adjusting to aging parents

VI. Later maturity

1. Adjusting to decreasing physical strength and health

2. Adjusting to retirement and reduced income

3. Adjusting to death of spouse

4. Establishing an explicit affiliation with one's age group

5. Adopting and adapting social roles in a flexible way

**6.** Establishing satisfactory physical living arrangements

By developing this list of age-related tasks, Havighurst has created a useful tool for the community counselor to use in assessing a client's skills (both assets and deficits) and level of functioning.

## Erikson's Epigenetic Stages

Erik H. Erikson (1963, 1968) proposed that normal human development takes place in eight successive stages. Based on his studies of development in a variety of cultures, he claimed that these eight stages are valid across cultures.

Although the stages are typically age-related, each stage must be substantially accomplished in order for the individual to move on to the next stage. Each stage is concerned with the resolution of a particular issue, the positive outcome of these being: (1) trust, (2) autonomy, (3) initiative, (4) industry, (5) identity, (6) intimacy, (7) generativity, and (8) integrity. Thus, the infant must develop *trust* in its parents and its surroundings before it can take the risk to try to function autonomously. Once, however, it gains *autonomy* of functioning, the young child can feel secure enough of its self-control to be able to *initiate* actions affecting its environment. Having proved to itself that it can have an impact on its surroundings, the child learns the habits and skills *(industry)* necessary for survival as a productive member of its society, that is, how to have an effective, goal-directed impact on its environment. By adolescence, the individual has a clear enough picture of personal strengths and weaknesses to develop a particular social, sexual, and vocational *identity* by which one is uniquely recognizable to oneself and to other people. Having established a secure identity, the young adult can become intimately involved with a significant other (person, career, and/or cause) without fear of loss of selfhood. *Intimacy* generates products—children, artistic creations, ideas, business ventures, and so on—which must be nourished and developed through the years of middle adulthood (the period of *generativity*). Finally, as one moves toward the end of life, one should be able to look back over one's life as a whole and see it as a positive, *integrated,* fulfilled experience, thereby freeing one to face death (the final passage) with equanimity.

In this theory, a series of successive, age-related life stages are defined. As with Havighurst's system, the counselor may use Erikson's model to suggest the skills and concerns a client typically could be expected to have at a particular time of life. Moreover, if a client is dealing with the issue of a stage that should have been resolved earlier in life, the counselor may infer at what point in life the client's problem began. Erikson has also defined the unsuccessful outcome that may occur at each stage; this may be used as an indicator of when the individual's problems arose. These negative outcomes for each stage are, respectively: (1) mistrust (failure to develop trust), (2) shame and doubt (failure to achieve autonomy), (3) guilt (failure to achieve initiative), (4) inferiority (failure to develop industry), (5) identify confusion (failure to form an identity), (6) isolation (inability to achieve intimacy), (7) stagnation (failure to attain generativity), (8) despair (lack of integrity).

Another point made by Erikson that is of importance to community counselors is that each culture develops institutions (such as rites of passage, role expectations, etc.) that serve to assist an individual to progress through the life stages. One example is the moratorium provided by the college years, which allows the late adolescent a relatively unpressured time in which to consolidate an identity. It is incumbent on the counselor to be aware of the particular institutions in the general culture and in the client's subculture that can support and facilitate the client's growth.

The counselor should regularly utilize these institutions as sources of environmental support in working with the client.

## Maslow's Need Hierarchy

Abraham Maslow (1954, 1962), based on his study of highly successful people, proposed that all people have a hierarchy of needs, and that each level of need must be substantially satisfied before the next level can be recognized and attended to. This hierarchy consists of the following, starting from the most basic level:

1. Physiological needs (food, shelter, clothing, etc.)
2. Safety needs
3. Needs for love and belonging
4. Need for esteem
5. Need for self-actualization
6. Need for cognitive understanding

For example, if one is starving (facing physiological need), one will take risks (not be driven by safety needs) in order to get food; and so on, up the hierarchy. As one moves up the hierarchy, one moves from survival needs to growth needs. Numbers 1 and 2 are clearly survival needs; numbers 5 and 6 clearly growth needs (Maslow, 1962). Most people never achieve the higher levels of the hierarchy because their needs at a lower level are never sufficiently met. Nonetheless, from the point of view of the community counselor, this model suggests a way of categorizing a client's problem, suggesting what has to be provided to resolve it, and predicting what needs will arise once that problem is solved (that is, once that level of need is met).

Hershenson (1982) proposed a model that combines Erikson's stages and Maslow's levels into a single system of six sequential developmental trends: survival, growth, communication, recognition, mastery, and understanding. Survival encompasses Maslow's physiological and safety needs and Erikson's issue of trust. As its name implies, this trend concerns the biological, psychological, and social survival and continuity of the individual. Growth encompasses Maslow's point of shift from survival needs to needs involving growth and Erikson's issues of autonomy and initiative. Having survived, the individual can manifest the trend of growth—physically, emotionally, intellectually, and socially. Writers in a wide range of fields, from biology to sociology, have attributed the trends of survival and growth to all organisms, from single-celled plants and animals to large human organizations and societies. Communication encompasses Maslow's needs for love and belonging and Erikson's issue of intimacy. The trend of communication entails the receiving and giving of love, closeness, and social interchange. Berelson and Steiner (1964, p. 65) stated, as one of the few scientifically verified findings concerning human behavioral development: "Normal adult human behavior develops only through the stimulation of other people." Recognition encompasses Maslow's need for esteem and Erikson's issue of identity. Recognition involves the acceptance by the person and by significant others of the person's individuality and worth. It involves self-respect and respect by and for others. Mastery encompasses Maslow's need for self-actualization and Erikson's issues of industry and generativity. Mastery involves the development of the ability to cope with one's environment in a competent, productive, and satisfying manner. Finally, understanding encompasses Maslow's need for cognitive understanding and Erikson's issue of integrity. This trend involves the development of a personally meaningful conception of one's world and of one's place within it.

It may be noted that the first two of these trends (survival and growth) relate particularly to the person's self, the next two (communication and recognition) relate to interpersonal functioning, and the last two (mastery and understanding) relate to task performance. The community counselor may use this sequence of trends as a framework within which to place a client's level of development and consequently to conceptualize the client's problem. For example, a client may have a problem with mastery in an area of life because of never having satisfactorily achieved recognition for the unique set of talents and abilities that identify the client as a capable individual, worthy of respect (self-respect and by others).

## Super's Theory of Career Development

While there have been a large number of theories of career development formulated during the past fifty years (Sharf, 1992), Donald Super's (1990) life-span, life-space theory is generally regarded as the most comprehensive. Super postulated that career development involves the implementation of occupational self-concepts that are developed through a process of synthesis and compromise among one's physical makeup, special aptitudes, and learned and rewarded roles. One's satisfaction from work depends on how well one has been able to implement these self-concepts. Moreover, since people are multipotentialed and occupations can be performed in a number of different ways, there is no single, ideal occupation for anyone. Super postulated that career development occurs in a series of five stages: (1) growth (birth to age 14); (2) exploration (ages 15–24), which contains the successive phases of fantasy, tentative, and realistic; (3) establishment (ages 25–44), which includes trial and stable phases; (4) maintenance (ages 45–64), and (5) disengagement (age 65 on). External events may disrupt this pattern, in which case careers may involve repeated cycles of new growth, reexploration, and reestablishment. Moreover, of particular

importance to community counselors, career involves more roles than just that of worker. For different individuals and at different times in their lives, the principal role may be child, student, "leisurite", homemaker, or citizen.

## Hershenson's Model of the Development of Work Adjustment

The two principal elements in this model (Hershenson & Szymanski, 1992) are the person and the environment. Within the person, three domains develop in sequence. The work personality, which is the focus of development during the preschool years while the child is primarily in the family environment, includes the person's self-concept as a worker and the person's system of motivation to work. Then, during the school years, the domain of work competencies is the focus of development. This domain includes work habits (for example, neatness, promptness, reliability), physical and mental skills applicable to jobs, and work-related interpersonal skills (for example, accepting supervision, getting along with one's peers). As the person approaches the school-to-work transition, the third domain of appropriate, crystallized work goals becomes the focus of development. These work goals reflect the environmental influences of the peer group, reference group, and societal values.

As these three domains develop and continue to function, they interact with each other and with the environment. As each domain develops, it reciprocally affects the continued development of its predecessor(s). Each domain can only initially develop to a level that is supported by its predecessor; however, the currently focal domain can affect its predecessor, thereby affecting (positively or negatively) its own potential level of development. For example, failures at school (work competencies) may force the person to revise downward an inflated self-concept as a worker (work personality) initially developed in an overprotective home environment. If that downward revision is too great, it may in turn induce further failures. The model further posits that, throughout an individual's life span, all domains continue to develop, although not as rapidly or dramatically as at the time they are focal. The three domains establish a dynamic, reciprocal balance, so that change in any one domain at any time in life will necessitate changes in the other two to restore balance.

The interaction of the domains with the work environment is called work adjustment. Work adjustment has three components: (1) task performance (that is, the quality and quantity of work output), which is primarily linked to work competencies; (2) work-role behavior (that is, acting appropriately in the work setting), which is primarily linked to work personality; and (3) worker satisfaction (that is, the degree of gratification resulting from one's work), which is primarily linked to work goals.

This model provides the community counselor with a set of concepts with which to assess and to plan interventions in work problems that clients present.

The group of theories just presented can provide the community counselor with a series of templates through which to view data about a client when trying to conceptualize where that client is in a particular aspect of his or her life, how the client got there, and where the client may need to change in order to resume unimpeded development. The counselor must take care, however, not to use a theory as a procrustean bed, crushing or stretching facts about the client to fit the theory.

## MODELS OF HEALTHY GROWTH AND FUNCTIONING

While theories of human development focus on the process of growth, models of healthy functioning suggest the goals toward which growth should be directed. Until recently,

models of healthy growth and functioning were relatively difficult to find (Schultz, 1977). For most of the past several hundred years, the models that were proposed tended to focus on psychopathology rather than on health. This is not surprising, since the field that dominated thinking on this topic was psychiatry, a branch of medicine. Medicine, by its very nature, is concerned with the diagnosis and treatment of disease. It was only with the work of the Joint Commission on Mental Illness and Health in the late 1950s (discussed in Chapter 1) that the focus began to shift toward thinking of health as something more than just the absence of disease. Indeed, the first monograph to come out of the Joint Commission, by Jahoda (1958), proposed the following as characteristics of positive mental health: (a) positive attitudes toward oneself, (b) growth and self-actualization, (c) integrated psychological functioning, (d) autonomy and personal independence, (e) adequate perception of reality, and (f) mastery of one's environment.

Thereafter, Kegan (1982) derived from Maslow (1954) "a set of traits characterizing an ideal healthy or fully functioning personality" (Kegan, 1982, p. 290). This list included the person becoming more: (a) realistic, (b) accepting of self and others, (c) natural and spontaneous, (d) problem focused, (e) autonomous and self-contained, (f) open to experience, (g) democratic, (h) creative, (i) discriminating in judgment, and (j) capable of deep interpersonal relationships.

As was noted in Chapter 1, a focus on promoting health and wellness has become a hallmark of the field of counseling. Therefore, it is not surprising that in 1992, the *Journal of Counseling and Development*, the principal journal of the American Counseling Association, published a special issue on wellness throughout the life span. In this issue, Witmer and Sweeney (1992) proposed a holistic, life-span model for wellness that involved the achievement of five life tasks: (1) spirituality, which included the dimensions of sense of wholeness and inner peace, purposiveness, optimism, and a strongly ethical set of values; (2) self-regulation, including sense of worth, sense of mastery, accurate reality perception, spontaneity and emotional responsiveness, problem-solving skills, creativity, sense of humor, physical fitness, and good health habits; (3) work as a psychologically, socially, and economically fulfilling task throughout the life span; (4) friendship and social support; and (5) love and intimacy. How well one achieves these five life tasks is affected by a number of environmental influences, including family, religion, education, community, media, government, and business and industry, as well as by the internal characteristics of the individual.

Having looked at some positive goals and outcomes of healthy development and functioning, we must also look at the formulations that have been made about less successful outcomes.

## PROBLEMS OF LIVING: BASES FOR DEFINITION

Problems of living imply aberrations and/or natural rough spots as one moves through the course of life-span development. The mental health disciplines have evolved a number of ways of conceptualizing and categorizing these problems. We shall deal first with the conceptual bases and then with systems for categorization. Some of these conceptual approaches are taxonomic, that is, concerned with identifying, describing, and classifying types of problems (just as biologists have classified species of plants or animals as a first step to understanding them). Other conceptual approaches are developmental, concerned not with the overt signs or symptoms of the problem but rather with identifying the issue in the course of development that provides the underlying cause of the problem. The advocates of the taxonomic approaches argue that unless

one establishes a typology, any attempt to remedy problems of living will be like trying to bail out the ocean one drop at a time. Without categories, one cannot apply what one has learned from one's past successes or mistakes, and each new case must be approached in total ignorance about what will work. Conversely, the advocates of the developmental approaches argue that the same problematic behavior may have any of a large number of causes, and one must find and treat the cause (not the symptom) if the problem is to be resolved. Thus, in a medical analogy, one does not get rid of every fever by taking out a person's appendix. Behaviorally, psychosis and adolescent acting-out may underlie behaviors (symptoms) that appear indistinguishable from each other, but that does not mean that they require the same treatment.

### Taxonomic Approaches

We shall now review some of the more common bases upon which systems of taxonomic classification of problems of living have been based and then offer some observations about developmental approaches to categorizing problems of living. Developmental approaches are necessarily tied to specific theories of development, that is, they represent the antithesis of what each of these theories posits to be the healthy course of development. For example, as noted earlier, Erikson defined failure for each of the eight stages through which, according to his model, the individual passes (mistrust as the failure to develop trust, shame and doubt as the failure to develop autonomy, and so on). Similarly, every other developmental theory suggests its own system for classifying and understanding problems of living, based on failure to achieve some aspect of appropriate development as defined by the theory. Taxonomic systems, however, are generally more independent of specific theories of human development. Frequently, they treat problems of living as a phenomenon in its own right, rather than as a by-product of some theory of development or of some approach to treatment. Most taxonomic approaches start from one or more of three bases for defining problems of living: (1) statistical deviance; (2) social disruption; or (3) subjective discomfort.

## Statistical Deviance

Statistical deviance is the extent to which a particular behavior departs from the behavior of most people in general when faced with a similar situation. Behavioral scientists generally assume that most human characteristics, including behaviors, follow a normal distribution. That is, they tend to cluster around a most common (average) value; the further one gets from that average, "normal" (i. e., the norm) value, the fewer the number of cases that will exist. For example, if the average height for adult men is 5'10", there will be many who are 5'9" or 5'11", fewer who are 5'6" or 6'2", and far fewer who are 4'10" or 6'10". Similarly, if most adults go out in public and maintain decorum (thus, "normal" behavior), then those who refuse ever to go out in public and those who go out but who shout threats or curses at strangers deviate from the statistical norm and are, therefore, considered to have a problem. One difficulty with this approach is in defining how far from the norm a behavior must be before it is considered problematic. This decision is largely influenced by cultural and subcultural expectations. For example, in some cultures hallucinations are seen as a sign of divine grace; whereas in others, they are seen as evidence of severe problems. Another difficulty with this approach to a definition is that sometimes the norm changes. Once one would have been considered to have a serious problem if he or she professed a belief that the earth was round; now the reverse is true, and those who assert that the earth is flat are viewed as problematic. A third difficulty is that, typically, the greater any departure is from the norm, the more it is assumed a priori to be problematic. The average or "normal" is, however, not necessarily the optimal state for a given characteristic. It may be that one extreme tail of the distribution of the characteristic is actually better, rather than worse than the norm (for example, intelligence). Thus, what was apparently a quantifiable, objective basis for defining problems of living is, in practical application, quite subjective.

## Social Disruption

A second approach to defining problems of living is based on a criterion that, by its very nature, has even less potential for quantification or objectivity than statistical deviance. That criterion is social disruption. By this approach, a behavior is defined as a problem of living if it causes danger or annoyance to a significant number of others in the environment of the person who is exhibiting the behavior. Thus, inflicting physical harm, making threats, or standing on a street corner shouting at an invisible object are all classifiable as problems of living, albeit of progressively less public concern. The greater the public menace, the more problematic the behavior is generally perceived to be and the more immediate the pressure to remove the perpetrator or to force that person to change the offending behavior. One problem with this approach is that the most menacing behavior need not reflect the presence of the most serious problem within the client. Indeed, the reverse may be true, as in the withdrawal (no menace to anyone else) that frequently precedes a suicide. Another problem with this approach is the cultural relativity of definitions of what constitutes social disruption. Behaviors that appear totally acceptable to one age, ethnic, socioeconomic, or educational group may be seen as socially disruptive to another group living within the same society. Who determines whether a given behavior is defined as problematic? Usually, it is the group with the most power to enforce their standards.

From the point of view of the community counselor, a problem arises in attempting to get a client to change a behavior from one that is accepted and sometimes reinforced in the client's own reference group (among whom the client may well spend the most time) to one that is approved by those who set the standards of what is socially acceptable. This conflict becomes even more intense when the dominant social group accepts the inevitability of certain behaviors it has designated as disruptive (and, hence, should be changed) and offers reinforcement for those who exhibit that behavior. Examples of this include use of addictive drugs, unwed parenthood, illegal immigration, chronic unemployment, and homelessness. These behaviors are publicly deplored by the arbiters of standards for the broader society; are widely accepted, prevalent practices within some subgroups of the society; and are supported by apparatus (for example, welfare services) set up by the very group that declared the behaviors disruptive in the first place. A dilemma arises for community counselors, who are frequently employed in agencies funded by those in power, that is, by those who decide which behaviors are disruptive and must be changed. It is difficult for counselors to "bite the hand that feeds them" by pointing out to those in the power structure their role in creating (if only by designating the behavior as disruptive) and sustaining the very behaviors they have employed the counselor to change. (For an extensive discussion of the role of society in creating and defining problems of living for certain of its subgroups, see Cochrane, 1983.)

### Subjective Discomfort

A third basis for defining behaviors (which includes thoughts and feelings, as well as overt actions) as problematic is subjective discomfort, that is, the degree to which they cause pain or distress to the person exhibiting the behavior. This would seem to be a reasonable basis for defining problems of living, comparable to using physical pain as a sign that one has a medical problem. There are, however, several inherent problems in using subjective distress as the defining characteristic of problems of living. One problem is that some persons (frequently labeled as "psychopaths" or "sociopaths") feel no discomfort or remorse for behaving in ways that are both statistically deviant and socially disruptive. If one uses only the criterion of subjective discomfort, these individuals (including some mass murderers) would have to be defined as problem-free. Another problem with this criterion is its subjectivity. People have different thresholds for discomfort. Therefore, is a behavior to be defined as problematic if only one individual out of a million finds that it causes personal distress? Also, how uncomfortable must a person be made by the behavior before it can be defined as causing "discomfort"? Because all perceptions are, by their very nature, subjective, it is inevitable that this basis for defining problematic behavior is a difficult one to apply consistently. This criterion is, however, of relevance to a particular counselor working with a particular client. If the client reports that a behavior causes subjective discomfort, it is clearly a problem for that client, even if no one else feels that way about that behavior.

We have briefly reviewed three widely used bases for defining problems of living: statistical deviance, social disruption, and subjective discomfort. Although each has some degree of validity, there are clearly limitations to applying any of these bases as the sole criterion for deciding if a behavior is problematic. A better (that is, more consistent, less open to exceptions) basis may be found in requiring that at least two of these criteria be met, that is, a behavior must be statistically deviant and socially disruptive, statistically deviant and cause subjective discomfort, or socially disruptive and cause subjective discomfort before it is to be considered problematic. This approach is not without its own limitations; for example, how much deviance, disruption, or discomfort is necessary to meet the combined criteria? Because there is no absolutely objective basis possible, the counselor must arrive at a definition that is both as objective as possible (that is, can be described to and applied by others) and fits best into the counselor's conceptual system of human development—problems of living—intervention.

## Developmental Approaches

Developmental systems for defining problems of living start from the premise that such problems represent departures from "normal, healthy development" as defined by the particular theory of human development. For example, by Erikson's schema, failure to move from autonomy to initiative means that one is left with the problem of shame and doubt. One difficulty with this approach is that it assumes that everyone (including the client) necessarily moves directly from autonomy to initiative. In this view, no one can move from autonomy right to industry. There is, however, some evidence that Erikson's sequence is not necessarily as invariable as he believed it to be. Another difficulty with this approach is the assumption that failure to achieve autonomy is the only cause of shame and doubt. Could not shame and doubt also result from failure to attain industry, identity, intimacy, or generativity? Thus, all developmental approaches are only as good as that group of persons to whom the theory of development actually applies; and it is not always possible for the counselor to determine immediately whether the client belongs to that group. Also, many of the links between developmental processes and specific problems of living are tenuous, at best. Therefore, it may be hazardous for the counselor to base the treatment plan on these assumptions. On the other hand, the theoretical models of development/problems that are used most commonly by mental health professions are those that were derived from clinical practice (such as psychoanalytic or client-centered approaches). Because such approaches create a logically circular process (practice X is used to generate theory Y, which is then used to justify practice X), they are of little use to the scientifically oriented community counselor.

Hence, the counselor is faced with a serious dilemma. The counselor needs a system for categorizing clients' problems, so that they can be approached systematically. Without such a system, the counselor can only flail about, treating each new problem of each client as a unique, random event. In that case, the counselor forfeits any claim to systematic knowledge or professional expertise. On the other hand, existing theories of human development and approaches to classifying problems of living are neither universally applicable nor totally valid. Therefore, the most effective and efficient solution to this dilemma may be for the counselor to use the concept of "failure to cope" with the reasons for that failure specified. As long as these reasons can be reliably given and suggest an appropriate intervention, this rather simplistic approach may well be the best alternative of any of the currently available bases for defining problems of living.

## PROBLEMS OF LIVING: SYSTEMS OF CATEGORIZATION

The system of categorization most widely used in the United States is the *Diagnostic and Statistical Manual of Mental Disorders* put out by the American Psychiatric Association (1994). This manual, now in its fourth edition, is popularly known as DSM-IV. Medicine, as a field of applied biology, has always approached problems with the belief that they had to be described and classified as a first step to understanding and, eventually, treating them. Considerable support for this approach may be derived from the progress medicine has made using it in the realm of organic disease. When, however, one attempts to apply this approach to problems of living (in medical terms, mental illness), one runs into severe difficulties because of the issues of multicausality (more than one cause for the same symptom) and of individual differences in the way that any single cause is expressed. One cannot arrive at the neat generalizations possible in biological medicine, for example, that fever usually is symptomatic of infection. In the behavioral realm, for example, hallucinations may result from any of a number of causes, including organic brain damage, certain drugs, psychosis, adolescent turmoil, lack of food or sleep, sensory deprivation, and so on. Nonetheless, since the time of the ancient Greek physician Hippocrates, physicians have tried to categorize "mental illnesses" as a basis for treating them, and those who follow the medical model have found these systems of categorization useful (or at least comforting to have available). It may, moreover, be noted that even if a community counselor does not accept the premises of the medical model, it is still useful to be familiar with the DSM-IV system, because many insurance forms used by third-party payers require that a diagnosis be submitted in terms of DSM-IV categories.

DSM-I was published in 1952, DSM-II in 1968, DSM-III in 1980, DSM-III-R in 1987, and DSM-IV in 1994. DSM-III and subsequent editions were significantly different from the earlier editions in that they redefined major conditions based on research findings; added new categories, more explicit diagnostic criteria, and a formal definition of "mental disorder"; and presented a multiaxial system for classification. Thus, an attempt was made to develop a classification system that could be more accurately applied, universally accepted, and clinically relevant than was the case with the earlier editions of DSM. DSM-III, III-R, and IV utilized a system of five axes to classify psychiatric problems. As applied in DSM-IV, Axis I included Clinical Disorders and Other Conditions That May Be a Focus of Clinical Attention (16 categories); Axis II included Personality Disorders and Mental Retardation (12 categories); Axis III included General Medical Conditions (16 categories); Axis IV included Psychosocial and Environmental Problems (9 categories); and Axis V involved a Global Assessment of Functioning (GAF), on a scale of 1 to 100. Of most immediate relevance to community counselors are the problems on Axis IV, the categories of which are: (1) problems with primary support group, (2) problems related to social environment, (3) educational problems, (4) occupational problems, (5) housing problems, (6) economic problems, (7) problems with access to health care services, (8) problems related to interaction with legal system/crime, and (9) other psychosocial and economic problems. For community counselors, ratings on Axes I, II, and III are primarily of interest for their impact on the problems on Axis IV and for the effects and side-effects of treatments used to address these problems. The GAF (Axis V) is clearly of use to community counselors and others concerned with a client's functioning.

One serious problem with the earlier editions of DSM was that psychiatrists and others who used it showed relatively poor agreement in classifying patients. Zigler and Phillips (1961) found identical symptoms in cases placed in different diagnostic categories and low correlations between individual symptoms and diagnostic decisions made. The revised approach used in DSM-III and DSM-III-R did not solve the problem of low reliability of diagnoses made according to this system (Garfield, 1993). Further, serious questions have been raised about the extent to which the diagnostic categories used in DSM-III and DSM-III-R (Garfield, 1993) and DSM-IV (Kirk & Kutchins, 1994, June 20) meet scientific standards for validity.

Another interesting approach to categorizing the problems for which clients seek counseling was proposed by Celotta and Teglasi-Golubcow (1982). They suggested that problems can be categorized as being on one of five levels:

Level 1  General expectation problems (the client sees self as the passive victim of a hostile environment).

Level 2  General cognition problems (the client is making broad maladaptive statements about self or others, on a conscious or an unconscious level).

Level 3  Specific cognition problems (the client is conflicted by ideas, attitudes, or beliefs that seem to affect the problem with which the client is trying to cope).

Level 4  Information problems (the client lacks necessary information or facts).

Level 5  Behavioral problems (lack or excess of some type of behavior).

As one moves up the hierarchy from Level 5 to Level 1, the problems: (a) increase in the general distress they cause the client, (b) have a longer history over the client's life, (c) affect more roles in the client's life (worker, student, friend, family member, etc.), (d) appear as more disturbed interpersonal behavior, and (e) will be less accessible to the client's awareness. The authors further suggested that different interventions may be appropriate for different levels, although this aspect of the model had yet to be validated.

A third approach of interest to the community counselor is that adopted by Holmes and Rahe (1967), who obtained average rankings from approximately 400 people of how stressful 43 events in a person's life are perceived to be. These events ranged in stressfulness from the death of a spouse (mean value of 100) to minor violations of the law (mean value of 11) and included, in descending order of stressfulness (mean value given in parentheses) such life events as: divorce (73), a jail term (63), death of a close family member (63), personal illness or injury (53), getting married (50), being fired at work

(47), retirement (45), pregnancy (40), change in financial state (38), death of a close friend (37), foreclosure on a mortgage or loan (30), change in job responsibilities (29), a son's or daughter's leaving home (29), begin or end school (26), trouble with one's boss (23), change in residence (20), change in social activities (18), change in eating habits (15), and going on vacation (13). Thus, counselors can be aware of the probable impact of certain events on their client or on those who might, as a consequence of the stress caused by these events, become their clients (Bloom, 1985). Obviously, for any given individual, the order and relative magnitude of stressfulness of these events will vary; and Leong, Tseng, and Wu (1985) have shown that the order of stressfulness varies systematically across different cultures and even across different regions within a single country. Nonetheless, Holmes and Rahe's idea of determining the relative stressfulness of various life events and their listing of these events are of value to counselors in conceptualizing client problems.

Finally, reflecting the discussion of theories of career and work adjustment development in the first section of this chapter, one may note that taxonomies of career and work adjustment problems have also been constructed. Campbell and Cellini (1981) proposed a taxonomy of adult career problems involving four categories, each containing a number of subcategories. These categories were: (1) problems in career decision making (including the subcategories of getting started, gathering information, generating and selecting alternatives, and making plans); (2) problems in implementing career plans (including those stemming from the individual and those stemming from the environment, such as economic conditions); (3) problems in performance in the work setting (including deficits in knowledge and skills, personal factors, and conditions in the work environment); and (4) problems in adapting to the work setting (including those at time of entry, changes over time, and interpersonal conflicts at work). Neff (1985) proposed a taxonomy of five patterns that lead to work maladjustment, including: (1) people with major lack of work motivation, (2) people who respond to work demands with fear and anxiety, (3) people who are excessively hostile and aggressive, (4) people who are overly dependent, and (5) people who are so socially naive that they lack a conception of work or appropriate work behavior.

## Prevalence and Incidence

Related to the question of classification is that of frequency of occurrence of a given problem. In public health terms, this breaks down into two factors: prevalence and incidence. Prevalence refers to the number of cases of a given condition found to be existing in the general population or a sample of that population. Incidence refers to new cases of a condition that come into being within a certain time frame. Prevalence is measured in terms of number of cases per hundred or per thousand persons, whereas incidence indicates number of new cases that develop within a specified population within a given time span. In a landmark study of the prevalence of mental health problems, Srole, Langner, Michael, Opler, and Rennie (1962) surveyed a random sample of more than 1,600 residents of a section of Manhattan in New York City during the mid-1950s, asking them to report all past and present physical and mental conditions and the degree to which any resultant symptoms interfered with their lives. Based on their self-reports, less than a quarter of the sample was judged to be "well" and almost 20 percent was judged to be psychologically "incapacitated." These results were shocking to many, including a large number of professionals, who had been estimating the prevalence of mental health problems as being much lower.

Within the overall issues of prevalence and incidence, the community counselor should be aware of the factors that have been shown to relate to the presence or frequency of certain mental health problems. These factors include socioeconomic status, sex, age, race, ethnicity, and urban-versus-rural community. In a famous study, Hollingshead and Redlich (1958) demonstrated that psychiatric diagnosis in the New Haven, Connecticut area was related to social class, in that those of higher class status were more frequently diagnosed as neurotic, whereas those belong to lower socioeconomic classes were more frequently diagnosed as psychotic. This phenomenon may reflect class differences in behavior patterns, including patterns of problematic behavior; or it may reflect the economics of treatment, in that psychiatrists could collect fees from upper class outpatients and hence gave them diagnoses that kept them out of the hospital, but could only get paid for treating lower-class patients who were hospitalized, and so gave them diagnoses that would allow them to be hospitalized.

Race, ethnicity, and urban-rural differences are often confounded with socioeconomic class, although Murphy, Wittkower, Fried, and Ellenberger (1963) showed ethnic, religious, social and urban-rural differences in the frequency with which particular symptoms were exhibited by schizophrenics in different cultures, in some cases apparently regardless of socioeconomic class. Reviewing the research on the relation between culture and symptomatology, Dohrenwend and Dohrenwend (1974) concluded that "symptoms can take on coloration from the culture... Research subjects from lower class backgrounds are more likely to express psychological distress in somatic terms than research subjects from higher class backgrounds... So are Puerto Ricans by contrast with Blacks, Jews, and Irish" (p. 432).

Age has been related to type and distribution of mental health problems in several ways, including (a) the biologically based senile degenerative conditions associated with aging, such as Alzheimer's disease, and (b) frequent reports of a higher incidence of certain mental problems among older persons. For example, Butler and Lewis (1983) cited studies indicating that the incidence rate of psychoses among those age 75 and over is double that of 35- to 44-year-olds and five times that of 15- to 24-year-olds. Finally, some mental health problems have been associated with traditional sex-role differences within the culture. For example, hysteria is more common in women (so much so that the name hysteria itself derives from the classical Greek word for womb), probably reflecting sex-role behaviors that were traditionally expected of women (emotionality, irrationality, seductiveness).

## AIMS OF INTERVENTION

We have now reviewed several models of human development and of healthy functioning and several ways of conceptualizing and categorizing the things that can go wrong in the course of development. Taken together, these provide bases for suggesting appropriate intervention to get development back on the proper course and for determining the goal toward which that course should be headed. Insofar as community counseling takes an educational, developmental approach to intervention, it is particularly important that the counselor have a plan that spells out the aim of each intervention.

Broad sets of aims for intervention have been defined along several different dimensions. For example, the aim of intervention may be seen as (a) behavior change, (b) adjustment or actualization, or (c) environmental modification. Another set of alternative aims reflects the three criteria for defining problems of living discussed in the third section of this chapter: statistical deviance, social disruption, and subjective discomfort. In this context, the aims of the intervention may be defined as (a) cure, (b) social adaptation, or (c) comfort, respectively. We shall briefly examine each of these aims and then look at the aim of intervention for community counseling suggested above, that is, coping.

Behavior change as an aim is most closely linked with the view that behaviors are learned and that intervention therefore consists of assisting the client to learn a better behavior than the one representing the problem of living. Defining the aim of intervention in this way has the advantages of giving the counselor an integrated system of human development (learned behaviors)—problems (bad learning)—interventions (improve that learning). Also, as emphasized by Krumboltz (1966), a strong advocate of behavioral counseling, this approach allows one to define a problem of living in terms of concrete, objective behaviors and thus to assess accurately how much the intervention has helped to change those behaviors. For example, if the problem is defined in terms of being plagued by repetitive thoughts about one's worthlessness, then the effectiveness of a particular intervention can be measured in terms of how many fewer times per day the client has such thoughts. If, however, the problem is merely defined as the client's feeling worthless, the counselor cannot say to what extent a client's global report of feeling better resulted from the intervention used, to what extent it was the client's desire to please the counselor, to what extent it reflected fluctuations in the client's mood, and so on. Thus, the fact that a learning theory–based aim (behavior change) requires an explicit definition of the behavior to be changed is one of the great virtues of this approach. One may, however, apply this principle and require an explicit definition of the problem (which by its very nature suggests an approach to change and a measure of that change) even if one does not otherwise adopt the premises and procedures of learning theory. The principal difficulty with the learning theory approach is, in general, that the more complex the problem behavior is, the less able this system is to explain and to offer techniques for changing it. Thus, although this system seems to work well with relatively specific, easily defined problems (for example, fear of snakes), it does not succeed any better than other approaches in working with broader, more pervasive problems, such as generalized feelings of anxiety. From the viewpoint of the psychodynamic theorists, moreover, those who define the aims of intervention in terms of behavior change are inappropriately focusing on symptoms, rather than causes. In this view, the personality is seen as a worn inner tube, such that if a patch is put over one leak (symptom), a new and possibly more serious leak will only spring up at another spot. Thus, to seek to treat only the symptom, rather than the cause, may well do more harm than good. Needless to say, the literature is full of arguments between behaviorists who claim to have changed a problem behavior (treated a symptom) without other problems arising and psychodynamicists who argue that the problem was a trivial one, the behaviorist did not know where to look for the new symptom, or the behaviorist did not wait long enough for the new symptom to appear.

Adjustment or actualization are the aims of intervention that derive from the psychodynamic model. The difference between these aims is that "adjustment" refers to meeting the minimal-to-average expectations set by the model, whereas "actualization" refers to fulfilling and exceeding those expectations. Thus, if the problem has to do with passing a course in physics, the aim of attaining a grade of at least C would represent adjustment; the aim of winning a Nobel Prize would be actualization. To some extent, the choice between these aims is dictated by: (a) what the theory states is sufficient, (b) the personality and level of aspiration of the counselor, and (c) the severity of the client's problem. In some instances, adjustment would be the most one could hope for; in others, anything short of actualization would leave the client unfulfilled. The argument against these aims is that they are too vague and subjective to be scientifically meaningful and so cannot be used as the criteria for a scientifically oriented approach to counseling. On what basis can a client and/or counselor assert that "adjustment" or "actualization" has been attained? To what extent is the decision a self-fulfilling fantasy: Because I want to believe it, it must be true? To what extent is it a rationalization: If I declare that the goal is achieved, I can quit this painful process? Another problem is that even if one can accurately assess "adjustment" or "actualization" in terms of a specific psychodynamic theory, who is to say that that particular theory and what it prescribes are appropriate for the given client in the particular life situation? Is a client who lives in a dangerous neighborhood better adjusted if he or she reduces the levels of suspiciousness and aggression in the personality, as is called for by some psychodynamic theories?

Environmental modification particularly fits with systems theory formulations but is also consistent with a learning theory–based approach. One of the arguments against relying totally on this approach is that the kinds of environmental change needed to solve the client's problem are often far beyond the powers of counseling. The community counselor cannot bring about the end of an economic recession so the client can find a job, nor can the counselor lower the crime rate in the client's neighborhood so the client will not be afraid to go to the grocery store. Another argument against relying on environmental modification is that it does not help the client learn to cope with situations that will arise in the future, that is, that it deprives counseling of its educational function. Nonetheless, removing environmental barriers and mobilizing environmental resources are valid and generally necessary parts of the community counseling approach.

Defining the aims of intervention as cure, social adaptation, or comfort reflect the problems with the specific criteria for defining problems of living to which each of them relates. Thus, "cure" (the aim of the medical model) faces the same problems as an aim of intervention that "statistical deviance" faced as a criterion for defining problems of living. That is, norms are not absolute, but vary with social and historical context, nor are norms necessarily the same as optimum states. Thus, what constitutes a cure is a relative decision cloaked in absolute terms. Not only are the terms misleading, but the choice of "cure" as the aim implies acceptance of the assumption that problems of living are a form of disease, an assumption that is rejected by community counselors.

The aim of "social adaptation," like the criterion of social disruption to which it relates, is even less objective and more relativistic than "cure" (although not necessarily more objectionable to community counselors). The counselor must always consider the norms to which the client is being expected to adapt and whether those norms are truly adaptive for the client's life situation and personal objectives. Thus the aim of social adaptation may be disastrous for the client, if it is actually attained.

The aim of "comfort," like the criterion of "subjective discomfort," is by its very nature totally subjective and so of little use in a scientific approach to counseling. This is not meant to imply that one does not wish to help the client to feel better, but rather to suggest that feeling better is a consequence of living more effectively than a sufficient goal in and of itself.

Having seen the benefits and limitations of the most commonly espoused aims of intervention, we may turn to the aim generally espoused by community counselors: assisting the client to cope with the problems of living for which help was sought. Coping generally entails:

1. Accurately assessing the problem.
2. Mobilizing the personal and environmental resources that are relevant to dealing with the problem at hand.

3. Developing necessary but currently unavailable resources for dealing with the problem.
4. Removing the personal and environmental barriers that are detrimental to dealing with the problem.

Is it possible to derive a summary, integrated model for community counseling from the variety of theories of human development, problems of living, and aims of intervention presented in this chapter? No doubt a number of such models may be derived, and each counselor should construct and amplify upon one that seems valid in light of that counselor's professional experience. To be valid, the model must be constantly subjected to evaluation. Does it help the counselor to help the client? If not, it is merely an intellectual exercise and of no practical significance. However, as Kurt Lewin has been frequently quoted as saying, "There is nothing more practical than a good theory."

We suggest the following model as one possible theory:

1. As people grow, they learn from their family, peers, subcultural group, and culture how to deal with certain situations. For dealing with many of these situations, these groups have evolved standardized patterns of behavior (responses) that seem to work at least much of the time. Many of these responses relate to matters that arise at a particular time in life and so are learned at that time.

2. Problems arise when the person confronts a new situation to which he or she has not learned how to respond or confronts an apparently familiar situation on which the known response does not produce the expected effect.

3. Coping comes through the person's analyzing the problem and calling up or developing responses that will achieve the desired result and/or changing the situation so that the person's responses will produce that result.

**4.** Community counseling assists the client to cope by: (a) defining and analyzing the problem; (b) determining and selecting among possible solutions, based on employing available or potential resources within the client and/or the environment; (c) implementing that solution; and (d) evaluating its effectiveness (and if necessary, repeating the process).

Obviously, the first important step is defining the problem in such a way that it can be analyzed, dealt with, and evaluated. This issue, and the subsequent steps in this process, will be discussed in later chapters.

**EXERCISE**

Now, review the theories presented in this chapter and try applying each of them to the following case. See what each approach contributes to your understanding of the client and to your thoughts about how you might be of help to this client. Also note what each theory fails to account for.

## Case Study

Helen, age 55, seeks counseling from the community mental health center at which you are working. Three years ago, Helen went to a psychotherapist for ten months, but she felt that she was not making progress and stopped going. She reports that since then, she has felt progressively more troubled, is "consumed by anger," and has "not been able to get anything done in my life." She further reports that a pattern of stammering and stuttering in her speech has been evident during the last two years. Helen has never married, has owned her home for twenty years, and for three years has been retired from her job as the director of billing services for a large general hospital. She took an early retirement because "my

work situation became so difficult since my workers were becoming so difficult to supervise." Helen has built another home in an exclusive recreation area, completed four years ago with the assistance of a carpenter. She collected the building materials over a period of ten years from auctions, junkyards, and from buildings that were being demolished. The home has been rented. Now the tenant of four years is leaving, and "I won't live in this house because my neighbors appear to have feelings against me... It is an exclusive society, and I don't think I am accepted with my beautiful house because my background is different." Helen receives income from a retirement fund and from periodic earnings she obtains from writing articles on different aspects of local history. She has a degree in accounting, has many hobbies, regularly attends her church, and loves animals. Currently she reports that she has eight cats and three dogs in her home. When she is driving and sees an animal that has been injured on the highway, she will stop her car, note the animal's location, and then go to the nearest phone and contact the local animal shelter.

Helen is an only child. After living by themselves in their own home some 500 miles away for many years, her parents became quite feeble. Helen and her parents decided that they should move closer to their daughter. Consequently, two years ago they bought a house two blocks away from Helen's home, and Helen then arranged for domestic help and caretakers for her parents. Helen claims that when her parents settled nearby, she began to deteriorate emotionally. She also exclaims, "I have always loved my father, but I despise my mother. She did nothing but criticize me all my life... never said anything good about me... always made me feel guilty... and now I am stuck with her." Her father died at the age of 92 six months ago, and Helen immediately moved her mother into a nursing home. She only visits her mother once every two weeks, for thirty minutes, to make sure that the care arrangements are proceeding appropriately. Helen reports that she finds it difficult to even look at her mother during the visits; and in the intake interview, Helen started to yell, "I hate that woman." The mother is 86, and though she suffered a stroke one year ago, is alert mentally and responsive to care from the nursing home.

Presenting problems stated by Helen are: "I don't have the energy to sell my parents' house, and I should. I am so angry that I now stutter and stammer. I don't get anything really accomplished now in my life, like cleaning my house (which has not been cleaned in over a year), or my writing, or seeing my friends, and I don't know what to do."

## REFERENCES

American Psychiatric Association. (1994). *Diagnostic and statistical manual of mental disorders, DSM IV* (4th ed.). Washington, DC: Author.

Bandura, A., & Walters, R. (1963). *Social learning and personality development.* New York: Holt, Rinehart & Winston.

Beck, A. T. (1976). *Cognitive therapy and the emotional disorders.* New York: International Universities Press.

Berelson, B., & Steiner, G. A. (1964). *Human behavior: An inventory of scientific findings.* New York: Harcourt, Brace & World.

Bloom, B. L. (1985). *Stressful life event theory and research: Implications for primary prevention.* Rockville, MD: National Institute of Mental Health.

Butler, R. M., & Lewis, M. I. (1983). *Aging and mental health: Positive psychosocial approaches.* St. Louis: C. V. Mosby.

Campbell, R. E., & Cellini, J. V. (1981). A diagnostic taxonomy of adult career problems. *Journal of Vocational Behavior, 19,* 175–190.

Celotta, B., & Teglasi-Golubcow, H. (1982). A problem taxonomy for classifying clients' problems. *Personnel and Guidance Journal, 61,* 73–76.

Cochrane, R. (1983). *The social creation of mental illness.* New York: Longman.

Dohrenwend, B. P., & Dohrenwend, B. S. (1974). Social and cultural influences on psychopathology. *Annual Review of Psychology, 25,* 417–452.

Dollard, J., & Miller, N. E. (1950). *Personality and psychotherapy: An analysis in terms of learning, thinking and culture.* New York: McGraw.

Ellis, A. (1962). *Reason and emotion in psychotherapy.* Secaucus, NJ: Lyle Stuart.

Erikson, E. H. (1963). *Childhood and society* (2nd ed.). New York: Norton.

Erikson, E. H. (1968). *Identity: Youth and crisis.* New York: Norton.

Flavell, J. H. (1963). *The developmental psychology of Jean Piaget.* New York: Van Nostrand.

Garfield, S. L. (1993). Methodological problems in clinical diagnosis. In P. B. Sutter & H. E. Adams (Eds.), *Comprehensive handbook of psychopathology* (2nd ed., pp. 27–46). New York: Plenum Press.

Havighurst, R. J. (1972). *Developmental tasks and education* (3rd ed.) White Plains, NY: Longman.

Hershenson, D. B. (1982). A formulation of counseling based on the healthy personality. *Personnel and Guidance Journal, 60,* 406–409.

Hershenson, D. B. (1993). Healthy development as the basis for mental health counseling theory. *Journal of Mental Health Counseling, 15,* 430–437.

Hershenson, D. B., & Szymanski, E. M. (1992). Career development of people with disabilities. In R. M. Parker & E. M. Szymanski (Eds.), *Rehabilitation counseling: Basics and beyond* (2nd ed., pp. 273–303). Austin, TX: Pro-ed.

Hollingshead, A. B., & Redlich, F. C. (1958). *Social class and mental illness.* New York: Wiley.

Holmes, T. H., & Rahe, R. H. (1967). The social readjustment rating scale. *Journal of Psychosomatic Research, 11,* 213–218.

Ivey, A. E., & Goncalves, O. F. (1988). Developmental therapy: Integrating developmental processes into clinical practice. *Journal of Counseling & Development, 66,* 406–413.

Jahoda, M. (1958). *Current concepts of positive mental health.* New York: Basic Books.

Kegan, R. (1982). *The evolving self: Problem and processes in human development.* Cambridge, MA: Harvard University Press.

Kirk, S. A., & Kutchins, H. (1994, June 20). Is bad writing a mental disorder? *New York Times,* p. A17.

Krumboltz, J. D. (1966). *Revolution in counseling: Implications of behavioral science.* Boston: Houghton Mifflin.

Leong, F. T. L., Tseng, W. S., & Wu, D. Y. H. (1985). Crosscultural variations in stressful life events: A preliminary study. *AMHCA Journal, 7,* 72–77.

Levinson, D. J., Darrow, C. N., Klein, E. B., Levinson, M. H., & McKee, B. (1978). *The seasons of a man's life.* New York: Ballantine Books.

Marx, M. H. (1976). Formal theory. In M. H. Marx & F. E. Goodson (Eds.), *Theories in contemporary psychology* (2nd ed., pp. 234–260). New York: Macmillan.

Maslow, A. H. (1954). *Motivation and personality.* New York: Harper.

Maslow, A. H. (1962). *Toward a psychology of being.* Princeton, NJ: Van Nostrand.

Murphy, H. B. M., Wittkower, E. D., Fried, J., & Ellenberger, H. (1963). A cross-cultural survey of schizophrenic symptomatology. *International Journal of Social Psychiatry, 9,* 237–249.

Muuss, R. E. (1975). Theories of adolescence (3rd ed.). New York: Random House.

Neff, W. S. (1985). *Work and human behavior* (3rd ed.). New York: Aldine.

Rotter, J. B. (1954). *Social learning and clinical psychology.* Englewood Cliffs, NJ: Prentice-Hall.

Schultz, D. (1977). *Growth psychology: Models of the healthy personality.* New York: Van Nostrand.

Sharf, R. S. (1992). *Applying career development theory to counseling.* Pacific Grove, CA: Brooks/Cole.

Srole, L., Langner, T. S., Michael, S. T., Opler, M. K., & Rennie, T. A. C. (1962). *The Midtown Manhattan Study: Mental health in the metropolis* (Vol. I). New York: McGraw-Hill.

Super, D. E. (1990). A life-span, life-space approach to career development. In D. Brown, L. Brooks, & Assoc. (Eds.), *Career choice and development: Applying contemporary theories to practice* (2nd ed., pp. 197–261). San Francisco: Jossey-Bass.

Witmer, J. M., & Sweeney, T. J. (1992). A holistic model of wellness and prevention over the life span. *Journal of Counseling and Development, 71,* 140–148.

Zigler, E., & Phillips, L. (1961). Psychiatric diagnosis and symptomatology. *Journal of Abnormal and Social Psychology, 63,* 69–75.

# PART II

# THE PRACTICE OF COMMUNITY COUNSELING

When clients seek help from community counselors, a variety of problems may be identified that demand different intervention approaches. Community counselors today need many counseling skills in order to deal with the difficulties that are presented by individuals, families, or other societal groups. Community counseling intervention is frequently on a short-term basis, and the many intervention approaches explained in Part II are accommodated to this brief time period. The chapters included in Part II also pinpoint the practice skills that community counselors need to have in order to effectively assist their clients.

Chapter 6 describes one important skill, assessment, which actually includes many tasks during the client evaluation process. The different approaches to client assessment are explained, and information pertaining to useful measurement tools that could be employed during evaluation is described. Importantly, a model for client assessment is suggested, providing an approach that can be utilized in many community counseling settings. Chapter 7 highlights an emerging area for community counseling practices, environment and

needs assessment. This chapter explains the needed skills for these forms of assessment, and a case example further illustrates how these skills can be implemented during counseling practice.

Since community counselors may work with individuals or groups, Chapters 8, 9, and 10 discuss these topics and provide information on selected strategies for individual and group counseling. Chapter 9 provides a model for the community counselor when intervening with families. This model is different from the traditional approaches to family counseling, yet does incorporate many of the concepts integral to family therapy strategies. The model represents a unique intervention that offers assistance to families who are attempting to cope with a family member undergoing a major life transition.

Community counselors often have the opportunity to develop programs, as well as to consult with organizations providing helping services. Many counselors come to realize that they can increase their effectiveness when they develop and provide programs or offer information to counseling-related organizations. Chapters 11 and 12 explain the counseling skills of programming, educating, consulting, and supervising. Case examples in each chapter suggest how these skills can be applied.

Three counseling skills that are often overlooked in community counselor training programs, but which can make a decided difference in the type and quality of services that are offered to clients, are the skills of case management and resource coordination, advocacy, and program evaluation. Chapters 13, 14, and 15 describe these skills and the varied ways that they can be used in different practice settings. A counselor's effectiveness is extended when the skills of advocacy and case management, for example, are incorporated into community counseling practice.

# 6

# CLIENT ASSESSMENT

A crucial step in the counseling process for the client is diagnostic assessment. It provides the strategic foundation for the provision of services, and establishes the necessary guidelines for appropriate client planning and the achievement of life adjustment goals. In one form or another, assessment has been practiced in a variety of settings and by different human service professionals for thousands of years (Hohenshil & Brown, 1991). Since the early 1980's, because of advances in technology and increased attention to the issues presented by diverse populations, such as the disadvantaged and varied ethnic groups, assessment has received renewed interest.

Client assessment is a comprehensive, usually interdisciplinary process of evaluating an individual's physical, mental, and emotional abilities, limitations, and obstacles in order to identify an optimal outcome for the client (Power, 1991). A frequently stated assessment goal is to determine whether a person is ready for career planning or what kind of productive activity the individual will be able to do. Added evaluation goals can be the identification of an individual's strengths and weaknesses relevant to necessary life adjustment, and the identification of those services needed to overcome the client's limitations that may

be barriers to efffective living, learning, and working (Anthony, 1980). Client assessment, consequently, is a method of acquiring information, a process to assist individuals to identify their functional competencies and limitations. As a process of diagnosis and prediction, client assessment as utilized in the counseling process is different, for example, from the process of medical assessment. The latter is traditionally viewed as a basis for determining a specific, appropriate treatment, whereas assessment in a counseling context may be directed to no definite intervention and may include the evaluation of a wide range of factors, such as age, education, mental status and ability, family dynamics, transferability of skills, and related phenomena (Hartlage, 1987).

This chapter will highlight the comprehensive nature of client assessment during the counseling process, explain a philosophy of evaluation and suggested criteria for selecting assessment approaches, discuss the important areas and the process of client evaluation, and identify the limitations of client assessment. With the methods of assessment as guidelines, a model of assessment will be proposed that applies several philosophical tenets explained earlier. The chapter will conclude with a brief discussion of the roles of the counselor during evaluation, new trends in assessment, and a case study which will illustrate the proposed assessment model. The purpose of this chapter is to provide an overview of client assessment as it is utilized during the counseling process in order to assist the community counselor both to continue to act as an enlightened consumer of evaluation practices, and to gain an understanding of how to use appropriate assessment methods with clients from varied cultural backgrounds.

## PHILOSOPHY OF ASSESSMENT

Methods of effective client assessment must be developed not only from acquired knowledge and continued experience but also from personal convictions that emerge from a counseling philosophy. In this book the authors propose viewpoints that include such tenets as (a) human behavior is a function of the interaction between an individual and that individual's environment at a particular point in time; (b) counseling embraces a developmental perspective that focuses on both individuals and the systems within which we all live; and (c) an individual's behavior is viewed primarily, not in terms of dysfunction, but how that behavior can be improved in proactive and positive ways. There are many implications of this philosophy for client assessment, such as:

1. The foundation of client assessment is that evaluation should be holistic and humanistic. A holistic approach encompasses issues of diversity, all relevant attributes of the individual, his/her existing or potential environments, and the interactions between the individual and the environment (Interdisciplinary Council, 1994).

2. Assessment should include a multifactorial approach, which promotes the exploration of a wide variety of client characteristics. A broad range of questions must be posed to determine what makes an individual as well as his/her abilities and needs unique. In using this multifactor approach, different methods and tools should be employed to verify assessment information.

3. Client assessment should be integrated into the counseling process and the continued interaction that takes place in counseling between the professional and the client. Evaluation, consequently, may be an ongoing and developmental process in client development, and certain individuals may need assessments of varying degrees given at different junctures over their lifespan (Interdisciplinary Council, 1994).

4. As much as possible, the client should take part in the assessment process. Often, clients have the expectation that they must place themselves completely in the counselor's hands and the counselor will provide answers to finding a suitable career or making appropriate life adjustments.

5. The assessment process should not only target a client's limitations and the obstacles to productive living, but also include a focus on the identification of the client's assets and needed skills to reach life adjustment goals as well as available resources in the environment that can reduce the client's problems of living and/or facilitate the client's ability to cope with these problems (Hershenson & Power, 1987). Assets may be defined as those personal qualities (traits, habits, behavior patterns, defenses, ways of thinking) that a client may apply to solving a given problem of living. Skills may be defined as physical, intellectual, and/or emotional techniques for achieving a specific objective.

6. Client assessment practices should be current, valid, and relevant (Interdisciplinary Council, 1994). Unfortunately, evaluation methods may be used that actually have not been developed for a population that is cur-

rently undergoing assessment. The context of assessment material may also contain items or guidelines that are outdated or inappropriate for a selected population, such as those with a severe mental or physical disability. Implicit in this tenet is the need for selecting assessment methods that are directed to exploring a specific individual's assets, skills, limitations, and available resources.

**7.** Client assessment should be an integral part of larger service delivery systems, such as career placement or community remedial services. In many agencies the assessment process is unnecessarily abbreviated or neglected altogether because of the perceived financial cost or the need to accelerate the client's job placement. The omission of evaluation services often implies that a particular agency always knows what is best for the client, or that effective client planning can be based on the knowledge of a specific client skill rather than on a more comprehensive understanding of how other factors, such as personality traits or current emotions, may influence the exercise of that skill. What is good for the agency is not always beneficial for the client (Power, 1991).

**8.** During client assessment, the process itself should be developed in such a way that evaluation becomes a source of esteem-enhancing efforts. The assessment process is not only one of diagnosis but also an opportunity to provide positive feedback to clients (Power, 1991). For individuals with disabilities, for example, assessment information can assist them to achieve a renewed understanding of themselves and assist them to identify those personal capabilities that could be utilized for successful coping or other life adjustment demands.

All of these principles provide a decided focus for the selection of assessment tools and influence the different purposes of client evaluation. If the assessment process, however, is to assist in determining an individual's cap-

acities, provide data contributing to career development, specify behavior patterns, and establish a foundation for an intervention plan, then the process itself should attempt to utilize all the available resources that can generate information. At the beginning of client assessment a determination should be made on the best type of evaluation for the client. There are many clients for whom the traditional measures of career assessment would not be appropriate. For persons with a severe disability, for example, the standard aptitude tests that emphasize verbal directions may provide little information that can be translated into suitable plans for education and training. Counselors should carefully appraise, consequently, the available evaluation resources and determine what resources would be best for planning purposes. There are criteria that can assist counselors to identify the appropriate resources, and these are now explained.

## SELECTING AN ASSESSMENT MEASURE

To understand the client assessment process, counselors should have a minimum understanding of selected tests and how they are developed. There are standards against which published instruments can and should be checked. Those standards extend beyond those assessment approaches that have an established reputation, beyond those instruments that fit within the practical limitations under which the counselor must function, and beyond those evaluation tools that meet one's own personal need (Womer, 1988). Though the counselor needs to relate the specific purposes and/or suggested uses of the measure to the needs for specific information, there are technical criteria that are important to follow in the selection of assessment approaches. These criteria usually consist of validity, reliability, and norms.

## Validity

The validity of an assessment tool is indicated by the extent this tool measures what it is designed to measure. A standardized test, for example, will usually be given for a specific purpose, and the extent to which it serves this purpose is a measure of its validity. Validity can be reported in different ways, such as (a) predictive validity, namely, the validity suggests how present status on an evaluation instrument predicts future status on a criterion variable; (b) content validity, which refers to how well the particular sampling of behaviors used to measure a characteristic reflects performance in the entire domain of behaviors that constitutes that characteristic; (c) construct validity, which refers to the "meaning" of a test—if the test is going to measure intelligence, for example, one would want to know how the concept of intelligence is operationalized or carefully defined and then the assumptions regarding the nature and extent of its relationships to other variables (school performance, learning ability, etc.) (Walsh & Betz, 1985); and (d) "face validity," which refers to the extent to which the instrument appears to look like what it is intended to measure. Face validity helps to establish rapport between the client and the one who will administer the instrument. It is a subjective appraisal of the degree to which a test appears to measure what it is designed to measure. A test that measures anxiety, for example, should have items that look as if they measure anxiety.

The concept of validity, therefore, responds to such questions as: Do selected observations truly sample the situations they are claimed to represent (content validity)? Does a particular test measure the attribute it is said to measure (construct validity)? The manual that is usually available with a specific assessment tool contains information about that instrument's validity.

## Reliability

Reliability refers to the consistency and dependability of an assessment approach, that portion of the client's performance that will remain constant over time. The most common way to estimate reliability is through the test-retest method, a procedure consisting of testing a group of individuals twice on the same instrument. The degree to which a group's test scores fluctuate from test to retest is expressed as a correlation between scores over time. A test that has a reliability coefficient of 0. 80 is more reliable than a test with a reliability coefficient of 0. 40. The closer the decimal is to 1, the more reliable the test.

Another way of estimating reliability is through the use of parallel tests, a method in which two separate tests designed to be parallel to each other are both administered to a group. Similar to parallel test reliability estimation is the split-half method, a procedure involving a comparison of scores on each half of a single test by summing and comparing the scores for odd-and even-numbered items.

Apart from understanding the concept of reliability, what a reliability coefficient means and how it is developed, the counselor should be aware of the factors that influence reliability. There are many, such as situational (the conditions of testing, i.e., number of distractions, light, ventilation, clarity of instructions), client-focused (health, fatigue, emotional strain, general skills and techniques of taking tests), and test factors themselves (length of test or level of difficulty). All of these factors should be considered during client assessment, but the question of what constitutes practical, minimal reliability is difficult to answer. It depends on the degree of precision one will accept, the type of evaluation instrument used, and the purpose of using the instrument. Different types of published tests, for example, report different ranges of reliability. The counselor must also determine whether there are influences caused by the instrument itself or the environment that may affect the client's assessment performance, and whether the client is actually ready at a specific time to be involved in evaluation.

## Norms

A norm is a standard of comparison, and in order to understand the results or scores of an individual's assessment, these results or scores should be compared with the scores other people have made. For this comparison to be credible, information should be provided about the kinds of people included in the norm groups. Normative data must be representative of the population in which a test is designed to be used. Norm groups may consist of a national sample, a fixed reference group, or local norms. Whenever possible, for example, if one is evaluating client achievement or personality functioning, persons should be used, as well as their performance rates, from a population similar to those being evaluated.

The majority of tests used in counseling or client assessment are classified as norm-referenced tests. The individual's performance is evaluated based on the performance characteristics of a standardized sample of a particular population. An evaluation manual should provide information about standardization procedures, including the number of individuals in the group sample, the representativeness of the sample population to the individual being tested, and the relevance of the norm group to the questions being asked (Hursh Kerns, 1988). When criterion-referenced tests are used, however, they can provide information about the individual's ability to perform specific behaviors, skills, or activities or to demonstrate mastery over a particular skill domain. The Functional Assessment Inventory is an example of a criterion-referenced instrument (Power, 1991).

In any client assessment situation, consequently, when a specific test or evaluation tool is to be used in making a decision about an individual or group, all the available evidence emerging from validity, reliability, and normative data should be studied before any attempt is made to interpret the results. But the major requirement for the usefulness of most psychological tests and related instruments in applied situations is their ability to predict some criterion measure (Betz & Weiss, 1987). This ability may not depend exclusively on a criterion-related validity coefficient, but how a particular measure can assist the counselor to make correct decisions concerning mental health functioning or career placement of individuals. The usefulness of an assessment tool may also depend on cost, the importance of the decision to be made, and the client's own involvement in the assessment approach (Betz & Weiss, 1987). What further facilitates a test's usefulness is when counselors themselves take a particular measure. The feedback resulting from this involvement enables counselors to develop an initial "feel" for its utility, and forces counselors to think about the type of information that may be helpful to the client (Womer, 1988).

The process of selecting the most appropriate assessment tools can either precede the initial client contact, when the counselor is aware of a presenting problem, or take place after the initial client interview, when the counselor has identified the difficulty that needs immediate attention. The assessment process then focuses on obtaining information relevant to this problem. Since client assessment is a comprehensive process of evaluating a wide range of client strengths and barriers relevant to the goal of problem remediation or resolution, there are many approaches in the process, as well as many dimensions of client functioning that are the target areas of these approaches. Counselors need to be aware of these many evaluation approaches that can provide information about an individual.

## VARIED APPROACHES TO CLIENT ASSESSMENT

Among the methods used by counselors to appraise clients are: (a) observation, which often includes behavioral assessment, (b) interviews, (c) life history, (d) psychometric instruments, and (e) functional assessment. Observation begins from the moment the client first contacts the counselor. The counselor may be able to observe how the client approaches the process of making an appointment for a first visit. Is the client tentative or assertive, self-effacing or self-assured, vacillating or decisive? When the client comes for the first meeting, how does he/she present him/herself: on time, early, or late; well groomed or poorly groomed; neatly dressed or slovenly? Does the client walk in with assurance? Is his/her handshake firm, too firm, or tentative; moist from anxiety or dry? As the counseling process proceeds, the counselor must observe the client's body language, whether the client distances him/herself from the counselor, when the client is tense, when relaxed, and so on. Observation is essential in understanding the client and the client's impact on others. The counselor must always be careful not to impose her/his personal values on the client's appearance or actions but must place them in the context of the client's own reference group.

Interviews may be structured (the questions and their order are all set ahead of time) or unstructured. Much of the counseling process is conducted in a relatively unstructured interview format. Structured interviews are, of course, less spontaneous; but they allow the counselor to gather specific information in an expeditious manner, and they provide a consistent frame of reference within which to compare the client's responses and way of responding with other people's behavior in the same situation. An interview guide is available in the Appendix. This detailed guide identifies the important areas that should be explored by counselors during most interview situations. It also suggests several questions that can be used to collect necessary information from clients.

The life history is important in establishing the client's strengths and limitations, past problems and how they were coped with, and what sorts of situations are problematic for the client. Understanding family history, medical history, educational record, work history, past and continuing social relationships, and past problems and how they were handled are all necessary parts of understanding the client. They provide the counselor with some insight into the actual facts of relevance to the client's life, and through the way in which the client tells these facts, they also provide insight into how the client feels about what he/she reports. Depending on the nature of the client's problem, the counselor will seek greater detail concerning relevant areas in the client's past. For example, if the client's problem relates to the relationship to his/her boss at work, the client's work history and relationship to past authority figures would ordinarily be examined in greater detail than the client's social friendships. Other, apparently unrelated areas of the client's life should not be disregarded, because they may offer suggestions as to how the client has coped successfully in the past and because problems in one area may really be the expression of deeper problems in some other area of life.

Psychometric instruments are extensively used during many assessment situations, and offer structured opportunities for counselors to identify an individual's emotional and cognitive functioning. Exercise caution, however, when using these tools since they may not be appropriate for certain client populations or for particular circumstances. Many of these issues were explained earlier in this chapter in the discussion of validity, reliability, and norming factors.

Psychometric instruments usually include four areas of assessment, each of which will now be explained. Within each area of discussion selected methods currently utilized to obtain information will be identified.

## The Interest Area

Because this area of client functioning may be the least threatening for clients when they undergo a process of self-exploration and identification of capabilities and weaknesses, it frequently receives the initial focus of assessment efforts. Currently, an evaluation of client interests is increasingly emphasizing (a) self-exploration, namely, more approaches are providing opportunities for individuals to examine the evaluation results and relate them to information about careers, personal qualifications, and experiences; (b) expanding the career options available to the client, and (c) attention to the sex fairness and multicultural factors of interest measures (Meyer, Fouad, & Klein, 1987; Levinson & Folino, 1990). Normative information used to develop the interest inventory is also receiving closer scrutiny, for the inventory is comparing the client's interests expressed on this measure with those typical of persons engaged, for example, in different occupations. With so many careers which traditionally were gender specific now more available to both men and women, the normative issue in test development becomes all the more important.

Interests can refer to a constellation of likes and dislikes, preferences cultivated during an individual's family, educational, leisure, and working experience. Interests act as motivators and reinforcers for an individual especially when confronted with a career decision. Generally there are three types of interests. Expressed interests are the likes and dislikes people express when they are asked what they do and do not enjoy. Manifest interests are usually expressed by the activities in which individuals voluntarily engage, and inventoried interests are the likes and dislikes reflected on standardized interest inventories (Levinson & Folino, 1990). Expressed and inventoried interests are usually the main targets of interest assessment for clients. Interest inventories were initially developed in the mid-1920s as a response to an established premise that linked occupational interest with job satisfaction (Phillips, 1978). These inventories were designed to identify individual areas of interest and compare subsequent subjective interest scores with the measured interest of successful professionals in a wide variety of occupations. Interest inventories usually provide the largest amount of knowledge relevant to the client's career preferences, likes and dislikes.

While the origin of interests is still a scientific mystery, career development theorists have indicated that interests tend to be relatively unstable during childhood and early adolescence; but once adolescents reach their middle teens, interests seem to stabilize enough to play a significant role for career planning (Levinson & Folino, 1990). Yet interests can change even during young adulthood, especially if such factors as educational, work, and family experiences have a decided impact on the individual.

Interest measures are used by counselors mainly for career planning purposes. When utilizing interest inventories or checklists, the following guidelines are suggested:

**1.** Interest tests measure the direction rather than the strengths of a client's interest. These tests don't answer the question "How much?" but rather, "What kind?"

**2.** Interest inventories measure likes and dislikes, not abilities. Most studies show a negligible relationship between inventoried interests and tested abilities (Walsh & Betz, 1980).

3. Interest inventories may be inappropriate for people with emotional problems. Individuals who are experiencing mental illness difficulties tend to make more negative responses and endorse more passive interests that do persons who are not disturbed (Levinson & Folino, 1990).

4. Interest inventories involve both acceptance and rejection of possible areas of activity. These tests provide the client with the opportunity to express a strong preference toward certain types of occupational or avocational behavior by responding to a wide number of items contained in the particular test.

5. The results of interest measures are the products of the interaction between the individual and the specific inventory and should not be considered separately in any way. If the test items reflect the interests of social workers, for example, one's interests as shown by a high score in that occupational area are to that extent like social workers.

6. Interest inventories are usually of limited value for people who are attempting to make rather fine distinctions, such as choosing between two types of medical specialities. Interest information must be supplemented with other information about the person, such as abilities, values, and previous work experiences.

There are several popular and frequently used interest inventories, and the following information provides a brief identification of these measures.

1. *Strong Interest Inventory.* This test has a 70-year history of use as a vocational interest tool and is designed to measure interests in areas including professional, technical, non-professional, and vocational-technical (Levinson & Folino, 1990). The inventory contains 325 items written at a sixth-grade reading level. All scoring is done by machine.

2. *The Self-Directed Search.* This test is a self-administered, self-scored, and self-interpreted vocational interest inventory based on Holland's theory of personality and work environments. The target population for this tool has a range of junior high school students to adults and can provide helpful information regarding matches between work environments and the personal information a client may possess about his/her own personal interests and skills (Campbell, 1988).

3. *Career Assessment Inventory (Enhanced Version).* This test has 370 items tapping preferences among three categories: activities, school subjects, and occupations. The reading level of the tool is the eighth grade, hand scoring is not feasible, and it is an inventory that is actually more useful for those who are not college bound (McCabe, 1988).

4. *Kuder Occupational Interest Survey, Form DD.* This inventory is for persons from grade 10 through college and adults of all ages, and measures occupational and college major interests. Hand scoring is not available. "The instrument is relatively time efficient, and the inclusion of an audio tape, designed to explain the interpretation of the inventory, is helpful" (Levinson & Folino, 1990, p. 120).

5. *Jackson Vocational Interest Survey.* This assessment tool explores general areas of interest; can be used for individuals considering such options as choice of college major, changing careers, or research in vocational interests and student characteristics; and is especially useful in working with adolescents early in the career development process (Davidshofer, 1988). The instrument can be hand scored in about ten minutes or computer scored, and the latter may be preferred because it provides additional information.

6. *Harrington O'Shea Career Decision-Making System (CDM).* This test is representative of a new generation of comprehensive instruments involving systematic self-assessment of vocationally relevant variables fol-

lowed by focused career exploration (Droege, 1988). Hand or machine scoring are both available, as well as computer software options. The inventory integrates five major dimensions in choosing a career—abilities, job values, future plans, subject preferences, and interests. The target population is from grades 7 to 12 and adults.

All of these suggested interest inventories sample different occupational areas and levels and can be used to support information gained from the client's interview. The vocational goals and aspirations of the client should be considered when selecting a specific interest tool, as well as the person's reading and educational levels. Since interest inventory results are strongly influenced by experiences, the counselor must be careful when interpreting the results to differentiate between low interest scores reflective of lack of experience and those reflective of lack of interest (Levinson, Folino, 1990).

## The Intelligence Area

This area of assessment can stimulate many conflictual issues for the counselor, because the evaluation of intellectual functioning depends on how one defines "intelligence," the competency one has for assessing this function, and how assessment results are to be used. There has been a resurgence of interest in more sophisticated redefinitions of intelligence (Anastasi, 1992). Intelligence assessment has generated controversy for decades, mainly because of the issues that emerge from the psychological testing of American minorities, including those with mental or physical disabilities. Also, most professional counselors have not had the specialized training to respond to the technical demands of many intelligence assessment tools. Consequently, in this area of assessment the role of the counselor is more as a consumer of information, as someone who will review specific test results

and then incorporate this information into client planning.

Intelligence tests represent a highly specialized field with a vast body of literature and research surrounding their use (Power, 1991). Intelligence itself is not a single, unitary ability, but rather a composite of several functions (Anastasi, 1992). It is the global capacity of the individual to act purposefully, think rationally, and deal effectively with the environment (Wechsler, 1981). Precisely what intelligence tests measure has been the subject of dispute since their origin. Generally, these tests identify the extent to which an individual's innate potential has been modified or developed within his or her environment (Power, 1991). Measured intelligence has been found both to reflect past schooling and to predict future school success, and the IQ score resulting from such tests could be viewed as "measured intelligence, not necessarily the adaptive intelligence used in everyday living" (Sundberg, 1977, p. 215).

When reviewing the results of measured intelligence functioning, the following guidelines are suggested:

**1.** The most commonly used tests of mental ability are highly reliable (usually in the 0. 80s or 0. 90s).

**2.** Because of the multitude of abilities and the complexity of mental activities, it is important not to base decisions for life adjustment, including career planning, on any single measure of ability. Several different kinds of assessment tasks, such as the interview or job tryout, should be utilized.

**3.** How the results of intelligence assessment are going to be used is a critical issue for the counselor and the client. In job placement, for example, a particular training environment or area of employment may not demand a specific level of IQ ability.

**4.** Particular attention should be given to the selection of IQ tests relevant to a specific disability or previous education. The WAIS-R is appropriate for most handicaps but has limited use with visually and hearing-impaired persons. The Shipley Institute of Living Scale is more useful for those clients who have at least some high school education (Shipley, 1986).

**5.** When evaluating the vocational potential of persons with disabilities, or those representing different ethnic minorities, many of the problems found in intelligence testing are magnified. Each culture, as well as each disability, has specific and characteristically definite strengths and limiting effects, especially in an assessment situation. These clients may reflect adaptive and learning behavior aspects of intelligence differently. Counselors should be aware of the capabilities, strengths, problems, and limitations that clients may bring to the evalation of their intelligence functioning.

**6.** Specific goals of client assessment may not warrant an assessment of intelligence. When the presenting problem is defined as anxiety or communication-interpersonal difficulties, it is usually not necessary to request information of this aspect of client functioning. A counselor's understanding of the meaning of intelligence and its function for varied life adjustment demands is important when considering intelligence assessment.

The following is a brief description of two popular instruments for intelligence evaluation that are utilized with adults:

**1.** *Wechsler Adult Intelligence Scale— Revised Edition (WAIS-R).* This widely used intelligence measure assesses general and specific intellectual abilities of persons ages 16 to 74. It consists of 11 subtests grouped under the Verbal and Performance Scales. Each scale explores particular dimensions of intelligence functioning such as information comprehension, arithmetic, similarities, digit span, vocabulary, digit symbol, picture completion, and object assembly. The verbal and nonver-

bal group may be administered separately or together to yield, respectively, a Verbal, Performance, and Full-Scale IQ. With a trained examiner and careful test preparation, this measure can provide very useful information in many areas of client functioning.

**2.** *Peabody Picture Vocabulary Test— Revised (PPVT-R).* This measure is an untimed individual intelligence test, orally administered in 15 minutes or less. It identifies an individual's receptive (hearing) vocabulary for Standard American English and provides, at the same time, a quick estimate of verbal ability as a component of scholastic aptitude. No reading is required by the client, and scoring is rapid and objective.

Other intelligence tests that could come to the counselor's attention are the Slosson Intelligence Test-R, Revised Beta Examination, the Raven Progressive Matrices, the Stanford-Binet Intelligence Tests, and the Otis-Lennon School Ability Test. Some of these instruments are individually administered; others are usually given in a group setting. The tests themselves reflect a particular understanding of the concept of intelligence, with an emphasis on verbal ability. For clients who belong to different minority groups, the counselor should exercise caution regarding the tests' applicability.

## The Personality Area

Assessment of the client's apparent personality problems can give valuable feedback for both treatment and rehabilitation. The purpose of a psychological evaluation is to provide a description of a person, where and how the individual functions effectively, and the pattern of the person's behaviors (Make, Pape, & Prout, 1979). When viewed in the broad sense, personality measurement identifies motivational, interpersonal, and attitudinal characteristics (Anastasi, 1988). This assessment can also identify the client's emotional strengths, an identification that traditionally has been neglected in personality evaluation. Because of the emphasis on discovering what is wrong with the client, personality assessment has not been widely used in career counseling. But developing an understanding and awareness of personality characteristics is one of the most important areas of self-knowledge for persons involved in the career decision-making process (Power, 1991).

The types of personality characteristics of interest to counselors depend upon one's professional orientation and practice. The psychological assessment of career functioning, for example, may identify such characteristics as motivation, self-concept, coping styles, interpersonal relationships, and the awareness and handling of feelings (Kaplan & Questad, 1980; Snyder & Wilson, 1977). When a client has a physical or mental disability, additional assessment goals may include the adjustment to the disability, dependency needs, satisfaction with work, and the influence of any secondary gain factors (De Nour & Czaczkes, 1975). For those counselors who focus on the client's problem as an expression of social and personal maladjustment, clinical instruments may identify the characteristics of depression, paranoia, severe anxiety, and hysteria.

There are hundreds of personality instruments available today, which can be divided into several types, i.e., diagnostic/clinical tests, descriptive tests, and those constructed to assess values (Brown, 1990). These tests can be categorized according to techniques—verbal, drawing, manipulative, visual, and objective. Both formal and informal approaches to assessment can provide information on the client's personality functioning. The client interview, the responses to drawings and checklists may all suggest the identification of the client's self-concept, inner conflicts, motivation, values, and interpersonal

strengths and difficulties. The Minnesota Multiphasic Personality Inventory (MMPI-2), the most widely used personality inventory, is designed to assess psychological dysfunctions. Other counselors may be more concerned with how healthy personality characteristics can facilitate personal, work, or family adjustment, and may utilize such instruments as the California Psychological Inventory, the Sixteen Personality Factor Questionnaire, the Tennessee Self-Concept Scale, the Edwards Personnel Preference Schedule, and the Rosenberg Self-Esteem Scale.

Established personality inventories may provide the same information but also report in their manuals extensive normative data and several reliability and validity studies. Personality inventories, however, present problems of reliability and validity different from those given by cognitive and ability tests.

Suggested guidelines to follow when selecting personality measures or understanding their results are:

**1.** Responses to a personality inventory comprise clients' attempts to describe for themselves and specific others, such as a counseling professional, how they see themselves in terms of the behaviors described in each inventory item. Such inventories provide a picture of the extent to which clients are able to face themselves or are willing to have others see them as they think they are. Consequently, conditions must be created in the assessment situation that assist the client in generating information useful in self-understanding or self-acceptance (Power, 1991). The test taker may wish to distort responses in a particular direction, or may answer deliberately to produce a certain image. Deliberate faking is a major problem in personality assessment, but response style can often be corrected through careful test construction practices and the preparation of the client for this area of assessment.

**2.** Behaviors that are necessary for the client to function well in a specific situation should be identified before the selection of a personality instrument. Personality assessment begins with the counselor's awareness of the close relationship between behavioral traits, for example, and job-related or other productivity-related adjustment.

**3.** The scores from a structured personality inventory are considered to be a description of *how* an individual behaves, not *why* a person does something. The *why* of behavior must be discovered through other assessment approaches, such as interest and value inventories. Frequently the client interview will provide information on the *why* of behavior.

**4.** Similar to all asssessment results, but especially with the client's personality results, every effort must be maintained to preserve confidentiality. These results could be particularly threatening to clients. Counselors should consider the overall purpose of the client's evaluation and how the results are going to be used.

**5.** For counselors whose primary professional work is to assist clients in career decision making, the assessment of values is especially important during the evaluation process. One's values can be the leading criterion when selecting between career options, and the understanding of the client's values may also indicate the *why* behind an individual's behavior.

**6.** Though promising personality tests and techniques exist, many procedures and instruments require specialized training and supervision for proper administration, scoring, and interpretation. This training is particularly true for the MMPI, the Thematic Apperception Test, and the Rorshach Ink-Blot Test.

**7.** The most effective use of a personality inventory or test occurs after the client understands its purpose and willingly under-

takes completion. The purpose of the measure should always be carefully explained.

## The Aptitude and Abilities Area

Although there is widespread use of aptitude and abilities tests in client assessment, especially for career decision making purposes, counselors usually do not have that many opportunities to administer these instruments. Research has demonstrated how specialized ability tests used in psychological assessment can enhance the counselor's ability to understand clients' aptitudes and learning needs as they relate to career and other related assessments (Capps, Heinlein, & Sautter, 1990). This understanding is most frequently achieved by the counselor's knowledge of the different types of aptitude and ability measures and what the results mean for client planning purposes.

Aptitude tests attempt to identify an ability or characteristic, mental or physical, native or acquired, that is believed or known to indicate a client's capacity or potential for learning a particular skill or knowledge (Power, 1991). Essentially, an aptitude is the capacity to learn, whereas the concept of achievement describes what has already been learned, or developed capacity (Walsh & Betz, 1985).

Aptitude tests are used primarily in the prediction of future performance, while achievement tests tend to be past and present oriented rather than future oriented. Aptitude tests can help older adolescents make specific vocational or educational decisions, and older adults may pursue aptitude testing to help facilitate career change (Capps, Heinlein, & Sautter, 1990).

There are several approaches to measuring aptitudes, and the specific approach generally depends on the individual, client needs, the purpose of evaluation, and the resources available, i.e., time and costs, for the testing. Capps, Heinlein, and Sautter (1990) categorize this assessment into approaches with specific suggestions for each approach.

**1.** *Paper and pencil tests.* These are the most commonly used aptitude tests, particularly in schools and the military. Two well-known instruments are the Differential Aptitude Tests (DAT), revised in 1982 and measuring the aptitudes of verbal reasoning, numerical ability, abstract reasoning, clerical speed and accuracy, mechanical reasoning, spatial relations, spelling, and language use; and the Armed Services Vocational Aptitude Battery, which measures academic and specific aptitudes much like the DAT.

**2.** *Performance tests.* These widely used instruments minimize the use of written or spoken language when measuring motor and spatial abilities. The major performance aptitude test in use today is the General Aptitude Test Battery (GATB), which Is developed and distributed by the United States Employment Service. It measures such specific aptitudes as verbal, numerical, and spatial ability, finger dexterity, manual dexterity, form perception, clerical perception, and motor coordination. Two instruments that are computerized and normed on special populations are the APTICOM and SAGE.

**3.** *Work samples.* These are performance tests that either simulate actual job operations or are conducted on the job. They are only used in limited settings and have been utilized for individuals with disabilities to assess their ability to function in various types of jobs. Both commercial and homemade work sample systems are available.

**4.** *Interview.* This approach can be utilized by counselors to gather information about the client's previous school and work history. The client's disclosure about these past experiences may indicate specific aptitudes or limitations to academic or occupational success.

Although aptitude and ability results may yield information that may predict future performance, these results should never be the sole determinant, for example, in career decision making (Capps, Heinlein, & Sautter,

1990; Power, 1991). During career counseling, the client's beliefs, values, interests, and temperament should also be considered. Success in various careers can depend on many factors.

Behavioral assessment, utilizing such techniques as observation and the completion of checklists, has gained increased interest as an alternative to traditional psychological evaluation. The approach assumes that behavior is observable and quantifiable, and can be stated in simple, understandable, and functional terms (Field, 1979). The approach also assumes that behavior occurs under certain conditions and often has identifiable consequences that affect the behavior. For example, rather than relying solely on a diagnosis of depression the behavior(s) referred to as depression would be described in operational terms and include such factors as frequency, intensity, and duration (Field, 1979; Power, 1991).

Functional assessment is a newer approach of particular relevance to community counselors. Cohen and Anthony (1984) have pointed out that psychiatric diagnosis or symptoms do not correlate with either a client's skills or rehabilitation outcome. On the other hand, skills do correlate with rehabilitation outcome. Therefore, a measure of skills is both one of the better predictive devices and a way of determining what resources the client has available and what resources the client needs to develop to solve the problem at hand. Granger (1975) called functional assessment

*a method for describing abilities and activities in order to measure an individual's use of the variety of skills included in performing the tasks necessary for daily living, vocational pursuits, social interactions, leisure activities, and other activities, and other required behaviors. (p. 24)*

Halpern and Fuhrer (1984) defined functional assessment as "the measurement of purposeful behavior in interaction with the environment, which is interpreted according to the assessment's intended uses" (p. 3). They cautioned, however, that "the results of functional assessment cannot automatically be assumed to generalize across different environments" (p. 4). They went on to note that a wide array of functional assessment instruments and procedures have been developed, and the rate of development of new measures is increasing. Measurement of skills has been one of the most prolific areas of activity in the field of functional assessment, particularly as represented by the many activities of daily living scales that have emerged over the years. These skills, among many that involve a client's functioning, can include learning ability, memory, vision, hearing, speech, hand functioning, endurance, stability of mental or physical condition, work history, acceptability to employers, access to job opportunities, work habits, social support system, accurate perception of capabilities and limitations, judgment, and problem-solving. Given the focus on resources that is present in community counseling, functional assessment represents a particularly relevant appraisal method for community counselors to become familiar with and to use.

Functional assessment may be used particularly by counselors who are working with clients who have been injured on the job but who wish to return to work. Both partial and total loss of capacity to work should be measured in a reliable and valid way. Functional assessment was originally developed for persons with physical impairments in connection with worker's compensation legislation. The counselor must attempt to achieve a fit between the individual's work-related characteristics and the demands of a particular job. This information and the accruing self-awareness can help persons weigh different options when choosing a particular occupational career.

In addition, the counselor also must appraise the environment in which the problem takes place. Cohen and Anthony (1984)

went so far as to state that person-focused assessment is only of value if accompanied by and coordinated with an environmental assessment. Do the human and inanimate environments really help the client to cope or do they complicate the client's life? Environments are often assessed by what people do in them, how people react to them, and how they are compared with other environments by those engaged in certain activities.

Figure 6–1 illustrates the comprehensiveness of client assessment, both in those areas that are evaluated and in the methods utilized to generate information. Yet client assessment still has many inadequacies.

## INADEQUACIES OF CLIENT ASSESSMENT

Since 1985 the debates concerning the use of standardized tests in client assessment have intensified. The conflicts focus on gender and cultural biases, the lack of development of appropriate evaluation instruments for those with a severe disability, the misuse of tests, and how environmental factors influence assessment performance. Many tests identified in this chapter are still culturally biased, with normative information collected from a white, middle-class population. Much of the criticism has been leveled against IQ and achievement tests, a criticism that responds to such questions as What is the nature of intelligence? and, What actually is the criterion for successful performance in basic educational skills?

The criterion problem in assessment is a major issue. To evaluate the client's emotional, intellectual, and vocational functioning, an index of the adequacy of performance is needed. This problem can be quite difficult when working with those with severe disabilities for career planning purposes. The concern is to help these clients select the best career, keeping in mind their specific strengths and limitations. The issue that emerges is, How

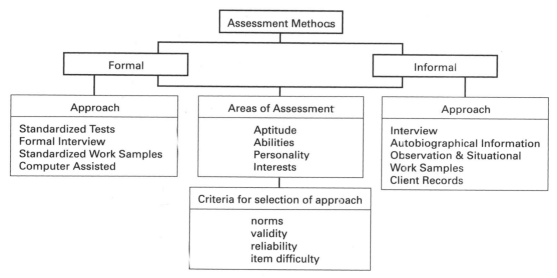

**FIGURE 6–1**  An Overview of Assessment

should actual performance in a career, a particular job, or a selected environment be measured? Since usually the best prediction of what a person will do in a given situation is what he or she has done the last time in that situation, the counselor may have to explore alternative ways to predict performance with certain populations.

Even with some modifications, when tests are used cross-culturally, there is usually an inherent cultural bias. All tests are developed within the frame of reference of the culture or society in which they originated (Smart & Smart, 1993). Great caution must be exercised, consequently, when using standardized tests with persons on whom the test was not standardized (Anastasi, 1988; Geisinger, 1991; Puente, 1990). Though many assessment procedures appear to offer certainty and exactitude because they yield numerical scores, we actually know very little about the applicability of most assessment tools when working with different ethnic groups (Smart & Smart, 1993). Mehvens & Lehman (1986) have stated that "if a test does tend to discriminate (differentiate) between races, sexes, or other sub-cultures, and if the differential scores are not related to what is being predicted (such as on-

the-job success), then the test is unfair" (P. 471). Counselors need to look beyond the apparent credibility of test scores and give careful thought to the validity and reliability of these procedures before generating career or other life-adjustment plans for the client.

Most criticisms of standardized tests have focused not on the tests themselves, but on how these tools are used (Anastasi, 1992). Counselors may use assessment instruments as quick solutions to difficult problems presented by clients, presuming that the tests can provide an easy answer to questions about career choice or interpersonal and emotional problems. The test itself may act as a substitute for the deliberative process usually needed in decision making. The counselor may lack sufficient information about the technical properties of a test, or about the behavior being evaluated. Other hazards in the utilization of tests include basing an individual's test performance on a single score or evaluating a person on the basis of the individual's performance on a specified test at a specified time (Anastasi, 1992).

When considering applicability issues with different populations, as well as gender concerns, psychological tests are generally imperfect. Reliability and validity factors, the ambiguity of test items found on many interest and personality inventories, and the lack of an established criterion on which to base predictive directions are just a few added difficulties contributing to the use of caution when selecting and administering assessment tools. Other difficulties include the orientation of the counselor who is performing the assessment and reliability factors that can influence the client's performance.

Because of their clinically-oriented academic training, counselors may be oriented primarily to identifying client deficits rather than the client's strengths, living, learning and working assets, and life adjustment and career needs (Power, 1991). This situation has often occurred with clients with various physical or mental disabilities. The counselor may focus on the disability and its accompanying handicapping conditions, and overlook a thorough exploration of the client's capabilities. Another counselor orientation may flow from the attitude that "I know what is best for you," and the counselor, consequently, does not attempt to encourage the client's active participation in the assessment process.

Often neglected but a decided deterrent to the reliability of an assessment situation are environmental and client-centered factors that can influence test performance. An environment in which evaluation is conducted may contain such properties as noise, excessive heat or light, all of which may represent a considerable distraction to the client who is undergoing assessment. Anxiety, low motivation, and language are client-centered factors that can inhibit evaluation performance, and with the environmental issues should be carefully considered either before assessment or when reviewing the client's assessment results.

When reviewing the literature on career assessment since 1975, moreover, one discovers that there has been relatively little systematic consideration of how interests, abilities,

and personality characteristics interact to determine career choice and the need for change (Lowman, 1993). There is an abundance of single-variable, single-domain measures that do not capture the aspects of persons that are relevant to career concerns. Career behavior is multidetermined and the areas of the client's emotional, intellectual, and physical functioning must be identified when developing appropriate career plans (Lowman, 1993). The environment in which the client will function must also be evaluated, since the greater the degree of fit between the individual and environmental demands, such as specific occupational characteristics, the greater is the likelihood that the career will be satisfying and motivating.

In considering these several limitations in career assessment, there are guidelines that are important for the counselor to understand when beginning the evaluation process. Barrett (1987) suggested the following:

1. The purpose of the assessment should be clear.
2. There should be information available on the specific training program, job, or environment the assessment is designed to measure.
3. The validity and reliability studies of all the instruments used should be known.
4. Information should be available to certify that the evaluation tools used are free from bias and discrimination.
5. The assessment findings should be correctly interpreted and used in the decision-making process.

## A MODEL FOR CLIENT ASSESSMENT

When community counselors begin to engage in client assessment, consequently, either by utilizing the interview as a diagnostic approach, by employing selected psychological tests, or by reviewing evaluation results provided by other resources, they are confronted with a number of concerns. These include the biases of a particular assessment method, perhaps the neglect of how environmental variables have influenced the client's performance, and one's own professional orientation, such as career preferences, a mental health treatment modality, or a specific measurement tool that corresponds to this professional orientation. A counselor should be aware of these limitations and perhaps even make necessary modifications in the assessment process to accommodate the client's distinctive needs and cultural background.

What can be of assistance to counselors is the availability of an assessment model that considers many evaluation limitations, but still provides a foundation from which appropriate assessment approaches can be developed. An evaluation model should also promote the belief that assessment can be continuous throughout the counseling process (Vacc, 1982). Evaluation is often viewed as a one-time experience, perhaps to determine eligibility for services or for the development of a treatment plan. But assessment can be considered as the touchstone for direction setting and feedback from successive phases of counseling. The following is a description of a model that targets the multidimensional activities of client evaluation, the multiple influences of the environment, and myriad responsibilities for the client, the counselor, and the context or system in which counseling services are to be delivered. This model also highlights the goals of assessment and emphasizes that evaluation is not only a comprehensive process, but a continuous one as well.

The model suggests three dimensions for conceptualizing assessment. One dimension is person vs. environment, the second dimension is resources vs. barrier factors, and the third dimension concerns the functions of assessment over the full course of the counseling process. The second dimension resource factors

include skills, assets, and for those with a mental or physical disability, residual capacities; barriers include symptoms and functional limitations. For the environment, resources factors include family and community resources and supports, while barriers include social and environmental limitations. The third dimension, focusing on the functions of assessment, includes:

1. Establishing a relationship
2. Client involvement
3. Client empowerment and self-determination
4. Awareness of self and issues
5. Awareness of family and cultural influences
6. Understanding of options
7. Reality testing
8. Goal identification
9. Reinforcement of progress
10. Evaluation of program and of progress

This suggested model provides workable guidelines for targeting the important areas of client assessment, and further suggests the many activities and different approaches that can be utilized during the evaluation process. The three dimensions of the model are illustrated in Figure 6–2.

An understanding of the ten functions of assessment are crucial to the appropriate utilization of the model, and each one is now explained.

1. Assessment may be used to establish and/or to provide a focus for a relationship with a client. The forms and tests used in evaluation can help the client to understand the aims of counseling and the role of the counselor in working with the client toward the fulfillment of those aims. Further, the "objective" nature of many tests may make involvement with the counseling process less threatening for those

Functions of Assessment

Establishing Relationship

Client Involvement

Client Empowerment & Self-Determination

Self & Issue Awareness

Family & Cultural Awareness

Understanding Options

Reality Testing

Goal Setting

Reinforcement of Progress

Evaluating Progress

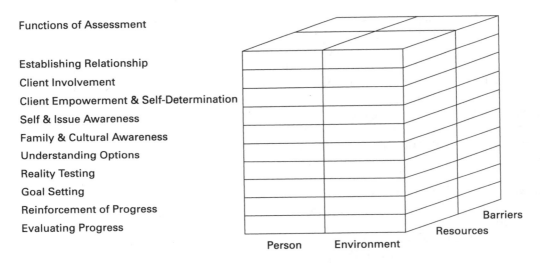

Barriers

Resources

Person     Environment

**FIGURE 6–2**   A Model of Assessment

clients who are not comfortable about self-disclosure of emotionally loaded content. Assessment can be a reinforcing experience for the client when emotional, physical, and intellectual strengths are emphasized and residual capacities are identified. This emphasis and identification facilitates the development of the counselor-client relationship.

2. Assessment necessarily involves the client in the counseling process and provides insights into the nature and depth of the client's involvement in that process. Is the client active or passive, enthusiastic or reluctant, cooperative or resistant? The client's approach to assessment provides insights into his/her level of involvement in the total counseling process.

3. The third function that assessment can serve is to show the client, by the way that he or she handles the assessment, that it is within his or her power to control the counseling process and outcome. This sense of empowerment and self-determination can generalize to the client's attitude toward overcoming the limitations imposed by disability or a life circumstance, such as a severe loss or a major transition (sudden unemployment; forced early retirement).

4. Assessment provides the client and the counselor with information about the client's self-perception and understanding of the issues that must be worked on during counseling. Since much of the counseling process focuses on assisting the client to change, a beginning step for this change is the person's own awareness of the obstacles that must be confronted and the resources to deal with these limitations. This self-knowledge is frequently achieved when the counselor explains assessment results, both at the client's level of understanding and in the context of the client's expectations for counseling outcomes.

5. Evaluation also can identify family and culturally imposed expectations and beliefs that the client maintains. These beliefs include culturally influenced perceptions of support, traditional customs that the family expresses concerning mental health services, an awareness of one's cultural identity, how the family has utilized resources, kinship bonds, family values, and such negative factors as racism, socioeconomic status, discrimination, and cultural stereotyping. This information is usually obtained during the client interview and, when

the opportunity arises, when the counselor speaks directly with family members.

**6.** The topics that are addressed in counseling can suggest options for training, mental health services, and career directions. These factors, including different coping styles, may emerge during the client interview or sometimes from just scanning the categories identified on test protocols. For example, a career interest checklist may suggest options that had not occurred to the client in the past. Yet if little information is available about resources for life adjustment, or if the counselor holds stereotypical beliefs about, for example, career opportunities or the residual capacities of the client following a major life transition, then client options might be quite limiting.

**7.** Reality testing is one of the implicit results of effective assessment. The objective results from evaluation provoke such questions as: Does the client have the skills needed to achieve a desired goal? Can the client really perform the tasks necessary for life adjustment? Concrete assessment procedures can steer the client clear of the Scylla of unrealistic omnipotence and the Charybdis of unwarranted self-limitation (Hershenson, 1993). "Breaking down" the client's denial, which is a limitation to appropriate planning, may be a major task for the counselor, but assessment results represent a confrontation with reality and can be another resource for the counselor when the client has unrealistic demands.

**8.** Client assessment is used to establish not only appropriate goals, but also to identify the planned steps that facilitate goal achievement. If the client has established a working relationship with the counselor, is involved in the assessment process, begins to be aware of the important issues, and understands the different options, then this function should naturally follow. Client denial may inhibit effective goal setting; and if the client refuses to consider the future and only "lives in the present," then assessment results might have to be reempha-

sized and short-term goals identified during the interpretation of test results phase of the evaluation process.

**9.** Assessment results provide a unique opportunity to reinforce the client's progress during the assessment process. The identification of the client's strengths in the intellectual, emotional, and physical areas of life functioning can assist clients to build their confidence as they embark on training, further involvement in mental health services, or the pursuit of a selected career direction. Though the client's depression, confusion, and high anxiety may be limiting factors inhibiting an awareness of his or her own strengths, the counselor's realization of these limitations from information gained during the interview or psychological testing may serve as a counseling focus during the assessment process.

**10.** When any assessment is done again during the counseling process, such as interest or personality measurement, this reassessment helps the client and counselor track progress, determine what is not working, and consequently know when to revise each stage of the counseling plan and when to view it as successfully completed. The client interview, when used as an assessment tool, can be useful to identify client progress during the counseling process, and particularly can provide feedback on how the counseling plan should be modified to accommodate new environmental or career demands.

Finally, two general principles of this approach to client assessment should be noted. First, all assessment approaches or techniques may serve more than one function. Evaluation tools can, for example, assist the client to acquire enhanced self-awareness and to understand treatment or career options, and can provide reality testing. Second, because of the counselor's awareness of assessment's multiple functions throughout the counseling process, evaluation can serve as an organizing principle, providing coherence and integration to that process for the client and the counselor.

## ROLE OF THE COMMUNITY COUNSELOR IN CLIENT ASSESSMENT

The information presented in this chapter suggests varied roles and functions for community counselors when involved in any aspect of the client's assessment. The counselor may have the opportunity, apart from using the client interview to identify needed directions for future planning, to administer selected evaluation instruments. If this is so, Herr (1988) believed that the counselor should continually learn about the instruments available for different populations and different purposes, be aware that many critics object to the influence that any form of testing exerts in American society, and be concerned about the technical or scientific aspects of a particular instrument and the social functions of the assessment. Social functions refer to the reality that when using assessment tools counselors can maximize the opportunity to assist clients to identify their strengths and limitations, and also be a gatekeeper, to exclude or include persons (Herr, 1988).

When the community counselor's role in assessment is primarily the referral of the client to evaluation resources or to review the client's assessment results contained in an evaluation report, then the counselor has definite responsibilities. These responsibilities include selecting the reason and time to evaluate, since identifying the appropriate time for evaluation after a major life transition or a disability inducing trauma can be a significant determinant in the usefulness of assessment results; formulating specific questions to be answered by the assessment resource; suggesting to this resource, from one's own understanding of assessment, what is the best type of evaluation for the client; preparing the client for a structured assessment experience by

explaining the purpose of evaluation and how the results can aid the client in achieving realistic counseling goals; imparting information and responding to the client's own questions and related concerns, which should be the focus of this preparation; and finally, evaluating the report of the client's assessment results. In other words, did the report answer specific questions? Was the evaluation directed to areas that were needed for planning? What are the recommendations for the client? Are there any unresolved discrepancies among the reported test evaluation results?

Whatever the responsibilities of the counselor during assessment, three roles are thematic in any assessment function, namely, (1) educator, i.e., using assessment as a learning experience in decision making, helping the client to develop an action plan based on assessment results, and having a knowledge of treatment and career resources; (2) facilitator, i.e., helping the client to become aware of his/her strengths and weaknesses and assisting the client to recognize abilities that will either help or hinder a successful life transition; and (3) communicator, i.e., establishing a trusting and helpful relationship with the client, being willing to listen openly so the client will respond genuinely and authentically to questions asked, and communicating the evaluation information at the client's level of understanding. All of these roles and responsibilities are necessary if client assessment is to become the foundation for establishing effective treatment or career plans.

## CONCLUSION

With the continued, emerging technological advances in the areas of client assessment, especially with the increased use of computers for evaluation, with the increased numbers of adults representing different ethnic minorities or experiencing major career transitions, and with the changing skills needed to function successfully in the workplace, community counselors must maintain the knowledge related to changes taking place in the economy, society, and the job market. A relationship between counselors and assessment is needed. When counselors understand how standardized tests should be interpreted to clients, and realize that evaluation instruments are not used exclusively for prediction purposes but also to assist individuals in their growth and development, then assessment feedback during counseling can provide unique personal insights into both the opportunities and current obstacles for development. Counselors who engage in client assessment will also require a basic understanding relating to the changing roles of men and women in the future (Ryan & Cole, 1990). Counselors must further understand cultural values and their relationship to the delivery of mental health services and to career values. Assessment in counseling provides a variety of methods to facilitate the client's achievement of identified goals, but the societal context in which these methods are utilized is ever-changing. For this reason client assessment is a dynamic process, ever-responsive to client needs and maintaining the flexibility to utilize different approaches in order to achieve the most appropriate information for planning purposes.

## EXERCISE

### Case Study

Ruth is a twenty-one-year-old African American woman who comes to you for career counseling. She is from a poor family. When she came in for her first counseling interview at a mental health agency where you are employed as a counselor, you noted her shyness and tenseness. She has been having trouble with anxiety, and she states that it interferes with her getting along with others and in making a decision about her future. She strongly feels the need to decide on an educational or vocational direction, and would like some help to "control my anxiety."

Ruth graduated from high school and took a general liberal arts program in high school, earning an overall GPA of B–. Her SAT scores were 950. Ruth states that her best subjects were history and English, and during high school she was involved in the glee club. She reports that she is also very active in her church; she has been a member of a youth organization and sings in the church choir. She has been working as a dispatcher for a small cab company since high school graduation, but feels she could do much better and there is simply too much job stress.

Ruth's father passed away many years ago and her mother supported Ruth and her two younger brothers as a hotel cleaner. Ruth helped with the family finances when she was in high school by working as a waitress. Her mother's sisters also assist in household matters. They live nearby and Ruth believes "they are a great support system."

Ruth is undecided about a future career choice. She has had a boyfriend who wants to marry her, but she insists that she wants to get "situated" in a career before she gets married. Also, she feels a continuing responsibility to contribute to the family income and help her mother support her two brothers.

You notice that during the first fifteen minutes of the interview she does not volunteer much information and appears to show some resistance to self-exploration or to explore career alternatives. She seems uneasy in your presence but is quite willing to proceed with counseling.

With this information, please answer the following questions:

**1.** What assessment approaches would you suggest that could be used to provide Ruth with her personality strengths and career interests, as well as her career options?

**2.** What difficulties do you believe would emerge during the assessment process?

**3.** What information do you believe is particularly important for you to gather during the interview with Ruth?

**4.** What problems do you foresee in establishing a counseling relationship with Ruth in understanding her cultural and family background?

---

## REFERENCES

Anastasi, A. (1988). *Psychological testing.* New York: Macmillan.

Anastasi, A. (1992). What counselors should know about the use and interpretation of psychological tests. *Journal of Counseling and Development, 70,* 610–615.

Anthony, W. A. (1980). A rehabilitation model for rehabilitating the pschiatrically disabled. *Rehabilitation Counseling Bulletin, 24,* 6–14.

Barrett, S. P. (1987). The legal implications of testing. In P. LeConte (Ed.), *Using vocational assessment results for effective planning* (p. 105–110). Stevens Point, WI: Department of Public Instruction.

Betz, N. E., & Weiss, D. J. (1987). Validity. In B. Bolton (Ed.), *Handbook of measurement and evaluation in rehabilitation.* (2nd ed., pp. 37–55) Baltimore, MD: Univeristy Park Press.

Brown, M. B. (1990). Personality assessment in career counseling. *Career Planning and Adult Development Journal, 6* 22–27.

Campbell, N. J. (1988). Self-directed search. In J. T. Kames & M. M. Mastie (Eds.), *A counselor's guide to career assessment instruments.* (2nd ed., pp. 116–120). Alexandria, VA: National Career Development Association.

Capps, C. F. , Heinlein, W. E. , & Sautter, S. W. (1990). Aptitude testing in career assessment. *Career Planning and Adult Development Journal, 6* 16–21.

Cohen, B. F., & Anthony, W. A. (1984). Functional assessment in psychiatric rehabilitation. In A. Halpern & M. Fuhrer (Eds.) *Functional asssessment in rehabilitation* (pp. 79–100). Baltimore: Brookes.

Davidshofer, C. O. (1988). Jackson vocational interest survey. In J. T. Kames & M. M. Mastie (Eds.), A Counselor's Guide to Career Assessment Instruments. (2nd ed., pp. 95–99). Alexandria, VA: National Career Development Association.

Denove, A. K., & Czaczkes, J. W. (1975). Personality factors influencing vocational rehabilitation. *Archives General Psychiatry, 32,* 573–578.

Droege, R. C. (1988). Harrington-O'Shea career decision-making system. In J. T. Kapes & M. M. Mastie (Eds.), *A counselor's guide to career assessment instruments.* (2nd ed., pp. 86–90). Alexandria, VA: National Career Development Association.

Field, T. F. (1979). The psychological assessment of vocational functioning. *Journal of Applied Rehabilitation Counseling, 10,* 124–130.

Geisinger, K. F. (1991). Fairness and selected psychometric issues in the psychological testing of Hispanics. In K. F. Geisinger (Ed.), *Psychological testing of Hispanics* (pp. 17–42). Washington, DC: American Psychological Association.

Goldman, L. (1972). Tests and counseling: The marriage that failed. *Measurement and Evaluation in Guidance, 4,* 213–220.

Granger, C. V. (1975). *Barthel index-granger adaptation.* Pawtucket, RI: Medical Rehabilitation Evaluation Center.

Halpern, A. S., & Fuhrer, M. J. (1984). *Functional assessment in rehabilitation.* Baltimore: Brookes.

Hartlage, L. C. (1987). Diagnostic assessment in rehabilitation. In B. Bolton, (Ed.), *Handbook of measurement and evaluation in rehabilitation* (2nd ed. , pp. 131–150). Baltimore, MD: Paul H. Brookes.

Herr, E. L. (1988). The counselor's role in career assessment. In J. T. Kapas & M. M. Mastie (Eds.), *A counselor's guide to career assessment instruments* (pp. 13–24). Alexandria, VA: National Career Development Association.

Hershenson, D. H. (1993, March). Integrating assessment in the rehabilitation process. Paper delivered at the annual meeting of the Interdisciplinary Council on Vocation Evaluation, Virginia Beach, VA.

Hershenson, D. H. , & Power, P. W. (1987). *Mental health counseling & theory and practice.* New York: Pergamon Press.

Hohenshil, T. H. , & Brown, M. B. (1991). The special issue on current practices in career assessment. *Career Planning and Adult Development Journal, 6,* 3–4.

Hursh, N. C. , & Kerns, A. F. (1988). *Vocational evaluation in special education.* Boston, MA: Little, Brown.

Interdisciplinary Council. (1994). *A position paper on vocational evaluation/assessment.* University of Wisconsin—Whitewater.

Kaplan, S. , & Questad, K. (1980). Client characteristics in rehabilitation studies: A literature review. *Journal of Applied Rehabilitation Counseling, 11,* 165–168.

Kaufman, A. S. , Clark, J. H. , & Flaitz, J. (1987). Intelligence testing. In B. Bolton (Ed.), *Handbook of measurement and evaluation in rehabilitation,* (2nd ed., pp. 59–74). Baltimore, MD: Paul Brookes.

Levinson, E. M. , & Folina, L. (1990). Career interest assessment techniques. *Career Planning and Adult Development Journal, 6,* 9–15.

Lowman, R. L. (1993). The inter-domain model of career assessment and counseling. *Journal of Counseling and Development, 71,* 549–554.

McCabe, S. P. (1998). Career assessment inventory. The enhanced version. In J. T. Kapes & M. M. Mastie (Eds.) *A counselor's guide to career assessment instruments,* (2nd ed., pp. 76–80). Alexandria, VA: National Career Development Association.

Maki, D. R. , Pape, D. A. , & Prout, H. T. (1979). Personality evaluations: A tool of the rehabilitation counselor. *Journal of Applied Rehabilitation Counseling, 10,* 119–123.

Mehens, W. A. , & Llehman, I. J. (1986). Using standardized tests in education (4th ed.) New York: Longman.

Meyer, A. B. , Fouad, N. A. , & Klein, M. (1976) Vocational inventories. In B. Bolton (Ed.) Handbook of measurement and evaluation in rehabilitatior (2nd ed., pp. 110–138). Baltimore, MD.

Phillips, J. T. (1978). Occupational interest inventories: An often untapped resource. *Journal of Applied Rehabilitation Counseling, 9,* 10–12.

Power, P. W. (1991). A guide to vocational assessment (2nd ed.) Austin, Texas: Pro. Ed. Publishers.

Puente, A. E. (1990). Psychological assessment of minority group members. In G. Golstein & M. Herson (Eds.). Handbook of psychological assessment (2nd ed., pp. 505–520). New York: Pergamon.

Ryan, C. W. & Cole, D. J. (1990) Career Assessment: Projections for the future. *Career and Adult Development Journal, 6,* 11–44.

Schaie, K. W. (1978). External validity in the assessment of intellectual development in adulthood. *Journal of Gerontology, 3,* 695–701. 6-17.

Shipley, W. C. (1986). *Shipley institute of living scale.* Los Angeles, CA: Western Psychological Services.

Smart, J. F. , & Smart, D. W. (1993). The rehabilitation of Hispanics with disabilities: Sociocultural constraints. *Rehabilitation education, 7,* 167–184.

Snyder, J. C. , & Wilson, M. F. (1977). Elements of a psychological assessment. *American Journal of Nursing, February,* 235–239.

Sundberg, N. D. (1977). *Assessment of persons* Englewood Cliffs, NJ: Prentice-Hall.

Vacc, M. A. (1982). A conceptual framework for continuous assessment of clients. *Measurement and Evaluation in Guidance, 15,* 40–47.

Walsh, W. B. , & Betz, N. E. (1985). *Tests and assessment.* Englewood Cliffs, NJ: Prentice-Hall.

Wechsler, D. C. (1981). Wechsler adult intelligence scale. New York: Psychological Corporation.

Womer, F. B. (1988). Selecting an instrument: Chore or challenge. In J. T. Kapes & M. M. Mastie (Eds.), *A counselor's guide to career assessment instruments,* (2nd. ed., pp. 27–36). Alexandria, VA: National Career Development Association.

# 7

# ENVIRONMENTAL AND NEEDS ASSESSMENT

Since 1970 there has been increased attention to the environment in which we live, learn, work, and socialize. The ecology movement and the national political focus on saving the natural environment have both been able to maintain the continued interests of countless people while tapping their creative capacities for effective advocacy. Many of these capacities have been directed to showing counselors how clients' environments can be utilized for more effective life and career adjustment. The growth of environmental interests, moreover, has formed the belief that many of the causes of mental health problems may reside in several features of society itself, including such problems as racism, sexism, unemployment, poverty, or restricted educational opportunities (Greenblatt, Emery, Black, & Glueck, 1967). In responding to these problems, environmental design projects, public policy programs, and relevant research studies have been developed (Stokols, 1992). While much progress has been made at local levels toward establishing healthier environments, the daunting challenge remains on how to incorporate environmental issues into client diagnostic assessment and appropriate planning.

This chapter attempts to respond to the issues concerning the relationship of the environment to client life planning and adjustment. The response entails identifying the varied meanings of environment, exploring the theories of person-environment interaction, focusing on the aspects of the environment that should be assessed by the community counselor, and then explaining the specific implications of environmental assessment for client intervention. All of this information should represent a resource for counselors when action is taken to formulate the most relevant diagnostic approaches for understanding the complexity of client problems. In addition, this chapter will discuss needs assessment approaches, which are essential tools for exploring environmental influences on client functioning. The authors of the book strongly believe that integral to the acquisition of skills necessary for assessing the client for productive living is an understanding of the needs that reside in the client's environment, including those of societal institutions. Stokols (1992) explained that "just as environments can be described in terms of their relative scale and complexity, the participants in those environments can be studied at varying levels ranging from individuals, small groups, and organizations to larger aggregates and populations" (p. 7).

## THE MEANING OF ENVIRONMENT

The term *environment* can include such ambient features as climate and elevation, temperature, light, color, hazards and natural disasters, personal and territorial space (family, school, residential and work environments), crowding, and the organizational and personal behaviors of those who occupy space in the environment (McAndrew, 1993). The term *ecology* refers to the interrelations between organisms and their environment, and an ecological perspective has provided a general framework for understanding the nature of people's transactions with their physical and sociocultural surroundings (Hawley, 1950; Rogers-Warren & Warren, 1977; Stokols, 1992). Bronfenbrenner (1979) conceptualized the ecological model as the "outcome of life-long engagements between person and environment... and desires or dysfunctional behaviors are best understood and most effectively prevented or treated within the environments where they occur." Walsh and Betz (1985), moreover, cited Kantor (1924), who distinguished between the physical and the psychological environment. The physical environment is described by Kantor as geographical region, temperature, and general ecological conditions; the psychological environment is defined within the context of a stimulus response model (Walsh & Betz, 1985). Because there is much ambiguity associated with the terms *physical* and *psychological* environment, Magnusson (1981) suggested viewing the environment as it is— the actual environmental variables that need to be distinguished: physical geographical, biological, and social-cultural. The combination of these three types of properties may be used for descriptions of actual environments and situations.

Environments have also been classified in terms of their resources, incentives, and constraints. Resources represent the material and symbolic content of the environment. Incentives are group-induced behavior reinforcers, and constraints are physical and social barriers to self-fulfillment (Anderson, 1963). All of these definitions, consequently, offer varied meanings of environment and environmental classifications. In this chapter environment will be understood as the interactions and relationships between people and the contexts in which they live, including behaviors, situations, attitudes, properties of places, and the sociocultural factors of norms, rules, and roles integral to work settings, families, organizations, and societies as a whole. The focus of this viewpoint is on the perception of the situation and the psychological meaning of the situation to the individual, as well as the reality of the situation environment. Since the counselor is concerned about the functioning of human behavior, the transactions between individual variables and environmental variables can usually provide the most complete explanations of this behavior (Huebner & Corazzini, 1984).

## THEORIES OF PERSON-ENVIRONMENT INTERACTION

In their review of the different approaches that explain the individual-environment interaction, Huebner and Corazzini (1984) identified models suggested by Walsh (1973) as those that have enjoyed the widest application in varied settings relevant to the work of counselors. These models are now explained, as well as their implications for the development of an environmental assessment approach.

**1.** *Behavior setting approach.* This model states that environments select and shape the behavior of their inhabitants. Behavior settings consist of physical components, overt behaviors, temporal properties, and the relationship between behavioral and nonbehavioral factors. When exploring an individual's life experience, those aspects of the setting that make a difference to the person's behavior would be identified. The setting aspects could include the physical size of the setting and the essential number of people in the setting (Barker, 1968). This specific model provides many target areas for assessment. When counseling clients who present problems apparently related to the family, for example, the professional would want to explore the number of family members and the physical makeup of the family home. Each factor might cause unusual stress in the client's life and stimulate behavior dysfunction.

**2.** *Need-press theory.* The focus of this approach is on the person's needs identified from behavioral self-reports, environmental influences or pressures, and the relationship between the needs and environmental "presses." A congruent person-environment relationship will produce satisfaction and fulfillment, resulting from a complementary combination of need and press. For example, if management expectations and the physical work setting are considered as environmental "presses," then the worker may be satisfied if his/her work-related needs are met by these expectations and physical work characteristics. If not, then discomfort or distress may result (Stern, 1964).

**3.** *Human aggregate model.* This model examines the match between an individual and the environment, and the "fit" contributes to higher performance, higher satisfaction, and less stress. The characteristics of both the person and the environment are identified. Of interest to the counselor is that this approach includes an individual's perceptions about self and preferences or choices for a particular environment (school, employment setting, community agency) (Pervin, 1968; Holland, 1966, 1973). An assumption of this approach

is that "individuals will perform better and report more satisfaction in environments that tend to reduce the discrepancy between their perceived actual selves and their ideal selves" (Huebner & Corazzini, 1984, p. 586).

A modification of this transactional approach is frequently used in career counseling and has formed the basis of such career development theories as trait-factor and John Holland's personality model. Characteristics of both the individual and specific careers or occupational environments are identified, and then a connection is suggested to the client. Integral to this identification is exploring how the person perceives both self and occupational environments suggested by the counselor.

**4.** *Social climate models.* Moos (1976) has been the leading proponent of this approach, and though he utilizes a person's subjective perceptions of the environment and reported behaviors in that environment, he conceptualized social climate dimensions as relationship, personal development, system maintenance, and system change. System maintenance and change refer to the extent to which the environment is orderly and clear in its expectations, maintains control, and is responsive to change (Huebner & Corazzini, 1984). If a counselor used this approach during client assessment, then the client's possible support systems would be identified, as well as the opportunities for personal growth existing in a given environment and how much this environment is responsive to change. A client presenting the problem of a major career or other life transition, for example, would be asked about available support systems, such as family members or significant others, the chances for personal enhancement in a proposed new career or life setting, and perhaps how accommodating the new environment would be.

All of these approaches have additional implications for assessment. Each model highlights identifiable characteristics of the environment and suggests that a specific environment can be positioned along a powerful-weak continuum. If one conceptualizes a client's environment in the perspective of physical factors, group characteristics, organizational structure, reinforcement consequences, and organizational or social climate, then these dimensions can have demonstrable effects on individual and group behavior and overall life functioning (Moos, 1973; Riger, 1984). Some people, however, are much more affected than others by the characteristics of environmental settings.

Even with an understanding of these four stated approaches, there are still lingering questions about which person and environmental variables should be measured and how these variables interact (Huebner & Corazzini, 1984). Another question is how these variables should be measured. In other words, can a valid response be given on a subjective self-report about the meaning of the environment, or should a "test" be administered that operationally defines discrete environmental variables? These questions will be further explored in the remaining sections of this chapter.

Before various environmental assessment techniques are explored, the targets of this assessment should be identified. Though such characteristics as physical factors, group characteristics, organizational structure, reinforcement consequences, and organizational or social climate have been mentioned, the environmental components of an assessment approach will also depend on the kind of environment that is having a negative or positive impact on the client's adjustment. A family environment may present different attributes from a work or organizational environment. Yet both environments, as well as others, such as schools or residential neighborhoods, may possess in common objective information (population or member size, member behaviors, including attitudes and expectations) and subjective data (perceptions, evaluations, and

opinions of people). Both types of information need to be explored in environmental assessment, though the perceptions that people have of a particular setting and the objective evaluation of that setting may not always coincide (Riger, 1984).

Riger (1984) provided an important contribution to environmental assessment when she explained that the community in which people live and work is a context for understanding human behavior and well-being. She viewed community both as a place and as relationships and resources. The concept of place refers to the social characteristics of the residents in a given area, the land use and the quality of the housing, and the presence or absence of such institutions and organizations as schools, churches, or civic groups. Community as relationships and resources implies informal social networks, which may not necessarily be located in one's neighborhood, neighboring functions, and the social organization of neighborhoods (Riger, 1984). Of interest to the counselor is the additional concept that emerges from understanding community as a place and as a resource for relationships, namely, a "sense of community." Riger (1984) cited the research of Chavis, Hogge, McMillan, and Wandersman (1984), who proposed four principles of a sense of community. These principles comprise: (1) membership—a feeling of belonging, a sense of relatedness; (2) influence—can an individual affect the group, and can the group put pressure on an individual to perform tasks; (3) sharing of values with integration and fulfillment of needs—the fulfillment of an individual's values by a group or community; and (4) shared emotional connection, which can be increased by interpersonal contact, the success of contact, and the importance of a shared event to individuals. These principles can be illustrated when the counselor explores, for example, a client's work environment after understanding that perhaps one of the major sources of the client's sustained depressive mood are job work pressures. The counselor would then evaluate if the client has a "sense" of connection to his/her place of employment, feels part of the "team," enjoys many working relationships, believes that the job fulfills his/her reported needs, perceives that the organization is putting too much pressure on him or her, and understands how much contact or shared activities he or she has with other employees. The counselor's recognition of these factors may contribute to understanding the impact environmental influences have on the client's problem.

With an awareness of the proposed theories of person-environment interaction and the possible target areas for an environmental assessment, the counselor can develop a specific assessment approach. This approach assumes that the counselor believes that the physical world affects the individual; if the source of the client's problem does not reside objectively in the environment, then perhaps the client's perception of his/her environment represents a major obstacle to effective life functioning. This belief and perception are particularly true for those with a significant physical or mental disability. Although an individual with a severe physical disability, for example, may be perfectly able to perform designated job duties, the unavailability of accessible, accommodated transportation or an accessible workplace may prevent employment. The counselor's understanding of how an environment is handicapping and of the client's perceptions of possible discriminating factors is an important step in providing appropriate assistance.

Several environmental assessment techniques have been explained in the literature, and each strategy can suggest concepts and other insights into the most workable assessment structure for a particular counselor. With any assessment approach, however, not only should the physical and social environments be described and evaluated, but also to be explored is how an individual's perceptions of

the environment may influence the way one behaves in that environment (Walsh & Betz, 1985). If an individual perceives the environment either as threatening or nurturing, then this perception will affect one's interpersonal relationships within that environment and the person's motivation to complete tasks.

One strategy for environmental assessment is largely descriptive and focuses on such variables as size of the organization, number of people in a specific organization or setting, perhaps the ability levels of the setting members, and the ratios within an organization, for example, of management to labor or faculty to students (Huebner & Corazzini 1984). This approach can also include identifying such additional characteristics of individuals and particular setting or occupation as geographic location, educational level of the members, and work functions, and assessing the resemblance of these characteristics to specific personality needs. The emphasis of this assessment approach is on the physical characteristics and related demographic factors of environments and how they tend to subsequently influence behavior (Walsh & Betz, 1985).

A second approach focuses on an individual's perception of the environment and includes such properties as value, beauty, social climate, stressors, and satisfaction. These properties include both descriptive and evaluative components (Walsh & Betz, 1985). A series of scales developed by Moos and his colleagues use the perceptual approach and each of these scales contains several subscales that measures such basic underlying dimensions of an environment as relationships, personal development, and system-changes (Huebner & Corazzini, 1984). Examples of these scales are the Social Climate Indexes and the University Residence Environment Scale (Moos & Gerst, 1974). Stern (1970) has also developed environmental indexes, i.e., the Organizational Climate Index and the Evening College Characteristics Index,

(Stern, 1970) in which an environment is also defined by considering activities that are perceived to occur in it. Perception is an important area to explore during this assessment strategy. The client's appraisal of his/her environment may indicate any differences between what is really happening in the client's life and the client's perception of what is happening. There may be quite a discrepancy between the real and the perceived. Such a discrepancy often emerges when clients attempt to blame their difficulties on others, i.e., family members, significant friends, employers, the economy, or imagined environmental barriers. Or during career counseling the client may become aware of the differences between the criteria for success in a specific career and the actual factors that facilitate a successful, satisfying career.

A third assessment approach targets the behavioral attributes of environments or behavior settings and includes an assessment of overt behaviors, the physical components or settings in which behavior occurs, and the temporal properties associated with behavior (Huebner & Corazzini, 1984; Walsh & Betz, 1985). Utilizing this perspective the counselor, when exploring the family environment of clients, for example, may identify such family behaviors as communication styles and role performance, the physical makeup of the home (size, number of rooms, geographic location), and the varied stimuli that elicit specific interaction patterns and communication behaviors.

A fourth strategy of environmental assessment focuses more specifically on a work organizational environment and includes the role of the environment in career assessment. Greenhaus and Callahan (1994) summarized that four facets of an environment are particularly important in career assessment and decision making: occupations, jobs, organizations, and families. Effective environmental assessment should assist a person to identify the setting in which he or she would most likely find

significant values and find expression for needs, interests, and a preferred lifestyle (Greenhaus & Callahan, 1994).

Each facet of the environment relevant to work and careers contains important information for assessment, and Greenhaus and Callahan (1994) summarized this information with the following factors:

| | |
|---|---|
| *Occupations*: | Task activities |
| | Ability/training requirements |
| | Financial rewards |
| | Social relationships |
| | Security |
| | Physical setting |
| | Lifestyle considerations |
| |    Work stress |
| |    Time commitment to work |
| *Jobs*: | Task variety |
| | Task significance |
| | Ability/training requirements |
| | Financial rewards |
| | Security |
| | Physical setting |
| | Social relationships |
| | Lifestyle considerations |
| |    Time demands |
| |    Work stress |
| | Amount of autonomy |
| *Organizations*: | Industry outlook |
| | Financial health of organizations |
| | Career path flexibility |
| | Career management policies |
| | Size and structure |
| | Reward and system |
| *Families*: | Spouse's career expectations and emotional needs |
| | Family members' needs |
| | Family's financial needs |
| | Family's desired lifestyle |
| | Family stage |
| | Self and spouse career stage |

Another approach that focuses on a work environment targets such factors as size, number of people, and the ability levels of the members within an organization. This approach also incorporates the personality style and expectation of the designated leader, associates (those individuals who have similar positions within an organization), subordinates, and the organization itself. The personality and expectation of an organization are determined by the history and tradition of the organization as well as by the organizational goals and objectives that reflect the style and expectation of present top management (Hersey & Blanchard, 1972). Hersey & Blanchard (1972) defined expectations as "the perceptions of appropriate behavior for one's own role or position or one's perceptions of the roles of others within the organization" (p. 111). Although diagnosing an environment can be difficult when the organization's leader has a dominant presence in the specific setting, this approach can be useful when clients are having many work-related problems and the counselor wishes to identify such possible stressors as overwhelming expectations for job performance and unusual commitment of time. A person may not share his/her expectations with a superior, and alleviation of this stressor may involve the person accepting his or her roles and the role of the other. Other situational variables relevant to this approach which could be explored during counseling are job demands, the time available for decision making, and an individual's potential for adaptability (Hersey & Blanchard, 1972).

A fifth approach, which has emerged from the research and practice of selected vocational evaluators, utilizes an ecological systems perspective (Seymula & Schleser, 1986). Seymula and Schleser (1986) explained this approach as an individual's behavior interacting with the family, school, occupation, and society. Individual differences are viewed from their cultural context, and behavior can best be understood by watching how individuals interrelate with their environment. The identification of the systems most important and most troublesome to the individual must precede any effective intervention. When adjustment problems are caused by a faulty interaction between a person and the environment, then perhaps these problems can be modified through the development of competencies, such as the acquisition of assertive skills or coping strategies for handling anger. Assumptions implicit in this approach are that different systems can influence an individual's behavior, and that failure to utilize such environmental measures as job analysis, labor market surveys, or family assessment increases the chance of poor adjustment between an individual and an employment setting or a family environment. When a counselor, for example, is working with those with severe mental illness who have been institutionalized for several months or years and are now being released, an evaluation of the person's family could be significantly important for his/her adjustment. An identification of the family's expectations, resources to cope with the individual, and possible family dysfunction would be crucial if the family is to serve as a supportive, even rehabilitative environment for their family member.

All of these five approaches assume that frequently the counselor is looking for the optimal client-environmental fit. The achievement of this fit may be particularly necessary for career counseling purposes, but when working with individuals who have other life adjustment problems, counselors are also attempting to identify such systems as school, work, local residential community, and available family and their possible contribution to the client's problems. Diagnostic assessment viewed, consequently, from an environmental systems perspective takes on a new emphasis and depth. It builds on the assumption that often the source both of clients' problems and their possible solutions resides in the person's environment.

Figure 7–1 illustrates the different components of the client's environment that could be explored when attempting to identify the source of clients' difficulties. Work, family, and the civic/geographical community also interact with each other. An individual's problems with the work environment can spill over to family relationships, and conditions of overcrowding and population density may have an impact on how family life is conducted. A key factor in the client's evaluation, however, is how this individual perceives his/her work, family, and civic environments. What may be stressors for one person, such as organizational unresponsiveness, unclear family expectations, or limited space for carrying out family responsibilities, may be ignored by another person.

During assessment one must consider how the counselor is to integrate and use all the information about a client and the client's environment that has been gathered through the evaluation process. Without such a framework, the mass of information confronting the counselor appears overwhelming, disorganized, and irrelevant. Appraisal is, however, intended to guide the selection and planning of the intervention. For community counselors, information about the client's competencies, goals, and dispositions and information about the client's environmental interactions are particularly to be sought out and examined in formulating the plan for intervention.

For current purposes, this model represents a "time slice" of the client and the client's environment. During the counseling process, several such time slices are necessary: (a) a time slice taken at the start of counseling; (b)

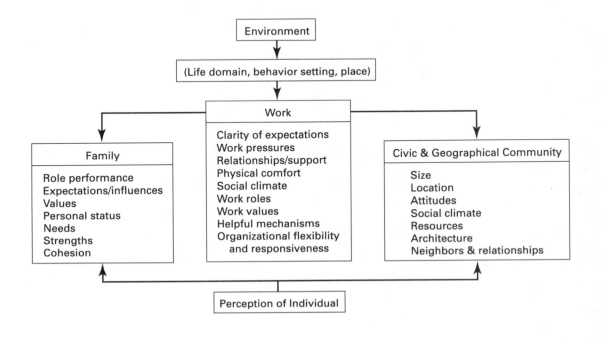

**FIGURE 7–1**   Areas for Environmental Assessment

a projected time slice as to what the situation should become on which to base the strategy of intervention; and (c) a time slice taken after the intervention to evaluate its success.

While the use of environmental assessment during the counseling process is increasing, there are still general problems to consider when employing this approach. Huebner & Corrazini (1984) explained that often the specific environment as the target of diagnostic efforts, particularly the physical environment, is not actually defined. It has also been difficult for both clinicians and researchers to decide what to measure, though evaluation decisions should be made in relation to problem areas that can be changed. Although many assessment measures primarily identify one's perceptions of the environment, the perceived environment may not reflect the actual environment.

Because of these limitations, guidelines should be developed for environmental assessment approaches, and Huebner (1980) has suggested the following:

1. Within the total environment, subenvironments and subgroups must be identified and studied independently and in relation to each other.

2. When instruments are used for decision-making purposes, the instruments must provide information about the causes or sources of pressure that influence the environment.

3. When developing intervention plans, locally developed instruments may prove more useful than standardized instruments.

4. Multiple measures and approaches must be employed and integrated to achieve a more complex and complete understanding of environments and person-environment relationships.

5. Relationships between the "objective" environment and the "perceived" environment must be differentiated.

6. Reliability and validity data on instruments that have been constructed must be obtained.

7. Instruments should be used for which there is available validity and reliability information and which have been used in previous studies.

The effects of the environment on people's behavior is a complex issue, and the counselor would be better served if he/she not only chooses those assessment resources that are the most appropriate for the client or project, but also uses instruments that have an established reputation. The following section identifies a few of these measures.

## SELECTED ENVIRONMENT ASSESSMENT MEASURES

Instruments that have been developed to measure environmental influences target both objective information (statistics, size, events, etc.) and subjective data (perceptions, beliefs, and opinions). There are several indices that yield this information, such as:

1. *The Stern Environmental Indexes.* These indices include the College Characteristics Index, the High School Characteristics Index, the Evening College Characteristics Index, and the Organizational Climate Index. They were developed to assess the perceived environment, and though considerable validity data have been reported, the indexes are waning in use (Walsh & Betz, 1985). A manual was published in 1959; since then, apparently there has been no concise and organized statement of the description, scoring, and technical information associated with Stern's indexes.

**2.** *The Moos Social Climate Scales.* Using primarily a rational approach to develop his social climate scales, Moos (1974) asked people individually about their patterns of behavior in certain environments (Walsh & Betz, 1985). Moos explored different types of environments, such as hospital and community programs, correctional institutions, military settings, companies, university student living groups, junior high and high school classrooms, work milieus, social, task-oriented and therapeutic groups, and families. Within these varied environments he studied both relationship, personal development, and system maintenance and change dimensions. Moos was concerned with the problem of why an individual does well in one environment and not so well in another (Walsh & Betz, 1985). Walsh and Betz (1985) concluded that "additional validity and normative data will contribute to the meaning and usefulness of the scales" (p. 316).

**3.** *Work Environment Preference Schedule.* This instrument consists of 24 items, is self-administering, has no time limit, and is appropriate for grades 11 through 16 and for adults. It attempts to identify individuals who are likely to be adaptable to bureaucratic settings, an orientation that reflects a commitment to the set of attitudes, values, and behaviors that are characteristically rewarded by bureaucratic organizations (Walsh & Betz, 1985). These attitudes, values, and behaviors consist of self-subordination, impersonalization, rule conformity, traditionalism, and compartmentalization. Normative data was obtained from high school and college students and occupational groups, but the manual indicates that the sample groups were very small. The manual does report adequate reliability information. This instrument could be used during career counseling, especially when interest assessment suggests occupational areas that represent large institutions, companies, or agencies.

All of these measures are able to provide information and insights into the person-environment interaction and suggest possible influences on client functioning. They give a focus to the possibilities of environmental change, a perspective that includes the changing of those alterable conditions that contribute to the client's life adjustment difficulties, such as lack of employment opportunities, family problems, discriminatory practices and inadequate education, housing, and transportation. If change in the person is ever to occur, then frequently the individual's available life environment must be addressed for the identification of limiting influences. Yet a question still remains for the counselor, namely, what environmental factors should actually receive attention? These will vary, of course, according to the nature of the problem, its intensity, and the orientation and skills of counselors. Two factors, however, have been recurrent themes in life functioning and represent negative influences on the client's achievement of appropriate adjustment goals. These themes are attitudes and stress, two realities, which if not understood by counselors as potential or ever-present obstacles for clients, can undermine many intervention efforts. The following sections discuss these factors.

## Attitudes

An attitude is a tendency to act toward or against something in the environment. It may be a residue of experience by which an activity is conditioned and controlled, and a mental disposition of someone to act for or against a definite object. Attitudes are reflections of beliefs, and they indicate the definitions of the situation held by the majority (Altman, 1981). These attitudes can be predictors of overt behavior, as well as structure the way society defines a problem and the framework within which behavior takes place. Discrimination toward different multicultural groups is an example of a behavior resulting from the way society defines the apparent problems between people of different racial backgrounds. Prejudice can influence the relationships with peers and significant others, the interaction with professionals such as social workers, teachers, counselors, and employers who may be important resources influencing a person's life direction, and one's relation to the general public whose reactions to an individual's presence in the community is part of everyday life (Altman, 1981).

For those with disabilities, the attitudes of family and close friends can be essential determinants of support and acceptance. Also, isolation of individuals with severe disabilities by their immediate peer group can result in the reduction of learned social competencies necessary for life adjustment. Counselors, moreover, are viewed by many as gatekeepers of information and services. Their attitudes can influence family and societal reactions to such major life transitions as chronic illness or retirement. Employer attitudes affect the hiring of those who are older or who have a significant disability. Public attitudes seem to be based on stereotypes, and the public's ignorance regarding a disability, racial heritage, and gender solicits different responses toward individuals representing these groups. Public attitudes, consequently, are a crucial component of the surroundings with which many people must contend. If a culture places a high premium, for example, on physical abilities for mastering the environment and on coping successfully with a problem, the counselor's effort to differentiate attitudinal factors from accepted standards for human performance may be a difficult endeavor.

The investigation of attitudes toward a specific client should receive emphasis when developing an assessment strategy. There are two main sources for this exploration, namely, the client interview and appropriate measuring instruments.

Counselors can explore with their clients their perception of attitudes of their family, community, peer, or work organizations. Such perceptions may frequently be useful determinants to why a client is displaying a certain behavior.

The cause of the attitude should also be identified as much as this can be discerned. The cause of a negative attitude can be a key factor for the focus of intervention approaches. In other words, the counselor is assisting the client to understand what shapes a specific attitude expressed by the immediate environment. A review of the literature indicates that most attitudes are shaped by the following determinants (Arokiasamy, Rubin, & Roessler, 1987).

**a.** *Perceived cause of the problem.* This factor includes religious beliefs, medical reasons, societal causes, i.e., economic conditions or the prevailing economic philosophy, and personal beliefs, which may include the belief that certain problems are inevitable or incurable. A person's belief about cause is particularly important with the problem of mental illness. Negative attitudes toward an individual with this disability may be softened by the belief that a medical explanation can be offered for the origin of the illness. Society, capitalism, and the family have also been blamed for mental illness.

**b.** *Perceived responsibility for a specific problem.* If an individual is held responsible for his or her difficulties, then that person is usually going to be treated adversely by others. The degree of negativity may be determined by the gravity of the problem and its effect on or implications for others. Obese people, alcoholics, sex offenders, persons with AIDS, and those with a criminal history generally elicit more negative responses from society then someone who was born with a disability or who is unemployed because of economic conditions. How ascribed personal responsibility can shape an individual's response is highlighted today by society's attitude toward the homeless, welfare recipients, and those with HIV-AIDS. Responsibility for an identified problem must be carefully explored during counseling, for the root cause of the client's dysfunction might be the belief and resultant behavior of a significant other. This attitude harbored by an important person in the client's life may represent the most important barrier to overcome. A man who has become head-injured due to an auto accident caused by his drunk driving may be facing a greater barrier from his employer's attitude about personal responsibility than from any architectural obstacle in the workplace.

c. *Perceived threat to one's personal safety.* Many people are today living with severe anxiety and are developing mental health problems because of their perception, for example, of recurrent violence in their local neighborhood. The fear of contagious or personal endangerment also seems to be an important factor in society's reaction to persons with certain diseases such as AIDS or tuberculosis, or those with a criminal record. Life adjustment problems are often encountered by public offenders because of the perception that they are too dangerous to live among other human beings. These perceptions usually emerge from societal stereotypes. Stereotypes are steadfastly maintained toward certain individuals, resulting in many interpersonal difficulties for these persons.

The utilization of a structured interview is not the only approach when identifying attitudes. Specific measures have been developed that investigate attitudes toward certain groups, such as those with a disability, women, gays and lesbians, and individuals representing different minority groups. From her review of the literature, Fassinger (in press), indicated that there are many inadequacies in the measurement of attitudes toward feminism, women's roles, and other related constructs. Definitional inadequacy, the difficulties of any instrument adequately discriminating beliefs that have occurred in the context of the rapid social change since the measures were developed, and the weak evidence of construct validity are just a few of the limitations in existing instruments that attempt to identify attitudes toward gender-role issues. Several instruments have been developed, however, which have taken into account these problems, and a sampling of the scales that measure societal attitudes toward persons with disabilities, women, and sex role egalitarian issues will be briefly explained.

**1.** *Attitudes Toward Disabled Persons Scale.* The ATDP was constructed to measure generalized attitudes toward persons with disabilities. It has two scales, each containing 30 items to which respondents express their agreement or disagreement about disabled persons on a standard six-point continuum. Another stated purpose of the instrument is the indirect assessment of the motivation and self-attitudes of individuals with disabilities. Extensive reliability and validity studies have been conducted on the ATDP, all of which support both high reliability and construct validity (Bolton, 1985).

**2.** *The Sex-Role Egalitarianism Scale.* This instrument was developed to provide information on attitudes toward equality between the sexes, with particular attention to including both items reflecting attitudes toward women in nontraditional roles and those reflecting attitudes toward men in nontraditional roles (King & King, 1986). The 95-item alternate forms represent the five content domains or role categories of marital, parental, employment, social-interpersonal-heterosexual, and educational. Adequate validity and reliability data have been developed, and the measure is particularly useful when exploring with university students the areas of sex roles (King & King, 1990).

**3.** *Attitudes Toward Women Scale.* This short (25-item) scale explores attitudes about the rights and roles of women in such areas as vocational, educational, and intellectual activities; dating behavior and etiquette; sexual behavior and marital relationships (Spence, Helmreich, & Stapp, 1973). Though developed in the early 1970s, the items describe attitudes toward the roles of women in society that different people still have. The scale itself is a shorter form of the original attitudes toward women scale generated by Spence, Helmreich, and Stapp, and the items in the briefer instrument evolved from an item analysis performed on the data from 241 female and 286 male students at a southwestern university. Normative data from student and parent samples were also collected (Spence, Helmreich, & Stapp, 1973).

**4.** *Attitudes Toward Feminism and the Women's Movement Scale.* This is a brief measure of affective attitudes toward the feminist movement, and reliability and validity studies on a sample of 117 female and male college students suggest a highly internally consistent and valid attitudinal measure (Fassinger, in press). It can be used by counselors and related human service professionals who need a very brief measure to identify individuals expressing a range of pro-feminist positions (Fassinger, in press).

Although these four instruments are only a very limited indication of those measures that explore attitudinal beliefs, they suggest that it is possible to identify societal attitudes toward certain populations. Attitudinal measures can frequently be used as a supplement to infor-mation gathered during a structured client interview. But the counselor should evaluate item content and the reported reliability and validity studies before using them in an assessment situation.

## Stress

Another factor very much represented in the client's environment are stressors, namely, the different demands made on the person. Demands are often conceptualized as originating within the person, such as adjusting to the aging process, an illness, or the loss of family members or friends. But many stressors are caused by the physical environment, such as overcrowding; the expectations of others in the workplace that one perform in a certain way; and family or work role ambiguity, overload, and insufficiency. Role insufficiency refers to a lack of challenge in an individual's work environment. Changing economic conditions and societal conflicts expressed in neighborhood violence can also cause stress. When living and working conditions, for example, stimulate frustration or if technology brings unaccustomed change, or there is pressure from imposed standards to behave in a certain manner, persons usually experience stress.

Although stress is an everyday event, the counselor's understanding of how the client's environment is producing unwelcomed stress will be an important factor when developing intervention plans. There are many environmental sources of stress, and because stress usually resides in the eye of the beholder, an evaluation of one's perception of life stressors is an integral part of eventual client adjustment. Variables that can assist counselors in their appraisal of client stress are the factors of controllability, predictability, familiarity, and imminence. If individuals believe, for example, that they have some control over predictable life events, such as retirement or geographic relocation, then the stressors could be reduced. Many stressors emanating from the environment, however, are neither predictable nor familiar, and occur suddenly, like unexpected layoffs, eruptions of violence, and natural disasters. The continued presence of harmful circumstances, specifically of the kind represented in role strains caused by work, family, or other community pressures, can slowly strip away the protection that people develop to insulate themselves against these threats (Pearlin, Lieberman, Menaghan & Mullan, 1981). All of these phenomena usually demand a period of readjustment during which the person's system struggles to reestablish a homeostasis.

A measure that has been frequently used by counselors to explore the impact of life events on clients is the Social Readjustment Rating Scale (SRRS) (Holmes & Rahe, 1967) discussed in Chapter 5. One concern with this measure is that the SRRS is dominated by events that are clearly negative or undesirable, events that generate great frustration, so that it is possible that frustration rather than the change itself is the stimulus for most of the stress. Stressors induced by the environment, as well as existing positive or negative attitudes, are important to identify during the client appraisal process. This identification can make a difference in whether plans are developed that will lead eventually to effective life functioning for clients. There is also another environmental dimension that should be identified, especially when considering the development of programs to address client problems. The results of a needs assessment can facilitate an appreciation of why certain programs adequately serve their clients, or why they do not. These issues will be discussed in the following section.

## NEEDS ASSESSMENT

The assessment of needs is perhaps the most important part of planning or evaluating any new program. Needs assessment has become an important concept in community mental health (Stewart, 1979). It is absolutely fundamental to evaluation, because there is no way to do a complete evaluation without knowing what clients need. Traditionally, needs assessment has been defined as a determination of the difference between what is and what ought to be, or between the actual and the ideal. Cook (1989) stated that a need assessment is bound by four general parameters: (1) the target of analysis must be determined; (2) a method to contact the target must be specified; (3) a measurement scheme must be developed; and (4) data must be interpreted to decision makers. Actually, needs assessment should be operationalized in terms of the several ways it has normally been done. Assessment of needs in community mental health and welfare has usually been related to the assessment of a deficit, the social problems involved, or the desire for new services that may demand analysis (Stewart, 1979). Scriven and Roth (1978) explained that the principal weakness in a needs assessment approach is that it appears to require that one know what the ideal state is in order to determine a need. These authors suggested, consequently, the definition of need as "the gap between actual and satisfactory" (p. 1). Need is a relative concept, however, and can be viewed "as a discrepancy from some recognized standard or as the gap between an individual's desired and actual situation" (Cook, 1989, p. 462). The word *need* can be both a noun and a verb, or it can describe a condition of lack, a want, or anything that is felt to be needed.

Stewart (1979) proposed the following definition of needs assessment: "A comprehensive needs assessment is an activity through which one identifies community problems and resources to meet the problems, develops priorities concerning problems and services, and is part of program planning and development of new or altered services" (p. 294). Needs assessments vary in comprehensiveness, complexity, cost, length of time to be conducted, information received, and relative effectiveness. Within these programs there can be many approaches, such as key informant, community forum, rates under treatment, social indicators, and field survey. An explanation for each approach follows:

**1.** *Key informant.* This is an activity based on information secured from those in the area who are in a position to know the community's needs and utilization patterns. The kinds of persons normally sought as key informants include public officials; administrative and program personnel in the health and welfare organizations of the community; health service providers from both the public and private sectors, including physicians and public health nurses; the program clinical staff of agencies such as community mental health centers, vocational rehabilitation organizations, guidance clinics, and others engaged in either the delivery of primary care or the administration of health programs. One of the disadvantages to this approach is the possibility of bias when the key informant is part of the program (Cook, 1989).

**2.** *Community forum.* This approach relies on individuals who are asked to assess the needs and service patterns of those in the community. Though similar to the key informant's approach, the circle of respondents is widened to include persons from within the general population. A forum study is designed around a series of public meetings to which all residents are invited and asked to express their beliefs about the needs and services of the community. Two limitations to this approach include problems in attracting a true cross section of program constituents and the possibility of obtaining mainly negative information (Cook, 1989).

**3.** *Rates under treatment.* This activity is based on a descriptive enumeration of persons who have utilized the services of the health and welfare agencies of a community. The underlying assumption is that the needs of the population in the community can be estimated from a sample of persons who have received care or treatment. This approach may overlook unserved groups that are most in need of services.

**4.** *Social indicators.* This activity utilizes inferences of need drawn from descriptive statistics found in public records and reports. The underlying assumption of this approach is that it is possible to make useful estimates of the needs and social well-being of those in a community by analyzing statistics or factors found to be highly correlated with persons in need. These statistics are regarded as indicators of need.

**5.** *Field survey.* This approach uses data from a sample or entire population of a community. This activity begins by conceptualizing and operationalizing the methods by which valid information can be obtained most practically and economically.

The methods employed to gather information about client or community needs are varied. They include the interview questionnaires, tests, group interviews, performance review, and records and reports study. Although the interview affords the maximum opportunity for free expression of opinion, it is time-consuming and usually can reach relatively few people. But the questionnaire can reach many people in a short time, is relatively inexpensive, and gives an opportunity of expression without fear or embarrassment. This method, however, may be difficult to construct and has limited effectiveness in getting at causes of problems. Tests are useful as diagnostic tools to identify specific areas or deficiencies but often lack validation for many specific situations. Also, needs have to be defined and the respondents should be able to place these needs in some order of priority. A Likert scale is often used as a response format, especially when the counselor is interested in individual difference between respondents. To achieve some prioritization of needs, rank ordering through paired comparison is usually the scaling method of choice. In this process a need is contrasted with each other need, and respondents choose one need from every pair of needs. The proportion of times a need is chosen results in a ranking of that need among all other needs rated (Cook, 1989).

The group interview can stimulate the giving of suggestions and promote general understanding and agreement, but it is also time-consuming and initially expensive. Performance reviews as a method for collecting information are also time-consuming, but they can produce precise information about a job or someone's performance. Finally, records and reports studies are able to provide objective evidence of results of problems as well as suggest clues to trouble spots. But they do not show causes of problems or possible solutions, and may not reflect the current situation or recent changes.

All of these methods are used in the many needs assessment approaches, with perhaps the interview, the questionnaire, and the examination of reports and records being the most frequently used. Also, any one specific needs assessment approach may use a variety of these methods to gather information. This can be illustrated in the following example.

As a community counselor, you wish to develop a program in your community mental health center to treat and reduce cocaine use among adults in your geographic or catchment area. To explore the usage situation, you could specify the target population of police officials, administrators of outpatient clinics in hospitals, and perhaps, if you have access to them, selected users of the drug. You would

be following a key informant and community forum approach in needs assessment with, when available, the rate-under-treatment technique, supposing that you can have access to those users who have utilized the services of a health agency in the community. When contacting the target population, you may utilize an interview or questionnaire method. Their use would depend on your available time and your knowledge of how to construct a questionnaire or to conduct an interview. These methods would be ways to find out as much as possible about the characteristics of the population using cocaine, for example, age, sex, frequency, how drugs are obtained, and specific client needs.

After collecting the information about cocaine and the relevant factors, you would analyze the data from the interviews or questionnaires to determine, in the Scriven and Roth (1978) framework, what your program should have to be, to be viewed as satisfactory. This determination could also include meeting with other program directors in the region and obtaining their ideas on the critical needs of these cocaine users, and also to discover what treatment modalities, if any, have worked. Talking with other individuals engaged in similar activities helps you to develop a program that is built on their successes and tries to avoid their failures.

Needs assessment, consequently, is comprehensive and develops information that is essential for program planning. Needs assessment is also an area in program evaluation that should always be considered when conducting any type of program evaluation activity. Many programs or agencies are begun without determining the needs of the target population. Frequently, an evaluator is requested to assess the effectiveness of a program, when the relevant question would be: "Was the program developed in harmony with an established client need?"

# CONCLUSION

As explained in this chapter, environmental assessment embraces many dimensions, each of which could make an impact on the client's living, learning, and working abilities. The following case example illustrates the importance of the counselor evaluating environmental factors that might influence a client's life functioning.

**EXERCISE**

## Case Study

Harry, age 41, married with four children, has been referred to you. You are a mental health counselor working with a large industrial company in its employment assistance program. Harry was hired six months ago because of his academic degree in mechanical engineering and had ten years experience in this field before his previous company relocated to another country. Feedback from his supervisor indicates that Harry has been late to work several times, becomes very angry when his team leaders try to improve his productivity, and tends to remain silent when co-workers attempt to engage him in conversation. At work he appears depressed much of the time. During the initial interview, Harry reveals that he liked his previous job very much. His wife didn't want to move, especially since now they are living close to his mother, who is an alcoholic and intrusive into their family affairs. Because of the high cost of living in his new location, their affordable home is quite small for six people. The neighborhood is also undergoing many changes, and Harry's two oldest children, girls who are 14 and 12, are afraid to walk home by themselves from school.

The initial interview suggests many environmental stressors that could influence Harry's work performance. These stressors are apparently perceived by Harry as pressures that demand appropriate coping responses. But at present, because of the several changes that have occurred for Harry and his family, it may be difficult for him to utilize these coping resources to combat the stressors.

**1.** Considering the material discussed in this chapter, what are the environmental factors that should be identified by the counselor?

**2.** Of the five environmental assessment approaches explained in this chapter, which one do you think is the most appropriate to use for Harry's assessment? Why?

## REFERENCES

Altman, B. M. (1981). Studies of attitudes toward the handicapped: The need for a new direction. *Social Problems, 28,* 1–5.

Anderson, J. E. (1963). Environment and meaningful activity. In R. H. Williams, C. Tibbitts, & W. Donahue (Eds.) *Processes of aging,* Vol. 1. New York: McGraw-Hill.

Arokiasamy, C. M., Rubin, S. E., & Roessler (1987). Sociological aspects of disability. In S. E. Rubin & R. T. Roessler (Eds.), *Foundation of the Vocational Rehabilitation Process* (3rd ed., pp. 91–121). Austin, TX: Pro-Ed.

Barker, R. E. (1968). *Ecological psychology: Concepts and methods for studying the environment of human behavior.* Stanford, CA: Stanford University Press.

Bolton, B. (1985). Measurement in rehabilitation. In E. L. Pan, S. S. Newman, T. E. Backer, & C. L. Vash (Eds.), *Annual Review of Rehabilitation, 4,* 115–148, New York: Springer.

Bronfenbrenner, U. (1979). *The ecology of human development.* Cambridge, MA: Harvard University Press.

Chavis, D., Hogge, J. & McMillan, D. (1986). Sense of community through Brunswick's lens. *Journal of Community Psychology.* Vol. 14, 1, pp. 24–40.

Cook, D. W. (1989). Systematic need assessment: A primer. *Journal of Counseling and Development, 67,* 462–464.

Fassinger, R. E. (in press). Development and testing of the attitudes toward feminism and the women's movement scale. *Psychology of Women Quarterly.*

Fassinger, R. E. (1944). Development and testing of the attitudes toward feminism and the women's movement (FWM) Scale. *Psychology of Women Quarterly, 18,* 389–402.

Greenblatt, M., Emery, P. E., & Glueck, B. (1967). *Psychiatric research report: Poverty and mental health* (No. 21). Washington, DC: American Psychiatric Association.

Greenhaus, J. H., & Callahan, G. A. (1994). *Career management.* Orlando, FL: Harcourt Brace College Publishers.

Hawley, A. H. (1950). *Human ecology: A theory of community structure.* New York: Ronald Press.

Hersey, P. & Blanchard K. H. (1972). *Utilizing human resources* (2nd ed.). Englewood Cliffs, NJ: Prentice Hall.

Holland, J. L. (1966). *The psychology of vocational choice: A theory of personality types and model environments.* Waltham, MA: Blaisdell.

Holland, J. L. (1973). *Making vocational choices: A theory of careers.* Englewood Cliffs, NJ: Prentice-Hall.

Holmes, T. H., & Rahe, R. H. (1967). The social readjustment scale. *Journal of Psychosomatic Research, 11,* 213–218.

Huebner, L. A. (1980). Interaction of student and campus. In E. Delworth, G. Hanson, & Associates, *Student services: A handbook for the profession* (pp. 117–155). San Francisco: Jossey-Bass.

Huebner, L. A., & Corazzini, J. G. (1984). Environmental Assessment and intervention. In S. D. Brown & R. W. Lent (Eds.). *Handbook of counseling psychology* (pp. 599–621). New York: John Wiley & Sons.

Kantor, J. R. (1924). Principles of Phychology (Vol. 1) Bloomington, IN: Principia Press.

King, L. A., & King, D. W. (1986) Validity of the sex-role egalitarianism scale: Discriminating egalitarianism from feminism. *Sex Roles, 15,* 207–214.

King, L. A., & King, D. W. (1990). Abbreviated measures of sex role egalitarian attitudes. *Sex Roles, 23,* 659–673.

Magnusson, D. (1981). Problems in environmental analysis: An introduction. In D. Magnusson (Ed.), *Toward a psychology of situation: An interactional perspective* (pp. 3–7). Hillsdale,, NJ: Lawrence Erlbaum.

McAndrew, F. T. (1993). *Environmental psychology.* Pacific Grove, CA: Brooks/Cole.

Moos, R. H. (1973). Conceptualizations of human environments. *American Psychologist, 28,* 652–665.

Moos, R. H. (1974). Systems for the assessment and classification of human environments: An overview. In R. H. Moos & P. Insel (Eds.), *Issues in social ecology.* Palo Alto, CA: National Press Books.

Moos, R. H. (1976). *The human context: Environmental determinants of behavior.* New York: Wiley-Interscience.

Moos, R. H. & Gerst, M. (1974). *University residence environment scale manual.* Palo Alto, CA: Consulting Psychologists Press.

Moos, R. H., & Trickett, E. J. (1974). *Manual: Classroom environment scale.* Palo Alto, CA: Consulting Psychologists Press.

Pearlin, L. I., Lieberman, M. A., Menaghan, E. G., & Mullan, J. T. (1981). The stress process. *Journal of Health and Social Behavior, 22,* 337–356.

Pervin, L. A. (1968). Performance and satisfaction as a function of individual-environment fit. *Psychological Bulletin, 69,* 56–58.

Riger, S. (1984). Ecological and environmental influences on the individual. In K. Hellerr, R. Price, S. Reinharz, S. Riger, A. Wanderrsman, & T. D'Aunno (Eds.), *Psychology and community change* (pp. 117–142). Homewood, IL: Dorsey Press.

Rogers-Warren, A., & Warren, S. F. (Eds.). (1977). *Ecological perspectives in behavior analysis.* Baltimore, MD: University Park Press.

Scriven, M., & Roth, J. (1978). Needs assessment: Concept and practice. *New direction for program evaluation,* 1.

Seymula, G., & Schleser, R. C. (1986). A reappraisal of vocational evaluation from an ecological systems perspective. *Rehabilitation Literature, 47,* 224–229.

Spence, J. T., Helmreich, R., & Stapp, J. (1973). A short version of the attitudes toward women scale. *Bulletin Psychoanalytic Soc., 2,* 219–220.

Stern, C. G. (1970). *People in content: Measuring person-environment congruence in education and industry*. New York: Wiley.

Stern, G. (1964). P = f(P.E.). *Journal of Personality Assessment, 28,* 161–168.

Stewart, R. (1979). The nature of needs assessment in community mental health. *Mental Health Journal. 15,* 287–295.

Stokols, D. (1992, January). Establishing and maintaining healthy environments. *American Psychologist,* 6–22.

Walsh, W. B. (1973). *Theories of person-environment interaction: Implication for the college student*. Iowa City, IA: American College Testing Program.

Walsh, W. B., & Betz, N. E. (1985). *Tests and assessment*. Englewood Cliffs, NJ: Prentice-Hall.

# 8

# COMMUNITY COUNSELING WITH INDIVIDUALS

In Chapter 2, we presented a model of community counseling in which counseling is one of six intervention skills needed by professionals in this field. The other five requisite skills (which will be discussed in future chapters) are educating, coordinating, programming, consulting, and advocacy. Counseling is, in many ways, the most basic of these six skills, since it establishes the relationship with the client that is also necessary for all the other skills to be fully effective. Counseling provides the client and the counselor with exploration and clarification of the problem that is of concern to the client and of the solution to that problem that the client hopes to achieve. It is where the contract between the client and the counselor is negotiated, and where the working alliance between the counselor and the client is established. This relationship permits both parties to attempt whichever interventions appear warranted and mutually acceptable in pursuit of their mutually agreed upon goal.

In Chapter 5, we reviewed some of the conceptualizations of human development, of the problems that arise in the course of that development, and of the aims for intervention in those problems. The community counselor must integrate these three elements into a consistent, personally useful system by which to

select the specific procedures to be used in counseling different clients. As stated at the end of Chapter 1, a number of broad principles underlie the counseling orientation, including:

1. Respect for the individual
2. The premise that given the opportunity, normal growth and development will naturally take place
3. That counseling is an educational process that requires active participation by the client
4. That counseling works primarily by building on strengths, rather than by attacking weaknesses
5. That counseling seeks to assist the client to learn to define realistic goals and to identify, mobilize, and develop the personal and environmental resources needed for achieving those goals
6. That in working with the client toward these purposes, the counselor utilizes scientifically validated techniques

Within this framework, each counselor must establish his/her own logically derived and empirically validated basis for determining which techniques should be used (or at least tried first) in helping a given client to cope with a particular problem or to achieve a particular goal.

## EFFECTING CHANGE

Implicit in any resulting conceptualization of the counseling process is the aim of helping a client to change (coping capacity and/or the situation). Therefore, another necessary consideration for the counselor in formulating his/her systematic approach to intervention is knowledge about how the process of change occurs. As with most of the broad-based phenomena that have been considered by the social sciences, a large number of competing models of the change process have been proposed. These models generally were developed out of different contexts, and consequently any one of them may be better or worse than other models in explaining change in a particular situation. (Presumably, the closer the particular situation is to the context in which the model was originally developed, the better the model will work in accounting for the situation. For example, a model derived from studying change in lower socioeconomic-class Hispanic women would probably do better at predicting change in a client of that gender, ethnic, and socioeconomic group than would a model derived from studying upper-class, Anglo-Saxon men.) In analyzing change in organizations, Beckhard and Harris (1977) proposed a principle that is equally applicable to individuals: that there is a natural tendency to resist change, even in an uncomfortable situation ("Better the devil you know than the devil you might meet"). Change will only occur when the present situation is felt to be sufficiently untenable that the person is moved to attain the necessary state of both high readiness and high capability for that change. Therefore, in some instances in which a change seems appropriate to both the client and the counselor, it may be necessary for the counselor to increase, rather than to diminish,

the client's anxiety or discomfort in order to precipitate the desired change. (Naturally, care must be taken that the anxiety or discomfort is not raised so high that it immobilizes the client.) Similarly, Wheelis (1975), a psychoanalyst, proposed a sequence of steps that he believed to be necessary for change: "The sequence is suffering, insight, will, action, change" (p. 102).

Once the inertia has been overcome, it is necessary for the counselor to have a model to guide his/her handling of the change process. One model of change in human systems (that is, individuals, families, groups, organizations, or communities) was proposed by Capelle (1979). This model suggests that change involves a nine-step process, these successive steps being:

1. Analyze the situation.
2. Assess the potential for change.
3. Set outcome criteria.
4. Generate alternative solutions.
5. Make a decision.
6. Develop a plan.
7. Implement the plan.
8. Evaluate performance.
9. Reward performance, following which, return to Step 1, analyze the changed situation, and proceed through the successive steps.

## PHASES OF TREATMENT

In most mental health professions, the nine steps just listed are usually collapsed into four phases of the treatment process: (a) assessment (Steps 1, 2, and 3); (b) planning (Steps 4, 5, and 6); (c) intervention (Step 7); and (d) evaluation (Steps 8 and 9).

The specific direction taken in these four phases by any mental health professional is determined by:

**1.** The ethos of the particular profession to which the professional belongs (thus, psychiatrists think in terms of diagnosing, treating, and curing an illness; community counselors, in terms of improving coping capacities and changing the environment to promote growth and development).

**2.** The professional's own conception of mental health, mental health problems, and the aims of intervention within the framework provided by the ethos of the profession.

**3.** The context of the particular client-counselor relationship (for example, is the client there voluntarily or under compulsion; are there other constraints on the counseling process, etc.).

**4.** The characteristics of the client, the client's problem, and the client's life situation.

Given these stipulations, we may now examine the four phases of the treatment process.

## Assessment

For the community counselor, the questions to be explored in the assessment process include:

**1.** What motivates the client to seek to change at this time?

**2.** How does the client see his/her problem?

**3.** How do I conceptualize the client's problem in terms that I as a professional can work with?

**4.** Are the answers to Questions 2 and 3 compatible with each other?

**5.** What does the client seek as the outcome of counseling?

**6.** What can I ethically and realistically work toward as the outcome of counseling?

**7.** Are the answers to Questions 5 and 6 consistent with each other?

**8.** Can this outcome be put in terms of measurable goals?

**9.** What are the client's perceptual, defense, and reasoning processes?

**10.** What is the impact of these processes on how the client sees the problem and on the desired outcome?

**11.** What is needed in order to attain the agreed-upon outcome?

**12.** What assets and skills does the client have that can be used in attaining that outcome?

**13.** What resources in the client's environment may be brought into play to support the desired change?

**14.** What additional skills must the client develop and/or what environmental changes must be effected in order to attain the desired outcome?

**15.** Are these changes in the client and/or the client's environment realistically possible?

**16.** Is the client sufficiently motivated to do what is necessary to bring about these changes?

**17.** Do the client and I feel that we will be able to work together effectively?

**18.** Can we define the problem, the possible ways to deal with it, and the criteria for determining how well it has been dealt with in terms that we both find acceptable?

**19.** What are the probable and the possible consequences for the client if counseling is not successful? That is, do the risks of failure outweigh the benefits of success? If so, should counseling still be undertaken?

## Planning

If the client and counselor can agree on these issues, then they may move on to the planning phase. In this phase, the client and counselor consider the advantages and disadvantages of each possible alternative approach to solving the problem, agree on one as worth trying first, and arrange the sequence of actions to be implemented. The choice of approach may be based on the one judged most likely to succeed, the one most likely to have the greatest positive impact, the one with the fewest negative consequences of failure, or the one that can be accomplished in the least time. The choice will at least in part depend on the nature of the problem and the client's capacity to deal with failure or with delay of gratification.

Brickman et al. (1982) pointed out that both the counselor's and the client's views of who is responsible for the problem (the client or someone else) and of who is responsible for the solution (the client or someone else) determine the approach that will be selected in trying to solve the problem. An incorrect attribution as to the responsibility for either the problem or its solution will lead to the choice of an inappropriate (and therefore probably ineffective) strategy of intervention.

## Intervention

Once the problem has been defined as a way that it can be attacked (that is, in terms of specified behaviors to be changed and, where possible, the sources of those behaviors within the client and the client's environment) and a plan of attack has been agreed on, it can be carried out. Naturally, no plan is ever able to foresee all the effects of each of its elements. Thus, evaluation of an intervention must be done along with, as well as at the completion of, the intervention phase. Where the ongoing evaluation indicates the need for it, the intervention may have to be modified or replaced and the plan may have to be changed.

## Evaluation

Assuming that no contradindications arose and the intervention was pursued to its completion, its results can then be evaluated. This evaluation should be structured in terms of how effective the intervention was in remedy-

ing the problem as originally defined (that is, the extent to which the originally specified behaviors changed in the desired direction).

As is implicit in the preceding paragraph, the method used for initially assessing the extent of the problem may sometimes also be used to evaluate how much the problem has changed following the intervention. It may be noted that one cannot necessarily attribute that change to the intervention. Conditions in the client's life outside of counseling may have changed, thus precipitating a change in the client's problematic behavior or removing the source of the problem. The client may have been ready to change on his/her own, and seeking counseling was a way to justify or to celebrate the change rather than to make it occur. Nonetheless, if the desired change has occurred, one must conclude that the aims of the counseling were fulfilled.

In pursuing the four phases of the treatment process, three established sets of professional tools are available to the counselor: (1) methods for assessing the client, the setting, and the problem; (2) techniques for intervening; and (3) methods of evaluation. Individual and environmental assessment were discussed in Chapters 6 and 7, respectively. The rest of this chapter will be devoted to a discussion of intervention. The third topic—methods of evaluation—is discussed in Chapter 15.

It doubtless will not have escaped the reader's notice that there is no section devoted to a discussion of the planning phase. This is because the systematic study of this phase is still at a relatively early stage of development, and those pioneering models that have been developed (for example, Beutler & Clarkin, 1990; Seligman, 1986, 1990) largely conform to a medial model, psychotherapy orientation. Butcher, Scofield, and Baker (1985) examined the effects of the counselor's problem-solving style on a simulated treatment planning task. In their review of the state of knowledge on this subject, Butcher et al. (1985) stated that research to date indicated that counselors tend to decide on a treatment strategy very early in their contact with a client; that counselors rarely consider more than a few alternative intervention approaches; that counselors resist changing their initial assessments, even when faced with contradictory evidence; and that competence in planning is not consistent but seems to vary with the nature of the case. These conclusions strongly point to the need for concerted study of the planning phase, so that effective techniques and skills of planning can be developed and incorporated into counselor education and counseling practice. The model presented in Chapter 2 (Figure 2.1) provides a potentially useful framework for planning within a community counseling orientation.

## TECHNIQUES OF INTERVENTION

To summarize the earlier discussion, the assessment phase of the treatment process seeks to determine three categories of information:

**1.** The nature, extent, and (if possible) causes of the client's problem

**2.** The potential for changing the client and/or the client's environment in such a way as to mitigate the problem and/or to enable the client to cope with it

**3.** The criteria to be used to evaluate the effectiveness of the intervention

From the assessment, the community counselor should thus have a picture of the client's problem, the environmental context of that problem, and the resources the client has available or can develop that will allow him/her to cope with that problem. The nature and extent of a problem determine the overall goals of an intervention, which may be for:

**1.** Facilitation: smoothing the path of normal development so that the individual's maximum potential in a given area can be realized.

**2.** Prevention: avoiding a problem that has not yet occurred but is likely to if no steps are taken.

**3.** Remediation: stopping the continued operation of a problem.

**4.** Rehabilitation: overcoming the residual effects of a problem that is no longer creating new difficulties.

**5.** Enhancement: improving the client's life situation above its present level (which may be good or bad).

The intervention for any of these levels may involve: (a) mobilizing and applying resources that already exist in the client toward overcoming the problem, (b) developing those other resources that are necessary for coping with the problem, and/or (c) changing the environment to mitigate the problem and/or to facilitate its solution.

Particularly important to the community counseling orientation is the mobilization and the development of the client's resources. A number of authors (Anthony, 1979; Goldstein, 1981; Hersen & Bellack, 1976; Jacobs, Kardashian, Kreinbring, Ponder, & Simpson, 1984; L'Abate, 1980; to name just a few) have proposed lists of necessary skills and ways of helping to develop them in clients who are experiencing mental health problems. In the introduction to his book, Goldstein (1981) catalogued about 30 prior articles by various authors, each of which lists a different compendium of skills. These skills include everything from problem solving to communicating, from assertiveness to empathy, from listening to negotiating. Goldstein himself compiled a list of 50 separate skills needed by mental health clients, which he grouped into five categories: (1) social skills, (2) skills for dealing with feelings, (3) skill alternatives to aggression, (4) skills for dealing with stress, and (5) planning skills. Goldstein went on to indicate how these skills could be taught to clients, using such social learning theory techniques as modeling, role-playing, feedback, transfer of training, and self-reward.

A discussion of techniques of skill building would be misleading if one did not point out that techniques are only as effective as the capacity of the counselor to enlist the client's active participation in learning and applying these skills. Thus, the community counselor must possess two sets of skills if interventions of the type discussed here are to be effective: (1) the skills of relating to the client so that the client takes an active role in the counseling process, and (2) the skills to teach needed techniques to the client.

In addition to mobilizing and, where needed, developing resources in the client, the community counselor always has under consideration the option of changing the client's environment to mitigate the problem being worked on. Is the client in a destructive living arrangement, in an overly stressful work setting, or facing economic collapse? Will helping the client effect a change in the situation be enough, on its own, to resolve the problem?

The counseling relationship provides a setting for exploring these alternatives. In the past, numerous "schools" of counseling (i.e., systems of theory and related methods of intervention) were formulated by practitioners who found them to be personally effective systems. The counseling literature contains a number of books that survey the theories and methods proposed by the better known schools (psychoanalytic, client-centered, behavioral, humanistic, etc.), for example, Corey (1991), Cottone (1992), and Prochaska and Norcross (1994). The literature also contains an even larger number of books by the founders or the proponents of individual schools, presenting their own particular approaches to intervention. As noted in Chapter 5, some of these approaches focus on the client's cognitive processes (for example, Ellis's rational-emotive therapy), others focus on the client's affective processes (for example, psychoanalytic approaches), and

still others focus on the client's overt behavior (behavioral approaches). Some emphasize providing a completely open, accepting forum for expression and exploration of feelings (for example, client-centered-counseling), while others emphasize setting strict limits like those the client must learn to deal with in real life (for example, Glasser's [1965] reality therapy).

In recent years, counselors have tended to move away from blind allegiance to a single school, and have instead tried to pick and choose specific methods or concepts from a variety of schools, applying them where it appears appropriate to do so. Eclecticism, however, has its own set of hazards, as indicated in the paper by Brabeck and Welfel (1985) and the rejoinders to it by Patterson (1985) and Rychlak (1985). Certainly, there were limits to the old approach of strict adherence to one school, even to the extent that in some instances counselors wrote off clients who did not respond to their approach as being "unmotivated" or "resistant" rather than questioning the appropriateness of the principles and practices of their school for that client. The danger of eclecticism, however, is that unless the counselor has a systematic basis for selecting among the wide range of available techniques, the choice of technique becomes haphazard and therefore not susceptible to scientific evaluation. Without knowing which technique is effective at what point in the counseling process with what sort of client facing what problem in what context, the choice of technique becomes random and the counselor loses any claim to professional expertise. Therefore, a number of systems have been proposed for organizing techniques and suggesting when to apply them. Among these are the ones proposed by Beutler (1983); Bruce (1984); Frey and Raming (1979); Hershenson (1982); Howard, Nance, and Myers (1987); L'Abate (1981); and Ponzo (1976).

Another approach to this problem has been to develop texts that emphasize general principles of relating to clients, rather than specific techniques. Carkhuff (1993), Egan (1994), Ivey (1994), and Young (1992) are among the more recent books that have adopted this approach. For example, Carkhuff (1993) proposed that the counseling process could be broken down into four phases: (1) attending, to facilitate the client's involvement in the process; (2) responding, to facilitate the client's self-exploration; (3) personalizing, to facilitate the client's understanding and ownership of his/her problems, goals, and feelings; and (4) initiating/facilitating the client's taking action to achieve his/her goals. Carkhuff further proposed that a counselor can be rated on a nine-item scale (from 1.0 for not even attending to 5.0 for initiating the client to take action, in half-point intervals), representing the hierarchy of counseling skills involved in being able to assist a client to move through the four phases of the counseling process. Carkhuff detailed each of the skills making up the hierarchy (1.5—attending; 2.0, 2.5, and 3.0—responding to content, feeling, and meaning, respectively; 3.0 and 4.0— personalizing meaning and personalizing problem, goal, and feeling; 4.5 and 5.0— defining goals and initiating steps, respectively). To take another example, Egan (1994) proposed a different three-stage process model for counseling: (1) reviewing problem situations and unused opportunities, (2) developing the preferred scenario, and (3) determining how to get there.

Finally, some authors have attempted to tease out one essential issue in the counseling process that transcends schools or techniques, to study that element in detail, and then to suggest an approach to counseling based on it. Thus, Janis and Mann (1977) studied the decision-making process; and based on their findings, Janis (1983) proposed a model for counseling about personal decisions. Likewise, Schlossberg (1984) studied adult life transitions, and she and others (Elliott, 1985) have written on counseling about these transitions.

It should be noted that the approaches mentioned here are representative, rather than exhaustive listings. Thus, the reader who is left with the impression that a bewildering array of theories, principles, methods, and techniques of intervention coexist (and sometimes compete) within the field of counseling has perceived the state of affairs accurately. At this point in the development of the field, systematic studies are needed to determine which of these elements are effective under what particular combination of client, counselor, problem, and setting variables. This is a never-ending process, because people and conditions are forever changing; but we cannot establish even broad principles unless we approach the task systematically. The counseling profession is now making a concerted effort on this task (Forsyth & Strong, 1986). There is good reason to expect that if properly controlled studies are done and appropriate outcome evaluation techniques are used, the field will be able to develop an empirically validated system for selecting and using particular interventions based on relevant, clearly specified parameters.

## SPECIFIC CONSIDERATIONS FOR COMMUNITY COUNSELORS

Since all counselor education programs include courses that provide detailed coverage of counseling theories and methods, it is not necessary for us to repeat that material here. We shall, however, suggest that in studying those theories, the community counseling student should be particularly concerned with how well each theory fits the premises of community counseling. For example, since community counseling is based on a premise of normal, healthy development, one should consider whether a given theory was derived from work with healthy, normally functioning persons or from the treatment of person with psychiatrically definable conditions (for example,

Freud's derivation of the principles of psychoanalysis from his clinical work with persons suffering from neuroses). As another example, since community counseling emphasizes the interaction between the person and that person's environment, one should consider whether the theory in question places essentially equal stress on the person and the environment; or like most theories proposed before World War II, neglects environmental factors. Further, since community counselors work with a broad cross-section of the community, one should consider how applicable the theory is to both men and women, to persons of different socioeconomic levels, to members of minority groups, to persons with disabilities, and to persons of different sexual orientations.

Of course, no existing theory of counseling meets all of these criteria; and so until such a theory is constructed (an unlikely prospect for some time to come), the community counselor must recognize the limitations of existing theories and must judiciously select those theories or parts of theories that best fit both the counselor's conceptualization and the principles of community counseling.

Based on a review of theories of development, Hershenson (1993) suggested that two dimensions on which counseling theories could be rated for appropriateness for inclusion were: (1) the degree to which the client's internal drive was conceptualized as growth seeking (as opposed to discomfort reducing), and (2) the degree to which the client's relationship to the environment was one of active negotiation (as opposed to one of passive recipient of environmental impacts). While client-centered theory, with its premise of self-actualization, approached the first of these two criteria and cognitive, contextualist (Steenbarger, 1991), and systems theories approached the second criterion; the counseling theories of Blocher (1987) and of Ivey and Goncalves (1988) were judged to best fit both of these criteria simultaneously.

Blocher (1987) proposed a theory of "developmental human ecology [that] represents a merger of ecological and developmental psychology" (p. 68) as best fitting the premises of counseling and providing it with a distinctive approach. This theory is based on two premises: (1) "that human beings are characterized by a basic drive toward competence or mastery of the environment" and (2) "that we need to understand more about the ways in which competence develops in natural environments" (Blocher, 1987, pp. 68–69). According to Blocher (1987), "A developmental human ecology is concerned…primarily with the transactions between individuals and their learning environments" (p. 59). Problems arise when "serious *discontinuities* between the coping capacities of the individual and the demands of the environment occur" (p. 60). The function of counselors is "to help developing individuals bridge major discontinuities and overcome the obstacles that they create to higher levels of human development…by creating and staffing special learning environments in which people can acquire the coping and mastery behaviors needed to bridge discontinuities" (p. 61). Specific learning environments will depend on the client's developmental level and particular needs, but all learning environments must contain three essential elements: (1) an opportunity structure in which new behaviors can be tried out, (2) a support structure that provides affective and cognitive supports for the person trying to change his/her behavior, and (3) a reward structure to reinforce positive changes. Thus, this model eschews the medical model approach of seeking to identify and root out psychopathology, instead taking as its "unit of analysis the 'ecosystem,' that is,…the immediate physical, social, and psychological context of the transactions between the individual and the environment" (Blocher, 1987, pp. 66–67).

The other model identified as best fitting the premises of community counseling is the one proposed by Ivey and Goncalves (1988).

This model conceptualized four stages of cognitive development based on a modification of Piaget's four-stage system (summarized in Chapter 5). The stages proposed by Ivey and Goncalves are: (1) sensori-motor (incorporating Piaget's sensory-motor and preoperational stages); (2) concrete (equivalent to Piaget's third stage); (3) abstract (equivalent to Piaget's fourth stage of formal operations); and (4) dialectic, defined as "the search for truth or for better and more complex levels of thinking" (Ivey & Goncalves, 1988, p. 408).

Based on an analysis of the client's problem, the client's developmental level, and the client's environmental context, the counselor selects an appropriate counseling style. As the client grows, the counselor shifts to a counseling style appropriate for the client's new developmental level (generally higher, but may also be lower). "No matter where the counselor begins with the client, the objective is to move through the different developmental levels" (Ivey & Goncalves, 1988, p. 411) . Clients at the sensori-motor stage cannot act on their emotions or respond appropriately to their environment. Therefore, they require control, direction, environmental structuring, and counseling strategies that "emphasize emotional, sensory experience in the here and now" (p. 410), such as are found within Gestalt approaches. For clients at the concrete stage, "the objective is to help clients begin to operate on their own actions and emotions and to help them understand some patterns of linear causality" (p. 411) that will permit them to act on their environment in an intentional way. Behavioral, decisional, and reality therapy approaches provide useful strategies for working with clients at this level. For clients at the abstract level, counselors "help clients in thinking about their actions, thinking, and emotions, assisting them in the mobilization of the cognitive and metacognitive operations" (p. 411). The client at this level should "find an appropriate environment that helps him or her develop the possibilities of formal operations before moving into other levels of development" (p. 411). Existential strategies are useful at this level. "Finally, the fourth environmental style, called dialectics, has two central objectives. The first is to help the client identify underlying epistemological and ontological issues and move on to new constructs about self and reality. The second is to introduce a dialectical interaction between the client and the environment" (p. 411). Here, certain cognitive and object relations strategies are applicable. According to Ivey and Goncalves (1988), counseling should be a developmental process through which people, by coming to know themselves, "construct their being....This being, in turn, is their developmental relationship with their environments and with each other" (p. 412).

Thus, both theories focus on healthy development and person-environment interaction (Ivey and Goncalves somewhat more heavily on the former and Blocher somewhat more heavily on the latter). These two theories are therefore particularly useful for community counselors seeking to construct their own personal working theory to guide their practice. It may be noted that the two theories are not necessarily mutually exclusive. For example, one might construct a theory that utilized Blocher's learning environments, with those environments structured according to Ivey and Goncalves's four developmental levels. Other community counselors might find neither Blocher's nor Ivey and Goncalves's concepts fit their experience or conceptual style. In that case, it is incumbent on those counselors to look elsewhere. Nonetheless, regardless of what sources are used and how they are put together, each counselor must end up with a personally meaningful theory of intervention to guide his/her practice. Without it, one cannot function in a professionally responsible way. We shall close this discussion by noting that the model of community counseling that we presented in Chapter 2 permits wide latitude in the choice of one's counseling approach, as long as that approach (1) includes an emphasis on the interaction of the person with the environment (that is, the client and the community), and (2) involves identifying and mobilizing the personal and environmental resources needed to attain a goal or to cope with a problem.

## SPECIAL ISSUES IN INTERVENTION

One cannot end a discussion of intervention without mentioning a few special issues that come up with great frequency in the practice of community counseling. These include: (a) crisis intervention, (b) issues of diversity, (c) career issues, (d) substance abuse, (e) psychoactive medication, and (f) rehabilitation procedures.

### Crisis Intervention

Ordinarily, one thinks of seeking counseling as the result of a carefully thought out decision, arrived at over time. There are, however, crisis situations that bring people to counselors with no prior preparation. Caplan (1964), one of the major contributors to the field of community mental health, noted this phenomenon and developed the concept of crisis intervention to address this need. Killilea (1982) summarized Caplan's conception of crisis as "a period of disequilibrium accompanied by psychological and physical distress of a relatively limited duration which temporarily taxes a person's ability to cope competently or to achieve mastery. Crisis can be predictable or unpredictable" (p. 164) Marriage, the birth of a child, retirement, or many of the other items on Holmes and Rahe's (1967) list discussed in Chapter 5 are predictable crises. Violence, spouse or child abuse, accidents, natural disasters (floods, earthquakes), acts of terrorism, the sudden death of a loved one, or an unplanned marital separation are unpredictable crises. It may be noted that the term

"crisis" has been overused recently by politicians and by the media, so that now a crisis has come to mean little more than an event that has risen to sufficient significance to merit being given attention. As Caplan used the term *crisis intervention,* however, it had more far-reaching implications. These implications included the potential for the counselor to use the crisis to improve the client's coping by assisting the client cognitively to take the following steps (Killilea, 1982):

**1.** Appraise the threat and actual danger in the situation.

**2.** Seek new information and perspectives about the situation, including new ways of dealing with it.

**3.** Seek appropriate role models for how to behave.

**4.** Reassure oneself that the situation can be mastered by referring to analogous past experiences that had been mastered.

**5.** Link the current situation to personal competencies that had been demonstrated in the past.

**6.** Obtain feedback about one's behaviors, plans, and goals.

**7.** Modify one's level of aspiration.

**8.** Acquire growth-promoting skills.

Thus, a crisis may provide growth experiences by using it as a learning experience and as an opportunity to expand the range of experiences in which the client has been able to cope successfully. Hence, the notion of a crisis may be restructured into a positive experience, rather than merely viewed as a potentially disastrous event.

### Issues of Diversity

When Frank Parsons opened the Vocation Bureau in 1908, one of his concerns was to assist the flood of Eastern European immigrants then arriving in Boston to enter the American workforce. Thus, from its foundation as a field, counseling has been confronted by issues of diversity. For the following half century, however, the issue of diversity was rarely addressed in the counseling literature, because the prevailing national view was that America was a "melting pot" to which all groups contributed and into which all groups were expected to submerge their separate identities in order to form a homogeneous American culture. While this goal was never achieved, it was only during the past three decades that an alternative paradigm has emerged. The currently prevailing national paradigm is multiculturalism, that America is composed of a large number of subgroups, none of which are expected to give up their special identity, and that these groups coexist and interact within a common legal, political, and economic milieu. Because of both the failure of the old paradigm to meet its needs and the emergence of the new one, the field of counseling has devoted ever-increasing attention to issues of multiculturalism and their effects on counseling. This topic has now become central enough to the profession that (as noted in Chapter 2) CACREP and NBCC have designated social and cultural foundations as one of the eight core areas of the counseling curriculum. Therefore, as with theories of counseling, we shall only touch upon this issue here, since it will be the topic of a full course elsewhere in the community counseling curriculum. One should not, however, infer from the limited coverage of this topic here that the topic is of less than major importance to community counselors.

Indeed, the *Journal of Counseling and Development* recently published a 250-page special issue that was completely devoted to the topic of multiculturalism as a central consideration in counseling (Pederson, 1991). Many of the central premises and expectations of American counseling do not hold true in other cultures or in many American subcul-

tures. These premises include reliance on verbal exchange as the primary mode of communication; acceptance of the importance of showing up for appointments on time; willingness to self-disclose; the value of insight; the benefits of delaying gratification while working on problems; the goals of self-actualization, of independence, and of individual success. Clients of different racial and ethnic backgrounds, religious beliefs, sexual orientations, socioeconomic backgrounds, disability statuses, and native languages must each be approached as individuals, but with sensitivity to their concerns and expectations as members of one or more diverse groups. Sue, Arredondo, and McDavis (1992) reported on proposed multicultural competences for all counselors. These competences include attitudes and beliefs, knowledge, and skills in: (1) awareness of one's own values, assumptions, and biases; (2) understanding the perspective of clients from other cultures; and (3) developing intervention strategies and techniques that are effective with clients from other cultures. Given the particularly diverse population with which community counselors come into contact, it is especially important that they develop these competencies.

## Career Issues

Since most adolescents in our society are making vocational choices (or prevocational educational choices) as they prepare to leave high school and since most adults engage in work, it is almost inevitable that community counselors will find themselves faced with clients who are having problems with career development and/or work performance. In some instances, the best course of action is to refer the client to a National Certified Career Counselor (NCCC), who specializes in these sorts of issues. In other cases, however (for example, where a relatively uncomplicated career issue arises in the course of counseling entered into because of a problem in some other area of functioning), the community counselor may decide that the best course of action is to deal with the career issue within his/ her already established relationship with the client. Indeed, a long-debated issue within the field is whether career counseling is distinct from personal counseling. A recent special section in *The Career Development Quarterly* (Subich, 1993) presented a number of viewpoints on this issue, including Super's (1993) suggestion that all counseling can be placed along a continuum, the two poles of which are situational and personal. The view held by the authors of this book is that career counseling is distinctive in terms of the problems addressed (that is, problems with career development or with work performance) and some of the technology used (for example, career interest and abilities tests, occupational and labor market information, and computerized career guidance programs), but is not distinctive from other types of counseling in its use of relationship building, counseling techniques used, or its use of the full range of other community counseling skills (that is, educating, coordinating, programming, consulting, and advocacy).

At the dawn of the field of counseling, Frank Parsons (1909) wrote;

> *In the wise choice of a vocation there are three broad factors: (1) a clear understanding of yourself, your aptitudes, abilities, interests, ambitions, resources, limitations, and their causes; (2) a knowledge of the requirements and conditions of success, advantages and disadvantages, compensation, opportunities, and prospects in different lines of work; (3) true reasoning on the relations of these two groups of facts.* (p. 5)

With a few additions (consideration of personal values and personality traits; recognition that career development is a lifelong, ongoing process and not a single one-time choice; greater sophistication about the decision-making process), this statement still guides much of contemporary career counseling. Yost and Corbishley (1987) have proposed an eight-stage model for career counseling: (1) initial assessment of the problem and agreement on a career counseling process and goal; (2) client self-exploration of values, interests, abilities, experiences, and personal issues that may impinge on the career counseling process; (3) synthesizing and making sense of the information gathered in the previous step, listing personal and environmental resources and barriers; (4) generating a list of possible career alternatives consistent with the picture formed in step 3; (5) obtaining occupational and labor market information about each of the alternatives generated in the previous step; (6) making a choice among these alternatives (or deciding to seek other options); (7) making plans to reach the goal chosen; and (8) implementing those plans. Brown and Brooks (1991) have suggested that before one proceeds with career counseling, one must assess a client's motivation and capacity for cognitive processing. They indicated that since career counseling involves information processing and logical thinking, the counselor should only proceed with career counseling if the client demonstrates the ability to think clearly and rationally. If the client fails to demonstrate this ability, that capacity should be developed (by personal counseling, environmental change, or medication) before career counseling is begun. Similarly, clients who demonstrate generalized indecisiveness (cannot decide on anything in their lives) must address that problem before approaching the task of career decision-making.

Once career counseling is undertaken, at least three specialized procedures are often applied: (1) specialized career testing; (2) use of occupational information, both from print materials and from computerized programs; and (3) development of decision-making skills. (One may note that these three areas directly reflect the three elements in Parsons's

[1909] original statement: knowledge of self, knowledge of career options, and "true reasoning" to connect these two bodies of knowledge.) Specialized career assessment instruments include measures of abilities, work values, career maturity, and interest inventories (such as the widely used ones developed by Strong, Kuder, and Holland). These measures are discussed in Brown and Brooks (1991), Yost and Corbishley (1987), and other books on career counseling, as well as in a number of books on the specific topic of career assessment (for example, Kapes & Mastie, 1988; Zunker, 1994). Similarly, both printed sources of occupational information (such as the U.S. Government's *Dictionary of Occupational Titles* and *Occupational Outlook Handbook* as well as publications of commercial publishers) and computerized career guidance programs (such as CHOICES, DISCOVER, and SIGI) are covered in detail in almost all books on career counseling.

Having the knowledge of self and knowledge of career options obtained from counseling and from the specialized techniques just discussed, the client must decide which option to pursue. Harren (1979) suggested that each person has a decision-making style composed of a mixture of three components: (1) rational (logical, planful, information-based), (2) intuitive (based on his/her emotions), (3) dependent (passively relying on others' views). Usually one component predominates. Rational decision-makers need help in locating information. Intuitive decision-makers need help in making sure that they take that objective information into consideration, and dependent decision-makers need help in taking responsibility for their decisions.

Aside from personal styles, decision-making skills can be taught. These include listing pros and cons of each alternative or rank ordering the factors entering into one's decision for importance and then ranking each alternative on each of these factors. For example, if the client values variety of work more than a large salary, a lower-paying option that offered variety should be chosen over a higher-paying, routine type of work.

In addition to career choice problems, people may experience other types of work problems such as layoffs, conflicts with supervisors, performance problems (for example, procrastination) or conflicts between work and other life roles. In all these cases, the principles and skills of community counseling may be applied. Personal and environmental resources needed to solve the problem should be identified, developed, and mobilized, and barriers should be removed or avoided. Work is clearly a major life activity for most people; thus, community counselors should approach work problems in essentially the same way that they would approach problems in other areas of living.

## Substance Abuse

Alcohol and drug abuse (to which some would add smoking, habitual overeating, compulsive gambling, and any other addictive, self-destructive behavior patterns) are personal problems that have direct social consequences (accidents caused by drunk drivers, crime by drug addicts seeking money to support their habits, dissolution of families and loss of work productivity due to abuse of drugs and alcohol). Although this is not a book on substance abuse or the treatment of substance abusers (which range from some countries that supply drugs to addicts at government expense to others that jail or even execute them), and although separate specialized courses and certification procedures for addiction counselors exist in the United States, community counselors are nonetheless very likely to encounter clients with one or another of these addictions.

Working with individuals with addiction problems raises particular problems for many mental health professionals for several reasons. One of these reasons is that most mental health professionals subscribe at some emotional level to a middle class ethic, which states that in last analysis, people have some personal responsibility for their actions. Addictions are generally seen as problems that one has gotten oneself into, because they involve the introduction of a substance into the body. Therefore, at some level, many mental health professionals (psychiatrists, clinical psychologists, psychiatric social workers and nurses, as well as community counselors) find addicts to be morally reprehensible people. Thus, the professional may unconsciously treat such clients in a less helpful, more punitive way. Coupled with this phenomenon is the fact that for many addicts, the attraction of remaining on the substance exceeds the appeal of getting off it. Therefore, these clients may act consciously or unconsciously to sabotage any treatment aimed at helping them get rid of the addiction. Many addicts have arrived at counseling under duress; the alternative given to them was to go to jail. Needless to say, the combination of a disapproving counselor and an unwilling client does not make the chances for successful outcome very great.

Therefore, frequently those individuals with drug or alcohol problems who are motivated to overcome their addiction have turned to professionals who themselves had the addiction and are therefore more likely to be sympathetic and nonjudgmental in their approach, or to nonprofessional self-help groups. Groups such as Alcoholics Anonymous and similarly designed self-help groups for drug addicts appear to have been more successful than professionals in helping many persons with addiction problems. Professionals, of course, have often tended to question these conclusions, basing their attacks on the fact that these groups do not follow scientific procedures in substantiating their claims of success. For example, professionals argue that because of the anonymity practiced by some of these groups, successes are counted over and over while failures drop out and cannot be traced.

Today, however, the territorial warfare between these self-help groups and the professions seems to have largely cooled off. Each side recognizes that the other has something to contribute to helping the person with an addiction. Therefore, community counselors should do all they can to link a client with an addiction problem to an appropriate self-help group, so that the client can gain the benefits of both professional and self-help interventions in a coordinated way. It is, however, important that the counselor be familiar with the self-help group to which the client is referred, so that the match is a good one. For example, inner city and suburban chapters of Alcoholics Anonymous may be totally different from each other in membership and in approach. Just to tell a client to "go to AA meetings" may do that client a disservice, if the client happens to come from a poverty-level environment and ends up at a meeting peopled only by upper-income, highly educated suburbanites.

## Psychoactive Medication

Although medicine (including psychiatry) is the only profession legally allowed (in most jurisdictions) to prescribe psychoactive medications, it is essential for a community counselor to know if a client is receiving such medications. Assessment or intervention without that information would be totally ill-advised. There are numerous books and journal articles devoted to the topic of psychoactive medication, which focus on the chemical structure, physiological effects, and/or clinical use of these drugs. The principal concern for the community counselor, however, is the effects of these drugs on the client's functioning both within and outside of the counseling process. Goldsmith (1977) and Ponterotto (1985) have particularly focused on the issue. Ponterotto (1985) emphasized the responsibility of the counselor to contact the physician prescribing the medication (after obtaining the client's permission to do so) in order to: (a) gain specific information needed for the conduct of the counseling process, (b) gain needed information about the action and side effects of the drug as they appear to be manifesting themselves in the counseling situation, and (c) coordinate the counseling with the chemotherapy so that they do not work at cross-purposes. It is incumbent on the counselor to know exactly what information is needed and why it is needed before contacting the prescribing physician. It is essential that the counselor and the physician work cooperatively toward goals that are agreed upon by the client, counselor, and physician. For example, it would be counterproductive if the physician was prescribing heavy doses of an antianxiety medication at a time at which the counselor was attempting to mobilize and channel the client's anxiety toward a productive goal, such as going to work. Thus, a balance may have to be sought between too much anxiety for the client to be functional and too little for the client to be motivated. This may require an adjustment in the client's medication that only the physician can make.

In general, psychoactive medications are divided into three major categories: (1) antipsychotic drugs, (2) antidepressants, and (3) antianxiety drugs. Antipsychotic drugs are those that reduce or control the symptoms of schizophrenia, manic-depressive psychoses, or psychotic depression. These include, among other drugs, the phenothiazines and lithium salts (the latter specific to manic-depressive conditions). Antidepressants, the two major classes of which are tricyclics and monoamine oxidase inhibitors (MAO inhibitors), relieve depression; they do not, however, cause happiness or euphoria. There are three major classes of antianxiety drugs: barbiturates, benzodiazepines, and antihistamines. These drugs are intended to relieve anxiety, fear, or tensions. (See Ponterotto, 1985, for an excellent summary of the effects, side effects, and counseling implications of these drugs.)

A final point on this topic is in order. Not all medications have the same effect on all clients. Thus, for some persons, a particular antianxiety drug may actually increase the person's feelings of tension or foreboding. In such cases, a different medication may be called for. If the counselor observes this phenomenon of contrary effects of a medication being given to a client, the counselor should have the client (or if that is not possible, the counselor should) inform the prescribing physician immediately.

## Rehabilitation Procedures

The area of mental health rehabilitation is gaining continuously increasing attention, particularly in work with clients who have had more severe, long-term mental health problems and/or who have been out of the mainstream of society because of institutionalization or incapacity. It is of interest that the earliest writings on mental health rehabilitation (e.g., Davis, 1946) focused on helping the client adjust to the mental hospital setting, whereas the current focus (e.g., Anthony, 1979; Anthony, Howell, & Danley, 1984; Lamb, et al., 1971) is almost exclusively on adjustment to the community. This, of course, reflects the shift from long-term hospitalization to deinstitutionalization, which has taken place over this time period. Moreover, Anthony (1979) has marshalled evidence to show that traditional psychodiagnosis, psychotherapy, or measures of hospital inpatient behavior are not predictive of rehabilitation outcome in the community. Therefore, Anthony has developed a system for assessing and acquiring the skills and the environmental supports a client will need for successful adjustment to living, learning, and working in the community. As a skill-based model, Anthony's approach is entirely consistent with the model of community counseling espoused throughout this book. It is, indeed, even difficult to draw a clear line between the roles of the community counselor, the mental health counselor, and the rehabilitation counselor when they are working in this area, other than that the rehabilitation counselor usually has greater responsibility for the client's vocational functioning (preparing for, obtaining, and keeping a job). Even so, a competent community counselor must understand the area of work and career behavior, and a competent mental health rehabilitation counselor must understand psychosocial functioning as well as work. Anthony, Cohen, and Pierce (1979) have produced (along with additional co-authors on several of the individual volumes) a set of six manuals, plus an instructor's guide, which comprise the *Psychiatric Rehabilitation Practice Series*. These manuals cover the skills the counselor needs in: (a) diagnostic planning, (b) rehabilitation programming,(c) professional evaluation, (d) career counseling, (e) career placement, and (f) community service coordination. The authors of the series assert that these are the empirically determined skills needed in order to be an effective practitioner of mental health rehabilitation. In turn, the counselor's skills attained through this series are used to assess and promote client skills and environmental supports needed for coping in the community setting. For example, the client skills needed to live in a halfway house may include skills in hygiene, relaxation, nutrition (self-selection of diet), responsibility (e.g., to take own medication), punctuality, interpersonal relationships, and dealing with crises. Other skills may be necessary for getting or keeping a job. The counselor must be able to work with the client to prepare a list of skills needed to achieve a particular goal, to structure a way for the client to gain those skills that he/she does not already have, and to assist the client in learning to apply those skills in the current situation. At the same time, the counselor, along with the client, must assess the environmental supports and barriers and work to maximize the former

and to eliminate or compensate for the latter. Thus, mental health rehabilitation (like rehabilitation of persons with physical disabilities) seeks to help the client achieve independent living and productive employment by building on the client's residual assets and by creating an environment that will help the client to succeed. Rehabilitation is becoming more widely recognized as a necessary part of the counseling process.

## EXERCISE

In this chapter, we have looked at individual intervention strategies and issues of particular relevance to community counselors. Now test what you have learned from this chapter by applying it to the following case.

### Case Study

Jack is 21 years old, tall, muscular, single, and unemployed. He is of mixed race, the oldest son of a woman who married when he was 3. Jack's natural father was killed by police in a house burglary after a long criminal history. His mother and stepfather have six other children. His stepfather is disabled and receives Social Security, and the maternal grandfather also lives in the family home. The family has lived in the projects on the southwest side of the city for 12 years and has been supported by public aid and the mother's regular part-time employment.

Jack's adjustment to school was marginal and characterized by poor grades, tardiness, absenteeism, shyness, boredom, inability to concentrate, frustration, alienation from peers, and few friends. He dropped out of school during his sophomore year. He engaged in a series of thefts and drinking sprees, which usually led to arrests. The agencies to which he was referred since the age of 17 include Job

Corps, Youth Corps, Technical Institute, Community Mental Health Outpost, County Department of Corrections, and the State Psychiatric Institute.

Jack was referred to numerous jobs and job-training programs during a four-year period. The explanation most frequently given by Jack and his mother was that he lost the job because "he could not take orders" and "do what was expected of him." He is thought to be lazier than the other children in the family, who are either working or in school. Two years ago Jack was diagnosed as depressed and "functionally borderline retarded" with a history of acting-out behavior.

Jack has been followed for the past three years by a counselor from the State Psychiatric Institute. He was requested to come in periodically to report "how things are going" and was seen by the counselor for unscheduled appointments when he would "stop by," because he was in the neighborhood of the hospital. In his interviews with the counselor, Jack indicated his desire to leave the city and to have a job, money, friends, a home, and a wife. He would frequently state desires to go to school and to learn what he had not learned, i.e., how to read, write, spell, and do arithmetic. His problems with drinking, holding down a job, keeping appointments, following through with plans, establishing relationships with people, and vagrancy have persisted. He complained that his mother pushed him to get a job. He had feelings of worthlessness, fears of going to jail or being killed. He wanted to stay out of trouble, have friends, and get away to make a new start somewhere else. Further reports from Jack had to do with his efforts to read and to "teach himself." He was unsuccessful in these attempts. His thinking has remained confused. He has been to Texas, Louisiana, and Oklahoma, where he has relatives. He is currently unemployed, receives public aid, is transient, and now wants to stay in touch with a counselor.

Jack's former counselor has recently retired from his job at the State Psychiatric Institute, and Jack has been reassigned to you for continued counseling. In his initial interview with you, he expressed the wish to "get it together…find a job…go to school…to find out who I am."

Employing a community counseling orientation, plan your treatment approach to working with Jack. Indicate: (1) your goals, (2) the steps in your plan to reach these goals, (3) the techniques you will try first at each step, and (4) how what you propose in your answers to parts 1, 2, and 3 are consistent with a community counseling orientation.

## REFERENCES

Anthony, W. A. (1979). *The principles of psychiatric rehabilitation.* Amherst, MA: Human Resources Development Press.

Anthony, W. A., Cohen, M. R., & Pierce, R. M. (1979) *The psychiatric rehabilitation practice series* (Vols. 1–6 plus instructor's guide). Amherst, MA: Carkhuff Institute of Human Technology.

Anthony, W. A., Howell, J., & Danley, K. S. (1984). Vocational rehabilitation of the psychiatrically disabled. In M. Mirabi (Ed.), *The chronically mentally ill: Research and services* (pp. 215–237). New York: Spectrum.

Beckhard, R. & Harris, R. T. (1977). *Organizational transitions: Managing complex change.* Reading, MA: Addison-Wesley.

Beutler, L. E. (1983). *Eclectic psychotherapy: A systematic approach.* New York: Pergamon.

Beutler, L. E., & Clarkin, J. F. (1990) *Systematic treatment selection.* New York: Brunner/Mazel.

Blocher, D. H. (1987). *The professional counselor.* New York: Macmillan.

Brabeck, M. M., & Welfel, E. R. (1985) . Counseling theory: Understanding the trend toward eclecticism from a developmental perspective. *Journal of Counseling and Development, 63,* 343–348.

Brickman, P., Rabinowitz, V. C., Karuza, J., Jr, Coates, D., Cohn, E., & Kidder, L. (1982) . Models of helping and coping. *American Psychologist, 37,* 368–384.

Brown, D., & Brooks, L. (1991). *Career counseling techniques*. Boston: Allyn and Bacon.

Bruce, P. (1984) . Continuum of counseling goals: A framework for differentiating counseling strategies. *The Personnel and Guidance Journal, 62*, 259–263.

Butcher, E., Scofield, M. E., & Baker, S. B. (1985). Clinical judgment in planning mental health treatment: An empirical investigation. *AMHCA Journal, 7*, 116–126.

Capelle, R. G. (1979) . *Changing human systems*. Toronto: International Human Systems Institute.

Caplan, G. (1964). *Principles of preventive psychiatry*. New York: Basic Books.

Carkhuff, R. R. (1993). *The art of helping* (7th ed.). Amherst, MA: Human Resources Development Press.

Corey, G. (1991) . *Theory and practice of counseling and psychotherapy* (4th ed.). Pacific Grove, CA: Brooks/Cole.

Cottone, R. R. (1992). *Theories and paradigms of counseling and psychotherapy*. Boston: Allyn and Bacon.

Davis, J. E. (1946) *Rehabilitation: Its principles and practice* (rev. ed.). New York: Barnes.

Egan, G. (1994) *The skilled helper: A problem-management approach to helping* (5th ed.). Pacific Grove, CA: Brooks/Cole.

Elliott, T. R. (1985) . Counseling adults from Schlossberg's adaptation model. *AMHCA Journal, 7*, 133–141.

Forsyth, D. R., & Strong, S. R. (1986). The scientific study of counseling and psychotherapy: A unificationist view. *American Psychologist, 41*, 113–119.

Frey, D. H., & Raming, H. E. (1979). A taxonomy of counseling goals and methods. *Personnel and Guidance Journal, 58*, 26–33.

Glasser, W. (1965). *Reality therapy: A new approach to psychiatry*. New York: Harper & Row.

Goldsmith, W. (1977). *Psychiatric drugs for the non-medical mental health worker*. Springfield, IL: Charles C. Thomas.

Goldstein, A. P. (1981). *Psychological skill training: The structured learning technique*. Elmsford, NY: Pergamon.

Harren, V. A. (1979). A model of career decision-making for college students. *Journal of Vocational Behavior, 14*, 119–135.

Hersen, M., & Bellack, A. S. (1976). Social skills training for chronic psychiatric patients: Rationale, research findings, and future directions. *Comprehensive Psychiatry, 17*, 559–580.

Hershenson, D. B. (1982). A formulation of counseling based on the healthy personality. *Personnel and Guidance Journal, 60*, 406–409.

Hershenson, D. B. (1993). Healthy development as the basis for mental health counseling theory. *Journal of Mental Health Counseling, 15*, 430–437.

Holmes, T. H., & Rahe, R. H. (1967). The social readjustment rating scale. *Journal of Psychosomatic Research, 11*, 213–218.

Howard, G. S., Nance, D. W., & Myers, P. (1987). *Adaptive counseling and therapy: A systematic approach to selecting effective treatments*. San Francisco: Jossey-Bass.

Ivey, A. E. (1994). *Intentional interviewing and counseling: Facilitating client development in a multicultural society* (3rd ed.). Pacific Grove, CA: Brooks/Cole.

Ivey, A. E., & Goncalves, O. F. (1988). Developmental therapy: Integrating developmental processes into the clinical practice. *Journal of Counseling & Development, 66*, 406–413.

Jacobs, H. E., Kardashian, S., Kreinbring, R. K., Ponder, R., & Simpson, A. R. (1984). A skills-oriented model for facilitating employment among psychiatrically disabled persons. *Rehabilitation Counseling Bulletin, 28*, 87–96.

Janis, I. L. (1983) . *Short-term counseling: Guidelines based on recent research*. New Haven, CT: Yale University Press.

Janis, I. L., & Mann, L. (1977). *Decision making: A psychological analysis of conflict, choice, and commitment*. New York: Free Press.

Kapes, J. T., & Mastie, M. M. (Eds.). (1988). *A counselor's guide to career assessment instruments* (2nd ed.). Alexandria, VA: National Career Development Association.

Killilea, M. (1982). Interaction of crisis theory, coping strategies, and social support systems. In H. C. Schulberg & M. Killilea (Eds.), *The modern practice of community mental health* (pp. 163–214). San Francisco: Jossey-Bass.

L'Abate, L. (1980). Toward a theory and technology for social skills training. *Academic Psychology Bulletin, 2*, 207–228.

L'Abate, L. (1981). Classification of counseling and therapy theorists, methods, processes and goals: The E-R-A model. *Personnel and Guidance Journal, 59,* 263–265.

Lamb, H. R., & Associates. (1971). *Rehabilitation in community mental health.* San Francisco: Jossey-Bass.

Parsons, F. (1909). *Choosing a vocation.* Boston: Houghton Mifflin.

Patterson, C. H. (1985). New light for counseling theory. *Journal of Counseling and Development, 63,* 349–350.

Pedersen, P. B. (Ed.). (1991). Multiculturalism as a fourth force in counseling (Special issue.) *Journal of Counseling & Development, 70*(1).

Ponterotto, J. G. (1985). A counselor's guide to psychopharmacology. *Journal of Counseling and Development, 64,* 109–115.

Ponzo, A. (1976). Integrating techniques from five counseling theories. *Personnel and Guidance Journal, 54,* 415–419.

Prochaska, J. O., & Norcross, J. C. (1994). *Systems of psychotherapy: A transtheoretical analysis.* Pacific Grove, CA: Brooks/Cole.

Rychlak, J. E. (1985). Eclecticism in psychological theorizing: Good and bad. *Journal of Counseling and Development, 63,* 351–353.

Schlossberg, N. K. (1984). *Counseling adults in transition: Linking practice with theory.* New York: Springer.

Seligman, L. (1986). *Diagnosis and treatment planning in counseling.* New York: Human Sciences Press.

Seligman, L. (1990). *Selecting effective treatments: A comprehensive, systematic guide to treating adult mental disorders.* San Francisco: Jossey-Bass.

Steenbarger, B. N. (1991). All the world is not a stage: Emerging contextualist themes in counseling and development. *Journal of Counseling & Development, 70,* 288–296 .

Subich, L. M. (1993). How personal is career counseling? (Special section). *Career Development Quarterly,* 42, 129–191.

Sue, D. W., Arredondo, P., & McDavis, R. J. (1992). Multicultural counseling competencies and standards: A call to the profession. *Journal of Counseling & Development, 70,* 477–486.

Super, D. E. (1993). The two faces of counseling: Or is it three? *Career Development Quarterly,* 42, 132–136.

Wheelis, A. (1975). *How people change.* New York: Harper Colophon.

Yost, E. B., & Corbishley, M. A. (1987). *Career counseling: A psychological approach.* San Francisco: Jossey-Bass.

Young, M. E. (1992). *Counseling methods and techniques: An eclectic approach.* New York: Merrill.

Zunker, V. G. (1994). *Using assessment results for career development* (4th ed.). Pacific Grove, CA: Brooks/Cole.

# 9

# COMMUNITY COUNSELING
# WITH FAMILIES

Marital problems are the most common reason for referral to counseling services (Sperry & Carlson, 1991). Sholevar (1985) estimated that marital difficulties were among the concerns addressed by 75 percent of clients seeking counseling. Furthermore, given that community counselors endeavor to promote healthy development by focusing on clients and their social environments, it follows that family functioning should be an important concern for community counseling regardless of the presenting problem. But apart from family difficulties that may be presented for the counselor's attention, family members can become major resources when the counseling focus is primarily on a client's life adjustment or rehabilitation goals. Family dynamics can have a direct bearing on the attitudes and behaviors of individuals with mental or physical disabilities, or those with other difficulties (Power, & Dell Orto, 1980; Power,1995). The family is also the social group most likely to be damaged by the clients' problems and the group that must be mobilized to help clients recover from problems. With many illnesses, family members are often recognized as the secondary victims (Morrissey, 1995).

Because the family has the potential to be the community counselor's greatest ally in treatment, it should be an important focus of attention in the delivery of community counseling services. An array of services may be needed by families to deal with the impact of a chronic illness, a major life transition, or a life-threatening situation. Though community counselors have many job-related responsibilities, any attention to a client's family does not have to compromise these duties. A counselor's intervention with families usually requires an enhancement and adaptation of diagnostic, relationship, and planning skills that many counseling professionals use regularly. Family contact invites a further application of these specific skills, as well as an understanding of specific strategies that have been developed for family counseling. Though many serious family problems demand the attention of a trained family therapist or a counselor specially equipped and specializing in long-term family intervention, it is a premise of this chapter that community counselors may also have the opportunity either to alleviate selected family concerns that could be addressed during a brief intervention framework, or to work with a client's available family to accomplish adjustment goals when the client is undergoing a major life transition.

The goal of this chapter is to assist the reader to appreciate that effective community counseling demands an understanding both of family dynamics and how family members can influence an individual's life adjustment. To gain this appreciation the following topics will be discussed: (a) a definition of family; (b) a portrait of the "modern" family and its implications for the practice of community counseling; (c) selected ways of understanding the family; (d) the different approaches that have been developed for helping families; (e) selected family issues that may require the attention of the community counselor; (f) suggested roles for the community counselor when working with families; and (g) a proposed intervention model that can be utilized by community counselors. Each topic area blends with the others to form a picture illustrating the relationship between community counseling and the family. A knowledge of the family today as well as of different client problems and how they affect family members, suggest issues that can receive attention from community counselors. In turn, these factors come into sharper focus when several theoretical approaches to understanding the family are explained. These approaches then generate a background for explaining briefly the history of family counseling and for identifying the leading established directions in family counseling. The roles and functions of the community counselor when assisting families, as well as a proposed model of intervention, can be more cogently understood when an awareness is gained of the accepted approaches for family intervention.

## WHAT IS THE FAMILY?

Family today conveys many meanings to different people. Current family structures include nuclear families (husband, wife, and children), extended families (nuclear family and grandparents, aunts and uncles), stepfamilies (a single parent marries a person who is not a parent), blended families (two single parents marry, bringing children born of previous relationships together into one family), single parent families (individuals with children who have never been married, are divorced, or widowed), families consisting of a grandparent or grandparents who have become parents to their grandchild/children, adoptive families (adults accepting permanent parental responsibility for children to whom they are not biologically related), foster families (adults accepting temporary parental responsibility for children whom they are not biologically related) and gay and lesbian families (persons of the same gender in committed relationships which may or may not include rearing children.) The U.S. Bureau of the Census defines the family as two or more people who are related by blood, marriage, or adoption and who are residing together (U.S. Bureau of the Census, 1989). Persons living under circumstances outside this definition are defined as nonfamilies. Clearly these definitions exclude a large number of people (30 percent of U.S. households) from being seen as involved in family relations (Waldrop & Exter, 1992). Also, these definitions do not take into account members of extended families who may live close by and who may have considerable influence on family life (Furstenberg, 1984; Wilson, 1989). Zisserman (1981) defined the family as a nuclear family composed of spouses or one parent and offspring, functioning as a smaller unit than the preindustrial, three-generation extended family.

Historically in America the nuclear family (as typified in the television show "Father Knows Best") was perceived as the national norm (Ford, 1994). Consisting of husband, wife, and children, it emerged as the twentieth century began and reached its peak in popular acclaim and social influence in the years following World War II through the 1950s (Conger, 1981). This form tends to be child-centered and emphasizes the family as a center of nurturance and affection. It also may be more of a state of mind than social reality (Shorter, 1975). Divorce rates had risen from an estimated 1 percent in 1804 to 17 percent by the end of the 1920s, and to as high as 50 percent by 1980 (Bohannan, 1985). In the 1990s, it is estimated that two out of five children will see their parents separate (Furstenberg & Teitler, 1994) and that 35 percent of American children will be part of a stepfamily by the time they are 18 (Glick, 1989). Given these statistics, it is important for community counselors to broaden their view of family beyond the historical perception of "Father Knows Best."

## A PORTRAIT OF THE AMERICAN FAMILY

Though marriage continues to be a nearly universal experience for adults, the size of the American family has decreased. Women of childbearing age are delaying the onset of childbearing and having fewer children. In addition, there is increasingly less likelihood that the household will include individuals outside the nuclear family (Melson, 1980). Dissatisfaction with the institution of marriage itself, moreover, has not risen; only the willingness to do something about an unsatisfactory marriage has increased. In 1978, divorces numbered 1,122,000, a rate of 22 divorces per 1,000 married women, indicating that 2.2 percent of marriages ended in divorce that year (U.S. Bureau of the Census, 1979). Since 1978 the rate of divorce has increased and it is now estimated that half of all marriages ended or will end in divorce (Beer, 1988).

Divorce is no longer universally considered a symptom of a society's moral decay or social instability. Of course, whether divorce is a disruptive factor or a useful adjustment depends on the culture and one's point of view. However, separation and divorce can precipitate a host of problems for the family.

Mothers who retain custody of their children are likely to find themselves in severe economic straits within a few years after divorce (Amato, 1993). Child-support payments may dwindle to nothing, and it has been very difficult to prosecute defaulting ex-husbands. Sixty-two percent fail to comply within the first year and 42 percent make no payments at all. After 10 years, 79 percent of all ex-husbands are in noncompliance (Weitzman, 1974). "The single mother's precipitous fall in economic status is translated for the child into a new neighborhood and new school, fewer toys, treats and outings, and perhaps communication of abiding resentment against the one-time provider" (Melson, 1980, p. 44). The material and emotional losses accruing from divorce, consequently, generate stressors within a family. In turn, these stressors can cause severe life-adjustment problems or deteriorating mental health conditions that need the attention of professionals.

As a phenomenon related to current divorce statistics, another important reality for the modern family is the increase in the number of single-parent households, particularly those headed by a female. This family change has been steadily increasing since 1980. The trend from 1960 has been for percentages of white female-headed households to increase at a relatively greater rate than nonwhite, which have actually decreased (Melson, 1980). There may be joint custody of children or, in a minority of single-parent families, the father may have custody of his children.

Mills (1988) estimated that 20 percent of families begin with the birth of a child to an unwed mother who is younger than 19. Rarely is the biological father incorporated into the child's life. Consequently, children are being raised by teenage mothers. Many of these mothers work or engage in other activities outside the home, resulting in the children being left to care for themselves. Five million American children under the age of 10 years have no one to look after them when they come home from school (500,000 of them under the age of 7) (Strickland, 1985; Whitehead, 1993; Bronfenbrenner, 1988). The growing absence of adult supervision of any kind places these children at risk of injury, abuse, and death. Despite the economic and interpersonal stress this family form sustains, there is evidence that parenting out of wedlock is a pattern followed repeatedly by several generations within some families (Mills, 1988).

Concurrent with rising divorce rates has been a rise in remarriage. It is estimated that 75 percent of persons who divorce remarry, and that about half of those who remarry have minor children in their household (Beer, 1988). Coupled with statistics on single parents who later marry, it has been estimated that 35 percent of children will spend some time in a stepfamily (Glick, 1989). Stepfamilies are faced with many challenges. Ninety percent of stepchildren are members or potential members of two or more households. Having a significant adult in their lives who lives outside their home can strain children's loyalties and put stress on remarried couples. Nevertheless, there is evidence that stepfamilies often function as well or better than did the original families before the divorce (Mills, 1988).

Another component of the fabric of the "modern family" is the dual-earner couple, a reality that has become the norm in American society. The pivotal year for mothers of infants through teens was 1979, the year in which more mothers worked than stayed at home on a full-time basis (American Council of Life Insurance, 1980). Financial reasons, expanding career options, the increased educational attainment of women, the isolation of the homemaker from the extended family and support system, and changing marital status, that is, divorced or widowed, have all been identified as influences for mothers to enter the workplace (Robinson, Rotter, & Wilson, 1982). Among middle-class professionals, the dual-earner couple must make a commitment of time and energy far beyond a nine-to-five

routine (Melson, 1980). Blue-collar parents have equally serious work pressures that affect their family life. They may have to take two Jobs to make ends meet and thus work as long as career professionals.

When portraying the "modern family," attention should be given to the increasing number of families in which one or more members is assuming the responsibilities of caregiver. Technological advances, that have increased the longevity of those who are chronically ill, and demographic trends, which indicate that about three-quarters of elderly persons in need of long-term care receive informal support from family and friends exclusively (Doty, 1986), suggest that caring for an elderly relative is now considered to be a normative family stress (Brody, 1985). Toseland, Smith, and McCallion (1995) believe that the combined influence of technology and demographic trends predicts a scenario in which (a) traditional division of caregiving roles by gender will be eroded, (b) all adult children will be more likely to assume caregiving roles, and (c) all adult children will have some involvement in family caregiving.

Concurrently, there has been a shift to more egalitarian power sharing within families. The feminist movement has resulted in women having greater authority throughout society, and this change is reflected in families as well. Wife battering, which was generally tolerated (if not condoned) fifty years ago, is now dealt with as a criminal offense (Waldo, 1987). Parents' exercise of authority over children no longer includes their being allowed to physically harm them, subject them to sexual abuse, neglect their needs, or emotionally abuse them. We believe each of these changes indicate positive evolution in our society's expectations for families. At the same time, they challenge families to break with old patterns and develop new skills. Community counselors can be instrumental in helping families achieve these changes.

## UNDERSTANDING THE FAMILY

A knowledge of the most widely accepted and utilized theories of family dynamics can lay the foundation for effective intervention by community counselors. Successful assistance to troubled families depends largely on how the community counselor perceives what is going on in family life. Three theories that can provide valuable insights into family dynamics are role theory, developmental theory, and systems theory. Each can be applied to the diverse forms of family identified earlier in this chapter. Each theory also provides a context to understand the differences between "healthy" and "dysfunctional" families.

### Roles in Modern Marriage

Overs and Healy (1973) believed "that increasingly the family has come to be seen as an integrated system of reciprocal roles" (p. 87). Thus, the family as a unit functions adequately or inadequately according to the degree of role perception and the interaction among the role performances of the various members. Marital success or adjustment can be defined by the degree of congruence between the husband's and wife's perceptions of their respective roles (Overs & Healy, 1973).

Parsons and Bales's (1955) theory has stimulated more research than any other role theory. They identify two main roles in marriage, the instrumental and the expressive. The instrumental role is getting things done, namely, earning money and maintaining the outside relationships with the economic and school systems. The expressive role is primarily concerned with maintaining satisfactory relationships within the family and with the expression of feelings that are a part of intimate relationships. These functions are not exclusively carried out by any one family member. Wives shop for groceries and call schools about their children, and husbands settle quarrels among the children. In other words, in many "modern" families husbands and wives increasingly share duties that in the past were customarily reserved for the husband/father or wife/mother.

In role theory there are four concepts that are basic in understanding mental health and the family. They are role complementarity, role change, role conflict, and role reversal. Role complementarity exists when family members play different roles, which complement each other in fulfilling family functions. For example, a stepfather may listen to children's problems and complaints and their mother may offer them guidance and correction. Family role complementarity enables the family members to re-pattern their lives in such a way that family needs can still be met in an efficient manner.

Role change involves family members responding to new demands on the family by changing roles. An example would be an adolescent daughter who moves from cared-for child to part-time care providing teenager when an infant is born into the family. But changes in family roles may also be problematic. Where both husband and wife are committed to their career, couples may have difficulty managing child care. Older siblings in single parent families may be thrust into parenting younger brothers and sisters before they are capable of assuming this kind of responsibility.

Role conflict refers to two or more family members conflicting over a role. An example would be a stepfather taking on a disciplinary role when his wife feels this is her responsibility. Role reversal involves family members temporarily assuming roles that are the opposite of the roles they typically play. An example would be an adolescent daughter imagining what would be appropriate disciplinary action for her mother to take if her daughter violated an established curfew.

When understanding the family today in the perspective of role theory, the counselor is aware that roles in families are becoming increasingly less rigid and defined. The changes in family life can reflect a high complementarity of roles. In many "modern" marriages the husband and wife are colleagues, and there is a blurring of the edges of primary responsibility with more sharing of tasks. Moreover, the assessment of family role complementarity, change, conflict, and reversal can offer community counselors insight into family dynamics and guidance on what is the most appropriate intervention approach to improve family functioning.

## Developmental Theory

When a mental health crisis, such as a divorce, separation, death, or illness occurs, it occurs at a definite stage in the family's life cycle. The reaction of family members to the illness of a husband or wife can be quite different in the earlier stages of a marriage and family life than when the couple and family have been living together for many years. For example, the roles family members fulfill, which are strong determinants of how a family copes with a crisis, will vary during different stages of family life. A crisis can disrupt the balance of roles and the extent of the disruption depends on the life stage of the family.

Severe depression illustrates the intermeshing of family life stage and the disorder. For example, when a husband becomes depressed after being married for many years, the family members might find it very difficult to meet his needs for self-esteem and competency. The husband may have served as a model of emotional strength and independence throughout the marriage. His self-esteem may be closely tied in with his ability to show strength and energy, so that the loss of this role is perceived as a loss of worth. In contrast, while the wife may have become accustomed to focusing caring concern on the children, she may not have had opportunities to offer these qualities to her husband. The inability of the husband to fulfill his strong role and the possible added demands

for fulfilling a nurturance role made on the wife could create conflict and disharmony for the couple. True, such conflict may occur whether the couple is newly married or has just celebrated a twenty fifth wedding anniversary, but because the roles in the home have been so well established in a couple with more longevity, the community counselor may have a more difficult task helping the family members change roles. Counselors are more likely to be successful if they employ interventions that take into account the family's development.

Within each stage certain family tasks emerge. These family tasks reflect the assumption that developmental tasks of individual family members have an impact on the nature of a family life at a given time. Adequately handling tasks at early stages also strengthens the family's ability to handle subsequent stages effectively. Crises within a family, therefore, can be better understood when each of the family stages is explored, because each stage has its own role demands, responsibilities, problems, and challenges. The way the family comes to terms with crisis may vary according to the respective family stage.

Many systems have been developed for understanding family life stages (Havighurst, 1953; Duvall, 1971; Rhodes, 1977), but Cavan (1974) merged different family developmental frameworks and named the stages:

1. Beginning families (married couples without children)

2. Child-bearing families (oldest child: birth to 30 months)

3. Families with preschool children (oldest child: 30 months to 6 years)

4. Families with school children (oldest child: 6 to 13 years)

5. Families with teenagers (oldest child: 13 to 20 years)

6. Families as launching centers (first child gone to last child leaving home)

7. Families in the middle years (empty nest to retirement)

8. Aging families (retirement to death of both spouses)

Concepts of family development have been productively integrated into community counseling with families (Carter & McGoldrick, 1988; Wilcoxon, 1985). It is important to note, however, that the description of stages offered above is based on a "traditional" nuclear family. Transitions such as divorce, single parenting, remarriage, blending families, and stepparenting complicate development and adjustment in families, potentially altering the picture of healthy development. Furthermore, stages of development derived from examination of majority culture traditional nuclear families may not offer an accurate picture of the development of minority families (Goldenberg & Goldenberg, 1991).

## Systems Theory

One of the most important concepts in understanding families, as well as the framework for many approaches to assist families in crisis or continued dysfunction, is systems theory (Everett, 1990). A basic assumption of this theory is that all parts of a family are functionally interrelated. The family system consists of four subsystems: the marital (husband-wife interactions), the parental (parent-child interactions), the sibling (child-child interactions), and the extrafamilial (nuclear family interactions with external systems and individuals) (Office of Special Education, 1984). As stated by Power (1995) and outlined by Doherty and Baird (1983) and Herr and Weakland (1979), a family system's perspective establishes several core assumptions about families, which are:

1. The family is more than a collection of individuals. Change or stress affecting one family member affects the whole family.

2. Families have repeating interaction patterns that regulate members' behavior. All families develop implicit rules for daily living, and how people interact with each other significantly influences how they function, for better or worse. The implicit rules that govern family interactions are called boundaries. Boundaries are determined by the degree of closeness or distance among family members, the family's adaptability, and family communication. Boundary rules usually define who participates and how family functions are carried out. All families develop implicit rules for daily living. They may be shown in mealtime patterns, the patterns of handling decisions, of celebrating holidays, and of relating to outside professionals such as the community counselor. Families may also have troublesome rule-like interaction patterns, such as family members interrupting each other's conversation at any time, or singling out a particular person for blame when something goes wrong (Doherty & Baird, 1983).

3. Individuals' symptoms may have a function within the family. A physical or psychosocial symptom, for example, may become incorporated into the family interaction patterns in such a way that it seems essential for the family's harmony.

4. The ability to adapt to change is the hallmark of healthy family functioning. In the face of change, family flexibility or adaptability should be stressed.

5. Family members share joint responsibility for their problems.

6. When some behavior arises and persists that is seriously distressing either to the individual or to others concerned about the behavior, other behavior must be occurring within the system of interaction that provoke and maintains the problem behavior inadvertently and in spite of efforts to resolve it.

Watzlawick and Weakland (1977) believed that if one phrase could be used to capture the family systems approach to understanding families, it would be the "interactional context" of human behavior and human problems. The theory emphasizes the interconnectedness of human beings in their intimate environment (Doherty & Baird, 1983). It offers a point of view rather than specific information about specific people. In examining the family system one thinks not in terms of unidirectional cause and effect, but in terms of ongoing interactions. Family systems theory suggests to community counselors that individuals' symptoms may have a function within a family. For example, if the family system goal is stability, a child's illness can be seen in the larger context of keeping the family together. The sickness may be functional in terms of stabilization for a family system because it allows the fighting parents to join around the child (Berman, Lief, & Williams, 1981).

The three theoretical approaches that have been discussed, namely, roles, development, and systems, provide important insights to understanding families. They also have stimulated the development of family therapy theory. There has been an integration of role theory, development, and systems with the clinical practice of treating family problems. Helping families undergoing a transitional crisis or alleviating a selected family problem are objects of professional attention for many community counselors.

Another framework for understanding family dynamics, a framework that suggests useful guidelines for the community counselor when one initially attempts to identify the family "problem" or to discover how family members can become a resource for the client's life adjustment, are the differences between healthy and dysfunctional families. The hallmarks of healthy family functioning have been described by Lewis, Beavers, Gossett, and Phillips (1976), Power (1991), Stinnett and DeFrain (1985), and Wilcoxon (1985). Family health or family strengths may be described in terms of individual characteristics of family members or solely in terms of family group properties, and according to the aforementioned researchers can include such factors as:

1. Demonstrate a warm and trusting attitude in familial interactions.

2. Are characteristically open and mutually respectful in their interactions and speak honestly and disagree without fear of retribution.

3. Have an ability to discuss and to focus their concerns on the present, rather than on past events or disappointments.

4. Have shared, common perceptions of reality within the family.

5. Use negotiation rather than power in problem solving.

6. Promote a definite yet flexible family structure with appropriate distribution of responsibilities and privileges between parents and children.

7. Demonstrate a high level of personal initiative and assume personal responsibility for their individual choices and interests, as well as for disability-related, mental health, or career transition problems.

8. Possess an ability to discuss and to focus their concerns on the present, rather than on past events or disappointments.

9. Have the ability to adapt to change, maintaining a balance of cohesion, adaptability, and communication. But this does not mean that healthy families are always balanced. Change is an ever-present challenge to families and in times of family stress, community counselors evaluate whether family members are supportive of one another, whether role expectations are clear and flexible, and whether family rules are clear and flexible.

10. Have a willingness to take good care of themselves, which includes the family's ability to use leisure time well; to relax; to seek a balance between family responsibilities, a paid job, and recreation; and to maintain the

conviction that they must, when living with a chronic illness or assuming continued caregiving responsibilities, take appropriate, good care of themselves.

While the identification of healthy family functioning suggests the family's capacity to adapt to transitions in family life, the awareness of those traits that characterize dysfunctional families are equally important to understand when designing family intervention efforts. There are many expressions of family dysfunction, which can include:

**1.** Pathological communication, which may take the form of double-bind messages or the use of mystification. In the former, the receiver of such a contradictory message is doomed to failure whatever response is made. In the latter, the recipient is confused and befuddled by a message whose intent is to cloud over any real conflict taking place.

**2.** Enmeshment, which means that family boundaries between subsystems are blurred and members are overinvolved in each other's lives; in extreme cases, to separate from the family is to betray them. Because family membership is all-important, individuals often fail to develop a separate sense of self. In disengaged families, boundaries are rigid and members feel separate and isolated from one another. Without the experience of closeness within the family, they often cannot form relationships to people in the outside world.

**3.** Scapegoating, when one family member is distinguished from the other members, usually being labeled as pathological and the cause of family disharmony. By displacing family conflicts onto this person, underlying sources of conflict within the family can be covered over. Another self-deceptive mechanism may involve the persistence of family myths, subscribed to by all family members and convincingly presented to the outside world. Through these myths, families may initiate, maintain, and justify many of their dysfunctional interactional patterns.

Severely disturbed families, moreover, are very threatened by change, express greatest resistance to separations, and show most difficulty accepting loss and adapting to normal life developmental process changes, including aging and death. Family members also have severe difficulty making decisions related to changes; and within enmeshed families, all decisions must be made by the family. In those dysfunctional families that are also characterized by disengagement, decisions are primarily individual, and there are weak coalitions among family members, with usually a family scapegoat (Olson, Sprenkle, & Russell, 1979).

A recognition by community counselors of healthy and dysfunctional family dynamics is an affirmation of the systemic properties of family interactions, is of assistance in the intervention process, and expresses the developmental nature of family life (Wilcoxon, 1985). Many community counselors intervene with families because of transition crises; and an understanding of previously successful coping strategies, and being able to link those to the current crisis is helpful for intervention. If a current trauma is not eroding healthy family processes, but those processes are only undergoing adjustment and change, then these strengths can be effectively utilized for any family assistance. Besides building upon existing family strengths, however, there are other, established family intervention approaches. Community counselors providing family interventions may be engaged, when working with families, to improve the quality of their interaction, the structure of their relationships, the functioning of the family unit, and the family's ability to be a resource for the life adjustment of the client. To accomplish these goals, an understanding is necessary not only of the predominant approaches to counseling families but also of the development of family counseling. (The terms *family counseling* and *family therapy* are often used interchangeably in the literature. Because this book is focused on the community counseling specialty, *family counseling* will be used in this chapter.)

## APPROACHES FOR HELPING FAMILIES

### History of Family Counseling

Family counseling dates from the 1920s, when Alfred Adler initiated child guidance clinics in schools and communities (Dinkmeyer & Dinkmeyer, 1985). Adler educated parents about family dynamics, sibling rivalry, and the effects of birth order and taught them ways of appropriately disciplining children. Adlerian approaches to family counseling are still prevalent, as evidenced in programs like Systematic Training for Effective Parenting (STEP) (Dinkmeyer & Dynkmeyer, 1985). The family counseling movement gained tremendous momentum in the late 1950s when Gregory Bateson, John Weakland, Jay Haley, Don Jackson, Theodore Lidz, Stephen Fleck, Murray Bowen, Robert Dysinger, Betty Basamaria, and Warren Brady became nationally known and began to know of each other's work (Goldenberg & Goldenberg, 1980). The main focus of these researchers and clinicians was on studying families with a hospitalized schizophrenic member. From their research and clinical practice, such concepts as double bind, family homeostasis, and family boundaries were developed. These terms were used to describe the family process and to conceptualize the entire family system as the patient.

The beginning years in family counseling were marked by an orientation to research and theory, with an emphasis on understanding the family of the schizophrenic (Okun & Rappaport, 1980). Family counseling was viewed as a new way of understanding and treating mental disorders (Goldenberg & Goldenberg, 1980). In the 1960s and early 1970s, however,

such clinicians as Jay Haley, Salvador Minuchin, Nathan Ackerman and Virginia Satir grew to realize that more than treating individuals in a family context, the dysfunctional family itself must be changed. Haley (1971) also indicated that the focus of treatment should be on changing the family structure and interaction patterns. Family members must learn to relate to each other in new ways and even, if appropriate, to modify their value system. An understanding of the family moved more and more toward viewing family members as interacting individuals whose behaviors influenced each other and not simply as providing "crazy-making" environments in which to grow up (Goldenberg & Goldenberg, 1980).

These years, moreover, also spawned new professional publications on family counseling, new families (e.g., nonwhite minority families), and new outpatient settings (e.g., community mental health centers). Many approaches were followed and innovative techniques were proposed, such as multiple family therapy, multiple impact therapy, and network therapy. Multiple family therapy is an adaptation of group therapy techniques to the treatment of whole families (Leichter & Schulman, 1981). Selected families meet with a counselor weekly during which they share problems with each other and help one another in the problem-solving process. Multiple impact therapy involves an entire family in a series of continuing interactions with a multidisciplinary team of community counselors over, perhaps, a two-day period. Developed by MacGregor and his associates at the University of Texas Medical Branch in Galveston, this therapy implies that a single family in crisis receives counseling full-time for two or more days (Goldenberg & Goldenberg, 1980). Network therapy attempts to mobilize a number of people who are willing to come together in a crisis to be forged into a therapeutic force. Originally developed from work with schizophrenics in their homes, network therapy is based on the assumption that there is significant disturbance in the schizophrenic's communication patterns with all members of his or her social network, not just within the nuclear family (Goldenberg & Goldenberg, 1980). The goal of this network intervention is to capitalize on the strength of the assembled network to facilitate changes in the family system.

In the 1990s, no single approach to helping dysfunctional families completely dominates the family counseling field. Current approaches to family counseling can be organized on a continuum, which could be described as ranging from covert and historical to overt and immediate. This continuum starts with approaches that look at subconscious or historical roots affecting family functioning (psychodynamic), then approaches that focus on family structure (structural), followed by approaches that examine the more immediate behavioral exchanges between family members (strategic), and lastly those approaches that focus primarily on the on-going communication between family members (communication). While the different approaches focus on levels of family phenomena, they share the conviction that the family system is of primary importance for understanding and affecting families. It is the system of psychodynamic, structural, strategic, or communication influences that is addressed. As is typical with efforts to categorize theories, no one approach to family counseling fits cleanly and completely into just one (even broad) area on the continuum. Also, it is not likely that community counselors will use only one approach to understand and to intervene when counseling families. Community counselors often use several approaches concurrently or in sequence when working with clients and their available families.

## Psychodynamic Approach

This approach applies the techniques and strategies of individual psychotherapy to fam-

ily situations. The family counselor believes that behavior and feelings of family members will change as each member gains insight about himself/herself and about other family members. Ackerman (1966), who was a psychoanalyst, explained that family counseling involves both helping a family to have a meaningful emotional exchange and assisting the family members to get in better touch with themselves. The latter is achieved through contact with the counselor, who not only helps influence the family interactional process but also withdraws as the family attempts to deal more constructively with its problems. Ackerman considered the influences of social psychology and role theory as important when treating families in the psychodynamic context. In his approach to families, he was always interested in how people define their role (e.g., "What does it mean for you to be a mother?") and what they expect from other family members ("How would you like your son to react to this situation?") (Goldenberg & Goldenberg, 1980).

## Dynamic Structural Approach

A family systems approach which takes into account intergenerational influences on how families are structured was developed by Murray Bowen. Bowen believed that families promote within their members varying levels of differentiated identities and emotional maturity (Bowen, 1981). Poorly functioning families or families that have been traumatized (for example, by the death of a child) tend to fuse their members into a single identity, with all members highly dependent on, and emotionally reactive to, each other. The parents in poorly differentiated families are unable to satisfy each other's dependency needs and may focus their emotional needs on one or more of their children. An emotional triangle forms between the parents and the child, resulting in the child failing to achieve healthy differentiation. As an adult, this child seeks a marital partner who has similar levels of emotional neediness. They then establish a new family system that is similar to their families of origin with regard to level of differentiation. In this way, Bowen proposed that family dynamics and structure are passed from one generation to the next. Community counselors employing Bowen's approach help family members develop insight into their roles in emotional triangles and learn how to differentiate themselves and other family members within the family system.

## Structural Approach

Like Bowen, Salvador Minuchin was interested in the dynamic structure of families. Minuchin, however, emphasized the current context of family interaction and restructuring the family system in the present through various strategies (Minuchin, 1984). As a therapist he joins the family as a leader, accommodating to the dysfunctional system, diagnosing, and eventually gaining agreement with the family on a contract for change. Minuchin conceived of family pathology as resulting from the development of dysfunctional sets or reactions. These family reactions, developed in response to stress, are repeated without modification when there is conflict. As an example, a mother verbally attacks her adolescent son, the father takes the son's side, and the younger children seize the opportunity to join in and pick on their brother. All family members become involved, various coalitions develop, but the family organization remains the same, and the dysfunctional sets will be repeated in the next stressful situation. Minuchin believed restructuring is necessary.

## Strategic Approach

Jay Haley (1976, 1980) and Cloe Madanes (1981, 1984) are perhaps the best-known proponents of the strategic approach. The strategic approach acknowledges that troubled families have dysfunctional dynamics and structure, but focuses attention on how this dysfunction is expressed in specific problem behaviors. Problem behaviors in families are seen as efforts to attain power and security. The family counselor's job is to devise strategies through which power and security needs can be met without use of problem behaviors. Because families will resist change, the counselor must be both clever and authoritative when prescribing strategies. When a family implements an effective strategy, the problem behavior no longer achieves the security and power goals it originally did; and the family develops a more functional structure.

## Communication Approach

A basic assumption of the communication approach is that families will naturally develop functional dynamics and structures if they engage in honest and compassionate communication. Dysfunctional structures and problem behaviors emerge from blocks in communication. Community counselors employing the communication approach to family counseling attempt to improve family communication. This can be done by directly teaching the family communication skills and assisting them to practice these skills (Gueney, 1990). It also can be done by holding a family meeting in which the counselor participates. Through the counselor's modeling of direct communication, challenging family members to honestly answer important questions about their relationships and offering empathic responses to family members' immediate experiences, the counselor serves as a catalyst to open up communication between family members (Satir, 1982). High-quality communication between family members is innately rewarding. Once initiated it is likely to continue, allowing the family to develop healthy structures and dynamics.

With these five approaches the community counselor has many theoretical resources to draw on when planning family interventions. When assisting dysfunctional families, many counselors integrate the different viewpoints and draw from whichever perspective appears to be most relevant to a particular family. There are many family situations that really do not necessitate long-term therapy. A brief intervention may be more appropriate, and this short-term involvement with families represents a rapidly growing area for community counseling efforts (Snyder & Guerney, 1993).

In fact, short-term intervention may be the only option available for community counselors when working with families. Agency guidelines, insurance demands, and even the nature of the graduate curriculum provided for the training of counselors usually dictates brief intervention for clients and their families. Most families, moreover, choose not to participate in long-term family counseling or therapy. There are many reasons for such lack of extended participation, such as financial costs, the stigma of being associated as a family with counseling or therapy, and the perceptions that those problems related to family management of members who have chronic physical or mental difficulties are really not serious enough to warrant long-term professional counseling (Power, 1995). Families are usually more amenable to outside assistance when they realize that it will be brief and problem focused, in contrast to a longer family involvement that targets changing the family as a system.

Although the need for systematic, professional intervention with families on a short-term basis has been well established, counseling approaches for working with different problems in a brief time framework, as well as for dealing with the possibility of using the family as a necessary resource for the client's life adjustment, have not been well developed. Approaches are usually based on the clinician or counselor's individual orienta-tion, a viewpoint that may not be adaptable either for brief assistance or for many specific family problems, i.e., intergenerational, family needs among the elderly, sudden unemployment of the principal family wage earner, or the family attempting to cope with HIV infection. Utilizing the contributions from family therapy, however, an intervention approach is suggested that includes (a) an identification of the issues that should be considered when planning short-term assistance, (b) the assumption by the community counselor of specific roles when engaging in family assistance, (c) the identification of goals that are attainable within a brief, intervention framework, (d) the process itself of intervention, and (e) the settings for family intervention. Many of these factors, which comprise the suggested intervention approach, are outlined in Figure 9–1.

Note that counselors can only offer intervention to the family. Whether family members are open to an intervention opportunity depends on their family structure (membership characteristics—family size, extrafamilial system; cultural style—ethnicity, religion, socioeconomic status, geographic location; and ideologic style—their beliefs, values, and coping styles), their history of interactions with health service professionals, and the counselor's ability to invite the family to reflect and act on their own problems (Wright & Leahey, 1994).

There are a number of issues that provide a context for family intervention by community counselors. The counselor's personal attitude towards specific populations or problems can influence one's choice of intervention strategies. The struggles of those who are dealing with difficult problems, especially those that may produce stigma, such as AIDS, child abuse, other criminal behaviors, or facial disfigurements, may demand that counselors explore their attitudes about disease, sexuality, dying, prejudice, and fear (Green & Bobele, 1994).

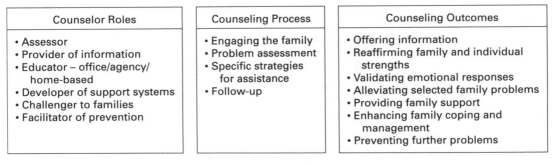

| Counselor Roles | Counseling Process | Counseling Outcomes |
|---|---|---|
| • Assessor<br>• Provider of information<br>• Educator – office/agency/<br>  home-based<br>• Developer of support systems<br>• Challenger to families<br>• Facilitator of prevention | • Engaging the family<br>• Problem assessment<br>• Specific strategies<br>  for assistance<br>• Follow-up | • Offering information<br>• Reaffirming family and individual<br>  strengths<br>• Validating emotional responses<br>• Alleviating selected family problems<br>• Providing family support<br>• Enhancing family coping and<br>  management<br>• Preventing further problems |

**FIGURE 9–1**    Counseling Intervention Model for Families

Additional issues influencing intervention approaches are the setting in which any counseling will take place, the resources available to the counselor that could be utilized for possible problem remediation, i.e., support groups, health care personnel, or other family members, the amount of burden or strain the family is currently experiencing related to the problem, the nature of the problem, previous ways that family members have managed other family difficulties, and the experience that family members may have had in articulating their needs and concerns to professionals or larger systems or organizations. A further issue is the ability of the counselor to recognize cultural diversity factors among families and changing family needs over the cycle of family life. A counseling approach that may be appropriate at one time may be irrelevant at another time. Family stressors and conflicts that emerge from various difficulties can be perceived differently at various points in the client's and family's developmental stage.

## INTERVENTION ROLES FOR COMMUNITY COUNSELORS

Intervention with families can comprise different activities. During family meetings, the counselor can assume varied roles. Five roles are identified that can be accommodated to short-term intervention. These roles are discussed here.

### Assessor

Wright and Leahy (1994) have proposed a number of questions that can be utilized during a family meeting, such as:

1. What is the agreed-upon problem that should receive attention?
2. At what area of family functioning should an intervention be aimed?
3. Could an intervention be linked to the family's strengths and previous useful strategies employed by the family?
4. Would a proposed intervention be consistent with the family's ethnic and religious beliefs?

Other areas that can be explored are:(1) the family's emotional reaction to a particular trauma and/or transition; (2) the unique composition of the family and the strengths and weaknesses inherent in that structure that could influence the family's life adjustment; (3) the amount of information the family has, and with this knowledge what expectations the family has about adaptive goals for themselves, for an ill family member, or for the individual that may be experiencing a significant transition; (4) family needs that relate to an identified presenting problem; and (5) the family's readiness for counseling intervention or for referral to another counseling resource when the counselor has the perception that long-term family therapy may be the only possibility for problem remediation.

Because of the briefness of the community counselor's usual opportunity to meet with families, assessment information may have to be obtained at more than one meeting. But regardless of the amount of time required to obtain information that suggests the "workable" family problem and that implies an appropriate intervention approach, the counselor needs to utilize basic communication skills and should create a setting during a family meeting in which people can, perhaps for the first time, take the risk of sharing their emotions and seek information about their concerns (Power, Dell Orto, & Gibbons, 1988).

## Provider of Information/Education

Family research has frequently indicated that in times of crisis, during a career transition of a family member, or when coping with a chronic illness or disability, what most families seek is timely and relevant information (Power, 1991); (Power, Dell Orto, & Gibbons, 1988). This information may focus on the important facts of a particular illness, disability, or transition, and community resources, which may include peer support groups, respite care, child day care, and financial aid opportunities. The family also needs to recognize their personal resources. Because many persons tend to overlook or underestimate their coping strengths, family members need help in acknowledging these assets.

Integral to this role of communicating information is educating families on factors that may be important for adjustment or prevention of a relapse. Education may comprise assisting an individual family to learn coping skills or other management strategies or developing psychoeducational programs for many families. Since 1985 different psychoeducational models for treatment of varied

chronic conditions such as schizophrenia and Alzheimer's disease have been developed (Keefler & Koritar, 1994). These programs target the reported needs of family members, the alleviation of the adverse effects on the families' physical and psychological health resulting from coping and daily management efforts, crisis intervention skills, improving the social functioning of the client and the family, and when possible, the prevention of relapse, especially with clients with mental illness. All of these objectives may result from the counselor's implementation of program development skills, discussed in Chapter 11.

## Developer of Support Systems

The identification of available support systems was discussed as part of the counselor's role of information provider. But family members may be reluctant to use external resources because of cultural, financial, or personal reasons, i.e., fear of stigma or embarrassment. The community counselor may then realize that he/she will be the principal source of support, or, when possible, the family members themselves are a support system to one another. Though many transitions involving one family member, such as unemployment or traumatic illness, have a considerable, even a devastating impact on the entire family system, the specific family member primarily affected by the loss needs encouragement and reassurance. As the family provides the best opportunity for growth and fulfillment, so the home is the place where individuals can receive accepting feedback and emotional support. Informal support can also be provided through the community counselor's communication of his or her availability to answer phone calls when family members have questions. This type of availability may be all that family members really need from the community counselor, since it demonstrates that someone cares about their welfare.

## Challenges to Families

In this role the counselor may challenge family members to work together for the benefit of the client and themselves, urge the family to maintain normal activities as much as possible as they attempt to manage caregiving responsibilities, and encourage them to seek appropriate new activities that could provide both a respite from providing care and a resource for enjoyment. Family members often have to be assisted, moreover, to confront unrealistic expectations about themselves and to find satisfaction in their own family role performances.

In the challenger role, the community counselor may also help the family to realize, when necessary, the importance of family counseling or therapy services. The recognition of serious family dysfunctional behavior may convince the counselor that family members need to receive assistance if the identified problem is ever to be resolved. Though resistance by family members to suggestions made concerning the value of extended family counseling is frequently encountered, many families become at least more willing to explore this possibility when it is cogently indicated how counseling/therapy intervention can make a decided difference in their own development of useful coping skills to deal with crises or disruptive life transitions (Power, 1988).

## Facilitation of Prevention

Anticipatory guidance can be of great assistance to many families who are confronted with a significant transition. Many events could cause a decline in family functioning, such as the birth of a child, a husband's heart attack, the unexpected death of a family member, or the discharge of a family member from a mental hospital. Early in their intervention community counselors should explore those areas within a family that may cause adjustment problems or difficulties for a patient's readaptation to a productive life. Poor family communication patterns, a family history of alcohol abuse, and isolation of family members from each other's needs, or poor coping abilities to deal with any problems could each be a barrier to family adjustment. Intervention efforts can include, consequently: (a) a search for information about family dynamics, (b) assisting the family to break down problems into manageable parts that can be handled one at a time, (c) encouraging them to be optimistic about their ability to handle whatever eventualities arise, and (d) focusing on what family members can do to ward off a possible serious strain on their relationship. Preparing for stresses by discussing them in advance and normalizing them after they occur are key strategies for preventive family intervention.

## THE COUNSELING PROCESS

As outlined in Figure 9–1, the suggested process comprises four steps, namely, (1) engaging the family; (2) problem assessment; (3) specific strategies for assistance; and (4) follow-up. Though family problems are frequently very complex, the time framework for most interventions by community counselors actually may be quite brief (3–8 visits); and the intervention process demands, therefore, an early identification both of a "workable" problem and of a plan to remediate or resolve the difficulty. In the context of this time-limited family assistance, each step in the intervention process is now briefly explained.

## Engaging the Family

Establishing a working relationship with the family is an important task, a relationship facilitated by the location of the family meeting and the helping style of the community counselor. Research indicates, for example, that certain traits and characteristics of helpers appear to affect the helping relationships positively (Okun, 1987; Power, 1995). The more in touch professionals are with their own behaviors, feelings, and beliefs, and the more able they are able to communicate this understanding genuinely, clearly, and empathically to family members, the more likely they are to be effective helpers.

The initial family contact usually takes place in an agency setting. But it is important for the counselor to consider offering the family an opportunity of at least a first meeting in their own home. Home-based family counseling is an approach used by community counselors for the preservation of families who are in severe crisis or beset by so many problems they are unlikely to, or incapable of, accessing traditional service within an agency (Woods, 1988). Community counselors provide home-based family counseling by meeting with families in the family's home. The frequency and duration of sessions is usually more flexible than in office-based counseling. Home-based counseling can occur for extended periods during a day, daily for several weeks, and/or be scheduled in brief, periodic check-in sessions with the family.

There are advantages of home-based family counseling both for assessing the family's needs and providing counseling interventions (Hodges & Blythe, 1992). With regard to assessment, visiting the family's home may result in the counselor having access to a larger number of family members (including extended family and significant others) than would be likely to come to his or her office. The counselor can observe living conditions (including financial situation, safety, cleanliness, geographic location) and family interaction patterns (including the influences of culture and religion) as they exist in the home. The counselor can assess what resources/obstacles exist in the environment that will assist or impede efforts to help the family. With regard to intervention, the counselor is likely to have stronger rapport and influence with the family because of his or her demonstrated willingness to work with them on their turf. The counselor can tailor counseling strategies to the specific problems that arise in the home and modify the strategies in response to how effective they are in actual practice. The counselor can incorporate all members of the family who are in the home in problem resolution. Changes that the family is able to make with the help of the counselor are more likely to be sustained in the counselor's absence because the changes occurred in the home setting rather than in an office setting, which is remote from the family's daily life.

Home-based counseling requires a high degree of flexibility on the part of community counselors. They must be able to adjust their treatment approaches and schedules to the needs and circumstances of the family. They also need to be appropriately assertive in helping the family to engage in counseling in the midst of potential distractions in their home, and must be well organized and prepared before beginning. They will not be able to reach into their office desk for a reference they would like to share with the family. Despite these requirements, there has been extensive growth in home-based counseling over the past ten years, suggesting that the approach is effective (Hodges & Blythe, 1992).

## Problem Assessment

Family assessment concerns were discussed earlier when the authors explained the intervention role of assessor for assisting families. An understanding of family problems usually emerges from the professional's theoretical orientation to family dynamics. But this understanding should also include a knowledge of family needs, expectations, strengths, and previous family history (Power, Dell Orto, & Gibbons, 1988). Apart from the counselor's exploration of the problem definition, specific services may be requested by family members, but the counselor should look beyond concrete requests in order to understand how a particular service is perceived by the family as well as what need it fulfills (Greene, 1989). An appraisal of selected areas of family functioning becomes the basis for the development of appropriate family helping strategies.

## Specific Strategies for Assistance

Chapter 8 of this book identifies different intervention goals for a community counselor, such as behavior change, adjustment or actualization, and environmental modification. Each of these goals could be utilized for family intervention. Goals planned for family assistance, however, usually will determine the choice of intervention strategy. Figure 9.1 lists many possible counseling outcomes. The achievement of each one will depend on the counselor's theoretical orientation, the cooperation of family members, and the counselor's competence in using a particular strategy. The different schools of family counseling and family therapy each offer a particular approach for the alleviation of family problems. Any one could be adopted by the community counselor if it is appropriate for the remediation of the presenting problem.

## Follow-Up

After the counselor has assisted the family with a particular problem, family members usually need periodic contact that shows support for the recommended intervention. The provision of support through a phone call or another form of brief contact should be an ever-present available resource for families as they continue to use, for example, newly learned skills to manage family difficulties (Power, 1995).

## CONCLUSION

Community counselors are continuing to express an interest in reevaluating the nature of their relationships with families. Family members are also demanding new approaches from professionals. The family is not dying, as some have suggested (Bretto-Kelly, 1979); it is diversifying. With this diversification, and combined with the complexity of economic, technological, and social change, many families will have many more difficulties in coping with the demands of modern living. The changes in family forms and the growing incidence of family crises provide an ideal opportunity for community counselors. The growth of the family counseling movement has given community counselors added options to treat troubled families. The new attention to the family as an invaluable resource for a client's life adjustment provides another important expansion of community counseling services. This resource can be illustrated in the following case example.

## EXERCISE

### Case Study

A young woman adopted a one-year-old child. With her husband she showed evidence of having adequately coped with and solved many problems concerning the rearing of this child, but their life pattern was suddenly changed when they left the supporting cultural and geographical area in which they had lived for a few years and came to an area where they had no contact with relatives or friends. At the same time, the wife's mother died and this precipitated a rather severe depression. Under the stress of her mother's death, the depression, loneliness, and lack of adequate support from the environment, the parents felt pushed beyond their strength. On one occasion the mother became impatient with her child and abused her, causing injury severe enough to warrant medical attention at the emergency room.

The mother reacted to this incident as if it were a surprising event in her life. The husband was also surprised, and became so angry with his wife that he left home for two days. When he returned, he told his wife that they both needed help.

1. What further information do you need before you can decide on an intervention approach?

2. Supppose that you can obtain this information. Outline your response to the four intervention steps as described in this chapter.

---

## REFERENCES

Ackerman, N. W. (1966). *Treating the troubled family*. New York: Basic Books.

Amato, P. R. (1993). Family structure, family process, and family ideology. *Journal of Marriage and the Family, 55*(1), 50–54.

American Council of Life Insurance. (1980). *Datatrack*. Washington, DC.

Beer, W. R. (1988). *Relative strangers: Studies of stepfamily processes*. Totowa, NJ: Rowman and Littlefield.

Berman, E., Lief, H., & Williams, A. (1981). A model of marital interaction. In C. P. Sholevar (Ed.), *The handbook of marriage and marital therapy* (pp. 3–34). New York: Spectrum.

Bohannan, P. (1985). *All the happy families: Exploring the varieties of family life*. New York: McGraw-Hill.

Bowen, M. (1981). Alcoholism as viewed through family systems theory and family psychotherapy. In G. D. Erickson & T. P. Hogan (Eds.), *Family therapy: An introduction to theory and technique* (2nd ed. pp. 197–205). Monterey, CA: Brooks/Cole.

Bretto-Kelly, C. (1979, October). *American families in the 1980's, implications for marriage and family therapy*. Paper presented at the 39th Annual Conference of the American Association for Marriage and Family Therapy, Washington, DC.

Brody, E. M. (1985). Parent care as a normative family stress. The *Gerontologist, 25*, 19–29.

Bronfenbrenner, U. (1988). Hectic times for families. *The Washington Post Health Focus* section-March 8th.

Carter, B., & McGoldrick, M. (1988). Overview: The changing family life cycle—A framework for family therapy. In B. Carter and M. McGoldrick (Eds.), *The changing family life cycle: A framework for family therapy* (2nd ed.). New York: Allyn and Bacon.

Cavan, R. S. (1974). Family life circle, United States. In R. C. Caven (Ed.), *Marriage and family in the modern world—Readings* (pp 91–104). New York: T. Y. Crowell.

Conger, J. J. (1981). Families, youth, and social change. *American Psychologist, 36*, 1475–1484.

Dinkmeyer, D., & Dinkmeyer, D. C., Jr. (1985). Adlerian psychotherapy and counseling. In S. Lynn & J. P. Garske (Eds.), *Contemporary psychotherapies: Models and methods* . Columbus, OH: Merrill/Macmillan.

Doherty, W. J., & Baird, M. A. (1983). *Family therapy and family medicine*. New York: The Guilford Press.

Doty, D. (1986). Family care of the elderly: The role of public policy. *The Milbank Quarterly, 67*, 485–506.

Duvall, E. M. (1971). *Family development* (4th ed.). Philadelphia: J. B. Lippincott.

Everett, C. A. (1990). The field of marital and family therapy. *Journal of Counseling and Development, 68*, 498–502.

Ford, D. Y. (1994). An exploration of perceptions of alternative family structures among university students. *Family Relations, 43*(1), 68–73.

Furstenberg, F. (1984) . The new extended family: The experience of parents and children after remarriage. In K. Pasley and M. Ihinger-Tallman (Eds.), *Remarriage and stepparenting* (pp.,42–61). New York: Guilford.

Furstenberg, F. F., & Teitler, J. O. (1994). Reconsidering the effects of marital disruption. *Journal of Family Issues, 15*(2), 173–190.

Glick, P. C. (1989). Remarried families, stepfamilies, and stepchildren: A brief demographic profile. *Family Relations, 38*, 24–27.

Goldenberg, I., & Goldenberg, H. (1980). *Family therapy: An overview*. Monterey, Ca: Brooks/Cole.

Goldenberg, I., & Goldenberg, H. (1991). *Family therapy: An overview* (3rd ed.). Monterey, CA: Brooks/Cole.

Green, S. K., & Bobele, M. (1994). Family therapists' response to AIDS: An examination of attitudes, knowledge, & contact. *Journal of Marriage and Family Therapy, 20,* 349–367.

Greene, R. (1989) . A life-systems approach to understanding parent-child relationships in aging families. *Journal of psychotherapy and the family, 5,* 57–69.

Guerney, B. G., Jr. (1990). Creating therapeutic and growth-inducing family systems: Personal moorings, landmarks, and guiding stars. In F. Kaslow (Ed.), *Voices in family psychology* (pp. 114–138). Beverly Hills, CA: Sage.

Haley, J. (1971). Approaches to family therapy. In J. Haley (Ed.), *Changing families: A family therapy reader.* New York: Grune & Stratton.

Haley, J. (1976). *Problem-solving therapy.* San Francisco: Jossey-Bass.

Haley, J. (1980). *Leaving home.* New York: McGraw-Hill.

Havighurst, R. J. (1953). *Human development and education.* New York: Longmans, Green.

Herr, J. J., & Weakland, J. H. (1979). *Counseling elders and their families: Practical techniques for applied gerontology.* New York: Springer.

Hodges, V. G., & Blythe, B. J. (1992). Improving service delivery to high-risk families: Home-based practice. *Families in society, 73*(5) , 259–265.

Keefler, J., & Koritar, E. (1994). Essential elements of a family psychoeducation program in the aftercare of schizophrenia. *Journal of marital and family therapy, 20,* 269–280.

Leichter, E., & Schulman, G. L. (1981). Multi-family group therapy: A multidimensional approach. In G. D. Erickson & T. P. Hogan (Eds.), *Family therapy: An introduction to theory and technique* (pp. 182–194) Monterey, CA: Brooks/Cole.

Lewis, J. Beavers, W. R., Gossett, J. T., & Phillips, V. A. (1976). *No single thread: Psychological health in family systems.* New York: Brunner/Mazel.

Madanes, C. (1981). *Strategic family therapy.* San Francisco: Jossey-Bass.

Madanes, C. (1984). *Behind the one-way mirror: Advances in the practice of strategic therapy.* San Francisco: Jossey-Bass.

Melson, G. F. (1980). *Family and environment—An ecosystem perspective.* Minneapolis: Burgess.

Mills, D. M. (1988). Stepfamilies in context. In W. R. Beer (Ed.), *Relative strangers: Studies of stepfamily processes* (pp. 1–28). Totowa, NJ: Rowman & Littlefield.

Minuchin, S. (1984). *Family kaleidoscope.* Cambridge, MA: Harvard University Press.

Morrissey, M. (1995, March). Prisoners of love. *Counseling Today,* 12–13.

Office of Special Education and Rehabilitative Services (1984). *Disability and families: A family systems approach* (vol. 7). Washington, DC: U.S. Department of Education.

Okun, B. F. (1987). *Effective helping; Interviewing and counseling techniques.* Monterey, CA: Brooks/Cole.

Okun, B. F., & Rappaport, L. J. (1980). *Working with families: An introduction to family therapy.* North Scituate, MA: Duxbury Press.

Olson, D., Sprenkle, D., Russell, C. (1979). Circumplex model of marital and family systems: I. *Family Process, 18,* 3–28.

Overs, R., & Healy, J. (1973). Stroke patients: Their spouses, families and the community. In A. B. Cobb (Ed.), *Medical and psychological aspects of disability* (pp. 87–117) . Springfield, IL: Charles C. Thomas.

Parsons, T., & Bales, T. R. (1955). *Family: Socialization and interaction process.* New York: The Free Press.

Power, P. W. (1988). An assessment approach to family intervention. In P. W. Power, A. E. Dell Orto, & M. B. Gibbons (Eds.), *Family interventions throughout chronic illness and disability* (pp 5–24). New York: Springer.

Power, P. W. (1991). Family coping with chronic illness and rehabilitation. In F. K. Judd, G. D. Burrow, & D. R. Lipsitt (Eds.), *Handbook of Studies on General Hospital Psychiatry* (pp. 207–224). New York: Elsevier Science.

Power, P. W. (1995). Understanding intergenerational issues in aging families. In G. Smith, S. Tobin, E. A. Robertson-Tchabo, & P. Power (Eds.), *Strengthening aging families* (pp 123–142) Thousand Oaks, CA: Sage.

Power, P., & Dell Orto, A. E. (1980). *Role of the family in the rehabilitation of the physically disabled.* Austin, TX: Pro/Ed Press.

Power, P. W. Dell Orto, A. E., & Gibbons, M. (1988). *Family intervention throughout chronic illness and, disability.* New York: Springer Publishing Company.

Rhodes, S. (1977, May). A developmental approach to the life cycle of the family. *Social Casework,* 301–312.

Robinson, S., Rotter, M., & Wilson, J. (1982). Mother's contemporary career decisions impact on the family. *The Personnel and Guidance Journal,* 60(9), 535–538.

Satir, V. M. (1982). The therapist and family therapy: Process model. In A. M. Horne & M. M. Ohlsen (Eds.) , *Family counseling and therapy.* Itasca, IL: Peacock.

Sholevar, G. (1985). Marital therapy. In H. Kaplan & B. Sadock (Eds.), *Comprehensive textbook of psychiatry IV* (vol. 2). Baltimore: Williams & Wilkins.

Shorter, E. (1975). *The making of the modern family.* New York: Basic Books.

Snyder, M., & Guerney, B. G., Jr. (1993). Brief couple/family therapy. In R. A. Wells & V. J. Giannetti (Eds.), *Casebook of the brief psychotherapies* (pp. 221–234). New York: Plenum Press.

Sperry, L., & Carlson, J. (1991). *Marital therapy: Integrating theory and technique.* Denver: Love.

Stinnet, N., & DeFrain, J. (1985). *Secrets of strong families.* Boston: Little, Brown.

Strickland, C. (1985, August 11). The fading American family. *The Atlanta Journal/The Atlanta Constitution,* pp. 1C, 8C.

Toseland, R. W., Smith, G. C. & McCallion, P. (1995). Supporting the family in elder care. In G. Smith, S. Tobin, E. A. Robertson-Tchabo, & P. Power (Eds.), *Strengthening aging families* (pp. 3–24) Thousand Oaks, CA: Sage.

Turnbull, A. P., Summers, J. A., & Brotherson, M. J. (1983). *Working with families with disabled members: A family systems approach.* Lawrence, KS: Kansas University Affiliated Facility at Lawrence, Bureau of Child Research.

U.S. Bureau of the Census. (1979. *Divorce, child custody, and child support* (Current Population Reports, Special Studies Series P-23, No. 84) . Washington, DC: U.S. Government Printing Office.

U.S. Bureau of the Census (1989). Household and family characteristics, March 988. (Current Population Reports, Series P-20, No. 437). Washington, DC: U.S. Government Printing Office.

Waldo, M. (1987). Also victims: Understanding and treating men arrested for spouse abuse. *Journal of Counseling Development,* 65, 385–388.

Waldrop, J., & Exter, T. (1992, March). The legacy of the 1980s. *American Demographics,* pp. 22–25.

Watzlawick, P., & Weakland, J. (Eds. (1977). *The interactional view: Studies at the mental research institute,* 1965–1974. New York: Norton.

Weitzman, L. (1974). Legal regulation of marriage: Tradition and changes. *California Law Review,* 62, 1169–1186.

Whitehead, B. D. (1993). Dan Quayle was right. *The Atlantic Monthly,* April, pp. 47–74.

Wilcoxon, S. A. (1985). Healthy family functioning: The other side of family pathology. *Journal of Counseling and Development,* 63, 495–499.

Wilson, M. N. (1989) . Child development in the context of the black extended family. *American Psychology,* 44, 380–385.

Woods, L. J. (1988). Home-based family therapy. *Social* Work, 33(3), 211–214

Wright, L. M., & Leahey, M. (1994). Calgary family intervention model: One way to think about change. *Journal of Marriage and Family Therapy,* 20, 381–395.

Zisserman, L. (1981). The modern family and rehabilitation of the handicapped. A macrosociological view. *American Journal of Occupational Therapy,* 35(1), 13–20.

# 10

# COMMUNITY COUNSELING
# WITH GROUPS

Community counseling in groups offers unique advantages for fostering clients' well-being. Individual client's strengths may be drawn out in the supportive atmosphere counseling groups provide (Yalom, 1985). The group situation can allow participants to share assets and build on each other's skills (Trotzer, 1989). Furthermore, groups may enable participants to develop a social network with other group members that can serve as a base for initiating environmental change (Zastrow, 1993). An example would be a group organized for victims of domestic violence at a battered women's shelter. Group work is often employed to help battered women practice assertion skills (Hudson, 1986). Interacting with other women, who understand what they have been through and recognize the strength they have demonstrated by surviving and dealing with abuse, helps enhance women's self-esteem (Vinson, 1992). Women in these groups also share concrete resources like child care, and learn from each other ways of avoiding dangerous situations and holding perpetrators accountable for their actions. Together they have formed organizations that lobby legislators for tougher battering laws and assist law enforcement agencies in effectively responding to domestic violence situations.

Group work is in many ways ideally suited to the environment and philosophy of the community counseling specialty. Groups employ the major resources within communities, the people of the community, as counseling change agents. In doing so, they make efficient use of professional resources by allowing one community counselor to help a number of clients during one session. Community counseling in groups broadens the impact of counseling by affecting more people within the community than could be reached by individual counseling methods. Because group work employs the strengths of the people within a community to assist each other, it embodies a central principle of community counseling presented in Chapter 2: identification and mobilization of client and community resources for goal attainment, coping, and growth.

The Association for Specialists in Group Work (ASGW) is the division of the American Counseling Association that focuses on group intervention methods. ASGW suggests group interventions can be categorized into four major modalities as follows (ASGW, 1992):

1. Task/work groups: Task forces, committees, community organizations, discussion groups, study circles, and learning

groups that serve to accomplish identified work goals.

2. Guidance / psychoeducational groups: Educational groups that teach group participants knowledge and skills for coping adaptively with potential and/or immediate environmental challenges, developmental transitions, and life crises.

3. Counseling/interpersonal problem-solving: Groups offering interpersonal support and an environment for problem-solving in which common career, educational, personal, social, and developmental concerns can be addressed.

4. Psychotherapy/personality reconstruction: Groups addressing in-depth psychological disturbance through reconstruction of major dimensions of group participants' personalities.

The ASGW categories include descriptions of both how the groups function (process) and their purpose (goals). In practice, groups may employ a process associated with one category (such as psychoeducational guidance) to achieve a goal from another (such as therapeutic personality change). For example, guidance in development of assertion skills can be offered to persons suffering from depression to help them to overcome tendencies toward passivity, which may contribute to their depression. To further clarify how groups are used in community counseling, six goals groups are commonly employed to pursue will be described below. It is important to recognize that the process through which these goals are pursued may include those categorized under any one or more of the ASGW group work modalities (task, guidance, counseling, psychotherapy).

1. *Action.* Groups can be organized to accomplish tasks that will improve the safety, adjustment, and development of members of the community (Gladding, 1991). Examples include efforts to develop youth recreation centers, educational and career opportunities for unwed mothers, "safe houses" in neighborhoods where children can go in emergencies, and mothers organized to prevent drunk driving.

2. *Enhancement.* Groups can be used to enhance the quality of life for people who do not have serious problems or mental disorders (Pearson, 1992). Within a group situation, participants can explore their reactions to events and relationships in the group. They can employ what they learn in the group to achieve better understanding of their lives, discovering greater depth in the meaning of their experiences. An example of this would be a marathon encounter group for college students.

3. *Facilitation.* Developmental transitions occurring for individuals can be facilitated through group counseling (Bowman, 1987). Clients will play out their responses to the transition within the group. Group counseling offers a safe environment for both examining these responses, and determining which responses are most beneficial for the participants. The group situation also allows counselors a forum in which to present information and skills that can help participants make the transition. Methods for addressing the transitions developed in the group can be generalized to situations outside the group, particularly when group members are consistently in contact with each other outside the group. An example would be a social interaction group for high school freshmen where they learn about the transition to high school, practice interpersonal skills for making friends, and develop relationships with other students in their school.

4. *Prevention.* Potential problems can be detected and addressed in a group environment (Maguire, 1986). Skills that will prevent development of problems can be presented by counselors and practiced among clients in a group.

If members of the group are in contact with each other outside the group, they can assist each other in use of the skills for problem prevention, and also work together to change the environment to prevent problems. An example would be a group to provide a hospital nursing staff with training in social skills.

5. *Remediation.* Identified problems can be treated in groups (Hines, 1992). Community counseling groups assist troubled people by offering them the support of other group members who are facing a similar problem, the opportunity to play out the problem and its solution within the immediate reality of relationships during the group, and the potential for members to continue to help each other outside the group. These benefits make community counseling in groups a potent method of problem remediation. An example of this is a parenting group for abusive parents.

6. *Rehabilitation.* Community counseling groups also have the potential for helping clients adjust to long-term disabilities (Livneh & Pullo, 1992). Counselors can present specific coping techniques and supervise their practice in a group. Clients can develop relationships with other clients that extend to involvement and support outside the group. Members of clients' social networks can also participate in groups where they can learn how to adjust to, and help with, clients' disabilities. Finally, clients and/or members of their social network can organize through group work to initiate environmental change to benefit the client. For example, after-care groups for stroke patients and their families are often offered to assist in adjustment directly following the patients' release from hospitals.

This chapter will offer an overview of group work in community counseling settings. It will include a definition of group work and descriptions of therapeutic factors in groups; a brief history of group work; a description of group dynamics as they develop over time; theories of group work; leadership functions for group counselors; selection, preparation, and integration of group members; examples of community counseling groups; and professional issues related to group work. Finally, the chapter will present, for discussion, a problem in group leadership a community counselor might face.

## DEFINITION

The Association for Specialists in Group Work (ASGW, 1992, p. 12) offers the following definition of group work:

> *...a broad professional practice that refers to the giving of help or the accomplishment of tasks in a group setting. It involves the application of group theory and process by a capable professional practitioner to assist an interdependent collection of people to reach their mutual goals, which may be personal, interpersonal, or task-related in nature.*

This definition is intentionally broad so that it can encompass a wide variety of group formats and goals, ranging from committees performing tasks to psychotherapy (Conyne, Dye, Kline, Morran, Ward, & Wilson, 1992). The breadth is especially appropriate when applied to groups offered by community counselors. For example, following a teen suicide, a community counselor might advise teachers and administrators, as they plan their response, to offer groups to help the teenager's friends and other students cope with their grief, hold a meeting for concerned parents on how to identify signs of suicide potential in their children, and start counseling groups for teenagers to prevent future suicide (Sherwood-Hawes, 1992).

The above definition, however, does not convey the rich benefits that can come from group work. Because community counseling focuses on development of strengths, perhaps the best definition of community counseling group work can be derived from examination of what such groups offer their members. Yalom (1985) provided descriptions of 11 therapeutic factors that research and clinical experience indicate occur in groups. The following is a brief description of the factors as they apply to community counseling group work.

**1.** *Hope.* Community counseling group members develop the belief that their problems can be overcome. This belief increases motivation and a sense of well-being, enabling members to become active in dealing with their problems. Hope is fostered by knowledge that the group was formed to help with members' problems, by the leaders' confidence in the group's effectiveness, and by examples of members who are successful in coping with the problems. Group members may be motivated to share their hope with persons suffering from similar problems in their community who have not yet sought help.

**2.** *Universality.* Community counseling groups help members overcome a debilitating impression that they are unique in having unacceptable problems. Hearing that others have similar concerns reduces their sense of isolation and allows validation of each member's humanity. Recognizing that others who have problems similar to their own are still worthwhile human beings allows them to view themselves as worthwhile people, in spite of their problems. They may become more tolerant and accepting of people in the community with similar or even very different problems.

**3.** *Catharsis.* Members of a community counseling group often enter the group having strong feelings about their problems. Interacting in the group may also generate feelings in group members. The group offers a safe environment for the expression of feelings that originate both within and outside the group. Expression of feelings relieves the emotional burdens of group members. They can express their anger, sadness, and fears rather than holding these feelings in. Releasing emotions reduces members' needs to employ ineffective defense mechanisms such as denial, projection, and acting out. It allows members to focus their emotions on creating productive change within themselves and in their community.

**4.** *Corrective recapitulation of the primary family group (family reenactment).* A community counseling group can allow a replay, both on conscious and unconscious levels, of experiences typical of a primary family group. The leaders are symbolic parents and other members are symbolic siblings. Joining a group constitutes a new birth and allows members an opportunity for positive development. The group can be a supportive, involved, accepting family that sets appropriate limits, unlike the real family of origin of many community counseling clients. Group members can get in touch with problems they acquired from their family of origin and correct those problems in the group. They may then go on to improve relationships with their families.

**5.** *Cohesiveness.* Membership in community counseling groups offers participants an experience of unconditional acceptance and belonging that enables them to accept themselves more fully and be congruent in their relationships with others. Cohesiveness raises self-esteem and motivates members to remain in the group and to behave in ways that the group approves. Members may change their behavior in appropriate directions because they do not want to let the group down. The strength of relationships within the group can enable the group to address problems in the community that no group member could tackle alone.

**6.** *Altruism.* By offering support, reassurance, suggestions, and sharing similar problems, group members can be helpful to one another. Seeing themselves as helpful to others raises members' self-esteem. Focusing on other peoples' problems turns their attention away from excessively dwelling on their own problems. Offering suggestions to others about how they can change makes it more likely that members will employ their suggestions toward dealing with their own problems. Members may also endeavor to help persons outside of the group, either directly or through affecting social policy.

7. *Interpersonal learning*. Interpersonal relationships define individuals' personality and adjustment. Clients have developed an interpersonal style that affects their relationships outside of the group. They carry this style into the group. There they reconstruct relationships typical of their life outside the group within the social microcosm of the group. However, unlike typical relationships outside of the group, in the group other members let clients know what effect their style has on them. Clients have an opportunity to change the way they relate, so that they can have the effect on others that they want to have. When they are successful in changing their style so that they get the reactions from other group members that they want, it results in a corrective emotional experience for clients. They are then in a position to improve the way they relate to others outside the group.

8. *Information (guidance)*. The group members and leaders provide a resource of knowledge and viewpoints through which clients can learn new information or have mistaken beliefs corrected. This can include factual information or different perspectives on psychological problems. The information can be employed by individuals or the group as a whole in making positive changes in their lives and their communities.

9. *Imitation (identification)*. Community counseling group members learn new behaviors by observing the behavior of the leaders and other members as models. They can imitate the behaviors they see working for others. Important components affecting learning include the status of the models, similarities between the models and observers, and rewards received by the models. Members can carry what they learn through imitation into their interactions outside the group.

10. *Socializing techniques*. Community counseling groups offer clients an opportunity to experiment with new behaviors. They try new responses in the group and are selectively reinforced for positive behavior. Negative behaviors are not reinforced, resulting in their extinction. Consistent reinforcement results in members becoming increasingly skilled in positive behaviors. Individuals from the group or the group as a whole may practice the new behaviors outside the group. This practice can include taking action to improve the physical and social environment of their community.

11. *Existential factors*. Clients usually cannot control who other members of a community counseling group will be, or how things will go for other members in their lives outside the group. This fact puts them in touch with the reality that there are many circumstances in their own lives that they cannot control. They also face their eventual termination with the group, which represents an end of life in the group. The time-limited nature of group involvement forces the members to recognize that their lifetimes are also limited. Finally, members recognize that although they have limited control and time in the group, they still have choice in how they respond to the group situation and responsibility for their choices. This recognition generalizes to accepting responsibility for the choices they make outside the group.

The therapeutic factors as they are described here may be seen as hallmarks of community counseling group work. Although they certainly would not all occur in all groups at all times, the existence of some of these factors at varying levels during the course of a group are necessary for the group to be an effective community counseling intervention.

## HISTORY

Perhaps because of the innate therapeutic factors they offer, small groups have made important contributions to people's mental health throughout human history (Brandler & Roman, 1991). Examples of such groups include nuclear and extended families, hunting bands, tribes, prayer groups, school classes, military units, guilds, and lodges.

Predecessors of current community counseling groups originated from three different approaches to helping clients, all of which emerged around the beginning of the twentieth century (Shaffer & Galinsky, 1989). These approaches can be classified as educational, therapeutic, and social action/self-help.

### Educational

In 1905, classes on tuberculosis were offered to patients suffering from the disease (Gazda, 1989). It was found that the effects of these classes on patients' attitudes and adjustment were extremely positive, particularly when patients were allowed to discuss their experiences with each other. The technique of offering classes about a disease to patients suffering from it was later successfully employed with schizophrenics. Class-like group guidance procedures were also used to educate professionals and parents in the psychological development of children. Other class-like guidance procedures emerged in the early twentieth century in public schools, offering students counseling in vocational, moral, and extracurricular activities. Currently, the class or structured group format is a prevalent community counseling approach, and corresponds to the ASGW Guidance/Psychoeducational category of groups. Examples include parent effectiveness training, career guidance workshops, and stress management courses.

### Therapeutic

Psychodrama was a therapeutic technique that developed early in the century and was a pre-decessor to group therapy (Weiner, 1984). Psychodrama offered individuals an opportunity to act out their concerns in groups by role-playing scenes of events that were bothering them. Psychoanalysis was another therapeutic technique that developed around the turn of the century, although it was not extensively applied in groups until the 1930s and 1940s. The economics of the depression and the crush of veterans returning from World War II who needed psychiatric help made the efficient use of professional resources particularly attractive at that time. Group counseling allowed a vast expansion of the number of clients who could be served by the same number of professionals. Currently, community counselors employ a wide array of therapeutic approaches in groups. These groups fit in the Psychotherapy/Personality Reconstruction- and Counseling/Interpersonal Problem-Solving categories of groups offered by ASGW. Examples include client-centered encounter, transactional analysis groups, gestalt groups, and rational-emotive therapy groups.

### Social Action/Self-Help

Social action and self-help groups also emerged around the turn of the century (Gladding, 1991). Groups were initially organized to help immigrants adjust to urban living in American culture. Alcoholics Anonymous started in 1935 to help problem drinkers maintain sobriety, and was followed by a number of other "anonymous"-type groups (Alanon, Narcanon, Gamblers Anonymous, Overeaters Anonymous). A major contribution to the social action and self-help group movement, and group work in general, was made in the late 1940s by Kurt Lewin and his associates (Bradford, Gibb, & Benne, 1964). Lewin's belief that a person's behavior is a function of the person in interaction with his or her environment gave rise to the study of group dynamics (which will be discussed at length in the next section). Many of these groups could be categorized as Task/Work groups by the

ASGW format. Contemporary social action and self-help groups include t-groups (which grew directly out of Lewin's work), consciousness raising groups, and parents without partners.

## GROUP DYNAMICS

Lewin (1951) suggested that the group is more than a collection of individuals; it is also a dynamic social environment. Full understanding of groups comes from examining not only the individuals who are members, but also the way they affect and are affected by each other. The sum of these ever-changing effects at any particular moment characterizes the dynamics of the group environment at that moment. Bion (1959) suggested that group dynamics may be characterized by viewing groups as responding as if they held one of three basic assumptions, in addition to the explicit or stated assumptions about why the groups have gathered to work together. The basic assumptions are that group members must act: (a) dependent because of their confusion and anxiety, (b) fight (aggressive) or flight (avoidant), because of their anger and fear, or (c) pairing (intimate), because of their caring and enthusiasm. Emotions that might accompany a group's responding to its explicit work assumption would include confidence and responsibility. Group dynamics can also be characterized as developing over time (Luft, 1984). The group as a whole can be seen as passing through different periods in its life, similar to the way individuals pass through periods in their lives. When a group first forms it is in childhood, then moves into adolescence, followed by young adulthood, then adulthood, and then maturity as it is about to disband. Crises occur in the group's life that are similar to crises that occur in an individual's life in each period (Erikson, 1963). Crises with which groups are faced at each period may be described as follows: childhood—trust versus mistrust; adolescence—identity versus

role confusion; young adulthood—intimacy versus isolation; adulthood—generativity versus stagnation; and maturity—integrity versus despair. The group's ability to resolve the crises at each period affects its progress and functioning through future periods.

Another perspective on the development of group dynamics over time is to view groups as passing through stages (Tuckman & Jensen, 1977). Each stage carries with it a concern for members about their roles in relation to the group. Each stage can be seen as generating dynamics associated with Bion's (1959) basic assumptions and crises described by Erikson's (1963) developmental theory. Each stage also may be seen as fostering members' experiences of specific therapeutic factors (Waldo, 1985). Table 10–1 lists the titles and descriptions of stages and examples of the following: major role concerns members have, basic assumptions that could be active, crises the groups face, and therapeutic factors that may be fostered.

## THEORIES OF GROUP WORK

A wide array of theoretical orientations toward counseling may be successfully applied in community counseling groups. Group work theories can be broadly categorized as being derived from learning, dynamic, and/or humanistic principles (Waldo, 1985). A potential problem with efforts to use theories from these categories to guide group work is that most were originally designed for individual counseling (Shaffer & Galinsky, 1989). Leading a group according to a theory that fails to take into account group dynamics can result in a restricted understanding of what is occurring in the group and limit the effectiveness of the procedures that are dictated by the theory. For example, the client-centered approach of demonstrating empathic understanding of deeply felt emotional material can result in frustration for both the group leaders and members, particularly when the group is in the forming stage and is unlikely to discuss such material. However, when group dynamics are taken into account, community counselors can employ dynamics within their groups to enhance the procedures dictated by various theories (Waldo, 1985). The following are examples of how learning, dynamic, and humanistic theories can be applied to make the best use of dynamics occurring at different stages of group development.

## Learning

Learning theories applied to group work focus on members learning new ideas, attitudes and behaviors that will help them adapt (George & Dustin, 1988). Forming stage dynamics of dependency enhance group members' receptivity to new ideas and behaviors. Storming stage dynamics of rebellion motivate group members to take action. Norming stage dynamics of

**TABLE 10–1**   Stages of Group Dynamics

### STAGE 1: FORMING

**Characteristics:** The group is often confused and very dependent on the leader and each other. Members want structure and guidelines. They need to see examples. They are particularly open to the leader's suggestions. They appreciate help figuring out how they can fit in.
**Role Concern:** Members are concerned with being a group member; Are they "in or out"?
**Basic Assumption:** Dependency, as the group struggles with trust vs. mistrust crisis.
**Therapeutic Factors:** Hope and universality.

### STAGE II: STORMING

**Characteristics:** Group members rebel against the leader, the structure, and each other. They want to express their opinions and feelings and to feel they are being heard.
**Role Concern:** Members are concerned with achieving a position in the group: Are they at the "top or bottom"?
**Basic Assumption:** Fight/flight, as the group in its adolescence struggles to achieve identity.
**Therapeutic Factors** Catharsis and family reenactment.

### STAGE III: NORMING

**Characteristics:** Having survived the "storm," the group is often caring, enthusiastic, and cooperative. Members are interested in knowing each other better and becoming more intimate. They decide on goals and ways of working together.
**Role Concern:** Members are concerned about their roles in caring for each other: Are they "near or far"?

**Basic Assumption:** Pairing, as the group struggles with an intimacy vs. isolation crisis in its young adulthood.
**Therapeutic Factors:** Cohesion and altruism.

### STAGE IV: PERFORMING

**Characteristics:** The group takes responsibility for its tasks. It is ready to progress fairly autonomously. Members appreciate an opportunity to be productive.
**Role Concern:** Members are concerned about their role in the work of the group: Are they "active or idle"?
**Basic Assumption:** Group dynamics may focus on the group's work at this stage as it strives to achieve generativity in its adulthood.
**Therapeutic Factors:** Interpersonal learning information, imitation, and socializing techniques.

### STAGE V: ADJOURNING

**Characteristics:** The members feel sadness at saying goodbye. They prepare to use what they have learned in their life after the group. They appreciate activities that offer closure and that will help them generalize their learning to their lives outside the group.
**Role Concern:** They are concerned with the meaning of their roles in the group: Are they "full or empty"?
**Basic Assumption:** Dependency may reemerge at this stage as the group tries to achieve integrity in the face of its dissolution.
**Therapeutic Factors:** Existential factors.

caring increase the reinforcement value of the group, members, and leaders and increase the likelihood members will imitate the appropriate behaviors they witness in the group. Performing stage dynamics of responsibility encourage members to practice new behaviors. Adjourning stage dynamics, which focus members on their life after the group, motivate them to internalize new behaviors and generalize them to situations outside the group.

Social skills training is an example of learning theory applied to groups (Hollin & Trower, 1986). Therapeutic factors likely to be prevalent in learning based groups include Hope, Information, Imitation, and Socializing Techniques.

## Dynamic

Dynamic theories focus on analysis-of members' unconscious dynamics that interfere with their adaptive functioning (Corey, 1990). Analytic principles applied to groups allow examination of the shared unconscious experience of group members. The shared unconscious is thought to be expressed through the topics the group addresses. Any member who is speaking at a particular moment serves as the group spokesperson at that moment. Although the shared unconscious is usually expressed through a metaphor, it always can be linked to the group's dynamics and their association with the way members feel about their relationships with each other and the leaders (often referred to as "transference" relationships). For example, a group member who speaks extensively about a love scene in a play he or she recently attended may be metaphorically expressing the group's desire for increased intimacy rising from norming stage dynamics. The dynamics of the first three stages of groups (forming, storming, and norming) generate feelings in members that are transferred from relationships early in their psychological life (oral, anal, and phallic periods, according to psychoanalytic theory). Reexperiencing these feelings in the group enables members to better understand and accept themselves. The performing stage allows interpretation of these feelings so that they can be appropriately integrated into the members' psychological makeup. The dynamics of the adjourning stage help members separate and individuate from the group.

Group psychoanalysis is an example of psychodynamic theory applied in groups (Hansen, Warner, & Smith, 1980). Therapeutic factors likely to be prevalent in groups based on dynamic theories include universality, catharsis, and family reenactment.

## Humanistic

Humanistic theories focus on facilitating self-actualizing tendencies within group members by offering them an environment in which they experience positive regard, congruence, and empathy with others (Corey, 1990). The forming stage can allow members' dependency to be met with unconditional positive regard. The storming stage can allow members to congruently express their rebellious and/or fearful emotions. The caring that typifies the norming stage fosters members' ability to develop empathy with each other. During the performing stage, ideally members will have developed the ability to relate to each other with unconditional positive regard, congruence, and empathy. The prevalence of these conditions in members' relations results in higher levels of self-actualization for every member. They carry this increased self-actualization out of the group when it adjourns.

Encounter groups are an example of humanistic theory applied to group work (Rogers, 1970). Therapeutic factors likely to be prevalent in humanistic groups include cohesion, altruism, interpersonal learning, and existential factors.

## Support and Mutual Help

Groups that could be referred to as self-help, support, and/or mutual help groups have been active throughout the twentieth century with ever-increasing numbers of members (Silverman, 1980). These groups do not all adhere to a similar theory (or necessarily any organized theory), but they do have some commonalities of orientation which allow grouping them together and differentiating them from other forms of group work (Shaffer & Galinsky, 1989). First, they assume that meetings of persons dealing with the same kinds of difficulties can be of tremendous help to those involved. Second, members of these groups can effectively offer direct assistance to each other, resulting in benefits both to the person receiving assistance and the person offering assistance. Third, professional leadership of the group is not necessary. Often the groups are guided by an ideology and/or written materials (like the Twelve Steps and Twelve Traditions in the "Big Book" that guides Alcoholics Anonymous). Experienced members serve as volunteer leaders whose primary functions are administrative (securing meeting places, scheduling meetings, starting and ending sessions).

Because support and mutual help groups are focused on specific concerns and are organized and offered with minimal professional involvement, they can be a tremendous asset to community counselors in providing their clients with comprehensive, affordable counseling services (Silverman, 1980). Examples of self-help groups include Alcoholics Anonymous, Parents Without Partners, and the American Schizophrenia Association. Therapeutic factors such groups foster include universality, hope, cohesion, altruism, imitation, and information.

## GROUP LEADERSHIP

Each of the theories mentioned above suggests goals and procedures for group leaders.

Although these (and many other theories) can, and often are, adhered to exclusively in running groups, research indicates that effective group leaders employ an eclectic approach that integrates leader functions associated with each of the theories. A factor-analytic study of a variety of groups (Lieberman, Yalom, & Miles, 1973) indicated that regardless of the leader's theoretical orientations or group format, leader functions could be characterized by the following four categories.

**1.** *Executive function.* The group leaders determine the purpose, procedures, time, and place of the group. They recruit clients and screen out people who would be inappropriate for the group. They educate clients about the group and what behaviors will be expected of them in order to prepare them for group membership. They set limits and suggest or set rules. They suggest goals and directions of movement. They manage time by sequencing, pacing, stopping, blocking, and interceding. They suggest procedures for the group or a person. They direct the content of group discussion toward topics that are of concern to members, but do not explore in depth any one member's personal experiences or feelings between members. An example of the content of group interaction encouraged by a leader in the executive function would be discussion of the principles of assertive behavior and how it can be learned.

**2.** *Emotional stimulation.* The leaders stimulate emotional reactions in participants by asking them to reveal feelings, personal values, attitudes, and beliefs. They ask provocative questions and provide an unsettlingly ambiguous atmosphere in the group. They often are not explicit about their intentions. They use challenge, confrontation, and exhortation. They frequently participate as members in the group, drawing attention to themselves and disclosing their reactions to group members. They direct the content of the group's discussion toward the intrapersonal emotional experience of group members. Members are encouraged to talk about "I" rather than "it." For example, a group member who is discussing the difficulty some people have finding a middle ground between passive and aggressive behaviors might be asked instead to express his/her own passive and aggressive emotions in the group.

3. *Caring.* The group leaders provide support and warmth. They demonstrate caring by offering friendship, love, and affection. They frequently invite members to seek and offer feedback, support, praise, and encouragement. They focus on how members feel about each other, directing the content of discussion toward interpersonal relationships between members in the group. Members are encouraged to talk about "we" rather than "I" or "it." For example, a member who was describing anxiety about self-disclosing to people outside the group would be encouraged to instead talk with another member in the group about what allows him or her to self-disclose to that person in the group.

4. *Meaning attribution.* The group leaders provide members with concepts for understanding their experiences, both in and outside the group. They offer members new insight, awareness, and knowledge by interpreting, explaining, clarifying, and providing frameworks for how to change. This function involves directing the content of interaction so that it integrates extrapersonal topics, intrapersonal experience, and interpersonal relations within the group. For example, group members might be encouraged to use principles of assertion to offer a balanced expression of their angry and passive emotions in relation to each other in the group.

All of the leadership functions described here are employed by eclectic group leaders. Some functions are likely to be stressed more when leaders are using certain theoretical orientations or are at certain stages in the development of the group, and each function may tend to generate specific therapeutic factors

(Waldo, 1985). Executive function primarily employs learning theories, fits the dynamics of the forming stage, and generates the therapeutic factors of hope and universality. Emotional stimulation employs dynamic theories, fits the storming stage, and generates catharsis and family re-enactment. Caring employs humanistic theories, fits the norming stage, and generates cohesion and altruism. Meaning attribution employs learning, dynamic, and humanistic theories, fits the performing stage, and generates interpersonal learning, information, imitation, and socializing techniques. Executive function also fits the adjourning stage, generating existential factors. Clearly, employing different leadership functions, guided by theory, in response to group dynamics requires a high degree of sophistication and flexibility on the part of community counselors.

## MEMBERSHIP

Because the majority of the benefits clients receive through participation in a group are the result of their relating to other group members, the selection, preparation, and integration of members in a group are essential for effective group work (Corey & Corey, 1992). These issues are of such critical importance that nine of the 15 ethical guidelines for group leaders address them (ASGW, 1989). Selection, preparation, and integration of community counseling group members will be examined in this section.

## Selection

A primary consideration in selection of group members is that there be similarities between clients in the group. Most important is the depth of clients' concerns. Similarity in the seriousness of clients' problems serves as a working bond between members. If there are vastly different degrees of problems among members (such as an individual struggling with severe, active alcoholism entering a single parents' group), outstanding clients are likely to become discouraged and alienated from the group and other members are likely to feel helpless and uninvolved with them. In addition to similarity in depth of concern, other areas of similarity help build relationships between members. These include gender, age, stage of psychological development, race, socioeconomic status, educational background, and level of commitment to getting help. Although it is neither possible nor desirable to have groups be homogeneous in all these areas, similarity in at least one of these areas with at least one other group member is critical for a client to feel comfortable in a group.

Other things to consider when selecting participants for community counseling group work include the following:

**1.** *Sources of stress in the client's life.* A recent death of a loved one, serious health problems, or difficulties with the expense, schedule, or location of the group may interfere with a client's benefiting from or continuing with the group.

**2.** *Sources of support in the client's life.* Family, friends, roommates, or romantic relationships can help clients benefit from groups by offering them support as they learn new things about themselves and how they relate to others in the group. If they do not have relationships outside the group, clients may be particularly vulnerable to negative experiences in the group. If their outside relationships are not supportive of their involvement in the group, they may be influenced to terminate membership.

**3.** *Past or present experience with counseling.* People who have been in counseling or psychotherapy may have had positive or negative experiences that will affect how they view group counseling. Persons who are currently in counseling should discuss being in a group with their counselor and get his or her agreement before joining.

**4.** *Past and present experiences in groups.* People who have always disliked being in groups are likely to have more problems in a community counseling group than those who have always enjoyed being in groups. Knowing the kinds of problems people have had in previous groups can be helpful in identifying and preventing similar problems from occurring in a community counseling group they are entering.

Information in each of these areas should be gathered on potential group participants prior to their joining a group. To save time, information can be gathered through telephone interviews, written applications, or in large pregroup meetings. Problems in any of these areas do not preclude a person participating in the group. If there are problems, it is worthwhile for the leader to discuss them with a potential member so that they can be resolved in a way that will allow the member to benefit from a community counseling group (for example, alleviating mistaken fears about groups, or having a member consult with his or her counselor about participating).

## Preparation

Clients who have been selected to participate in a group need to be prepared for the experience (Yalom, 1985). Members who know what they want and have realistic goals are likely to achieve their goals in a community counseling group. On the other hand, members who are unclear about their goals or have unrealistic expectations are likely to end their involvement with a group feeling confused and/or disappointed. This can be avoided by offering clients proper preparation for group participation. Carefully addressing the following points (Yalom, 1985) will prepare clients for optimum participation in community counseling groups:

**1.** Value of group work (history of group work, therapeutic factors in groups, development of social contracts, research evidence).

**2.** Explanation of the group's goals and theoretical orientation.

**3.** Exploration of match between the group's and the client's goals.

**4.** Description of necessary client behaviors (listening, self-disclosure, impression sharing).

**5.** Exploration of potential problems in participation (client's misperceptions about group, prior negative group experiences, withholding important concerns).

**6.** Detailed description of the group's methods and procedures (possibly including a role play or demonstration).

**7.** Description of other group members (age, gender, race, concerns).

**8.** Discussion of ground rules necessary for a productive group, including:

**a.** Confidentiality—expected but not guaranteed with regard to members; legal, research, and supervision constraints for the counselor.

**b.** Attendance—punctual, consistent, drug free; clients have the right to exit the group; counselors have responsibility to determine membership.

**c.** Participation—expectation of involvement; right to temporarily decline involvement; counselor responsibilities to guide involvement.

**9.** Client's understanding and agreement on these points.

Research suggests that when a member prematurely drops out of a group both that member and the group experience a setback (Lieberman, Yalom, & Miles, 1973). Feelings of failure, guilt, rejection, and anger may occur for everyone involved. The member who dropped out may be reluctant to seek help again. Remaining members may worry about the safety of the group, who will be next to leave, and if the group is going to survive. For these reasons it is important for community counselors to select and prepare members carefully, with the goal being that each member will have the greatest likelihood of successful group participation. When members end their involvement in groups, it is important to offer them referral to alternative services, when appropriate, and to discuss in the group the reactions other members have to the loss.

## Member Integration

Following selection and preparation, the integration of clients into meaningful involvement with other group members is a critical and ongoing process that is essential for productive community group counseling. Research has shown that clients receive the greatest benefits in group work from their interaction with other group members (Yalom, 1985). A variety of methods may be used to integrate group members. The methods may be adjusted in relation to the developmental stage of the group and pursued through a variety of leader functions. For example, in the performing stage of a group, greater member integration could occur from a leader pointing out that he or she noticed some friction between two members and inviting them to discuss it with each other. In the performing stage it is likely that the members would be in a position to productively act on that suggestion. However, during the forming stage, the same suggestion might result in extraordinary discomfort for the members and one or both dropping out of the group. Table 10–2 offers suggestions about methods for integrating group members through use of leader functions that match specific stages of group development.

Another method of promoting member integration is to analyze the role each member plays in the group, such as initiator, opinion seeker, evaluator, and so on. (Hansen, Warner & Smith, 1980). If a member consistently seems to take a negative role (blocker, cynic)

**TABLE 10–2**  Methods for Group Member Integration at Different Stages of Group Development

| GROUP STAGE | LEADER FUNCTIONAL | METHOD |
|---|---|---|
| Forming | Executive | Have members pair up and exchange non-threatening personal information. Then have members, introduce their partners to the group. |
| Storming | Emotional stimulation | Have members draw pictures of themselves and the group, and of how they would like to be in the future. Have members describe their feelings about the pictures to each other. |
| Norming | Caring | Demonstrate understanding and respect for the positive feelings members have for each other. |
| Performing | Meaning attribution | Point out an unexpressed conflict between members, interpret its meaning, and suggest they give each other direct feedback. |
| Adjourning | Executive | Ask members to identify an important insight they learned during the group and describe how they will use this insight after the group is over. |

steps can be taken, with the member and/or the group, to change that member's role to one that makes a constructive contribution to the group.

A final method of member integration is to assess and act on the immediate interaction occurring in a group. This can be done through the following steps:

**1.** Select a particular member and attend to his or her verbal and nonverbal behavior.

**2.** Using the information from Step 1 and background information on the member (personal history, concerns, previous behavior in group), make an empathic judgment about what the member is currently experiencing, and what he/she wants from other group members.

**3.** Attend to the verbal and nonverbal responses of other members in response to the selected member.

**4.** Similar to Step 2, make an empathic judgment about what other members are experiencing and want in response to the selected member.

**5.** Determine in what ways the relationship between the selected member and other members can be modified, within the context of their experience in the group and the group's current dynamics, so that they will be more effective at fulfilling what they want with each other.

**6.** Intervene by acknowledging the experience of the members and suggest how they might work together more productively.

For example, a member who constantly gives advice to other members may be nervous about his or her role in the group and want to be helpful to others. If other members are ignoring this person's comments, they may be frustrated with the constant advice, wanting this member just to listen and understand. By actively listening and demonstrating understanding, the member could satisfy his or her desire to be helpful and other members' desire to be understood. The following statement could be made by the leader to the selected member during a group's performing stage to work toward integrating the member into the group:

"You work hard to give suggestions to others to solve their problems. Among other things I think that shows you care. I'm worried, though, that sometimes others miss the caring message because it is buried under the advice. I know that I, and I think others too, would appreciate knowing that you understand our problems and that you are concerned. Rather than advice, I'd like you to tell us what feelings you hear people having about their problems."

## EXAMPLES OF COMMUNITY COUNSELING GROUPS

This section will offer specific examples of the practice of group work in communities. Examples will be offered of groups with the six different types of goals described earlier in this chapter: action, enhancement, facilitation, prevention, remediation, and rehabilitation. A different setting will be offered for each example and the theory, leadership function, and therapeutic factors that are characteristic of the example will be suggested. It is important to remember that although the theory, leadership function and therapeutic factors presented may typify these groups, it is likely that other theories, functions, and factors will play important roles during the life of the group. Also, although the groups and settings that will be presented are typical of action, enhancement, facilitation, and so on, it should be remembered that they are by no means exclusionary. For example, assertion training is a typical form of prevention in a community mental health center, but it is also used for remediation in psychiatric hospitals and for rehabilitation in drug treatment centers.

## Action

Groups have formed to advocate for protecting the rights of persons suffering from serious mental illnesses and improving services to them (Silverman, 1980). These groups are usually made up of primary consumers (persons suffering from mental illness), secondary consumers (family and friends of persons suffering from mental illness), or service providers (mental health professionals). Often groups include combinations of primary and secondary consumers and providers. Such groups have been successful at increasing employment and housing opportunities for persons suffering from mental illness within their communities, assisting police officers in differentiating behaviors motivated by criminal intent from behaviors resulting from delusions or disorientation, and affecting legislation. In addition to the benefits such groups promote by directly achieving their goals, there are additional benefits from their work together including increased group and personal efficacy, development of social networks, and improved relations between subgroups (consumers, their family members, and providers). Learning theories often guide these kinds of groups with the leaders operating in executive function. Therapeutic factors include hope, universality, cohesion, altruism, and socializing techniques.

## Enhancement

Marriage encounter groups are offered by religious congregations to enhance the quality of marriages (Gladding, 1991). Although often open to the public at large, the groups are primarily attended by members of a congregation. They are held in churches or in retreat settings. Based on humanistic theory, they involve marital partners taking time to address together issues that are pertinent to their marriages. There is time allotted for all participants to share what they are learning within their marriage with other couples. The leaders function primarily to provide caring. After establishing the time and place for the meetings and offering a structure for couples' discussions (executive functions), they are likely to convey support and understanding to the couples as they work. Therapeutic factors include interpersonal learning and socializing techniques within a couple, and cohesion and universality between couples. Marriage encounter builds on individual marital partners' assets and also causes environmental change, in that it strengthens marriages and builds stronger social networks within a congregation.

## Facilitation

Quality circle discussions in industry offer an example of group facilitation (Napier & Gershenfeld, 1985). In such groups, members of a working unit discuss how to increase their mutual effectiveness to achieve higher productivity and satisfaction. The goals may be seen as humanistic, that is, the fulfillment of individual and group potential. Leaders function in a caring capacity, offering members support as they examine conflicts and detriments to efficient co-worker relations and explore solutions. Predominant therapeutic factors include cohesion, altruism, interpersonal learning, information, and imitation. Quality circles build on individuals' strengths, increasing their career clarity and commitment, and strengthen relations between co-workers and management. Discussions often result in changes in the environment of the workplace.

## Prevention

Groups for international students offer an example of prevention-oriented groups (Bochner, 1986). International students face a dramatic transition when they begin to study in a host country. The students face the loss of their extended family and the task of assimilating into the host culture. In an effort to prevent adjustment problems that could affect the student, groups employ learning theory to provide training in the host country language, culture, and customs. The groups also allow partici-

pants the opportunity to discuss their feelings about their transition into the new culture. Leaders primarily serve an executive function. Benefits to members include hope, universality, cohesion, information, imitation, and socializing techniques. In addition to preventing adjustment problems through development of skills and confidence in dealing with the host culture, potential problems for students may also be forestalled by the social network that develops among members. These groups may also take an advocacy role, influencing the environment to be more supportive of foreign-born students.

## Remediation

Therapy groups are often held in psychiatric hospitals to help patients overcome a variety of mental disorders (Yalom, 1983). The groups encourage members to discuss the function of their symptoms and usually involve careful examination of the members' interactions and relationships. Based on dynamic theories, the groups seek to deal with the interpersonal manifestations of the patients' disorders. The leaders function as sources of emotional stimulation by calling on participants to examine their feelings, as well as serving as symbolic parent figures. Therapeutic factors fostered by the groups include catharsis, corrective recapitulation of the primary family group, and interpersonal learning.

## Rehabilitation

Assertion training in groups is often offered to recovering alcoholics (Clark, Blanchard, & Hawes, 1992). Participants learn how to be more direct in asking for what they want and how to refuse unwanted requests or pressure from others. Assertion skills are seen as important for recovering alcoholics because they need to refuse offers of alcohol if they are to maintain sobriety. Also, assertion skills help alcoholics get more of what they want in life directly from people, rather than turning to alcohol to fulfill unmet needs or to express aggression in a passive fashion.

Learning theories are used to guide leaders' behaviors, which usually are predominantly executive functions. Therapeutic factors in such groups include information, imitation, and socializing techniques. Catharsis also plays a major role as participants get in touch with their true feelings about situations in preparation to practice asserting themselves. Concurrent meetings of the members of the alcoholics' families are often held in which family members learn assertion skills they need to help with the alcoholic's recovery. Meetings with family members also have a preventive effect because the social support that participants experience helps them deal with the stresses associated with being related to an alcoholic.

## PROFESSIONAL ISSUES

Group work is a powerful and complex form of community counseling intervention which merits careful professional attention. The American Counseling Association (ACA) includes a division devoted to professional issues related to group work, the Association for Specialists in Group Work (ASGW). ASGW serves as a network for maintaining contact between counselors working with groups. It arranges presentations at national and regional ACA conventions and publishes the *Journal of Specialists in Group Work*, which reports research and innovative practice with groups. In addition to these activities, the association has generated "Professional Standards for the Training of Group Workers" (ASGW, 1992), which focuses on core competencies and necessary training experiences for group workers. The association also publishes *Ethical Guidelines for Group Counselors*, which addresses ethical issues specifically as they apply to group counseling (ASGW, 1989).

As mentioned earlier, the majority of ethical standards for group counselors address selection, preparation, and integration of group members during group counseling (including rights of clients to exit groups, to confidentiality, not to be coerced, to receive equitable treatment, and to receive referrals). Other areas covered by the ethical standards include use of techniques, imposition of counselor's values, dual relationships, goal development, between-group consultation, and evaluation/follow-up. It is incumbent on community counselors who engage in group work to be fully knowledgeable about and adhere to the *Ethical Guidelines for Group Counselors* provided by ASGW.

Research evaluating the processes and outcomes of community group counseling is an important responsibility for community counselors involved in group work. Through research, the complex interaction of variables that affect group process and outcomes may be examined (George & Dustin, 1988). These variables include (but certainly are not limited to): purpose of the group; personalities of leaders; theories guiding groups; group activities; duration of meetings; setting; nature of members' problems; and composition of groups with regard to members' ages, gender, personality, development, and so on. Research on group work has been extensive (Zimpfer, 1976, 1984). However, because groups are so complex, there are many methodological problems associated with group research. Also, because each group is unique, there is danger in generalizing findings from one study to another. Extensive programmatic research efforts are needed to advance understanding of group work.

## CONCLUSION

This chapter has presented an introduction to group work, an efficient and potent form of community counseling. An attempt has been made to acquaint the reader with a variety of applications of group work and the theories, functions, and methods typically employed by group counselors, as well as to provide a description of the professional structure of group work. For more detailed exposure to the area of community counseling in groups, readers are encouraged to examine the references for this chapter, in particular the introductory texts (Corey, 1990; Gazda, 1989; Shaffer & Galinsky, 1989; Yalom, 1985), and bibliographies that offer extensive references on specific uses of groups (Zimpfer, 1976, 1984).

## EXERCISE

### Problem in Group Leadership

Imagine you are leading a counseling group for adolescents who were ordered by the court to live in a group home after having been arrested for various crimes (repeated vandalism, truancy, burglary, auto theft). The group's goals are both remedial (changing attitudes that promote criminal behavior) and preventive (helping the adolescents develop knowledge and skills that will protect them from being drawn into permanent deviant lifestyles). It is the third meeting of the group and one member is yelling at another for having informed the house parents that he was smoking cigarettes in their room after lights out. "You're a narc!" the member shouts. The member he is shouting at looks down and remains silent. The non-verbal behavior of the other members suggest they are intensely involved in the interaction. Please discuss the following questions:

1. What stage of development might this group be in and what group dynamics might you expect to be active?

2. What theory or theories would you choose to guide your leadership at this time?

3. What leadership function might you try to fulfill now?

4. In what ways would you try to integrate members of the group to promote productive group interaction?

5. What therapeutic factors would you hope to help the group achieve?

6. What are the ethical concerns of group leadership that arise from this interaction?

### REFERENCES

Association for Specialists in Group Work. (1989). *Ethical guidelines for group counselors.* Alexandria, VA: Author.

Association for Specialists in Group Work. (1992). Professional standards for the training of group workers. *The Journal for Specialists in Group Work, 17,* 12–19.

Bion, V. R. (1959). *Experiences in group.* New York: Basic Books.

Bochner, S. (1986). Training inter-cultural skills. In C. R. Hollin and P. Trower (Eds.), *Handbook of social skills training: Vol. 1. Applications across the life span* (pp. 155–184). Oxford: Pergamon Press.

Bowman, R. P. (1987). Small-group guidance and counseling in schools: A national survey of school counselors. *School Counselor, 34,* 256–262.

Bradford, L. P., Gibb, J. R., & Benne, K. D. (1964). *T-group theory and laboratory method: Innovation in re-education.* New York: Wiley.

Brandler, S., & Roman, C. P. (1991). *Group work: Skills and strategies for effective interventions.* New York: The Haworth Press.

Clark, J., Blanchard, M., & Hawes, C. (1992). Group counseling for people with addictions. In D. Capuzzi & D. R. Gross (Eds.), *Introduction to group counseling* (pp. 103–119). Denver: Love.

Conyne, R. K., Dye, H. A., Kline, W. B., Morran, D. K., Ward, D. E. & Wilson, F. B. (1992). Context for revising the Association for Specialists in Group Work Training Standards. The *Journal for Specialists in Group Work, 17,* 10–11.

Corey, G. (1990). *Theory and practice of group counseling* (3rd ed.). Pacific Grove, CA: Brooks/Cole.

Corey, G., & Corey, M. S. (1992). *Groups: Process and practice* (4th ed.). Pacific Grove, CA: Brooks/Cole.

Erikson, E. H. (1963). *Childhood and society* (2nd ed.). New York: Norton.

Gazda, G. M. (1989). *Group counseling: A developmental approach* (4th ed.). Boston: Allyn & Bacon.

George, R. L. & Dustin, D. (1988). *Group counseling: Theory and Practice*. Englewood Cliffs, NJ: Prentice Hall.

Gladding, S. T. (1991). *Group work: A counseling specialty*. New York: MacMillan.

Hansen, V. C., Warner, R. W. & Smith, E. J. (1980). *Group counseling: Theory and process* (2nd ed.). Chicago: Rand McNally.

Hines, M. (1992). Group counseling with couples and families. In D. Capuzzi & D. R. Gross (Eds.), *Introduction to group counseling* (pp. 205–218). Denver: Love.

Hollin, C. R., & Trower, P. (Eds.). (1986). *Handbook of social skills training: Vol. 1. Applications across the life span.* Oxford: Pergamon.

Hudson, B. L. (1986). Community applications of social skills training. In C. R. Hollin & P. Trower (Eds.), *Handbook of social skills training: Vol. 1. Applications across the life span* (pp. 239–265). Oxford: Pergamon.

Lewin, K. (1951). *Field theory and social science.* New York: Harper & Row.

Lieberman, M., Yalom, I., & Miles, M. (1973). *Encounter groups: First facts.* New York: Basic Books

Livneh, H. & Pullo, R. E. (1992). Group counseling for people with physical disabilities. In D. Capuzzi & D. R. Gross (Eds.), *Introduction to group counseling* (pp. 141–164). Denver: Love.

Luft, J. (1984). *Group processes: An introduction to group dynamics* (3rd ed.). Palo Alto, CA: Mayfield.

Maguire, P. (1986). Social skills training for health professionals. In C. R. Hollin & P. Trower (Eds.), *Handbook of social skills training: Vol. 2. Clinical applications and new directions* (pp. 143–166). Oxford: Pergamon.

Napier, R. W. & Gershenfeld, M. K. (1985). *Groups: Theory and experience* (3rd ed.). Boston: Houghton Mifflin.

Pearson, R. (1992). Group counseling: Self-enhancement. In D. Capuzzi & D. R. Gross (Eds.), *Introduction to group counseling* (pp. 81–102). Denver: Love.

Rogers, C. R. (1970). *Carl Rogers on encounter groups.* New York: Harper & Row.

Shaffer, J., & Galinsky, M. D. (1989). *Models of group therapy* (2nd ed.). Englewood Cliffs, NJ: Prentice Hall.

Sherwood-Hawes, A. (1992). Group counseling for issues related to suicide. In D. Capuzzi & D. R. Gross (Eds.), *Introduction to group counseling* (pp. 236–261). Denver: Love.

Silverman, P. R. (1980). *Mutual help groups: Organization and development.* Beverly Hills, CA: Sage.

Trotzer, J. P. (1989). *The counselor and the group* (2nd ed.). Muncie, IN: Accelerated Development.

Tuckman, B. W. & Jensen, M. A. (1977). Stages of small group development revisited. *Group and organizational studies, 2*, 419–427.

Vinson, A. (1992). Group counseling with victims of abuse/incest. In D. Capuzzi & D. R. Gross (Eds.), *Introduction to group counseling* (pp. 165–181). Denver: Love.

Waldo, M. (1985). Curative factor framework for conceptualizing group counseling. *Journal of Counseling and Development, 64*, 52–58.

Weiner, M. F. (1984). *Techniques of group psychotherapy.* Washington, DC: American Psychiatric Press.

Yalom, I. (1983). *Inpatient group psychotherapy.* New York: Basic Books.

Yalom, I. (1985). *The theory and practice of group psychotherapy* (3rd ed.). New York: Basic Books.

Zastrow, C. (1993). *Social work with groups: Using the class as a group leadership laboratory* (3rd ed.). Chicago: Nelson-Hall.

Zimpfer, D. (1976). *Group work in the helping profession: A bibliography.* Washington, DC: Association for Specialists in Group Work.

Zimpfer, D. (1984). *Group work in the helping profession: A bibliography* (2nd ed.). Muncie, IN: Accelerated Development.

# 11

# EDUCATING AND PROGRAMMING

Chapter 2 of this book identified and explained several roles and functions of the counselor. Two roles, however, have assumed increased importance for the effective delivery of counseling services. They are the roles of educator and program planner. Several factors have contributed to these emerging counselor responsibilities, such as the need for many agencies to implement cost-effective interventions, the importance of developing preventive approaches for mental health problems, and the necessity of assisting people to develop specific skills to manage varied but continued life-adjustment problems. In particular, the literature suggests that underlying such widespread mental health concerns as extreme anxiety, isolation, and depression may be the difficulty of poor social functioning (Wilkinson & Canter, 1982). A program developed to teach clients social skills may eventually facilitate the remediation of their problems.

This chapter will discuss the two counselor roles of educator and program planner, and outline a social skills program training approach that could be adapted to different practice settings. In explaining the specific role and functions of educator, such questions as "How do clients learn?" and "How can the

counselor practice the educator role most effectively?" will be addressed to provide an understanding of the important implications for the counselor, who can be an agent for the communication involved in sharing information and acquiring knowledge. Involved in the educator role are many responsibilities, and if these functions are to be performed successfully, then the counselor must be aware of client learning styles and effective educational practices. After highlighting the principles of program development, this chapter will conclude with a case study example.

## COUNSELOR AS EDUCATOR

The counselor's work extends not only to the alleviation of individual difficulties, but also embraces the goal of helping clients to develop skills for improved emotional and intellectual functioning. This orientation is fundamental to the philosophy of counseling practice that is espoused in this book. Skill development could take place on an individual basis. For the most appropriate use of counselor time and client availability, however, the teaching of these skills may be better achieved in a group setting. This learning environment frequently provides the best opportunity for both the counselor and client to teach and to understand important life skills. One issue that enhances the effectiveness of an educator's efforts is to be knowledgeable about how clients or adult students learn.

## FACTORS INFLUENCING HOW ADULTS LEARN

Several factors influence adult learning, such as the needs, background experiences, attitudes, goals, and competencies of the learner (Seaman & Fellenz, 1989). Added to these characteristics is the situation in which the learning activity can occur and the content of the education itself. If the goal, for example, of an educational program is to communicate important health-related information to the participants, especially to those who may have a difficult time understanding the concepts to be learned, then the subject matter and the presumed learning difficulties will influence the practitioner's teaching style. The learning environment plays a vital role in the client's acquisition of new information and skills. A key ingredient for successful learning is the client's realization that participation in learning experiences will facilitate the achievement of desired goals. When a client realizes, for example, that enrolling in an educational program emphasizing the learning of stress reduction techniques will reduce continued anxiety and apprehension, the individual's motivation to engage in the necessary learning activities will be enhanced. This realization emerges from the participant's understanding of his or her own personal needs. The educator's knowledge of these needs is fundamental for the development of a successful program.

A general knowledge of program participants' learning styles further contributes to the educator's effective performance. Different learners have different ways to grasp, understand, and retain information, and these differences emphasize the truth that learning is a complex interaction of the client's needs, competencies, motivation, the setting, the practitioner's teaching style, and the individual manner by which the program participant understands the program content. Grasha and Riechmann (1975) identified many learning styles, such as:

1. Students who prefer to think for themselves, work on their own, are confident in their learning abilities, and are willing to listen to the ideas of others during a program presentation. These students generally remain distant from the instruction and look at the program content quite objectively.

2. Students who learn more effectively by sharing their ideas and who view the program setting as a source for social interaction as well as content learning.

3. Students who show little intellectual curiosity, learn only what is required, and view the program presenter and peers as sources of support. These students want to be told what to do and will contribute few ideas during a program. They may feel intellectually incompetent, are very concerned about how their program performance will be evaluated, and usually are anxious in a program setting.

4. Students who enjoy going to educational programs, take the responsibility for getting the most out of the specific program, and believe that one should take part in as much of the program-related activity as possible. The main concern of this educational group is understanding the material.

5. Students who show low self-esteem and pessimism about how the program will help them. They offer many criticisms during the program, and often convey the impression that they are hostile toward the educator.

6. Students who do not participate verbally in the program, and are characterized less by what they do during the program than by what they do not do.

Many of these learning styles or participant characteristics overlap one another, and demand the use of varied, instructional formats to satisfy their learning needs. Group discussion, the use of visual aids, a planned structure to the instructor's presentation, and other teaching techniques are necessary to use in order to reach the experiential, ability, and motivational varieties that students have during a program. In most situations when a counselor is offering an educational program to a large group, it is difficult to be aware of individual learning differences. But any attempts to understand these differences may be pivotal for the achievement of successful program goals. Effective education by a counselor implies more, however, than the identification of varied learning styles and the utilization of different teaching techniques.

Good instruction includes the educator's knowledge of the subject matter and his or her motivation to transmit knowledge in a way that lets participants learn. The good educator is willing to make appropriate accommodations to students' needs, is enthusiastic about instruction, and presents the material in a clear and interesting fashion. Counselors who are good educators are able to reach the students' minds, teach by example, and create sustained interest in the topic. They are willing to take risks by attempting to use different teaching techniques, and are organized and caring.

During an educational program, a participant will process information, hopefully integrate the new information with past experience, and then develop an understanding of the subject matter. If the goal of understanding is to be achieved, then educators must show that they care and are concerned about the learning of their students. During the program they encourage collaborative efforts between themselves and participants, as well as provide prompt feedback to students on their performance, communicate high expectations for what is to be learned, and show respect for the diverse talents and varied ways of learning that program participants may exhibit (Chickering & Gamson, 1987).

Coinciding with the opportunity to educate persons within a large program format is the additional counselor responsibility of program planning. Program development is integral to effective education, since educational goals are best achieved when careful planning has occurred. The next section will discuss program development.

## PROGRAM DEVELOPMENT: A COMPREHENSIVE APPROACH

Program development is a comprehensive term that can apply both to individuals and to organizations within the community. Individual program development could comprise, for example, the formulation of plans to assist a client to better life functioning. If the goal, for example, is to restore to deinstitutionalized clients their capacity to function in the community, then specific plans may be developed to assist these persons to progress from their present level of functioning (Anthony, Pierce, Mehren, & Cohen, 1979). Agency or organizational program development utilizes, on the other hand, a broader range of information and usually involves many more steps in the planning stage. For the busy and harassed community counselor, program planning may appear to be a dull or luxurious pastime. But the planning generally involves systematic action and the formulation of realistic and vital goals. Goals are the starting point in program planning. They chart the course and provide the destination for all that follows (Aubrey, 1981).

Before explaining the steps in program development, we should highlight a basic issue in program development, namely, "What makes an effective program work?" Bond and Wagner (1988) and Bartlett (1985) have identified several factors contributing to successful program development. They are summarized as:

**1.** A multisystem, multilevel perspective is important, which includes the forces or influences affecting the individuals targeted in the program. For example, a program designed to assist individuals with disabilities to learn job-seeking skills should consider not only the disability-related issues, but the perspective of the family, the attitudes of the employer, and the current economic picture in the clients' community.

**2.** Programs that emphasize the acquisition of skills and the promotion of their competent application enable clients to develop strategies for adaptively responding to the changing demands of their environments. The learning of important skills may also help individuals to restructure conditions so that they are conducive to their own well-being.

**3.** Through varied strategies incorporated into the program both individuals and groups should become empowered to deal with problems of living. Realizing this sense of empowerment, clients can believe they have many options and even control over many events. For example, programs that instill this empowerment communicate the belief that life transitions are not simply crises to be coped with, but are opportunities for change and development. A program that incorporates structured group interaction with others who find themselves in similar situations can provide opportunities for problem identification, problem solving, and giving help and support. As individuals engage in group decision making and contribute to the support of others, they can gain the confidence, power, and skills to make choices in their own lives as well.

**4.** Sensitivity to the developmental process includes not only attention to the age of the participants but also to the specific needs that emerge at particular periods, for example, in one's career, marriage, and personal life. A program, consequently, has to have the flexibility to address the needs of individuals who may be at different stages in the life transition.

**5.** Programs should be guided by a well-established theoretical perspective. Working from theory allows program planners to maintain a focused direction. A career program that is guided by Super's career development theory, for example, provides a structure that influences program design and goals.

**6.** Program planners need to thoroughly specify the participant behaviors or skills desired at the program's conclusion and identify the obstacles to performing those behaviors and skills.

**7.** A combination of both educational and behavioral strategies within a program is frequently more effective than simply one method. Information is necessary but generally is not sufficient for behavior change or the acquisition of skills. Programs should, therefore, be oriented not only to what the participant should know, but also to what the individual should do to change a particular situation.

**8.** There should be longitudinal tracking of the program's effectiveness. A longitudinal plan for program evaluation can contribute to process issues of further program development and evaluation. A perspective of time tends to generate greater consideration of how the particular program outcomes fit into the original program goals and even the life-span needs of the participants.

Effective programs are based, consequently, on an organized, sequential, comprehensive series of activities and experiences; on initial and even subsequent needs assessment of clients, program instructors, and policy makers; and on measurable, realistic, and specific objectives. A variety of resources and procedures are used to achieve the stated outcomes. Both the program objectives and the different resources used for program implementation should be in harmony with the identified needs of the participants.

The comprehensive sequential approach encompasses the components of planning, developing and implementing, all of which are basic steps or phases in program development.

## Planning

This phase involves determining what the staff and perhaps the consumers/clients want to accomplish and then integrating this goal with system or institutional needs. This is largely a data-gathering phase and uses information collected from needs or environment assessments. The key to good foundation building for a program is identifying the important needs of that programs's consumers. This phase also implies that the agency has articulated its philosophy, has determined how an existing program is functioning, and then based on these data, formulates needs statements and establishes a workable set of program goals. In other words, desired outcomes are identified and the current status of program resources, allocation of resources, and the current status of program consumers are evaluated. With all of this collected information, then, program goals are developed. Though initially these program goals may be formulated as global, abstract statements, it is important that as program plans continue to evolve, these goals become more specific. Generalized goal statements often fail to indicate exactly what the program consumers should be able to accomplish within the particular program.

An example of this planning is a community agency that seeks to start a program to prepare clients to live productive lives after retirement from their employment or profession. The staff who wish to begin this intervention will review the literature on the issue of postretirement life. Then they will target the intended population within a specified community and develop an approach to ascertain future client needs. Interviews with people about to retire or questionnaires may be utilized to collect data from future consumers. The staff may also wish to talk with counseling personnel who have been chosen for identifying client needs, and then select the format that would best suit the purposes of the staff and the abilities of the consumer to respond to the requested information. After these data are collected, a generalized goal for the program will be formulated, such as to help postretirement persons increase their productivity.

## Developing

In this phase, three steps are usually involved: (1) specifying immediate program participants and objectives; (2) investigating, selecting, and structuring program procedures, and (3) communicating and evaluating program structuring decisions and activities. The first step implies that the target population may have to be narrowed down further because staff and other resource availability, that is, financial or space, may necessitate a reduction in original program participants. Examining demographic data is one way to obtain more precise estimates of the target population. A crucial part of this step is to identify the specific goals that the program participants are to achieve. If possible, these should be measurable and priorities should be established among these goals. The second step focuses on identifying those particular events or activities that will be developed and used to achieve the planned objectives. The third step involves promoting the program itself within the community and evaluating through outcome measurement whether or not the program objectives have been attained.

To apply these steps to the designated example, the first demand for the staff might be to review again whether agency resources are sufficient to meet the identified needs of the target population. Though this was initially done in the planning phase, added information from the needs assessment may demand a reexamination of who in the target population can actually be served. Also, more specific program objectives will be developed that might include vocational, educational, personal-social, health, and leisure goals. As an example of educational goals, behaviors in this area might involve exploring and pursuing educational opportunities independent of, or not immediately having, vocational concomitants. In the second step activities will be selected and structured in the vocational, education, personal-social, health, and leisure areas. This will demand, of course, that the staff develop these activities in harmony with information collected from the needs assessment and the recognized capabilities of the program participants. Finally, once these activities have been planned, they are advertised among the intended target population. As the program begins, moreover, an evaluation approach can be designed that will assess the achievement of the program's activities.

## Implementing

In this phase the activities are begun and the program participants have an understanding of the program objectives. Prior to the implementation, program staff will have to be selected and perhaps staff development activities will also be initiated. Before all the activities are implemented, however, a counseling agency may wish to field test or "pilot" a particular activity in order to evaluate participant involvement and the feasibility of the design of the acitivty. When initiating the program for recent retirees, for example, the agency may want to begin with a personal-social activity in order to assess (a) whether it will appeal to the population, even though the needs assessment emphasized the activity, and (b) whether the way in which the staff has designed the personal-social activity really is capable of helping the postretirees to meet the stated objectives.

The three phases of planning, development, and implementation explained here comprise one systematic approach to program development. It is based on comprehensive data, and each of the phases involves many individual tasks for the program staff. The systematic nature of the program development does not remove the need for hard work. An illustration, however, that highlights different phases of program planning is a social skills training program. The suggested program also identifies the many functions that comprise the counselor's role as educator and program developer.

## SOCIAL SKILLS TRAINING

Social skills training is concerned with changing social behavior (Wilkinson & Canter, 1982). This training program is intended to give participants a sense of empowerment to deal with many problems of everyday living. Wilkinson and Canter (1982) believed that social behavior is learned, and many persons never acquire the skills for making satisfactory social relationships or for dealing with a wide variety of situations. Failure to learn these skills may result in extreme anxiety or depression. The extent of a person's deficit may vary, from a particular behavior as a lack of assertiveness when interacting with a spouse to include every aspect of social behavior, verbal and nonverbal. When an individual becomes more socially skilled, he or she then may become less anxious and feel less inadequate and more confident in handling social interactions.

Utilizing the framework of planning, development, and implementation, the program format that a counselor may adopt for social skills training can include such guidelines as: (a) the intended outcomes of training, (b) subject matter or content, (c) assumptions and normative beliefs, (d) intended audiences, and (e) methods of practice (Thomas & Arcus, 1992). The training itself is a planned, systematic teaching of the specific behaviors needed and consciously desired by the individual in order to function in an effective and satisfying manner (Goldstein, 1981). The program, consequently, should be well organized, have designated steps for learning, and teach specific behaviors. An assumption in the development of such programs is that they will relate to a client's needs, and that the participant is motivated to acquire the skills to be taught. Prior to the training the counselor should identify the social behavior needs of the clients who comprise the intended audience. After the identification of these needs, the counselor can follow the suggested program considerations that follow when developing training formats.

## Intended Training Outcomes

Different goals are developed, of course, for different populations. For those who have never learned a number of basic social behaviors because of poor instruction or lack of adequate models, then such skills that involve enhanced interpersonal communication may be taught in a training program. Further, because of a trauma, such as brain injury or stroke, many previously learned skills may have be be relearned, or long periods of institutionalization by persons with a mental impairment may diminish language and related communication skills. The deterioration of needed social skills may include nonverbal behaviors, i.e., facial expression, posture, and personal appearance. Social behaviors are perceived, consequently, as skills, and those that need remediation or development will depend on the needs of different clients. The literature that addresses the question of training outcomes for social skill programs does not identify a common goal for these programs, and the literature that specifies particular goals for a training program on social behaviors does not adequately reflect whether the focus of the training is on "enrichment" "enhancement," "remediation," (Ellis

& Whittington, 1981; Goldstein, 1981; Wilkinson & Canter, 1982). Yet Goldstein (1981) explained that the goals of training should emphasize effectiveness and satisfaction. Effectiveness pertains to the impact on others emerging from one's newly acquired skills, and satisfaction might be the inner feeling that is a consequence of overtly effective skill behavior.

## Subject Matter/Content

A review of the literature indicates that there is considerable diversity concerning the context of social skills training. Goldstein (1981) stated that social behavior comprises interpersonal and personal skills. Interpersonal skills are those competencies that individuals must use in their interactions with other individuals or groups of individuals, such as communication, leadership, relationship, and conflict management skills. Personal skills are emotional, cognitive, observational, or skills that relate to practical aspects of daily living in work, school, or home environments, such as self-control, decision making, goal setting, preparing for stressful conversations, and setting problem priorities. Ellis and Whittington (1981), in citing Trower et al. (1978), provided a useful organizational framework to understand both the diversity and the comprehensiveness of social behaviors. This framework with selected examples, is now explained:

1. Observation skills: Getting information about a situation; getting information about the other's attitudes and feelings
2. Listening skills: Reflection of feelings; attention feedback; questioning
3. Speaking skills: Disclosure of information; disclosure of feeling

| | |
|---|---|
| 4. Expression of attitudes: | Matching another's style and choosing a different style in order to influence the person |
| 5. Social routines: | Greetings; farewells; requests; gaining access to strangers; offering compliments, praise, encouragement, congratulations; sympathy; explanations; apologies; assertion |
| 6. Nonverbal: | Gaze, glance; facial expression; proximity and orientation; voice quality—pitch, loudness, speed; gestures accompanying speech and expressing emotions; posture—relaxed, tense, dominant or submissive |
| 7. Appearance: | Image conveyed by hair, grooming, clothes |

In citing Goldstein et al. (1976), Ellis and Whittington suggested an aditional framework for identifying social skills; the list of 59 skills is divided into five series of basic skills and a series of application skills tied to specified situations. The list consists of:

| | |
|---|---|
| Series I | *Conversations*: beginning skills: includes starting, stopping, carrying on, listening |
| Series II | *Conversations*: expressing oneself: includes expressing praise and encouragement, affection, anger, complaint, asking for help, giving instructions |
| Series III | *Conversations*: responding to others: includes responding to praise, persuasion, complaint, anger, confusion, empathy, apologizing, following instructions |
| Series IV | *Planning skills*: includes setting goals, priorities, gathering information, concentration on task, evaluating own abilities, preparing for stress, decision making |
| Series V | *Alternatives to aggression*: includes identifying emotions, determining responsibility, making requests, relaxation, self-control, negotiation, helping others and assertiveness |
| Series VI | *Application skills*: presituational skills that range from job seeking and moving into an apartment through marital situations to dealing with bereavement |

Ivey (1971) identified microcounseling skills which were developed from behavior modification strategies and include attending skills, interpersonal influence (self-expression, giving direction, expressing feelings and information, summarizing, and self-disclosure), and empathy (positive regard, warmth, concreteness, immediacy, confrontation, and genuineness). Many lists of social skills that are targets for training have been developed, and some skills appear more frequently and in more than one setting. Ellis and Whittington (1981) believed that such skills include greeting, asking questions, and giving praise.

## Assumptions and Normative Beliefs

In social skills training it is assumed that learning will be structured and participants will be exposed to expertly portrayed examples of the specific skill behaviors to be learned (Goldstein, 1981). The focus is to enable trainees to become better at interacting with other people (Ellis & Whittington, 1981). At the beginning of training, educators should make quite explicit their own views on social skills and training. When pursuing the direction of structured learning, a behaviorist approach will be implied, which puts emphasis on the features of the learner and on the environment, including the importance of learning through observation. This behavioral paradigm further implies that learning is encouraged through operant and classical conditioning. Both of these approaches seek to identify the ways in which behavior changes in relation to observable events. Social skills must be operationalized, consequently, in terms of observable behavior, and be reduced during training to subscales for easier learning. Reward is an important aspect of training (Ellis & Whittington, 1981). The learning process is facilitated when complex skills are reduced to simpler components, and the associations between action and the consequences of action are provided.

Though the training is structured, individual differences among the participants should be recognized. During the social skills program the trainee should experience the skill to be learned and report that he or she has done so, and an appropriate range of human problems should be presented to the participant. This type of training assumes that social interactions are analyzed, particular skills are identified for learning, and the relationship between these skills and their desired outcomes after training is explained.

## Intended Audiences

As stated earlier in this chapter, poor social functioning can cause a variety of client problems, such as loneliness, rejection, or poor self-image. The audiences for training will vary according to the problems that need remediation or the social behaviors that need development for specific clients. Clients are usually referred for training following an assessment interview. The interview can provide social and interactional data about the client, though one may initially talk about personal problems in terms of unhappiness, anxiety, or depression, rather than the inability to deal with social relationships (Wilkinson & Canter, 1982). The counselor who is aware of the deficits caused by poor social behaviors may have to structure the interview around specific interpersonal relationships and situations. After gaining information about the client's social functioning, the counselor should establish what changes the client would like to make and the extent to which the client is prepared to work toward making these changes (Wilkinson & Canter, 1982). The client's daily living and working environments should also be explored during the interview, since expectations from others can influence social behavior.

## Methods of Training

Goldstein (1981) believed that social behavior skills training can lead to trainer effectiveness and satisfaction "over an extended period of time and in a variety of positive, negative, and neutral contexts" (p. 4). The training methods utilized in a social skills program consist largely of principles derived from social learning theory principles and include instruction, modeling, role playing, and feedback. Instructional texts, simulations, and warmup exercises, structured discussions, behavioral rehearsal (roleplay), reinforcement, rewards, and homework assignments can also be part of the training methodology. Each training session is designed around a particular topic, which might be a nonverbal or verbal behavior or a particular situation that should elicit a special social skill, such as eye contact or assertive communication.

Wilkinson and Canter (1982) explained that "behavioral rehearsal forms the core component of social skills training." (p. 46). After a specific social skill needed for appropriate interaction is identified, the trainee is assisted to enact a brief scene that simulates the identified real-life situations, and is further instructed how to vary the usual set of responses and to try out new behaviors. The instructor prepares the role play, and perhaps prompts the client during the simulation. Other techniques used during the training are:

**1.** *Warm-up exercises*: Before the actual training of a specific social behavior, the client might practice a social skill not related to the actual situation, such as eye contact or tone of voice.

**2.** *Reinforcement*: This represents some form of feedback, such as rewards of praise and encouragement given immediately after the behavior rehearsal. The rewards must be appropriate to the need satisfactions of the specific client. Money has been used, for example, with institutionalized psychiatric populations; as rewards for learning different social interaction skills. But any feedback should focus on the behavior to be learned and not the person, and be given only to those skills taught in a particular session.

**3.** *Homework assignments*: Clients should have the opportunity to try out newly learned skills in real-life conditions. These assignments promote the transfer of behaviors acquired in a training context to real-life situations. The assignments will focus, of course, on skills taught in a particular session. Before the homework is actually given, it is helpful to have the trainee describe the actual situation in which the behavior will be attempted and indicate any possible obstacles. This information can be discussed and then a homework plan developed that considers how the trainee can best achieve success in skill implementation (Wilkinson & Canter, 1982).

All of these methods will be used during training in a variety of ways. They also may be utilized for group or one-to-one training and in individualized or standardized programs. The extent of their use in social skills training will depend, of course, on the length, number, and frequency of sessions. The length of each session will be influenced by whether training is on an individual or group basis and the difficulty in learning a particular skill. Also to be considered when planning the frequency of sessions is the client's time availability and the nature of the client's social behavior problem. For clients who have been shy and withdrawn for many years, leading to problems of extreme anxiety and avoidance related to social situations, the learning of assertion skills, for example, may take many sessions conducted over a long period of time.

Utilizing the teaching of assertive skills as an illustration of a social behavior training program, a program is now suggested that contains steps, phases, or components that can be applied to other social skills programs. Assuming that assertiveness involves duration of eye contact, tone of voice, speech fluency, facial expression, number of questions asked, and duration of responding (Ellis & Whittington, 1981), then a skills training program is implemented that includes the following steps (Wilkinson & Canter, 1982; Ellis & Whittington, 1981; & Goldstein, 1981):

**1.** *Preparing the client*. Following the assessment of the problem social behavior, details of the training arrangements should be carefully explained to the client. Punctuality, regular attendance, commitment, and full cooperation should be emphasized. The counselor may wish to use motivational procedures to ensure regular program attendance, such as selected reinforcements or incentives.

**2.** *Selection of the training setting.* With individual, one-to-one instruction it may be in the counselor's office. With groups a large room that engenders comfort and availability for easy movement during training is a necessity. The room must be large enough to conduct behavioral rehearsals.

**3.** *Actual training.*

**a.** *Introduction* to social skills training, and in later sessions, introduction and careful explanation of the specific, social skill to be learned, including its importance and function.

**b.** *Instruction.* The emphasis is on how a particular skill can be acquired and the specific situations in which it can be used. At this time, the different components of assertive skills, for example, can be explained and their use in a particular social situation can be illustrated.

**c.** *Warm-up exercise.* Perhaps the trainee can practice, with the goal of learning assertive skills, tone of voice and eye contact. The client may read a passage from a selected book to be aware of voice tone, or practice eye contact with a partner.

**d.** *Role play.* The instructor develops a simulated situation and then models, for example, the specific assertive skill. This may have to be repeated many times and then the client will practice the skill behavior, again perhaps many times. Each practice should be followed by the giving of some feedback, such as praise and encouragement. In a group session these practices may be done in pairs and then presented to the group for feedback and rating.

**4.** *Homework.* A specific assignment will be given by the instructor and details of how the behavior is to be practiced will be carefuly explained. The homework assignments stimulate the transfer of training, a vital component in social skills programs. The target of these assignments should be on the behavior being taught, and questions asked at the beginning of the training session about homework tasks should always be phrased in behavioral terms.

The sustained emphasis throughout training on the client's social skill behaviors that need improvement highlights the focus that it is essentially new behaviors that should be learned. Though clients bring to training their own feelings and attitudes, and while some of these feelings, such as anxiety and fear, might increase temporarily during training because of the role-play situations, it is important in social skill programs to maintain concentration on the client's behavior when working with social skill difficulties.

Social skills training is a highly structured form of learning requiring the insightful identification of the client's skill deficits and the careful preparation of the program and the client. The counselor may find such training extremely useful for the remediation of many of the client's problems (Wilkinson & Carter, 1982). Social skills training has been adapted and applied across a wide range of clients, settings, and circumstances, and the literature reports that there is enough positive evidence to merit its continued use as an intervention strategy (Ellis & Whittington, 1981).

Besides a social skills program, another approach is suggested, however, that is even more systematic in its program development. It is a model that is relevant not only to organizational needs, but also to the community counselor working with an individual client. One of the assumptions of this approach is that if the client is to function productively in the community, then he or she will usually have to be taught appropriate, needed skills (Anthony et al., 1979).

# A PROGRAMMING MODEL

The material that will be used to explain this approach is taken from Anthony et al. (1979) and modified for community counselors. These authors believe that although it is most important to diagnose client needs, behaviors, strengths, and deficits, another skill is required to enable clients to act on those diagnosed strengths and deficits. Thus, to identify community needs is essential for program planning; to act upon these identified needs necessitates an orderly, very systematic approach. In other words, if the diagnostic process is to assist clients to develop insights into their problems, then program planning is to help to develop client action. The stages and skills of this programming model are as follows:

1. Exploring the client's/organization's unique programming needs
   a. Establish priorities for the client's/organization's goals
   b. Develop the overall program plan
2. Understanding the specific program steps
3. Implementing the specific program steps

## Exploring the Client's/Organization's Unique Programming Needs

### Establish Priorities for the Client's/ Organization's Goals

The process of assigning priorities involves assessing client and organizational issues from three perspectives: (1) life functioning urgency; (2) client and organization motivation; and (3) client level of skill functioning or organizational level of resource availability. Life functioning urgency refers to deficits or needs that, if not overcome or met, will limit the client's ability to survive. Client motiva-

tion refers to the client's desire to either overcome or ignore specific skill deficits; organization motivation implies that the agency wants to expand to meet the widening demands of the population. Client level of skill functioning differentiates between the skill areas where the client is functioning relatively well. Organizational level of resource availability is concerned with, for example, an identification of adequate resources, namely, staff, financial, or space, and what is needed to function in a manner that better serves the particular goal.

### Develop the Overall Program Plan

The goal of this step is to describe the responsibilities of the person(s) who will be held accountable for the program. Usually the person who develops the program is the person responsible for writing and sequencing the necessary program steps. In some cases, however, a number of people may be involved in the development, implementation, and monitoring process. This is particularly true when an agency is developing a program that will have an impact on the community. One of the key components in this development, however, is the monitoring process. Often, well-designed programs go awry because no one maintains responsibility for determining on a periodic basis whether the program is being implemented. Also, on an individual client basis, the person who monitors the program assures, when possible, that differential reinforcement occurs as a result of the client's successful or unsuccessful program performance. Another important component of the plan is the determination of when the plan will begin and end, because there should always be a target date for each part of the program.

With individual clients, the community counselor might wish to specify on the plan the specific client behaviors that should be changed, or what skills should be acquired or enhanced if the client is to achieve productive living. Anthony et al. (1979) emphasized that the goal specified on the client's plan should be observable. For example, after evaluating the client's problem, the counselor might believe that the client's physical, emotional, and intellectual functioning will have to improve if the client is going to make a suitable adjustment. The main problem might be a continued state of anxiety that is preventing the client from making decisions in his/her life.

For example, a client reports that she feels badly about being overweight and this covers a feeling of inferiority and loss of confidence in herself. Yet as a single mother of three children, she must make continued decisions about home and school issues and about problems that occur at her job as an accountant. Because she unnecessarily delays making these decisions, she believes she is living in a constant state of anxiety. To alleviate this anxiety, the client might have to feel better about herself physically, begin to utilize her intellectual capabilities, and perform activities that will help her to have peace of mind. Each area—physical, emotional, and intellectual—would have to be identified in the plan for improvement. An example of an observable goal in the physical area might be, "In 4 weeks, the client will lose 5 pounds." A modification of a sample program planning chart as devised by Anthony et al. (1979) for this client is illustrated in Figure 11–1.

## Understanding the Specific Program Steps

In the second stage the counselor would develop the major program steps. On an organizational level, once a programming goal has been identified (for example, implementing a primary prevention program for substance abuse among adolescents), this might involve using brainstorming sessions with the agency staff to identify how a program can be promoted and then initiated in the community, defining the current prevention efforts in the specific community, and finding the "ideal" prevention strategies. The steps to promote and implement the program would be created and each step would be written, if possible, in behavioral terms. On the client level the development of the major program steps would include: (a) defining the client's present and needed skill functioning in observable terms, such as the physical area, the needed weight loss; (b) involving the client in the program development; (c) using brainstorming questions to identify the steps that will advance the client from where he/she is to where he/she needs to be; (d) listing the steps as they are created; and (e) writing the steps in behavioral terms.

For the client who is having decision-making problems because of overwhelming anxiety, once the counselor has identified weight loss as one approach to alleviate the problem,

**FIGURE 11–1**    Program Planning Chart

Goal: To reduce client's anxiety and increase client's decision-making skills in the homemaking and employment areas:

| Area | Program Developer | Program Monitor | Date of Implementation | Date of Completion |
|---|---|---|---|---|
| Physical To Lose 5 lbs. in 4 weeks | Counselor | Counselor | As soon as possible | 4 weeks from beginning of plan |
| Emotional | | | | |
| Intellectual | | | | |

then the counselor will explore with the client the ways to lose this weight. Exercise and diet can both be discussed, and once a method is agreed on, the specific steps to pursue regular exercise or to change eating habits will be noted. Engaging in regular exercise might involve the specific steps of (a) identifying what kind of exercise is the most feasible; (b) deciding where this exercise could be performed; and (c) establishing a schedule to do the exercise.

## Implementing the Specific Program Steps

The third stage includes, according to Anthony et al. (1979), setting time lines for program implementation; creating reinforcement steps; implementing, when necessary, the teaching steps; and then monitoring client performance. The setting of time lines is a valuable component in program development because these guidelines give clients or organizations a target for which to aim and a structure to keep them on the program's schedule. Time lines also serve as criteria by which client performance can be evaluated, and are set for the completion of each major step. For example, if the community counselor is to recommend weight loss as one approach to alleviating the client's severe anxiety, then the client's self-expectation might be enhanced with the guidelines of a time framework. This framework might even increase the client's motivation to lose weight.

Another dimension of this stage that is quite helpful for programming efforts is the development of reinforcement steps. Although perhaps not as applicable to organizations as to clients, reinforcements can act as motivators and rewards for acquiring new skills. These reinforcers should come from the client's frame of reference, namely, the client must perceive the reinforcer as actually reinforcing. The counselor's perception of a certain behavior as reinforcing may not necessarily be what the client considers reinforcing (Anthony et al., 1979). Even the counselor can be a potent reinforcer to clients, and this is particularly true of counselors who have demonstrated a high level of interpersonal skills with their clients. Yet the unique things and activities that each client finds to be reinforcing can be learned by observing the client, by questioning the client, and/or by soliciting the observations of significant others.

Both of the approaches to program development discussed here—the comprehensive model and the programming model—use systematic methods in their planning efforts. The effectiveness of planning for human services depends not only on the involvement and cooperation of the target community and the participation of agency staff and clients in the planning process, but also on the skills of program developers to focus on specific strategies that can prevent or remediate particular problems. When planners are faced with many attractive alternatives to alleviate community problems, there is the temptation to run off simultaneously in all directions. If a counselor in a substance abuse rehabilitation agency wants to develop, for example, a program to prevent adolescent substance abuse, there are many options to pursue. A systematic approach to planning provides guidelines for the selection of options. Furthermore, the planner must distinguish between short- and long-term objectives, because they may be antithetical. Providing remedies to those young people who are already using drugs, for example, can be of immediate benefit to these people, but it may reduce the community's support for the more fundamental and long-range changes needed to alter the substance abuse cycle. There are many issues to consider, consequently, when conducting program development. Effective program development can make a difference in how the community influences the client's own attainment of life adjustment goals. The community itself can also become a therapeutic resource for clients.

## EXERCISE

## Case Study

The following case study can provide an example of what is needed to develop an effective program for a designated population. As a community counselor, you have been asked by a local health clinic to develop and present a workshop for seven families who have a member who has been diagnosed with AIDS during the past four months. The clinic is in a rural area, and the physician who has been treating the individuals with AIDS contacted the mental health facility because he feels that these families "need help," and some of the family members have showed reluctance to assume any of the caregiving responsibilities. There is no hospice or similar facility in the county, and home care will be the most viable option for care as the disease progresses to its more severe state. All the family members have agreed to attend the first session of the planned workshop, but have reservations about their continued involvement in any program. The physician has been practicing medicine in the county for over 15 years, and apparently is widely respected in the community. He also has a master's degree in public health. Within the families, both the father and mother have at least part-time jobs in the surrounding towns. It is mainly an agricultural area, but the farms are quite small and family income must be supplemented by other jobs. There are also two factories in the county, and many of the family members work for these companies. Within each family there is a nuclear family-mother and father still living, with at least one sibling besides the individual with AIDS. No sibling is younger than 18 years of age. Those with AIDS range from 24 to 33 years of age, and three are still working in the local economy.

What are the steps that you would follow in developing this workshop program accord-ing to the material explained in this chapter that particularly focuses on planning, developing, and implementing?

## REFERENCES

Anthony, W. A., Pierce, R. H., Mehren, R., & Cohen, M. (1979). *The skills of diagnostic planning (psychiatric rehabilitation practice series: Book 1).* Amherst, MA: Carkhuff Institute of Human Technology.

Aubrey, R. C. (1981). Program planning and evaluation: Road map for the 80's. *Elementary School Guidance Counseling, 17,* 51–52.

Bartlett, E. E. (1985). Eight principles form patient education research. *Preventative Medicine, 14,* 667–669.

Bond, L. A., & Wagner, B. M. (1988). *Families in transition. Primary prevention programs that work.* Newbury Park, CA: Sage.

Chickering, A. W., & Gamson, Z. F. (1987). Seven principles for good practice in undergraduate education. *The Wingspread Journal, 9,* 1–4.

Ellis, R., & Whittington, D. (1981). *Guide to social skill training.* Cambridge, MA: Brookline Books.

Goldstein, A. P. (1981). *Psychological skill training.* New York: Pergamon Press.

Goldstein, A., Sprafkin, R., & Gershaw, N. (1976). *Skill training for community living.* New York: Pergamon Press.

Grasha, T., & Riechmann, S. (1975). Student learning styles. In W. Bergquist, & S. Phillips (Eds.), *Handbook for faculty development.* Washington, DC: Council for Advancement of Small Colleges.

Ivey, A. (1971). *Microcounseling: Innovations in interviewing training.* Springfield, IL: Charles Thomas.

Seaman, D. F., & Fellenz, R. A. (1989). *Effective strategies for teaching adults.* Toronto: Merrill.

Thomas, J., & Arcus, M. (1992). Family life education: An analysis of the concept. *Family Relations, 41,* 3–8.

Trower, P., Bryant, B., & Argyle, M. (1978). *Social skills and mental health.* London: Methuen.

Wilkinson, J., & Canter, S. (1982). *Social skills training manual.* New York: John Wiley & Sons.

# 12

# CONSULTATION AND SUPERVISION

Because community counseling focuses on maximizing the resources available in clients' communities to foster their development and growth, it follows that community counselor will dedicate considerable effort to strengthening the effectiveness of community resources. Two of the primary ways in which this can be accomplished are through community counseling consultation and supervision. Consultation has been defined as "...tripartite interactions in human service agencies. The consultant (a specialized professional) assists consultees (agency employees who are also professionals) with work-related concerns (the third component)" (Gallessich, 1982, p. 6). The third component typically is clients and/or services to clients. Supervision has been defined as "...an experienced counselor helping a beginning student or less experienced therapist learn counseling by various means" (Bartlett, 1983, p. 9). Usually, the

"various means" include review of the less experienced counselor's services to clients.

Clearly there is a good deal of overlap between the two activities. An experienced and expert counselor helps a less experienced counselor to learn and improve his or her work. There are important differences as well, most of which are associated with authority and evaluation. Supervisors typically have authority over supervisees and responsibility to evaluate their performance (Bernard & Goodyear, 1992). This is usually not the case with consultation. Consultation and supervision will be addressed separately in this chapter.

## CONSULTATION

Since passage of the Community Mental Health Act in 1963, consultation has become recognized as a more broadly defined helping process (Kurpius, 1978). This act specifically stated that consultation services were to become an "essential" part of the community mental health programs of the future. Kurpius (1978) explained that the "intent of this early legislation was to urge the helping professions to move from individual and small group remedial activities as the primary caregiving intervention toward more developmental and preventive approaches" (p. 32).

There is no one universally agreed upon definition of consultation (Mannino & Shore, 1986), but a number of diverse definitions delineate its key components, which results in consultation having its own identity (West & Idol, 1987). Ohlsen (1983) defined it as "an activity in which a professional helps another person in regard to a third." (p. 347). Kurpuis (1978) agreed and stated "…by definition the process …tends to be triadic (consultant, consultee, and client or client system)" (p. 335). The ethical code of the American Counseling Association (1988) goes one step further and defines consultation as "a voluntary relationship between a professional helper and help-needing individual, group or social unit in which the consultant is providing help to the client(s) in defining and solving a work-related problem or potential problem with a client or client system" (p. 3). Perhaps the most succinct and current definition is offered by Dougherty (1990, p. 12):

*A type of helping relationship in which a human services professional (consultant) delivers assistance to another person (consultee) in order to solve a work-related or caretaking-related problem the consultee has with a client system.*

Caplan (1970) believed that it is important to distinguish consultation from other community counseling activities with which it is sometimes confused. Bloom (1984) stated that consultation can be differentiated from supervision on the grounds that (a) the consultant may not be of the same professional specialty as the consultee, (b) the consultant has no administrative responsibility for the work of the consultee, (c) consultation may be irregular in character rather than continuous, and (d) the consultant is not in a position of power with respect to the consultee. He added that consultation can be distinguished from education on the basis of (a) the relative freedom of the consultee to accept or reject the ideas of the consultant, (b) the lack of a planned curriculum on the part of the consultant, (c) the absence of any evaluation or assessment of the consultee's progress by the consultant. Consultation is different from counseling because in the latter there is a clear contractual relationship between an individual designated as a client and another individual designated as a counselor (Bloom, 1984). Also, the goal of consultation is improved work performance rather than improved personal adjustment. Consultation is different, moreover, from collaboration, because in the case of the former there is no implication that the consultant will participate with the consultee in the implementation of any plans. The task of the consultant is to assist the consultee in meeting his or her work responsibilities more effectively.

In its earliest stage of development during the late 1940s and early 1950s, consultation was viewed as a direct service to clients or to client systems (Kurpius, 1978). As more experience was gained with this direct service approach, it was recognized that it would be beneficial to include the consultee in the problem-solving process. By the end of the 1950s, consequently, a major breakthrough in consultation resulted—the consultee became active in the consultation process. During this time Gerald Caplan's work became decisive in formulating a direction for consultation. Among his contributions was the innovative concept of "theme interference," defined by Caplan (1964) as a "symbolic inhibition of free perception and communication between consultee and client and a concomitant disorder of objectivity" (p. 223). Themes are symbols of unresolved problems that result in an assumption of likely failure (Rogawski, 1978). Theme interferences reduce the consultee's effectiveness in working with clients, and the technique of theme-interference reduction employed by the community counselor is designed to modify the line of reasoning being followed by the consultee as well as the consultee's feelings (Bloom, 1984).

In the 1960s, the consultant was established as a trainer. With the assumption that the consultant has expert knowledge and skills in a problem area, organizations hire consultants to educate their members in areas of need (Conoley & Conoley, 1982). Consultants can directly teach consultees solutions to problems and/or teach them how to learn about their problems and generate solutions (Lippitt & Nadler, 1979; Beer, 1980). Although the training function of consultation continues, a more generic purpose of consultation has emerged in which the consultant facilitates the consultees' use of their own skills and knowledge to resolve difficulties (Berkowitz, 1973; Brokes, 1975). In what is often referred to as the Process Model (Schein, 1969, 1978, 1987), the consultee provides less structure than would a trainer (Brown, Pryzwansky, & Schulte, 1987), and instead collaborates with the consultant in a joint effort (Goodstein, 1978).

Models of consultation have developed that guide how consultation is offered (process) and who or what is the focus of consultation (content). Both the process and content of community counseling consultation will be addressed below, with examples. It is important to remember that whatever model is employed, consultation is likely to progress through stages. The stages have been described by Dougherty (1990) as entry, diagnosis, implementation and disengagement. Each will be discussed in further depth later in this chapter. Keeping in mind the universal

application of stages in consultation, models of consultation process will be addressed first, followed by a description of categories of content upon which consultation can focus.

Four models of consultation process have been identified by Kurpius and Brubaker (1976):

**1.** *Provision.* In this type of consultation, the consultant provides a direct service to consultees who do not have the time, inclination, or perceived skills to deal with a particular problem area. Historically, this mode of consultation was the first to develop (Kurpuis & Robinson, 1978) and was used extensively in the 1940s and early 1950s. The advantage of the model is that experts can handle difficult problems and thus leave consultees free to manage their own duties without work conflicts. Schein (1978) referred to this form of consultation as the expert model because of the role the consultant plays. Examples of expert provision of consultation by community counselors following the stages suggested by Dougherty (1990) might be found in counselors consulting with a battered spouses' shelter. Shelter workers may be uncertain how to assist their clients in making decisions about their plans after leaving the shelter. The consultants develop relationships with the shelter staff and assess the circumstances of shelter clients identifying what inhibits their decision making. If impediments to decision making include the shelter clients not having had an opportunity to clarify and resolve conflicts in their values, the consultants could periodically provide two-hour workshops on values clarification and conflict resolution for shelter clients. The consultants could assess the effectiveness of the workshops by asking for feedback from the clients and checking with shelter staff about their clients' success in planning their departure from the shelter.

**2.** *Prescription.* This form of consultation does not require the consultant to bring about a change or "cure" as in the provision model.

Instead, the consultant advises the consultee about what is wrong with the targeted third party and what should be done about it. A good way to conceptualize this method is to draw an analogy with the traditional medical model, where a patient's problem is diagnosed and a prescription to rectify the situation is given (Schein, 1978). Using the situation depicted under provision, prescription would involve community counselor consultants giving shelter staffs formats and directions for the staffs to provide values clarification workshops for their clients. The staff members instead of the consultants would lead the workshops.

3. *Mediation*. In this model, consultants act as coordinators. Their main function is to help unify the services of a variety of people who are trying to solve a problem. They accomplish this goal in one of two ways: (a) coordinate the services already being provided, or (b) create an alternative plan of services that represents a mutually acceptable synthesis of several solutions. Mediation consultation applied to assisting with shelter clients planning for leaving the shelter might involve community counselors in consulting with police departments, family services agencies, employment agencies and housing services. The services of each of these agencies could be coordinated to offer shelter clients a variety of options to choose from in planning for their safety and well-being after leaving the shelter.

4. *Collaboration*. Consultants who operate from this position are facilitators of the problem-solving process. Their main task is to get their consultees actively involved in finding solutions to the present difficulties they have with clients. Thus, consultees must define their problems clearly, analyze them thoroughly, design workable solutions, and then implement and evaluate their own plan of action. Setting up an atmosphere in which this process can happen is a major task for collaboration consultants. It requires the use of a number of interpersonal counseling skills, for example, empathy, active listening, and structuring. In addition, to make the process work, consultants must be highly intelligent and analytical thinkers, who are able to generate enthusiasm, optimism, and self-confidence in others. They must be able to integrate affective, behavioral, and cognitive dimensions of problem solving and know how to use each appropriately. Community counselors offering collaboration consultation to shelter staff would hold meetings with the staff during which the staff would define the problem of facilitating their clients' planning and design their own efforts to overcome it.

Bloom (1984) explained another perspective on the different types or models of consultation, which addresses who or what consultation focuses on (content). He described the four varieties of consultation suggested by Caplan (1964), which are:

1. *Client-centered case consultation*. In this variety of consultation the primary goal is to help the consultee deal with the presented case, and the case, or client, is the focus of the consultation. To accomplish this goal, the consultant uses his or her specialized skills and knowledge to assist the consultee in making an assessment of the client's problem and to recommend how best to deal with the problem (Bloom, 1984). The content of the consultation sessions is discussion of the consultee's clients. For example, community counselors offering consultation to adolescent group home houseparents would focus consultation on discussion of the houseparents' adolescent clients. The consultant would assess the adolescents' strengths and problems and make suggestions to the houseparents on how to best serve the adolescents.

2. *Consultee-centered case consultation*. The consultant attempts to identify the consultee's difficulties in handling the case and to

remedy these difficulties, whether they stem from insufficient skill, knowledge, self-confidence, or objectivity. The content discussed during consultation is the consultee. Continuing the example from the adolescent group home, consultee-centered consultation would focus on the houseparents' concerns in dealing with their adolescent clients. Community counseling consultants might help houseparents develop communication skills, learn stress management techniques, or gain insight into their emotional responses to their clients.

3. *Program-centered administrative consultation.* The consultant's primary goal is to suggest some actions the consultee might take in order to affect the development, expansion, or modification of a clinic or agency program. The content discussed during consultation is the consultees' program of services. The consultant draws not only on general mental health skills, but also on his or her understanding of the functioning of social systems and of the principles of mental health program administration (Bloom, 1984). For example, a community counselor offering program-centered administrative consultation to adolescent group homes might suggest the homes establish behavior modification programs, study hours with volunteer tutors and a system through which each adolescent is assigned one houseparent to be his or her personal advocate.

4. *Consultee-centered administrative consultation.* In this instance, the consultant attempts to identify difficulties in the consultee that appear to be limiting his or her effectiveness in instituting program change. The content discussed is how the consultees administer services they deliver. An example might be a community counselor exploring with houseparents their difficulty in consistently monitoring the adolescents' positive behavior as part of a group home's behavior modification program.

The process and content dimensions of consultation described above can be looked at simultaneously, allowing any act of consultation to be categorized regarding the process employed and the content addressed. Table 12–1 presents a matrix for categorizing consultation process and content simultaneously.

There are specific skills involved in offering consultation, which are applicable in each of the consultation models described above. These include interpersonal (Kurpius, 1986), communication (Parsons & Meyers, 1984), assessment (Kurpius & Brubaker, 1976), problem resolution (Maris, 1985) and organizational (Egan, 1985) skills.

Kurpius and Robinson (1978) pointed out critical teaching skills consultants employ when functioning as trainers, including recognizing "significant content details of the related problem situation and characteristics of the audience or client system members" (p. 32), which are then employed in planning and implementing training.

In addition to skills, Bloom (1984) pointed out that an effective consultant needs to have both substantial competence in the areas that are of concern to the consultee and certain general personality traits. He explained that "these traits should include the capacity to be permissive and accepting, the ability to share ideas constructively, the ability to relate effectively to other people, personal warmth, and an awareness of the subtleties of interpersonal relationships" (p. 123).

There are many skills, consequently, that the consultant should possess. All of these skills are utilized when actually performing the work of consultation. Dougherty (1990) suggested a four-stage model of consultation along with counselor techniques and behaviors that go with each. He described four phases that occur within each stage. Dougherty (1990) presented the stages as generically applicable within different models of consultation.

**TABLE 12–1** CONSULTATION PROCESS AND CONTENT MATRIX

| Process Dimension (methods for addressing topics) | Content Dimension (topics that are addressed) | | | |
|---|---|---|---|---|
| | 1. Client Centered | 2. Consultee Centered | 3. Program Centered | 4. Administrative Centered |
| 1. Provision | provide service to clients | provide service to consultees | design/develop/ offer programs | engage in administration |
| 2. Prescription | prescribe actions for consultees to assist clients | prescribe actions to consultees for their improvement | prescribe actions for consultees to improve programs | prescribe actions for consultees to improve administration |
| 3. Mediation | coordinate services to clients | coordinate activities of consultees | coordinate programs | coordinate administration |
| 4. Collaboration | facilitate consultees problem solving regarding clients | facilitate consultees solving their problems | facilitate programs | facilitate administration |

Stage one, entry, involves phasing in to the organization and developing relationships. It centers on establishing contacts and agreeing on a contract for consultation. The consultant at this juncture in the process uses such skills as active listening, self-disclosure, and empathy. A basis of trust is thus promoted. There are four phases to the entry stage: exploring needs, contracting, and physically and psychologically entering the system.

Stage two, diagnosis, consists of problem identification and clarification. At this time, consultants use focusing skills to help determine goals and ways of achieving those goals. They may also employ other counseling techniques such as paraphrasing, restatement, and genuineness. The four phases of diagnosis are information gathering, problem definition, goal setting, and generating interventions.

Stage three, implementation, is when specific actions are taken to achieve the goals that were set in stage two. Feedback is an important part of this process. Flexibility, dealing

with resistance and negative feelings, and patience are other counselor skills involved. The four phases of stage three are selecting interventions, planning their implementation, carrying out the interventions, and evaluating their effectiveness.

Stage four, disengagement, concentrates on assessing the results gained from the consultation process and bringing closure to previous activities. Some relationship skills, such as empathy and genuineness, are again employed. Giving and asking for feedback at this time are also important. It is vital that the consultant and consultee evaluate what was most profitable for each and what aspects of the procedure were less effective. The four phases of stage four are evaluation, planning how to maintain the positive effects of consultation, following up while reducing involvement, and terminating.

Dougherty (1990) pointed out that the four generic stages of consultation listed above are not discrete. Many of the skills and activities listed in one are necessarily repeated in another. Also, consultation does not always progress in an orderly fashion from one stage to the next. For example, if evaluation during the implementation stage suggests progress is not being made, it may be necessary to return to the diagnosis stage. The stages (and phases within stages) provide a developmental framework for understanding and planning consultation independent of the process or content model being employed. They can help community counselors avoid putting the consultation cart before the horse (for example, implementing interventions before thoroughly assessing the problem or establishing relationships), or failing to complete the process (for example, terminating before planning with the consultee about how gains will be sustained).

Consultation is an efficient means of improving counseling services and it is highly likely that a community counselor will be called on to offer consultation during the course of her or his career. Because of the many skills, extensive knowledge, and high degree of professional maturity required to perform consultation effectively, it is advisable that community counselors enter consultation with a strong background of training and experience.

## COMMUNITY COUNSELING SUPERVISION

Counselors are increasingly called on to offer supervision of counseling and counseling-related activities (Corey, Corey, & Callanan, 1993). By offering supervision, community counselors can increase the quantity and quality of services available to clients. Community counselors supervise counselors who have less experience than they do, including graduate students who are in the beginning stages of their training. They also supervise paraprofessionals who are not seeking graduate degrees but who are involved in offering counseling-

related services. And they may supervise professionals who were not originally trained in counseling but are offering counseling within their work setting, such as nurses or social workers.

Supervision has many similarities to consultation. In both activities community counselors are seeking to promote high-quality services to clients indirectly through their work with the persons who are serving the clients. In both activities community counselors are endeavoring to foster learning and development in the persons providing service as well as in the clients receiving it. Supervision may be seen as different from consultation in that supervisory relationships are typically of longer duration than consulting relationships (Bernard & Goodyear, 1992). Supervisors usually are employed in the same setting where the supervisee is providing service. Supervisors typically have more authority over their supervisees than consultants have in relation to consultees. Generally, when supervisors offer direction to supervisees, it is the expectation of both parties and the employment setting that those directions will be followed. In consulting relationships, it is more likely and acceptable that consultees will exercise their own judgment as to whether to follow or disregard consultants' suggestions. Supervisors are responsible for the professional behavior and development of their supervisees. Lastly, supervisors usually have responsibility for evaluating the performance and development of their supervisees. These evaluations may determine if the supervisee progresses through an academic program; receives a degree, licensure, or certification; and/or is retained in employment. Consultants' evaluations of consultees, when performed, rarely hold such direct consequence for the professional life of the consultee.

Supervisors carry a high degree of responsibility concomitant with their authority (Harrar, VandeCreek, & Knapp, 1990).

Supervisors can be and often are held liable for harm to clients resulting from incompetent or unprofessional behavior on the part of their supervisees. Furthermore, supervisors are responsible for the professional development of their supervisees, and can be held accountable if their supervision fails to promote supervisees' progress. Ethical standards dictate that supervisors must be skilled not only in counseling practice, but also in communicating training expectations, teaching, assessing limitations, and locating remediation resources for their supervisees (ACA Ethical Standards, 1988).

A great deal has been written about counseling supervision (Bartlett, 1983; Bernard & Goodyear, 1992; Borders & Usher, 1992; Stoltenberg & Delworth, 1987). In fact, the Association for Counselor Education and Supervision (division of the American Counseling Association) publishes the journal *Counselor Education and Supervision,* which is continually presenting literature on supervision. The vast majority of this literature addresses one or more of the following aspects of supervision: theories of supervision, the content and process of supervision sessions, and evaluation of supervision. Each of these aspects will be addressed below.

## Supervision Theories

Theories of counselor supervision have been derived from the same theoretical foundations that have spawned theories for understanding human nature, people's problems, and counseling (Goodyear, Bradley, & Bartlett, 1983). Learning, dynamic, and humanistic theories have each been applied to understanding and guiding supervision (Bernard & Goodyear, 1992).

Learning theory suggests that supervision is essentially a learning event (Russell, Crimmings, & Lent, 1984). Supervisees are endeavoring to learn about clients and counseling, and supervisors are, like teachers, assisting them in learning. Supervisors promote cognitive learning (the acquisition of information, concepts, and attitudes) by directly teaching. Social learning occurs when supervisors model effective counseling for supervisees. This can be done in response to tapes of clients or through role plays where the supervisees act the part of the client and the supervisors act the part of the counselor. Behavioral learning can occur when supervisees try new counseling skills with clients and their supervisors reinforce them when they are effective. Behavioral learning can also occur by practicing new responses to what clients have said while reviewing tapes of counseling sessions, during role plays in which the supervisors act the part of the client while the supervisees act the part of the counselor, or by the supervisees trying new counseling strategies while working with their clients. In the last instance, reinforcement to supervisees may come directly from the clients through their statements of appreciation and/or improved progress in counseling.

An example of a supervision session being offered according to learning theory principles might proceed in the following manner. The supervisee and supervisor are viewing a videotape of the supervisee offering counseling to a middle-aged male client suffering from depression. The client says he has felt no change in his mood, and he is really getting discouraged. The counselor remains silent. At this point the supervisor might stop the tape and tell the supervisee that it would be a good idea to reassure the client that eventually his depression will lift. The supervisor might go on to explain to the supervisee that knowing that he is going to feel better could give the client hope, which will help him deal with the low point in a depressive cycle. The supervisor would be providing an opportunity for cognitive learning for the supervisee through these statements. The supervisor might then demonstrate, "What I would say to this client is, 'it feels real bad right now. What I've observed about depression is that it comes in cycles. I'm confident that within a month you're going to feel some improvement in your mood.' By making this statement the supervisor is modeling for the supervisee. The supervisor might then ask the supervisee to formulate and practice a statement of reassurance to the client. The supervisor could replay the videotape of the client expressing discouragement and allow the supervisee to try a new response. The supervisee might say, "I could have said, 'You're really feeling discouraged. Research on depression shows that it usually occurs in cycles. It is very likely that your mood will improve over the next month' or something like that," to which the supervisor might respond, "That would be great." In this way the supervisor is reinforcing the supervisee for trying a new counseling skill.

Dynamic theories of supervision are concerned with the underlying emotional exchanges that occur between clients and supervisees (Moldawsky, 1980). Supervision includes exploration of the client's subconscious activity. Particular attention is paid to the client's unconscious reactions to the supervisee and the feelings the client unrealistically transfers onto the supervisee from past relationships. Supervision helps supervisees understand and deal with these transferred feelings productively. Because clients' unconscious feelings are likely to touch and affect supervisees at unconscious levels, supervisory attention is often paid to the reactions the supervisees are having to their clients (Ekstein & Wallerstein, 1972). Analyzing their own reactions can help supervisees understand and deal with their clients' unconscious reaction's to them. Dynamic theories suggest that what is referred to as parallel process feelings clients unconsciously transfer onto supervisees might, in turn, be transferred by supervisees onto supervisors (Friedlander, Siegel, & Brenock, 1989). For this reason, supervisees' responses to supervisors may be explored during supervision. Insight into the supervisees'

reactions to supervisors could assist the supervisees in understanding and working with their clients.

Using the example of the supervisee working with the depressed client, a supervisor working from a dynamic perspective might remain largely silent during the first part of the supervision session while the tape is playing. After a while the supervisee might shut off the tape and say, "I haven't been able to make any progress with this client. I just don't know how to help him." The supervisor might reply, "I wonder what feelings come up for you as you tell me this." The supervisee might say, "I'm feeling helpless…lost." The supervisor could respond, "Helpless…and I'll bet a little frustrated, wanting me to provide some solution and I'm not giving any." The supervisee might respond, "Yes! Well, yes…I mean I would like your help with this." The supervisor might respond to these statements with the following interpretation: "You have a feeling of helplessness and desire for me to do something to assist, in a sense to take care of you. I wonder if a similar dynamic is occurring between you and your client. Perhaps your client has a strong desire to be taken care of, and he is unconsciously presenting his discouragement to you in hopes that you will be moved to care for him. His continuing depression could be an unconscious effort to get people, in particular you, to take care of him." The supervisee might see some validity to the interpretation and subsequently explore it with the client. Insights the client gains from exploring his needs in relation to the supervisee could help him move out of depression and find effective means of dealing with his desire to be taken care of. In this way the supervisor would have applied an analysis of the dynamics occurring between the supervisor and supervisee to understanding and modifying the dynamics between the supervisee and client, ultimately fostering the supervisees's learning and the client's improvement.

Humanistic theories suggest that supervisees are engaged in a process of becoming counselors, which is motivated by their internal potential to grow (Rice, 1980). To foster this growth, supervisees need relationships with supervisors that are characterized by respect, honesty, and understanding. Also referred to as unconditional positive regard, genuineness, and empathy, these qualities in supervision allow supervisees to address their important concerns and find answers within themselves for how to best serve their clients. Supervisors who consistently provide these qualities in supervision nurture their supervisees' innate talent to be therapeutic with their clients.

Again using the depressed client example, a supervision session guided by "humanistic" orientation might include the following dialogue:

*Supervisee:* "I haven't been able to make any progress with this client. I just don't know how to help him."

*Supervisor:* "Really feeling discouraged and inadequate."

*Supervisee:* "Yes. It's like there's a brick wall there. I can't get through."

*Supervisor:* "Frustrating. And also, kind of lonely."

*Supervisee:* "Really. Like I'm in the room by myself when I'm working with him."

*Supervisor:* Remains quiet, listening intently to the supervisee.

*Supervisee:* You know, I wonder what it is like for him, if he feels there is a wall between us. I'll bet he's lonely, doesn't feel understood. Maybe scared, too. Afraid of what would happen if he let himself be known.

Following this dialogue the supervisee could be in a better position to understand the client and to share this understanding during counseling sessions with him in an honest and respectful fashion. This could reduce the client's sense of isolation and improve his self-esteem and mood. The respect and honest understanding the supervisor offered the supervisee can be seen as allowing the supervisee to become increasingly honest, respectful, and understanding with his client.

## Content and Process of Supervision

In addition to identification of guiding theories, supervision can be understood by examining the content that is discussed and the process that occurs during supervisory meetings. Content reflects what is actually discussed and process describes how it is discussed.

The content (Brammer & Wassmer, 1977) of supervision sessions can be characterized as focusing on the client; on the supervisee-client relationship; on the supervisee; and/or on the supervisee-supervisor relationship.

Client focus includes examining clients' problems, diagnosis, dynamics, goals and methods that might be most effective for achieving them. Supervision of a counselor working with an adult male suffering from schizophrenia might focus on the client's stress level, resources, and reality testing. The supervisor might inquire of the counselor, "What kinds of social support are available to him now?" and "Does he show signs of psychosis?" The counselor's responses would focus on her understanding of the client. The supervisor might suggest additional support resources the counselor could encourage the client to become involved with, or methods of unobtrusively assessing reality testing during counseling interviews.

Supervisee-client focus includes the quality of rapport, the effectiveness of interaction, and negative or positive reactions. Using the example of counseling with the client with schizophrenia, the supervisor might ask for the supervisee's impressions of the client's reactions to her, for example, "What allows him to trust you?" or "In what ways are you able to reach mutual understanding with him?" Reviewing tapes of recorded counseling sessions, the supervisor might comment, "When you confronted him about the importance of taking his medication he smiled a little bit, like he enjoyed hearing that you care about his well-being."

Supervisee focus includes examination of the supervisee's knowledge, skills, development, and internal dynamics, which may contribute to or detract from competent counseling. The supervisor of the counselor working with the client from schizophrenia might comment, "Knowing the seriousness of your client's diagnosis probably has had an impact on your feelings about working with him. Please talk for a while about your reaction," or "It will be important for you to become comfortable with prolonged silence."

Supervisee-supervisor focus includes examination of the dynamics in the supervisory relationship, which may reflect the supervisee's relationship with the client, the supervisee's internal dynamics and/or aspects of supervision that are contributing to or detracting from the supervisee's development and service to the client. If the counselor working with the client with schizophrenia found him to be resistant to her suggestions, her supervisor might invite her to explore resistance within their supervisory relationship. For example, the supervisor might say, "There have been a number of times I have made suggestions during supervision that you did not agree with. I wonder what feelings come up for you when I make suggestions and whether your client may not be having similar reactions when you make suggestions to him."

The content of supervision may be influenced by the theory of supervision being employed. Supervision from a learning perspective may be more likely to focus on the client and client-supervisee interaction than on the supervisee's internal dynamics or the

supervisee-supervisor relationship. Supervision from a humanistic perspective is likely to focus on the supervisee's experience, while supervision guided by dynamic theories is likely to explore the supervisee and how the supervisee is relating to clients and to the supervisor.

The process of how supervision is conducted is another variable that can be used to characterize different supervisory styles (Hart, 1982). Supervision usually involves supervisees discussing the counseling they offer clients with their supervisors, often including review of recordings of counseling sessions. Whether recordings are reviewed or not, supervisors can provide supervision by directly teaching, questioning, or empathically listening to their supervisees. These three styles—teaching, questioning, listening—can be seen as corresponding to theories of supervision. Learning theories would suggest teaching, dynamic theories suggest questioning, and humanistic theories suggest listening. As has been demonstrated in counseling, however, the theories supervisors follow do not necessarily correspond with the process they employ. Dynamic supervisors might teach their supervisees about dynamics and learning-based supervisors might seek to increase their supervisees learning by questioning.

Similar to consultation, the process and content of supervision can be examined simultaneously, allowing any act of supervision to be categorized regarding the process employed and the content addressed. Table 12–2 provides a matrix for categorizing supervision process and content simultaneously. Under each process dimension, the body of theory that typically guides that process is listed in parentheses.

## Evaluation

Evaluation is a critical and often difficult component of supervision (Pope & Vasquez, 1991). Whereas in counseling and consulta-

**TABLE 12–2**   SUPERVISION PROCESS AND CONTENT MATRIX

| Supervision Process | Supervision Content | | | |
|---|---|---|---|---|
| | Client | Client-Supervisee | Supervisee | Supervisee-Supervisor |
| Teaching (learning theory) | supervisor teaches the supervisee about the client | supervisor teaches the supervisee about the client-supervisee relationship | supervisor teaches the supervisee about the supervisee | supervisor teaches the supervisee avout the supervisee-supervisor relationship |
| Questioning (dynamic theory) | supervisor questions the supervisee about the client | supervisor questions the supervisee about the client-supervisee relationship | supervisor questions the supervisee about the supervisee | supervisor questions the supervisee about the supervisee-supervisor relationship |
| Listening (humanistic theory) | supervisor listens to the supervisee discuss the client | supervisor listens to the supervisee discuss the client-supervisee relationship | supervisor listens to the supervisee discuss the supervisee | supervisor listens to the supervisee discuss the supervisee-supervisor relationship |

tion evaluation is usually a service performed explicitly for the educational benefit of the client or consultee, evaluation in supervision carries with it the supervisor's responsibility to assess the progress of supervisees and determine if they are competent to advance to further training and/or independent practice (Levy, 1983).

Essentially supervisors serve as gatekeepers, helping the profession advance talented counselors and weed out those not fit to move forward. Obviously this aspect of evaluation in supervision can raise both supervisees' and supervisors' anxiety.

Evaluation in supervision can focus on a wide variety of criteria including supervisees' development of knowledge and skills, their clients' progress, their use of supervision and/or supervisees' professional and personal development (Dimick & Krause, 1980; Grann, Hendricks, Hoop, Jackson, & Traunstein, 1986). Whichever criteria are used, supervision is likely to be more effective and

congruent with ethical standards if supervisees are aware at the outset of supervision of the criteria on which they will be evaluated (Bernard & Goodyear, 1992).

Evaluation of supervision can and, we believe, should include the evaluation of the supervisor. Dimensions of supervisor evaluation can include supervisors' professionalism, demonstration of knowledge and skills, the quality of relationships they achieve with supervisees, the supervisee's development of knowledge and skills, and the progress the supervisee's clients make in counseling (Borders & Leddick, 1987).

## AN INTEGRATIVE DEVELOPMENTAL APPROACH

Perhaps the most comprehensive model for supervision and evaluation of counselor development is provided by Stoltenberg and Delworth (1987). These authors based their model on an extensive review of theory and research on supervisees and supervision. They proposed that supervisees progress through developmental stages as they learn counseling. In the first stage supervisees are focused on their own skill development and are dependent on supervisors for instruction. In the second stage supervisees are more focused on their clients, and the supervisor serves as a supportive catalyst (among other functions) to assist the supervisees in exploring their client's dynamics and their reactions to them. At level three supervisees are integrating their identity as counselors and their understanding of their clients. They need supportive, collegial relationships with supervisors who can offer their wisdom to assist the supervisees in deepening and consolidating their development.

The integrative developmental model proposed by Stoltenberg and Delworth (1987) draws from each of the theories, content focus, and processes described above and matches them to the needs of the supervisees. Stoltenberg and Delworth also offered methods for assessing the progress of supervisees at each stage and establishing goals.

## ETHICAL ISSUES RELATED TO SUPERVISION

Supervisory relationships may be seen as governed by the same ethical standards that direct other professional behavior for counselors, including those related to respect for supervisees' integrity and promotion of their welfare (Sherry, 1991). However, supervision is in some ways more ethically complex than counseling. Community counselors offering supervision are not only responsible for their supervisees' integrity and welfare but also for that of their supervisees' clients. Supervisors have been described as particularly vulnerable to ethical misconduct because of differences in power between supervisees and supervisors, because supervision is not therapy but in many ways is similar, and because supervisees and supervisors have potentially conflicting roles (for example, a confident and ambitous but inept novice counselor and a supervisor who is dedicated to protecting future clients by serving as a gatekeeper for the profession). Assistance in negotiating the potential ethical pitfalls of supervision is offered by Corey, Corey, and Callanan (1993). As in all situations where ethical concerns arise, consultation with other experienced professionals is advisable.

## EXERCISE

### Case Study

Imagine you are a community counselor serving as a consultant for a family services agency that is working with abusive parents. The agency offers individual, family, and group counseling and coordinates services to the families with the schools, social welfare, substance abuse clinics, and law enforcement. The director of the family services agency says she would like your assistance in improving services to families who have been identified as engaging in child abuse.

1. What steps would you follow in providing consultation to this agency?
2. Offer examples of how you might perform the following types of consultation:
   a. Provision
   b. Prescription
   c. Mediation
   d. Collaboration
3. What would you be talking about with the agency director if you were using each of the following models of consultation:
   a. Client-centered case consultation
   b. Consultee-centered case consultation

c. Program-centered administrative consultation

d. Consultee-centered administrative consultation

4. The agency director says she is having difficulty keeping her staff motivated, given their large caseloads and the overwhelming needs of the families they serve. Characterize the diagnosis, implementation, and disengagement you could imagine occurring during consultation with the director about this specific concern.

## Case Study

Imagine now that you are a community counselor who has been employed for a number of years in the family service agency described above. You are supervising a counselor who has been hired directly after graduating from a community counseling program. The counselor is talking with you about a divorced father he has been working with who has a nine-year-old and a seven-year-old son. The older son has been in trouble at school and been arrested for shoplifting. The father had punched the son repeatedly in the face during an argument, which resulted in the father's referral to the family service agency. The counselor says the father spends each session talking first about how the son is "going wrong and going to drag his brother down with him," and second about how unfair the system is that requires him to get counseling when the son is the one with problems. The counselor says he doubts he is benefiting this client and is at a loss for what to do with him.

1. Describe how you would approach supervising this counselor from learning, dynamic, and humanistic perspectives and what you would hope to accomplish.

2. Given what you know about this counselor, how would you assess his development and needs?

3. What content would you focus on with this counselor and what process would you follow?

---

## REFERENCES

American Counseling Association. (1988). *Ethical standards.* Alexandria, VA.

Bartlett, W. E. (1983). A multidimensional framework for the analysis of supervision of counseling. *The Counseling Psychologist, 11,* 9–17.

Beer, M. (1980). *Organizational change and development: A systems view.* Glenview, IL: Scott, Foresman.

Berkowitz, G. (1973). A collaborative approach to mental health consultation in school settings. In W. C. Claiborn & R. Cohen (Eds. ), *School intervention* (pp. 53–64). New York: Behavioral Publications.

Bernard, J. M., & Goodyear, R. K. (1992). *Fundamentals of clinical supervision.* Boston: Allyn and Bacon.

Bloom, B. L. (1984). *Community mental health: A general introduction* (2nd ed. ). Pacific Grove, CA: Brooks/Cole.

Borders, L. D., & Leddick, G. R. (1987). *Handbook of counseling supervision.* Alexandria, VA: Association for Counselor Education and Supervision.

Borders, L. D., & Usher, C. H. (1992). Post-degree supervision: Existing and preferred practices. *Journal of Counseling and Development, 70,* 594–599.

Brammer, L. M., & Wassmer, A. C. (1977). Supervision in counseling and psychotherapy. In D. J. Kurpius, R. D. Baker, & J. D. Thomas (Eds.), *Supervision of applied training* (pp. 43–82). Westport, CT: Greenwood.

Brokes, A. A. (1975). Process of consultation. In C. A. Parker (Ed. ), *Psychological consultation: Helping teachers meet special needs* (pp. 185–207). Minneapolis: Leadership Training Institute.

Brown, D., Pryzwansky, W. B., & Schulte, A. C. (1987). *Psychological consultation: Introduction to theory and practice.* Boston: Allyn & Bacon.

Conoley, J. C., & Conoley, C. W. (1982). *School consultation: A guide to practice and training.* New York: Pergamon Press.

Caplan, G. (1964). *Principles of preventive psychiatry.* New York: Basic Books.

Caplan, G. (1970). *Theory and practice of mental health consultation.* New York: Basic Books.

Corey, G., Corey, M. S., & Callanan, P. (1993). *Issues and ethics in the helping professions.* Pacific Grove, CA: Brooks/Cole.

Dimick, K. M., & Krause, F. H. (1980). *Practicum manual for counseling and psychotherapy.* Muncie, IN: Accelerated Development Press.

Dougherty, A. M. (1990). *Consultation: Practice and Perspectives.* Pacific Grove, CA: Brooks/Cole.

Egan, G. (1985). *Change agent skills in helping and human service settings.* Pacific Grove, CA: Brooks/Cole.

Ekstein, R., & Wallerstein, R. S. (1972). *The teaching and learning of psychotherapy* (2nd ed. ). New York: International Universities Press, Inc.

Friedlander, M. L., Siegel, S., & Brenock, K. (1989). Parallel processes in counseling and supervision: A case study. *Journal of Counseling Psychology, 31,* 149–157.

Gallessich, J. (1982). *The profession and practice of consultation.* San Francisco: Jossey-Bass.

Goodstein, L. D. (1978). *Consulting with human service systems.* Reading, MA: Addison-Wesley.

Goodyear, R. K., Bradley, F. O., & Bartlett, W. E. (1983). An introduction to theories of counselor supervision. *The Counseling Psychologist, 11,* 19–20.

Grann, I., Hendricks, B., Hoop, L., Jackson, G., & Traunstein, D. (1986). Competency-based evaluation: A second round. *The Clinical Supervisor, 3.* 81–91.

Harrar, W. R., VandeCreek, L., & Knapp, S. (1990). Ethical and legal aspects of clinical supervision. *Professional Psychology: Research and Practice, 21,* 371–41.

Hart, G. M. (1982). *The process of clinical supervision.* Baltimore:University Park Press.

Kurpius, D. J. (1978). Consultation theory and process: An integrated model. *The Personnel and Guidance Journal, 56,* 335–378.

Kurpius, D. J. (1986). Consultation: An important human and organizational intervention. *Journal of Counseling and Human Services Professions, 1,* 58–66.

Kurpius, D. J., & Brubaker, J. C. (1976). *Psychoeducational consultation: Definitions—functions—preparation.* Bloomington, IN: Indiana University Press.

Kurpius, D. J., & Robinson, S. E. (1978). An overview of consultation. *The Personnel and Guidance Journal, 56,* 321–323.

Levy, L. H. (1983). Evaluation of students in clinical psychology programs: A program evaluation perspective. *Professional Psychology: Research and Practice, 14,* 497–503.

Lippitt, G. L., & Nadler, L. (1979). Emerging roles of the training director. In C. R. Bell & L. Nadler (Eds. ), *The client-consultant handbook.* Houston: Gulf Publishing.

Mannino, F. V., & Shore, M. F. (1986). Understanding consultation: Some orienting dimensions. *The Counseling Psychologist, 13,* 363–367.

Maris, T. L. (1985). Characteristics of successful management consultants. *Consultation, 4,* 258–263.

Moldawsky, S. (1980). Psychoanalytic psychotherapy supervision. In A. K. Hess (Ed. ), *Psychotherapy supervision: Theory, research, and practice* (pp. 126–135). New York: John Wiley and Sons.

Ohlsen, M. M. (1983). *Introduction to counseling.* Itasca, IL: F. E. Peacock Publishers.

Parsons, R. D., & Meyers, J. (1984). *Developing consultation skills.* San Francisco: Jossey-Bass.

Pope, K. S., & Vasquez, M. J. (1991). *Ethics in psychotherapy and counseling: A practical guide for psychologists.* San Francisco: Jossey-Bass.

Rice, L. N. (1980). A client-centered approach to the supervision of psychotherapy. In A. K. Hess (Ed. ). *Psychotherapy supervision: Theory, research, and practice* (pp. 136–147). New York: John Wiley and Sons.

Rogawski, A. S. (1978). The Caplanian model. *The Personnel and Guidance Journal, 56,* 324–327.

Russell, R. K., Crimmings, A. M., & Lent, R. W. (1984). Counselor training and supervision: Theory and research. In S. D. Brown & R. W. Lent (Eds. ), *Handbook of counseling Psychology* (pp. 625–681). New York: John Wiley and Sons.

Schein, E. H. (1969). *Process consultation: Its role in organization development.* Reading, MA: Addison-Wesley.

Schein, E. H. (1978). The role of the consultant: Content expert or process facilitator? *The Personnel and Guidance Journal, 56,* 339–343.

Schein, E. H. (1987). *Process consultation: Lessons for managers and consultants* (Vol. II). Reading, MA: Addison-Wesley.

Sherry, P. (1991). Ethical issues in the conduct of supervision. The *Counseling Psychologist, 19,* 566–584.

Stoltenberg, C. D., & Delworth, U. (1987). *Supervising counselors and therapists.* San Francisco: Jossey-Bass.

West, J. F. & Idol, L. (1987). School consultation (Part I): An interdisciplinary perspective on theory, models, and research. *Journal of Learning Disabilities, 20,* 388–408.

# 13

# CASE MANAGEMENT AND COORDINATION OF RESOURCES

For many years there has been an ongoing debate, both in the professional literature and in counseling practice, on the varied roles of the counselor. Should the counselor's job function consist primarily of providing direct services, or should the counselor be a case coordinator, managing different services identified for assisting the client to a designated goal? These questions will continue to be argued among agency administrators and community counselors. But the two responsibilities of providing direct counseling assistance and offering case management services do not have to be completely distinct. These functions can frequently overlap because both roles require a strong alliance with the client, the available family, and other parties that can influence the direction and quality of counseling services (Dixon, Goll, & Stanton, 1988). In other words, since 1985 a strong interdisci-

plinary model for counseling intervention has emerged, which implies that when planning interventions for many clients, the counseling process is an interactive one in which a community counselor works as a member of a team that understands one another's technology and expertise that affect the client's care and eventual life adjustment.

The counselor, by virtue of the philosophy of the profession, must assist the client in bringing to bear those environmental resources that can facilitate the client's coping with his/her problem. In order to perform this function, the community counselor must possess a specialized set of knowledge and skills. This specialized set may be termed case management and/or the coordination of resources. This coordination involves: (a) knowledge about existing resources; (b) knowledge about where to find information about such resources; and (c) skills in coordination, including accessing, referral, linking, networking, and evaluating resources. Other chapters in this book have focused on the roles of the counselor as a direct service provider in the areas of assessment, evaluation, programming, education, advocacy, consultation, and providing direct service for clients' specific life adjustment concerns. This chapter will discuss the community counselor's role as a case manager/coordinator, which includes the functions of coordination and resources utilization. This chapter will also provide information on programmatic resources and related professionals, both integral components of the topics of case management and resource utilization.

## CASE MANAGEMENT

This topic will be discussed under five headings: (1) definition of case management; (2) the skills of case management, including coordination; (3) the process of case management; (4) environments for counselors performing as case managers; and (5) salient factors in case management. Public policy has served to stimulate and establish a significant increase in the number of case management programs, but little is known about their characteristics, including a universal, accepted understanding of what case management means (Center for Psychiatric Rehabilitation, 1991).

### Definitions of Case Management

As distinguished from counseling itself, case management "refers to the monitoring of the client's progress through the intake, appraisal, planning, intervention, evaluation, follow-up, and closure steps of the agency's routine and the coordination of resources outside the agency that have been enlisted on the client's behalf"(Hershenson & Power, 1984, p. 168). The term can also include the counselor's time management and paperwork flow. Green-

wood (1982) identified several definitions of case management, such as:

*The use of techniques…to control the distribution, quality, quantity and cost of all aspects of case work activities in order to accomplish the program goals of the agency.* (Third Institute on Rehabilitation Services, 1965, p. 12)

*How to work with more than one case at a time, how to select which case to work with, how to move from one case to another, how to establish a system to insure movement of all cases, how to meet objectives one has established. (*Henke, Connally, & Cox, 1975, p. 218).

*The process of ensuring that clients move sequentially through the appropriate statuses without undue delay.* (Thompson, Kite, Bruyere, 1977, p. 3).

All of these definitions indicate that case management has been practiced in various forms and domains for a long time. Frank Baker and James Intagliata (1992) reported that case management has emerged in response to the rapid expansion of human service programs in general, and to the deinstitutionalization of the mentally ill. The need for and availability of community services, consequently, has increased significantly.

In mental health settings, hospitals, and state rehabilitation agencies, case management has been practiced informally by physicians, social workers, discharge planners, and rehabilitation counselors for many years, especially as these practitioners are confronted with the dilemma of large caseloads and limited resources with which to effectively allocate and promote appropriate services for their clients (Dixon, Goll, & Stanton, 1988). The focus of case management is on continuity of care, which includes services that are comprehensive, coordinated, intergrated over time, responsive to changes in a person's needs, accessible, and accountable (Baker Intagliata, 1992).

The distinction between counseling and case management, however, is an administrative rather than a clinical one. It may also be used in circumscribing the role of supervision in the agency. Thus, an individual may have a senior counselor supervising counseling techniques and an administrator overseeing the case management aspects of the caseload. In many settings this distinction is not made.

## The Skills of Case Management and Coordination

Since the case management system is a process with multiple functions, the different functions suggest a variety of skills. Most of these skills are identified in the Rehabilitation Skills Inventory developed by Leahy, Shapson, & Wright (1987), and include the following:

**1.** Refer clients to appropriate specialists and/or special services.

**2.** Identify and arrange for functional or skill remediation services for clients' successful job placements.

**3.** Collaborate with other providers so that services are coordinated, appropriate, and timely.

**4.** Provide information regarding your organization's programs to current and potential referral services.

**5.** Interpret your organization's policy, laws, and regulations to clients and others.

**6.** Select appropriate adjustment alternatives such as counseling centers or educational programs.

**7.** Coordinate activities of all agencies involved in a counseling plan.

**8.** Use functional assessment information in determining counseling service needs.

**9.** State clearly the nature of clients' problems for referral to service providers.

**10.** Consult with medical professionals regarding functional capacities, prognosis, and treatments plans for clients.

**11.** Identify and challenge stereotypic views toward persons with disabilities.

**12.** Obtain regular client feedback regarding satisfaction with services delivered and suggestions for improvement.

**13.** Explain the services and limitations of various community resources to clients.

**14.** Educate clients regarding their rights under federal and state laws.

**15.** Understand the applications of current legislation affecting the employment of individuals with disabilities.

**16.** Read professional literature related to business, labor markets, medicine, and rehabilitation.

**17.** Apply principles of community mental health and career/employment legislation to daily practice.

Another perspective to skill identification, which focuses more on the organization of a counselor's workload, is provided by Greenwood (1982), who listed the functions of caseload management as: (a) planning for effective allocation of one's time and skills across one's caseload; (b) managing the plan to make best use of one's skills, resources, and time; and (c) reviewing client progress periodically to assess the effectiveness of services.

To carry out these tasks, the counselor must have at least six sets of knowledge and skills:

- knowledge of counselor roles and functions
- knowledge of planning procedures
- decision-making skills
- time and management skills, which involve analyzing and prioritizing the counselor's time and delegating selected activities

- administrative skills, which can include maintaining current copies of records required to operate a counseling practice, financial records related to a counseling practice, and clinical records for all persons the counseling practice serves, including clients, significant others, consultees, and referral organizations
- progress review skills, which demands reviewing the type of assistance you are utilizing to help your clients

Each one of these skills assumes importance for the community counselor when he/she considers that everyone involved in a client's rehabilitation or life adjustment is highly interested in the counseling outcome being maintained over time. For the client, it may mean an opportunity for continued growth; for the client's available family, it could mean movement toward a more stable lifestyle, and for an insurance carrier, it may mean a cost-effective use of resources (Dixon, Goll, & Stanton, 1988).

## The Process of Case Management and Resource Utilization

There are many active processes of case management and they generally follow some sequential pattern. Many aspects of the process may take place simultaneously and are frequently revisited. The process itself involves the implementation of the skills previously identified in this chapter. Several writers have contributed to the conceptualization of the many processes of case management, including the specific skills of resource utilization (Dixon, Goll, & Stanton, 1988; Backer & Trotter, 1986; Greenwood, 1982; Henderson & Wallack, 1987; Lewis & Lewis 1983; and Schwartz, 1986). The processes are assessing, accessing, organizing, coordinating, referral and linking, networking, negotiating, and evaluating and reassessing.

### Assessing

Assessment can be shared by many professionals, and should include the identification of all the factors related to the client's problem, including fiscal and legal realities.

### Accessing

Accessing is the skill of obtaining information about and entry into the resource that can best meet a client's need. For this purpose, many counselors maintain indices or card files of agencies and contact persons on the intake staff of those agencies with whom they have had prior contact. These files indicate (or are classified by) the particular services rendered by the agency; and where possible, some indication of the quality of performance of the agency in delivering each of those services. In many communities, the local council of social service agencies publishes a directory of agencies, including a list of the particular services offered by the agency and the key persons to contact. In some communities, this is called "the social service blue book,"or some similar name (frequently reflecting the color of its cover). The counselor should obtain and regularly use one of these directories (making sure that it is the most up-to-date edition; they are frequently loose-leaf). This should supplement but not replace the counselor's personal file of resources.

### Organizing

This includes the organization of assessment information, as well as organizing the expectations of the client, family, and different personnel or resources involved in the delivery of services to the client.

### Coordinating

Accomplished through communication with all the persons involved in the client's counseling, it includes coordinating all the information obtained from different services providers, and the family, into a feasible counseling plan that details the sequence of services to be delivered.

### Referral and Linking

Having accessed the most appropriate agency, the counselor must next connect the client with that agency. Some writers (for example, Lewis & Lewis, 1983) distinguish between referral (turning a client over to another agency and surrendering any further regular contact with the client) and linking (sending a client to one or more other agencies for particular services while maintaining regular contacts with the client on one's own caseload). Others, however, use the term referral to indicate surrendering responsibility for only one specific service to be given to a client. Agencies and individual counselors also differ as to whether they require feedback from agencies referred to and/or from the clients who are referred. Some counselors require feedback in order to evluate the agency for future possible referrals. Other counselors view such follow-up as a responsibility owed to the client who was referred.

The referral/linkage process may be seen as having several dimensions including: (a) the range of services the second agency is asked to provide to the client, (b) the responsibility taken for a client after the client is put into contact with the second agency, and (c) the feedback expected from the second agency and/or from the client. Clearly, the needs of the client should be the primary factor in determining what point along each of these dimensions is to be sought.

### Networking

The referral/linking process focuses on client needs; the networking process focuses on agency capabilities. Networking involves the coordination of agencies to share resources, to divide responsibilities on a systematic basis, or to integrate their functions. Networking may involve getting a number of agencies to work on different problems of a single client or getting each of several agencies to assume responsibility for working on one designated problem presented by a number of different clients. The intent of networking may be economic efficiency or the fostering of specialized expertise not presently available within a community. In order to promote networking, the counselor must possess both negotiating and leadership skills (such as persuasiveness). Backer and Trotter (1986) summarized the five basic rules of effective networking as: (1) keep a clear, specific focus to the network and avoid dispersion of goals; (2) keep in touch regularly with the others in the network; (3) keep the network small (many small, focused networks work better than one large one); (4) keep it simple and inexpensive; and (5) reciprocate, if you wish the network to stay together.

### Negotiating

When working with a client, the community counselor may have to negotiate with other service providers about the length of career or life adjustment evaluation, alternative settings that are environmentally appropriate and cost effective for his/her treatment, and services and equipment not normally covered by an insurance carrier. The success of a client's counseling plan may not only depend on how well it is formulated, but on how much cooperation is developed between the client, the family, and different service providers (Henderson & Wallack, 1987).

### Evaluating/Reassessing

Counselors must engage in a continuous process of evaluation of agencies and of particular staff members at those agencies. Decisions about referral, linking, and networking are based on who does the best job of providing each particular service. This information comes from evaluations, insofar as possible based on objective criteria. This step usually requires the continuous monitoring of the services provided, as well as the evaluation of their effectiveness. For many conditions, for example, such as traumatic head injury, this reassessment may be the most important aspect of case management. This function can generate a constant loop back into the other processes.

Pervading the different process steps of case management are the skills of planning, time management, and progress review. This process implies that the community counselor must plan services for the client, besides those that will be provided by the counselor himself/herself, as well as allocate time to a host of other activities. The process also demands that, when appropriate, the counselor often interacts with significant others involved in the delivery of services, for example, families of clients, the client's friends, and community resource personnel who have a contribution to make to the client's life adjustment goals (Greenwood, 1982). The process steps of assessing, counseling, and reassessing can all be used with the skill of progress review. The counselor should periodically determine whether the client's goals identified in planning have been achieved, and this function may demand further assessment, counseling on selected issues, and reassessing the original goals. The process of case management ensures, therefore, that through the practice of specific skills the client will move without undue delay through appropriate, designated steps to an appropriate goal.

## Environments for the Process and Skills of Case Management

The environments in which case management is practiced can vary according to the complexity of the client's problem. When a community counselor is assisting clients in handling career transitions, for example, case management can be utilized not only in the counselor's specific agency, but also prac-

ticed with insurance companies, the family, facilities that specialize in diagnostic assessment or work adjustment, and employers. Persons with severe mental and physical disabilities usually have many service providers contributing to their case and rehabilitation. The issues of cost-avoidance, time limits, and the selection of the most effective services may lead to different perspectives on both the skills and process of case management, and also may depend on who sponsors case management, namely, worker's compensation resources, long-term disability insurance companies, or private payers. The case management focus, consequently, can look quite different depending on the sponsors or payers of the activity (Dixon, Goll, & Stanton, 1988).

## Salient Factors in Case Management

Frank Baker and James Intagliata (1982) explained that the two basic structural elements in a case management system are the case manager and the core agency. When counselors practice the role of case manager, they should attempt to develop the most effective intervention appropriate to a specific problem, and successful intervention usually depends on timeliness, thorough decision making, remaining aware of the comprehensive needs of their clients, and linking clients to services that will meet their needs. The ability to accomplish this has significant implications for the process and skills of case management. When the community counselor is both aware of specific case management skills and understands the pertinent factors of a case, then services can be coordinated in a meaningful and sequential manner as clients move towards adjustment goals (Dixon, Goll, & Stanton, 1988). Added to this awareness and knowledge is the necessity for the counselor to understand all aspects of the counseling process and its component tasks, to utilize the principles of time management, and to implement periodic progress reviews. If counselors practice these skills, they can facilitate the use of optimal services for persons with complex problems and/or severe disabilities (Greenwood, 1982).

The other structural component in a case management system is a core agency, which can act as a catalyst to assure that the comprehensive needs of a population in a designated area are met (Baker & Intagliata, 1992). This agency would initially evaluate those needs, negotiate interagency linkages and agreements necessary to provide necessary support services, and develop new service components to remedy any gaps in the existing service network. In remedying service deficiencies, a core agency may be a more effective change agent than a case manager (Baker & Intagliata, 1992).

Now that we have briefly viewed the skills and the process the community counselor must use when functioning as a case manager and coordinating resources on behalf of a client, we may look at some of the major categories of resources to which those skills are to be applied. In addition to having the skills necessary to perform the functions we have just discussed, the counselor must know the major types or resources available and as many local examples of each of those types as is possible. The counselor must also be familiar with examples of effective resources not locally available in order to work with the community to establish such a resource locally, so clients can use it. To accomplish this, the counselor will need other skills, such as those involved in advocacy, in community development, and In using the political process, all of which are discussed in Chapter 14.

## PROGRAMMATIC RESOURCES

### Resources Discussed Elsewhere in This Book

It is difficult to separate resources distinctly from some of the topics dealt with in other parts of this book. For example, the most significant resource is often the client's family, a topic discussed in Chapter 9. The family may be the client's greatest source of support, difficulty, or both of these simultaneously. In any case, where a family is significantly involved in the client's environment, the counselor must work with them to maximize their helpfulness to the client and to minimize their contribution to the client's problem. Religious institutions are another resource that can serve as a powerful source of support for many clients. Social service agencies provide a wide range of resources, in terms of both direct services and money to purchase other services (and even, in some instances, for economic support while services are being rendered). Likewise, educational institutions are resources for teaching clients new skills. Given sufficient ingenuity, a community counselor may employ almost any community service or facility as a resource on behalf of some client. Although the number of such resources is almost infinite, we shall limit the rest of this discussion to four categories of resources: (1) those related to working, (2) those related to living arrangements, (3) financial resources, and (4) health-related resources.

### Resources Related to Work

Be it for good or for ill, work is a necessary major life activity for most persons, consuming the largest single block of their waking hours. Work is a phenomenon that has been an aspect of the human condition since time immemorial. At different times, this phenomenon has been viewed with greater or lesser pleasure. Thus, to the writers of the Bible, work was a curse imposed on humanity as a result of Adam and Eve's disobedience to God in the Garden of Eden. In the Reformation, conversely, work became associated with gaining eternal salvation for one's soul. As technology has changed the nature of work—such as the development of agriculture, the Industrial Revolution, or robotics—the meaning of and attitudes toward work have correspondingly changed. For a fascinating discussion of the changes in the meaning of work throughout history, see Tilgher (1930).

Work has been seen as an index of personal and social adjustment, a way of promoting or restoring mental health, and a cause of poor adjustment. Frequently, mental health professionals have held all three of these views of work at the same time. Slocum (1974) listed the functions of work in modern industrial society as providing: (a) a source of subsistence (income), (b) regulated activity (work time/free time), (c) patterns of association (coworkers, unions, professional groups), (d) an identity or label by which to define oneself, and (e) meaningful life experiences (successes, failures, topics of conversation).

Given these multiple major functions, it is small wonder that work has been considered to be tied to mental health. Generally, either too little work ("lazy," "dependent," "passive," etc.) or too much work ("workaholic") are viewed as symptomatic of poor coping skills. At the same time, work can be either destructive (e.g., job stress, role conflicts, etc.) or restorative (work therapy) of mental health.

From the point of view of the community counselor, work may be classified as competitive or sheltered. Competitive work is that which exists on the open labor market. Sheltered work—in workshops or training programs—may be either transitional (short-term, in preparation for movement into competitive employment as the goal) or long-term (where there is little hope of successful placement in competitive jobs). Depending on the client, any of these settings—including long-term sheltered work—can be stressful or a source of satisfaction. It is up to the counselor to work with the client to create a situation and a frame of mind in which work is a positive aspect of the client's life.

Recently, an increasing number of companies have come to realize that workers who have personal problems are less productive, have significantly greater absenteeism, and can disrupt company operations. Therefore,

companies have been establishing or contracting for "employee assistance programs" (EAPs), which are frequently staffed by community counselors. These programs vary in scope from some that deal only with substance abuse problems to others that are concerned with any aspect of worker functioning (retirement planning, family life, career change, handling stress, etc.). Because EAPs meet our definition of practice settings, they are discussed in detail in Chapter 3. Labor unions are also assuming greater concern and responsibility for their members' personal adjustment.

A community counselor may, with a client's permission, work with the EAP counselor or job supervisor at the client's place of employment to make the client's work situation more positive. Thereby, work may become a setting in which a client attains success, improves self-confidence, and develops life skills that are applicable both at and away from work. In some sheltered work settings, such goals can be the primary focus for the client's experience. In competitive employment, of course, the employer must be concerned with productivity above all other considerations. Nonetheless, with appropriate structuring, the counselor can use almost any type of work setting as a positive resource.

In addition to work itself as a resource, the community counselor should be aware of resources that prepare clients for work. Among these are the vocational training obtainable through the state divisions or bureaus of vocational rehabilitation (for any person judged to have a physical or mental condition that interferes with employment and that could be expected to be ameliorated by intervention), through the Veterans Administration (for veterans of military service), and in many locales through voluntary agencies. Some of the state and/or federally funded programs provide not only training but even the tools necessary to pursue the line of work for which the person was trained. Training may involve the development of prevocational skills (such as promptness, neatness, reliability, appropriate socialization in the work setting, etc.) in a sheltered workshop or vocational skill training in a training or apprenticeship program or a school.

Finally, the community counselor may use employment services as a resource to assist a client. These services may be either state or private. In the latter, the fee may be paid by either the client or the employer. Placement may be open or selective, that is, in a job uniquely structured to meet the client's needs and capacities. Where possible, the community counselor should have the client try to work through a professional employment counselor. It must, of course, be pointed out that getting a job is only half the battle; the other half is keeping the job. Thus, a community counselor should not treat a client's work life as a totally resolved issue once a job has been found. The counselor must also work with the client to develop job maintenance skills if the client does not already have them.

## Resources Related to Living

Clients without family homes or individual or group living arrangements have a primary need for shelter as a basic resource. Clients needing to establish their independence, battered spouses, elderly and physically handicapped clients, among others, may benefit from independent living facilities.

The term independent living center has come into current use to categorize facilities that provide at least the following services: housing assistance, attendant care, peer or professional counseling, financial and legal advocacy, and community awareness and barrier-removal programs (Frieden, 1980). Such centers may be residential or nonresidential (e.g., storefront service centers); may provide services themselves or may refer clients to collaborating agencies; may be run largely by the residents, largely by the professional staff, or largely by a board of directors; and may

seek to provide transitional or permanent living arrangements. The needs of the client should determine which sort of center is most appropriate. Another consideration in choosing a center is who is to pay for the client's use of the facility—public agency or the client (out of earnings or savings). Usually, the most important decision factor is whether the facility is transitional or ongoing. Transitional facilities (often called halfway houses or some variant of that term, such as "quarter-way houses" for clients needing a more structured environment) serve to prepare clients to live on their own, just as transitional sheltered workshops prepare clients for competitive employment.

Another category of resources for living is shelters for homeless persons. The presence of increased numbers of homeless persons living on city sidewalks, sleeping on heating grates in order to try (not always succesfully) to keep from freezing to death, and wandering aimlessly during daylight hours cannot escape public attention. As funds for social services have become diminished, many agencies sought to avoid taking on new classes of clients in order to preserve their dwindling resources to serve their traditional clientele. The result has been a chaotic pattern of attempting to avoid or shift responsibility for this population, rather than to serve them in an effective, coordinated way. Clearly, all the homeless need shelter, and those with mental health problems need treatment, as well. So far, relatively few professionals have championed this cause. Equally true, however, is the rejection by the homeless of the sorts of help professionals offer. This, however, does not free professionals from the obligation of trying to bridge the gap and provide appropriate, effective, attractive resources fox this potential client group. Community counselors have a role to play in developing effective service delivery systems for this most needy group. These services must begin with the establishment of resources for living.

## Financial Resources

Community counselors must be familiar with financial resources available or possibly applicable to their clients. These generally include a number of government programs and private insurance plans. The principal government programs are tied to workers' compensation laws, vocational rehabilitation, and the Social Security system. For a detailed review of these programs, see Erlanger and Roth (1985).

Lesser (1967) pointed out that during the 1960s, workers' compensation laws came to be construed by the courts as no longer requiring the worker to prove a causal relationship between employment and the disability, as long as it could be shown that the disability occurred on the job. Thus, in a number of cases compensation has been awarded to workers for emotional problems that they claimed were the result of a physical injury or of stress suffered in the course of doing the job. A client may be entitled to long-term financial support if her/his emotional problems can be shown to be work-related. It must, however, be pointed out that this can be a two-edged sword: Receiving workers' compensation payments may act as a disincentive to recovery, because the person who recovers may have to work hard to attain the same level of income now provided by remaining incapacitated.

Workers' compensation is paid for out of insurance funds that employers are legally required to carry. Depending on the state law, this insurance may be from either a private insurer or a state fund. The cost of insurance to the employer depends on the number of persons employed, the hazards involved in their work, and the past record of claims upheld against the company. The process of adjudicating workers' compensation claims is generally a quasi-legal one, involving awards by a board with legal appeal of their decisions to the courts possible. Because workers' compensation laws are written at the state level, there is wide variation from state to state as to procedures and benefits.

Although workers' compensation laws go back to 1911 and the legal precedents for them go back much further, it was not until 1918 (for disabled veterans) to 1920 (for civilians) that the United States government undertook a program of vocational rehabilitation for the physically disabled (Berkowitz, 1979). The impetus for the original vocational rehabilitation law was World War I, but it was not until the time of World War II, in 1943, that the law was expanded to include persons with mental health and mental retardation problems. It should be noted that workers' compensation laws, as their name implies, provided compensation for injuries sustained while one was working. Vocational rehabilitation, however, did not require that one's disability resulted from prior employment; rather, this law was aimed at assisting persons with disabilities that stood in the way of their employment (even if the disability was there from birth) to attain the training and medical help that would allow them to become employed. Thus, the tests for qualifying for vocational rehabilitation services are: (a) the presence of a documented disabling condition, (b) evidence that this condition interferes with one's ability to be employed, and (c) an evaluation that providing services will be likely to make the person employable. No prior work history is necessary. The program is administered in each state by a state agency (generally called the division or bureau of rehabilitation services), with funds coming primarily from the federal government. The funding to each state depends on the size of the state's population and its record of successfully rehabilitated cases during the prior year. The state rehabilitation services offices are staffed by rehabilitation counselors, and the community counselor would refer a client to such a co-professional for service by that agency.

Under the vocational rehabilitation program, a client would first be evaluated for eligibility for service and, if deemed eligible according to the three criteria just noted, would then be evaluated as to what services would be needed to make the client employable. These services could involve the purchase of medical and dental treatments, prosthetic devices, prevocational and vocational training, further formal education, related transportation, the purchase of tools of a trade, and/or the provision of counseling services. Naturally, only those services actually required by the client would be provided in each case. The rehabilitation counselor and the client would then agree on a written plan (the Individualized Written Rehabilitation Plan or IWRP), signed by both of them, which outlines the services, time-lines, and goals of the rehabilitation program for that client.

The next group of financial resources with which the mental health counselor should be familiar are those connected with the federal Social Security program (Detlefs & Myers, 1991). Social Security Disability Insurance (SSDI) provides a worker whose disability—including mental health problems—is expected to prevent him/her from engaging in substantial employment for a period of at least 12 months with payments equal to his/her Social Security retirement benefits, including dependents' allowances. To qualify for SSDI, the person must have worked and been covered by Social Security in 20 of the 40 quarters prior to the onset of the disability period. Benefits under SSDI may be offset by other benefits (e.g., workers' compensation benefits) and may be terminated if the recipient earns more than a specified amount.

Another benefit possibly available to one's clients under the Social Security program is Supplemental Security Income (SSI), which provides a minimum income to elderly and disabled persons. Unlike SSDI, no prior record of Social Security contributions or employment is required; however, also unlike SSDI, a client must pass a "means test"(that is, demonstrate financial need) in order to qualify for SSI benefits.

Associated with these two Social Security programs are two sets of benefits to help recipients defray the costs of health care. Medicare provides partial coverage for the costs of hospital and outpatient treatment for persons below the age of 65 who have qualified for SSDI coverage for 24 months, as well as for all persons over age 65 who qualify for Social Security retirement benefits. Medicaid provides partial coverage of health care costs for those whose income falls below a certain level. All persons who either receive or qualify for SSI meet this "means test." Medicare is an insurance program, paid for out of the deductions from one's salary made for Social Security. Medicaid, however, is an assistance program, funded by the federal and state governments out of general tax revenues, rather than by contributions of the participants. States vary in their approach to Medicaid, some states providing supplementary funds to recipients; but Medicare is a uniform program nationally.

Applications for SSDI, SSI, and Medicare are made through the client's local Social Security Administration office. Applications for Medicaid are made through the local office of the state department of social services. The regulations governing all of these programs are quite complex. A good overview of them is provided by Detlefs and Myers (1991).

A large number of programs provide benefits to veterans of the armed forces, particularly those who have a service-connected disability. These programs are run or coordinated by the Department of Veterans Affairs, which is a federal agency. If one's client is veteran of the military, the counselor should direct that client to the local Veterans Affairs office to explore possible benefits to which that client is entitled.

Finally, there are a number of health insurance plans, both private and government-sponsored, that provide coverage for health services. These include the Civilian Health and Medical Program of the Uniformed Services (CHAMPUS), which covers the civilian dependents of military personnel, Blue Cross/ Blue Shield, an many commercial plans. These programs all tend to change both their benefits (proportion of costs paid) and lists of services covered (specific treatment and type of professional who may provide it) frequently. Therefore, the community counselor should advise the client to check with his/her insurer, or if not yet insured, to check with a number of insurers about the coverage they provide before obtaining coverage from any one of them.

## Health Resources

Health resources that the community counselor should utilize, as appropriate, to meet clients' physical and mental health needs include hospitals and clinics, hospices, community service programs, self-help groups, and hotlines.

Hospitals may be publicly (municipal, state, United States Public Health Service, Veterans Affairs) or privately (religious groups, for-profit or not-for-profit corporations, etc.) supported. Community clinics are generally state supported and cover the population living within a certain defined area of the state. The state, in turn, may get part of its funding for these clinics from federal block grants. Many hospitals and some clinics provide facilities for persons experiencing severe emotional distress. Indeed, hospitals and clinics range from those that provide services only for problems of physical illness to those that deal only with mental health problems to those that offer service to both sorts of clientele. On occasion, a client may become so distressed as to require or to benefit from the environmental controls that many of these facilities can provide. Generally, admission to these facilities requires a physician's signa-

ture confirming the appropriateness of inpatient treatment. Clients may, of course, also require hospitalization for physical conditions. If one's client requires hospitalization, the community counselor should work out with the institution's professional staff a plan to continue or to coordinate treatment for the problems being worked on in counseling. Some institutions allow the counselor to visit the client and continue counseling while the client is an inpatient; other insitutions do not allow professionals not on their staff to treat their inpatients. If the client is entering one of the latter sort, the counselor should make it clear to the client that the counselor is not abandoning him/her, but is prevented from pursuing the counseling process during the time that the client is in the institution.

The hospice movement is a relatively recent phenomenon, arising in good part from medical advances that have prolonged life and extended the dying process. Hospices aim to provide for the physical and emotional care of individuals who are terminally ill and, in some instances, for the social and emotional needs of members of their families. Some hospices offer residential facilities, whereas others provide supportive services for the home care of the terminally ill person. Some hospices concentrate on children with terminal illnesses, but most work primarily with adults or elderly persons. In cases in which a client or a member of the client's immediate family is facing terminal illness, a hospice can be an excellent resource in helping the client to cope with the attendant set of problems. Hospices generally provide some combination of medical, nursing, social work, religious, and counseling services. The counselor and/or client should determine which services each locally available hospice program offers and make the selection among them on that basis.

A major resource for community counselors is self-help groups. Paskert and Madara (1985) noted that there are over 100,000 different self-help groups throughout the United

States, with over 3 million active members. These authors suggested that these groups may be broadly classified as (a) those that assist clients/patients and their family members with almost any specific major physical illness or mental health problem; (b) those that offer behavior modification programs for a wide range of addictive behaviors (e.g., alcohol abuse, drug abuse, smoking, overeating, gambling); (c) social support groups for persons facing life transitions (e.g., parenthood, divorce, bereavement); and (d) advocacy groups for special population groups (e.g., elderly, gays, racial or ethnic groups). Self-help groups are valuable in that they not only allow a sense of community and of empowerment in coping with a problem, but they also give a client an opportunity to take an active role as a helper, thereby helping themselves as well.

The relationship between self-help groups and professionals has not always been a smooth one. The self-help groups have accused professionals of acting out of self-interest, being unsympathetic or ineffective because they have not personally experienced the condition they are treating, and treating their clients as experimental subjects rather than as suffering fellow human beings. Conversely, professionals have accused self-help groups of acting unprofessionally (not a surprising observation), of being too committed to their agenda to be willing to stop and see if they are really helping those in need, of distorting their success rates by failing to apply scientific standards, and of helping themselves more than they help others with the same problem. Over time, however, these accusations on both sides have been attended to, and today, one is less likely to find the kind of mutual hostility that typified professional–self-help group relations in the past. Professionals recognize the unique effectiveness of certain self-help groups, such as Alcoholics Anonymous. If anything, professionals may be able to learn what make certain self-help groups effective, so that they may assist other self-help groups to apply or to adopt those principles to make themselves more effective. Also, as mutual distrust and competitiveness decrease, professionals and self-help groups are becoming more willing to learn from each other ways of benefiting those individuals they both seek to serve. Gartner (1982) emphasized both the sense of independence and empowerment and the cost-effectiveness of self-help groups, in that they can turn problems into resources for coping with those problems.

Community counselors must familiarize themselves with the range of self-help groups and refer clients to them when it is appropriate to do so, given the type of problem involved and the compatibility of the client and the particular group.

Finally, hotlines are telephone services maintained by either volunteer or professional organizations to provide immediate, crisis response to a particular problem (e.g., spouse abuse, potential suicide, runaway children, poisoning, infectious diseases, consumer problems). Given the specific knowledge required of persons who work on many of these hotlines, they may provide excellent resources for clients facing the specific problems toward which these hotlines are addressed.

## RELATED PROFESSIONALS

Community counselors clearly do not function in a realm that is devoid of other professionals who simultaneously are seeking to help their clients. These professionals can be seen as resources for assisting one's clients. Some of these professionals work generally with clients; others focus on serving a specialized need (e.g., job placement). Because of this multiplicity of fields, there is a good deal of complementarity; that is, one profession serves a particular need for a range of clients, while another profession serves a different need of the same client groups. There is, however, also inevitably a certain amount of over-lap of function across professions; and it is at these points that interprofessional frictions arise. To function to the benefit of the client, the community counselor must be familiar with these other, related professions, what specialized services their practitioners can offer to his/her client, and how to interact with these professionals. Moreover, when referring a client to a practitioner of one of these professions for a specific service, the counselor is obligated to evaluate that practitioner's performance of that service, so as to know whether to refer other clients to that practitioner for that service in the future.

Much of the information concerning the occupations discussed below was obtained from the *Occupational Outlook Handbook,* a publication of the U.S. Department of Labor (1992), which describes the preparation, duties, and employment opportunities in many fields of work and is regularly used by counselors doing career counseling.

## Psychiatrists

Psychiatry is the medical specialty that seeks to study, diagnose, and treat "mental ill-ness."As a branch of medicine, it is only natural that psychiatry would conceptualize emotional problems of living as a category of "illness," because the role of physicians is to treat illnesses. However, some psychiatrists (e.g., Laing, 1967; Szasz, 1961) have questioned the appropriateness of the illness model for mental health problems, suggesting that the term illness served the sociopolitical needs of the profession and/or its host society more than the therapeutic needs of the patient (the medical term for client). Psychiatrists receive extensive education: three to four years of a college premedical program, four years of medical school, a year of internship in a hospital, followed by a residency of three or four years in length. Of this education, however,

only the residency period is exclusively focused on working with mental health/mental illness problems. During the rest of the psychiatrist's training, "mental illness" is treated as only one of the many medical conditions studied. Psychiatrists are uniquely qualified to prescribe psychotropic medication (tranquilizers, antidepresssants, etc.), and all other professionals must turn to physicians if such medication is needed by their clients (although this prerogative is now under attack by clinical psychologists). Although any licensed physician is legally able to prescribe these medications, psychiatrists are generally more knowledgeable about the effects, side effects, indications, and contraindications of psychotropic medicines. Also, psychiatrists are uniquely qualified to prescribe and administer various physical treatments for mental health problems, such as electroconvulsive shock. In the main, however, most psychiatrists spend most of their working hours either in office private practice or in outpatient clinics, doing verbal psychotherapy; or in psychiatric hospital treatment and/or administration. Some psychiatrists pursue research into the neurological, physiological, or biochemical basis of mental illness. Until recently, psychiatrists were the only mental health professionals who could hospitalize a patient, but in the past few years, some mental health inpatient facilities in some locations have also allowed one or more nonphysician service providers (clinical psychologists, psychiatric nurses, etc.) to hospitalize clients and treat them in that inpatient setting (sometimes independently, sometimes only under medical supervision).

A subgroup of psychiatrists are psychoanalysts. These psychiatrists choose to undergo several additional years of specialized training and supervision, as well as a personal psychoanalysis, to qualify themselves to practice psychoanalysis (that is, the therapeutic technique originally developed by Sigmund Freud, discussed in Chapter 5).

Finally, it should be noted that not all physicians who practice psychiatry have necessarily undergone the special training or passed the medical specialty board in psychiatry. In the United States, any physician licensed to practice medicine can choose to limit his/her practice to a particular type of illness. Thus, a physician with just an internship in general medicine may hang out a shingle stating "practice limited to psychiatry." Consequently, counselors should familiarize themselves with the credentials of the psychiatrists to whom they refer clients for medication, physical treatments, or hospitalization. Generally, board-certified psychiatrists are more likely to possess the greatest knowledge of the field.

## Clinical, Counseling, and School Psychologists

From its establishment as a psychological specialization early in this century, clinical psychology has been concerned with the diagnosis of psychological problems. While the field originally focused on the diagnosis of children's learning problems, in the 1930s its role expanded to include the diagnosis of adult mental health status. It was not, however, until World War II that clinical psychologists became involved in the treatment as well as the diagnosis of mental health problems. Just after that war, the Veterans Administration provided a tremendous impetus to the growth of clinical psychology in seeking to meet its need for therapists for veterans of the war.

Clinical psychologists are trained in graduate programs in university departments of psychology or in independent schools of professional psychology. In most cases, those trained in universities are awarded the PhD degree, while independent schools give the PsyD degree. Doctoral training generally involves at least four years of graduate school, including a one-year internship and the writing of a doctoral dissertation. Some states require graduation from a doctoral program in clinical psychology that is approved by the American Psychological Association for licensure as a clinical psychologist. In many states, however, any PhD in psychology (experimental, developmental, industrial, etc.) can become licensed by passing the required examinations. Thus, just as not all physicians practicing psychiatry are board-certified or specialty educated, so, in many states, not all PhD-licensed psychologists practicing clinical psychology have gone through a clinical psychology academic program. The best indication of a clinical psychologist's professional competence is if he or she is a diplomate of the American Board of Professional Psychology in clinical psychology. This is the equivalent of specialty boards in psychiatry as an indication of expertise in one's profession.

Because PhD programs require a considerable amount of study of statistics and research methodology and require that the student designs and carries out an original research project for the doctoral dissertation, clinical (and other) psychologists are generally perceived as particularly competent in research. Most PsyD programs place less emphasis on research training than do PhD programs.

Graduate education in clinical psychology continues to involve more intensive study of psychodiagnostic testing than is taught in other mental health professions. Therefore, most diagnostic work-ups that involve objective and/or projective testing are performed by clinical psychologists. These work-ups may be necessary in order to determine if a particular behavior has an organic basis, such as brain damage, or whether it is symptomatic of a problem of living. Such determinations are necessary in order to decide what mixture of physical treatments, medications, and/or counseling is called for.

As with psychiatrists, clinical psychologists may work in mental health clinics, hospitals, or private practice. Some are employed in teaching and/or research in clinical psychology graduate training programs.

Other psychology specializations with which community counselors may come into contact, although probably less frequently than with clinical psychologists (who are more numerous), are counseling psychologists and school psychologists. As with clinical psychologists, fully qualified counseling psychologists and school psychologists should hold a doctorate from a program that is approved by the American Psychological Association and a diploma in their specialization from the American Board of Professional Psychology.

As its name implies, counseling psychology has been essentially a bridge field, drawing its theory and knowledge bases both from counseling and from psychology. The boundary between counseling psychology and clinical psychology remains vague, at best. Counseling psychologists generally are conceived of as emphasizing work with essentially mentally healthy persons and as having particular expertise in vocational behavior, whereas clinical psychologists are seen as tending to work with those facing more severe mental health difficulties and as having greater expertise in the diagnosis and treatment of psychopathology. In actual practice, however, the degree of overlap in function is greater than any difference between these two specialties (Watkins, 1985). Even the theoretical differences between the two have begun to blur, as counseling psychologists have come to work with clients having more severe emotional problems and as clinical psychologists have placed greater emphasis on identifying clients' assets (traditionally the orientation of counseling and of counseling psychology) as well as their pathology. Because of their doctoral-level training in research methodology combined with their knowledge of counseling process, counseling psychologists are of particular use to community counselors as consultants on research.

School psychologists assess children for school readiness, grade placement, learning difficulties, and behavior problems. They consult with teachers, parents, and school administrators as to how to help the child cope with the problem. Occasionally they offer direct treatment, such as play therapy with younger children; but usually the demand for diagnostic work-ups does not leave much time for the school psychologist to do therapy. Community counselors may seek work-ups from school psychologists for younger clients who are still in school and may seek to enlist the school psychologist to help a student whose parent or other family member is experiencing problems.

## Psychiatric Social Workers

Social workers are traditionally trained in three approaches: casework (providing social services and counseling to individuals and families with medical, legal, economic, or social problems); group work (working with youth groups, senior citizen groups, minority groups, etc., in community or institutional settings, to assist these groups to formulate and achieve their goals); and community organization (working with civic, religious, political, or industrial groups to develop community-wide programs to address particular social problems that exist in that community). Social workers frequently work in family and children's service centers, child welfare and adoption agencies, hospitals and nursing homes, and correctional institutions. Psychiatric social workers (generally using casework approaches) assist psychiatric patients and their families to cope with the social and economic problems associated with illness, hospitalization, and return to home and the community. They may work in mental hospitals, mental health clinics, community mental health centers, halfway houses, or community-based programs. In the course of their work, psychiatric social workers engage in verbal psychotherapy with persons experiencing problems of living, just as do the other mental health professions. Their unique expertise is their knowledge and utilization of the community welfare resources available to the client and the client's family.

The fully qualified professional social worker can be recognized by having the master's degree (generally, MSW) and the professional certification ACSW (Academy of Certified Social Workers). Many states also require licensure of psychiatric social workers, which is frequently designated by the initials LCSW (licensed clinical social worker).

Because clinical social work requires a two-year master's degree training program, emphasizes the use of social supports, and utilizes verbally oriented treatment approaches, it is generally perceived as more similar to community counseling than any of the other fields discussed here. This should be apparent from the wide variety of settings, discussed in Chapter 3, that hire members of these two professions on an almost interchangeable basis. As with clinical and counseling psychologists, one must search for distinctions between the two fields. One clear distinction is that clinical social work espouses the medical model while community counseling espouses the developmental model. This can affect the approach taken in working with a client.

## Psychiatric Nurses

Psychiatric nurses possess a master's degree (generally, master of science in nursing), obtained following the completion of an undergraduate degree in nursing and passing the examinations to qualify as a registered nurse (RN). In their graduate work, psychiatric nurses undergo specialized training in the care of mental patients. Generally, psychiatric nurses work in mental hospitals or clinics or in visiting nurse programs. Some are in private practice as nurse practitioners. In hospitals, psychiatric nurses supervise patient treatment regimens and administer wards. In outpatient settings, they are more involved in supervising treatment regimens and in performing individual therapy.

It should be pointed out that although the practitioner's degree in psychiatric social work and in psychiatric nursing is the master's degree, one may go on for further education and obtain a doctorate in both these fields (as is also true of counseling) if one wishes to qualify for academic, research, or some administrative positions.

From the viewpoint of the community counselor, it is important to know about the professional qualifications and unique expertise of each of these professions in order to obtain appropriate services for one's clients. To summarize, psychiatrists should be board-certified in psychiatry and can assist community counselors in the prescription of psychotropic medication, in the use of physically based therapeutic interventions, and in hospitalizing clients who are in need of that environment. Clinical and counseling psychologists should hold the American Board of Professional Psychology (ABPP) diploma in their specialization. Clinical psychologists can assist community counselors by doing psychodiagnostic work-ups of clients; counseling psychologists can assist in designing research studies; and either specialization, if they are trained as behaviorists, can assist in constructing behaviorally based treatment programs for particular clients. Social workers should hold the clinical social worker credential (LCSW); they can assist counselors in locating and obtaining social services for clients and the families of clients. Psychiatric nurses should hold a master's degree in psychiatric nursing; they can assist in developing ways of keeping clients on treatment regimens. All of these groups also offer verbal psychotherapy, just as counselors offer verbal counseling. Not surprisingly, in their extensive study of psychiatrists, psychoanalysts, clinical psychologists, and psychiatric social workers, Henry, Sims, and Spray (1971) found that the four professions had much more in common than they had separating them in their professional practice, and that taken together, they constituted a "fifth profession" of psychotherapists.

## Other Counseling Specialties

In addition to practitioners of these other helping professions, community counselors also work with counselors in other specializations such as (1) marriage and family counselors/therapists, who seek to resolve marital or family discord by working with the family unit as a system; (2) clinical mental health counselors, who work with persons with diagnosed mental illness; (3) career counselors, who assist individuals from mid-teens to old age to explore, decide on, and implement career plans and to deal with work-related issues; (4) rehabilitation counselors, who assist persons with physical, mental, emotional, or social disabilities to attain productive employment and/or independent living; (5) school counselors, who help elementary and secondary school students with their emotional, social, and behavioral adjustment to the school environment, the learning process, and their postschool plans; and (6) gerontological counselors, who work with older persons on issues of social and emotional functioning. Professionals in all of these fields hold a master's or doctoral degree in counseling and a specialized credential: (1) certification by the American Association for Marriage and Family Therapy (AAMFT); (2) Certified Clinical Mental Health Counselor (CCMHC); (3) National Certified Career Counselor (NCCC); (4) Certified Rehabilitation Counselor (CRC); (5) National Certified School Counselor (NCSC); and (6) National Certified Gerontological Counselor (NCGC), respectively. Each of these specializations is represented by a division in the American Counseling Association.

Other counseling-related fields with which community counselors may work are employment counselors, addictions counselors, and correctional counselors, who work with legal offenders. These fields do not necessarily require a master's degree, but they are represented by divisions within the American Counseling Association, and addictions counselors should hold the credential of Certified Addictions Counselor (CAC).

Just as with clinical and counseling psychologists, practitioners of different counseling specialities sometimes have more in common (for example, a common philosophical and knowledge base in counseling) than they have separating them (for example, their focus on a particular set of issues or segment of the population). Turf problems can arise when a client presents a set of issues that overlap specialty areas (for example, an older person with an emotional disability who is seeking a way to reenter the labor market—thus potentially coming within the purview of gerontological counselors, clinical mental health counselors, rehabilitation counselors, career counselors, and employment counselors, as well as community counselors). As in all instances of professonial overlap, it is essential that the issue be resolved in a way that best serves the interests of the client, rather than in a way that meets the needs of potentially competing professionals, who usually are acting out of the genuine conviction that their specialty has the most important contribution to make in assisting the client.

## Vocational Evaluators

Vocational evaluators are trained at the baccalaureate or the master's degree level to assess an individual's current capacity for work and what sorts of changes must be induced to prepare that person for entry into a work role. These changes may involve learning work habits (neatness, promptness, reliability), job skills, or social skills (relating to co-workers and bosses); or they may involve unlearning behaviors that prevent the person from getting or keeping a job. Work evaluators are employed in sheltered workshops, work evaluation programs, job retraining and placement agencies, and rehabilitation programs. They should be certified (Certified Vocational Evaluator, CVE) by the Vocational Evaluation and Work Adjustment Association, a division of the National Rehabilitation Association. Community counselors should refer clients to work evaluation programs to determine how ready these clients are for a given level of employment (sheltered, transitional, or competitive) and what they will need to do to prepare themselves to enter or return to work at any specified level. Clients may have to go through work adjustment programs in order to attain needed skills, or they may be able to overcome some deficits as part of their counseling "homework."

## Occupational and Recreational Therapists

Occupational therapists are trained at either the baccalaureate level or in master's degree programs. Graduates of either type of program must pass the occupational therapy registration examination, which earns them the designation OTR. Occupational therapists apply activities to diagnose and help correct musculoskeletal, neurological, and psychiatric problems. Some occupational therapists specialize in working with persons with mental health problems, using activities to promote socialization, feelings of competence, and release of anger or tension. Some occupational therapists specialize in the diagnosis and treatment of learning disorders, using activities to promote neurologic integration. Others work with the upper extremity physically disabled, to help them overcome or compensate for arm or hand dysfunction. (Generally, physical therapists work with lower limb and mobility problems.)

Individuals are trained in academic programs in therapeutic recreation at the junior college, college, and master's degree levels.

Recreational therapists are generally required to hold a state license or professional registration if they are to be employed in hospitals or nursing homes. In these settings, they utilize recreational activities to promote therapeutic change. As with a number of other helping professions, the boundary between occupational therapy and therapeutic recreation remains unclear, and there are unresolved issues between the two fields as to professional domain. When their clients are receiving occupational or recreational therapy, community counselors should regularly consult with those providing the service about the progress of their clients.

## Paraprofessionals and Other Helpers

In addition to the professional groups discussed above, there are a variety of other helpers whom the community counselor can use as resources in assisting a client. These include paraprofessionals such as mental health technicians, aides, and indigenous workers.

Mental health technicians generally are educated in two- or four-year undergraduate college programs. They perform routine tasks, such as taking family histories or contacting referrals. They are employed in hospitals, clinics, or community mental health centers, thereby freeing the time of the fully qualified professionals to serve more clients with their specialized skills. They may also work in daycare or residential programs for formerly hospitalized individuals or others in need of such services.

Aides and indigenous workers require, at most, a high school education. These workers receive in-service training to perform less skilled tasks than are required of mental health technicians. In some instances, however, these tasks are no less vital just because they are technically less skilled. For example, an indigenous worker may be accepted by a client belonging to the same cultural group of which the worker is a member, whereas a white, Anglo, middle-class professional may face suspicion or resistance. Aides and indigenous workers may serve in such capacities as case-finding, getting clients to clinic appointments, gathering data about the community, and talking to clients' relatives about the clients' behavior.

Another essential group of persons who should also be mentioned are volunteers. These individuals generally are not paid for their work, but act out of personal concern with the needs of their community. Volunteer workers may assist with administrative tasks at community agencies, serve to meet the public at agencies, work at establishing relationships with individual clients to assist them to reenter the community, serve on agency boards or committees, speak on behalf of particular agencies or issues in their community, or work on fund-raising campaigns. In essence, volunteers may assist with almost any and all aspects of programs. It is incumbent on community counselors to show respect for the work of volunteers and to learn how to assess and to utilize the talents of individual volunteers most effectively, so that the volunteer feels fulfilled by services donated and the agency benefits from the volunteer's efforts.

Undoubtedly, no group is turned to for help by persons experiencing problems of living as much as are family members, friends, and co-workers. Unfortunately, these groups are also the least systematically trained to assist persons having problems to deal with them. A major role of community counselors is to assist families and friends to cope with the demands placed upon them. Feelings of anger at being required to give help, frustration at the apparent failure of their efforts, and fatigue from trying to help the person in need while meeting the demands placed on them by their own work and family responsibilities are common. Thus, self-help groups for the families and friends of individuals with various

problems have become prevalent. At these groups, often organized on a community basis, friends and relatives of those with a particular problem gather on a regular basis to share their experiences and feelings, learn new ways of coping for themselves and of being helpful to the person experiencing the problem, and gain comfort from the awareness that they are not alone in facing this set of circumstances and the feelings it evokes in them.

Finally, in working with their clients, community counselors often interact with physicians, nurses, and allied health professionals (such as physical therapists or speech pathologists); members of the clergy; welfare workers; and police, parole officers, lawyers, and judges. In working with their clients' environments, community counselors may interact (frequently in advocacy roles) with employers, community planners, and politicians. Community counselors must be prepared to assist these persons who are turned to by large numbers of persons with social or emotional problems, even though these professions do not present themselves to the public as specialists in treating such problems (Mechanic, 1980). Conversely, practitioners of these professions must recognize when to consult or to refer clients to community counselors or other professionals who are trained to assist with particular problems of living. It is, therefore, incumbent on community counselors and related professionals to educate other professions about when, how, and to whom to refer persons in need of counseling services.

Similarly, community counselors must make their presence and availability known to the families, friends, and co-workers of those experiencing problems. Community counselors must assist these groups to help their relative, friend, or co-worker in need of help and to maintain their own health and stability while being of help to the person in need. Community education programs, public service announcements in the print and broadcast media, and direct contact with local support groups can all be used to inform family, friends, and co-workers of the availability of professionals who are ready and able to help.

At the same time, it is necessary for the community counselor to know what services these groups can offer the clients, to assist in the recovery process. Thus, a community counselor will refer clients to a physician to determine whether there is a physical basis for emotional symptoms, to treat co-existing physical illness that can debilitate a client and exacerbate mental health problems, and to prescribe psychotropic medication if no board-certified psychiatrist is available. Counselors should refer those clients expressing religious concerns to clergy, for assistance in meeting the clients' spiritual needs. Such help may greatly assist some clients in dealing with their problems of living. Counselors should know when and how to refer clients in need to welfare or other public services. Finally, community counselors must know how to enlist the help of family, friends, employers, and/or co-workers in their client's treatment, so that the client's environment facilitates, rather than impedes, the client's adjustment.

## CONCLUSION

Throughout this book the fact has been emphasized that an individual functions within an environmental context, and that this context may facilitate or hinder effective coping. This principle is as true for counselors as it is for clients. The counselor does not practice his/her profession in a vacuum, even if she/he is engaged in a one-person, full-time private practice. One cannot function as a community counselor without frequent interactions with many of the categories of professionals and other helpers discussed in this chapter. Just as the counselor must assist the client to identify, develop, and apply personal skills to changing the environment so that it will be supportive, so the counselor must develop and apply professional skills to making the client's environment of professionals and other helpers as facilitative for the client as possible. Thus, interacting with these groups of persons on the client's behalf (either directly or through the client) is as much a part of the counselor's professional duties as is sitting alone with the client in an office counseling session. Therefore, it is as important for the community counselor to know in what ways these persons or groups can help the client and to know how good a job they can do in their area of competence as it is know the different techniques of individual counseling and when to use each one. It is as important for the counselor to know how to refer clients and how to maintain contact with the helper so as to maximize the help needed by the client as it is to know how to establish a counseling relationship with a client. Neither individuals nor professions exist in isolation; and so the knowledge and skills to mobilize these resources are a necessary part of community counseling.

This chapter has reviewed a number of the major categories of resources that community counselors may bring to bear to assist their clients to cope with specific problems of living. Where these resources exist in the counselor's community, the counselor should know of them and how to access them. When a needed resource does not exist, the counselor should use her/his skills to involve the community in establishing that resource, as discussed in Chapter 2. Resources are a major element of the environmental context that can be used to help clients to cope with all sorts of problems of living. Involving the appropriate resources in the solution of problems is an essential part of any treatment plan, and the knowledge of how to do so is a basic professional skill that every community counselor must possess.

## EXERCISE

The following case study provides a framework to identify the many functions that are necessary when a community counselor assumes the role as a case manager.

### Case Study

Matthew, age 26, married with two children, ages 3 and 1, is concluding the in-hospital phase of his medical rehabilitation after a serious, closed head injury occurring 11 months previous to the preparation plans for his hospital discharge. You have been asked, as a community counselor, to act as Matthew's case manager during the outpatient period of Matthew's rehabilitation. Prior to his injury, Matthew worked as a landscaping specialist for a large nursery, and when his physical and mental functions are restored, his previous employer is willing to rehire Matthew, depending, however, on his physical and mental capabilities to perform his earlier job duties.

Currently, Matthew is experiencing memory deficits, conceptual limitations, and difficulties with prolonged standing and walking. He is receiving regular payments from an insurance carrier, since he was struck by another car while riding his motorcycle and the other driver was cited as responsible for the accident. During the discharge conference the community counselor is told that many resources will be necessary for Matthew's outpatient rehabilitation and eventual return to employment. Matthew's wife has been a homemaker since she was married, and the couple reports that, within 75 miles of their home, they have no relatives, but do have a few close friends. The wife states that she would like to be employed, especially if Matthew is unable to return to his former job. Also, they have large mortgage payments on their home, and another income would alleviate financial stress. The wife has a two-year associates degree in American history.

With this information, please respond to the following questions:

1. What functions of case management do you believe the community counselor would use when responding as a case manager for Matthew?

2. What other resources, besides the outpatient hospital services, should be identified as necessary to assist Matthew and his family?

3. Would related professionals be utilized in the case management process with Matthew, and if so, who?

4. What do you foresee as the biggest difficulty in coordinating services for Matthew?

### REFERENCES

Backer, T. E., & Trotter, M. W. (1986). Networks in the rehabilitation field: Local to international. *American Rehabilitation, 12*(l), 28–31.

Baker, F., & Intagliata, J. (1992). Case management. In R. P. Liberman (Ed.), *Handbook of psychiatric rehabilitation* (pp. 213–243). Boston, MA: Allyn and Bacon.

Berkowitz, E. D. (1979). The American disability system in historical perspective. In E. D. Berkowitz (Ed.), *Disability policies and government programs.* New York: Praeger.

Center for Psychiatric Rehabilitation. (1991). *National survey of case management practices.* Unpublished survey. Boston, MA: Center for Psychiatric Rehabilitation, Boston University.

Detlefs, D. R., & Myers, R. J. (1991). *Mercer guide to Social Security and Medicare: 1992.* Wm. Mercer.

Dixon, T. R, Goll, S., & Stanton, K. M. (1988). Case management issues and practices in head injury rehabilitation. *Rehabilitation Counseling Bulletin, 31,* 325–343.

Erlanger, H. S., & Roth W. (1985). Disability policy: The parts and the whole. *American Behavioral Scientist, 28,* 319–345.

Frieden, L. (1980). Independent living models. *Rehabilitation Literature, 41,* 169–173.

Gartner, A. (1982). Self-help/self-care: A cost effective health strategy. *Social Policy, 12*(4), 64

Greenwood, R. (1982). Systematic caseload management. In R. T. Roessler & S. E. Rubin (Eds.), *Case management and rehabilitation counseling* (pp. 159–172). Baltimore, MD: University Park Press.

Harold, M. (1985, September 5). Many of nation's homeless beset with mental disorders. *American Association for Counseling and Development Guidepost, 28*(3), 1, 12.

Hatfield, A. B. (1981). Self-help groups for families of the mentally ill. *Social Work, 26,* 408–413.

Henderson, M. G., & Wallack, S. S. (1987, January). Evaluating case management for catastrophic illness. *Business and Health,* 7–11.

Henke, R. O., Connolly, S. G., & Cox, J. G. (1975). Caseload management: The key to effectiveness. *Journal of Applied Rehabilitation Counseling, 6,* 217–227.

Henry, W. E. , Sims, J. H., & Spray, S. L. (1971). *The fifth profession.* San Francisco: Jossey-Bass.

Hershenson, D. B., & Power, P. W. (1987). *Mental health counseling: Theory and practice.* Elmsford, NY: Pergamon Press.

Laing, R. D. (1967). *The politics of experience.* New York: Ballantine Books.

Leahy, M. I., Shapson, P. R., & Wright, G. N. (1987). Professional rehabilitation competency research: Project methodology. *Rehabilitation Counseling Bulletin, 31,* 94–106.

Lesser, P. J. (1967). The legal viewpoint. In A. A. McLean (Ed.), *To work is human: Mental health and the business community* (pp. 103–122). New York: Macmillan.

Lewis, J. A., & Lewis, M. D. (1983). *Community counseling: A human services approach* (2nd ed.). New York: Wiley.

McLean, A. (Ed.).(1970). *Mental health and work organizations.* Chicago: Rand McNally.

Mechanic, D. (1980). *Mental health and social policy* (2nd ed.). Englewood Cliffs, NJ: Prentice-Hall.

National Council on the Handicapped. (1986, February). *Toward independence: An assessment of federal laws and programs affecting persons with disabilities—with legislative, recommendations.* Washington, DC: Author.

Paskert, C. J., & Madara, E. J. (1985). Introducing and tapping self-help mutual aid resources. *Health Education, 16,* 25–29.

Schwartz, B. (1986). Decide to network: A path to personal and professional empowerment. *AMHCA Journal, 8,* 12–17.

Slocum, W. L. (1974). *Occupational careers: A sociological perspective* (2nd ed.). Chicago: Aldine.

Szasz, T. (1961). *The myth of mental illness.* New York: Paul B. Hoeber.

Third Institute on Rehabilitation Services. (1965). *Training guides in caseload management for vocational rehabilitation.* Washington, DC: Vocational Rehabilitation Administration, DHEW.

Thompson, J. K., Kite, J.,C., & Bruyere, S. M. (1977). *Caseload management: Content and training perspective.* Paper presented at the American Personnel and Guidance Association Annual Convention, Dallas.

Tilgher, A. (1930). *Work: What it has meant to men through the ages* (D. C. Fisher, Trans.). New York: Harcourt, Brace.

U.S. Department of Labor. (1992). *Occupational outlook handbook: 1992–93 edition.* Washington, DC: U.S. Government Printing Office.

Watkins, C. E., Jr. (1985). Counseling psychology, clinical psychology, and human services psychology: Where the twain shall meet? *American Psychologist, 40,* 1054–1056.

# 14

# POLICY FORMATION AND ADVOCACY

Training programs for counselors have traditionally emphasized the acquisition of skills that are targeted for one-to-one or group relationships The educational focus has been on the awareness of individual problems and how they may affect not only the client, but also the family, school, and work environments. Little attention in counselor education has been directed to the counselor's role in the development of policies. Yet policies can not only address problems affecting a large group of people, but they also spawn progress, generate mental health services, and influence the allocation of resources. Policies reflect the values held by individuals who are concerned about societal and individual problems, as well as imply expectations and assumptions about the physical and behavioral attributes that people ought to possess in order to survive or to participate in community life

(Hahn, 1988). Income maintenance, health care, vocational rehabilitation, and family policies, for example, have been developed by people concerned about quality of life issues and committed to assisting individuals to independence, enhanced living, or to the exercise of their legal rights. If counselors better understood how policies are generated and effectively implemented, and their own role in policy development, then they might begin to play more of a part in advocating for the rights and opportunities of their clients.

This chapter will identify the definitions and scope of policy, discuss how policies are usually developed, and explain the main players in this development. Advocacy as a function of the counselor's roles will then be highlighted, followed by the description of a case example illustrating advocacy strategies.

# POLICY: DEFINITION AND SCOPE

Policy usually addresses the basic and often neglected problems of individuals in relation to society. Policies ultimately emerge from such societal and individual values as equity, life, rights, quality of life, and perhaps efficiency. Issues such as achieving greater independence for those with disabilities, protection from spousal abuse, welfare for the homeless, and job programs all involve values. When a group of people responsible for the rights of individuals and the recognition of societal difficulties agree upon a course of action to remedy specific problems, then there is a process of collective decision making, usually governed by rules and reflective of the decision maker's values (Zimmermann, 1988). Consequently, a stated policy that responds to a particular problem is the result of choices or decisions to support an agreed course of action for the achievement of a planned goal or a stated value.

The term policy can be applied to many levels of human endeavor, such as individual, family, organization, state, national and international. The notion of "policy" conveys a different meaning than the word "politics." Policy is concerned with normative issues, values, and standards, whereas politics includes interest and pressure groups, namely, those who wish to influence policy in terms of what gets on an agenda, newly elected officials, and even a "national mood" (Kingdom, 1984). To illustrate the difference, the Americans with Disabilities Act, landmark legislation for those with physical and mental disabilities that was enacted in 1990, represents both policy and politics. The act provides new employment and daily living opportunities for persons with disabilities, and addresses other issues that pertain to enhanced quality of life. During the development of this policy, the values of independence, freedom, and equal opportunity, as well as employment and living standards implicit in the just rights for all citizens, were carefully woven into the policy prescriptions of this law. But politics acted as a facilitator for the eventual passage of this policy by the United States Congress. A "national mood" was a context that provided an accepting atmosphere for the further extension of basic human rights implied in the policy legislation. There were lobbying groups of parents, legislators, and people with disabilities who exerted considerable pressure on lawmakers to develop and to enact this disability policy. Though they are different realities, politics and policy can meet to produce an effective response to the people's needs.

Each level in an individual's environment contains policies, moreover, to guide one's actions (Zimmermann, 1988). As discussed in Chapter 4, counselors are acquainted with policies generated by professional organizations that guide ethical behavior. They are also cognizant of policies related to mental health care, the delivery of vocational rehabilitation services to those with a disability, and those affecting family life. In other words, social policies have generally created the most attention for counselors. Zimmermann (1988) cited Baumheier and Schorr (1977) when defining social policy "as consisting of principles and procedures that guide any course of action dealing with individuals and aggregate relationships in society" (p. 17). This type of policy includes purposive action, rules that specify both who is to do what, where, and when and tools that may provide incentives and motivation (Nagel, 1990). These tools may include grants, educational programs, and even penalties and persuasive communications. Policies, therefore, manifest themselves in guidelines, laws, and programs as well as in the routines and practices of public organizations, and they "work through people to achieve results" (Nagel, 1990, p. 8).

Social policies can perform a number of functions, including providing partial compensation for handicapping conditions or for disservices caused by society, protection for individuals and society, and the offering of services for personal well-being, such as libraries and parks. Social policies, therefore, can affect a very large number of people and target a vast array of societal problems. Attention to these problems often reflects current public opinion and cultural values. These values are usually an expression of how individuals understand the world in which they live or think it should be (Zimmermann, 1988). If independence is a value highly treasured by members of a society, then policy will promote this belief in order to give individuals the sustained opportunity to be as independent as possible.

Jones (1984) identified three approaches for studying the formation of policy. One is to examine the substance of the issues and to explore the implications for the development of public policy. Second, the processes of institutions, i.e., legislatures, courts, and political parties, are analyzed to determine how they work, how they produce, and how the institutions connect with each other. The third approach focuses on groups that are an essential factor in the policy making process and studies how they function. Approaches to policy formation, consequently, can be divided into two categories: those that focus on the person or a group of persons, and those that focus on the institution, organization, or system (West, 1988). After reviewing the literature on policy development, West (1988) identified many guidelines for the policy making process, and the following steps reflect the contributions of many authors (Wergin, 1973; May & Wildavsky, 1978; Anderson, 1982; Cobb & Elder, 1982; Jones, 1984; Weimer & Vining, 1992).

## 1. Problem Identification and Definition

A problem must gain the attention of a large number of people if it is ever going to attain legislative resolution. Integral to problem identification, and a component of problem analysis, is understanding the problem. This knowledge involves evaluating the conditions that concern the client and then sifting through the conditions of concern and the variables that can be manipulated through policy. Assessing client concerns or symptoms usually demands determining their empirical basis. In other words, data should be located that help put the symptoms in a quantitative perspective (Weimer & Vining, 1992).

When considering problem identification, the question can be asked: "Why does one issue gain attention and not another?" Kingdom (1984) believed that both indicators and focusing events can be means by which policy makers can learn about specific issues. Indicators can include such events as highway deaths, the rising incidence of disease, and consumer prices. A focusing event may be a natural disaster, such as a flood or earthquake, or even a fiscal crisis.

These events or crises can stimulate careful studies conducted during a given time, and the studies may pinpoint the magnitude and challenges of a problem. Problems can, therefore, eventually develop into policies for their resolution, and politics may facilitate both progress development and implementation of policy. The problem, policy, and politics actually are essential factors for any issue being brought to public attention. This is particularly true for social and economic problems.

Problem identification also includes an understanding of the needs of a particular client population. Policy is most successful when it attends to the specific desires and needs of those who may benefit from the stated policy. Services may be perceived as helpful by counselors, for example, but not viewed as such by the client. Perception of need by both the client and the client's significant others should play a major role in a policy that defines how services are to be provided (Brubaker & Brubaker, 1995).

For the community counselor, policies related to certification and licensure and the access to services for those with life adjustment concerns are especially important for problem identification and definition. Different countries and states have different policies for counselor certification and licensure, as well as what fiscal and health services are available to individuals with problems needing intervention. How certification and licensure are defined during the policy development process can facilitate a timely response by political and professional constituencies responsible for eventual policy legislation and implementation. These issues affecting counseling practice receive more attention than perhaps other counselor concerns because of this problem identification and the entire process by which legislators learn about the seriousness of counselor credibility and available access to needed services.

## 2. Agenda Setting

Once policy makers begin to give attention to a specific social problem, for example, this item must appear on their agenda for possible policy development. Again the process by which certain items appear on the public agenda for action and others do not is a topic of considerable interest to policy researchers (West, 1988). Walker (1977) suggested that three factors determine if an issue reaches the agenda, namely, (1) impact on a large number of people and a broad appeal, (2) perception that it is a serious problem, and (3) the solution to the problem is easily understood. If all three factors are in place, the chances for the item to reach the agenda are good; and if a solution is attached to a problem, the chances of it reaching the agenda are even increased (West, 1988). Policy makers, of course, must also deal with old issues that are habitual or regularly recurring (e.g., budget), but new

issues may again emerge from the reaction of a decision maker to a certain situation or because of massive public demand.

## 3. Policy Formulation

This step involves the development of appropriate and acceptable proposals for resolving selected problems. This is usually a technical exercise during which decisions are made about what sort of action is needed on a particular problem and what the substance of the policy proposal should be. Criteria that may be used during this process for policy development are the values held by members of the policy community, monetary constraints implied in selecting different choices of policy action, technical feasibility, and the capability of the policy to be eventually implemented. During this step, the vested interests of the policy makers will also have an impact on decision making. But if policies are to benefit the individuals to whom services are directed, then as they are formulated the policies should take into account the personal characteristics of the client, as well as the characteristics of the environment in which the client lives and works (Brubaker & Brubaker, 1995). Policy enhances the delivery of services when it recognizes the complexity of the client's situation. Such complexity should be initially recognized during the program identification step.

Policy formulations frequently appear to be more reactive, namely, they explore forms of assistance after a problem has become serious and disruptive to client or family functioning. When community counselors are offering assistance to such groups as family caregivers of the elderly or parents of children with a chronic illness, they might consider initiating policies that will offer preventive, more proactive services. Such policies are needed if costs are going to be reduced for family care.

## 4. Policy Adoption

Bargaining and compromise characterize the adoption phase of the policy process. A particular proposal may need to be weakened or strengthened in exchange for an individual committee member's vote. Final adoption usually requires the formation of a number of majorities as the policy is considered by various groups.

Depending on the counselor's professional opportunity, the practitioner may be involved in each of the four steps. One step, however, that needs reemphasis for community counselors is problem definition. These professionals are often aware of specific, societal problems that affect their client's life functioning. After becoming aware of a specific, even widespread problem, the counselor can assume the responsibility and function as an advocate. Advocacy issues will be discussed later in this chapter.

## HISTORY OF POLICY

An understanding of the aforementioned guidelines for the policy-making process represents a context for understanding the history of public policy. Unlike the many guidelines or rules that are handed down from scientists to practitioners, for example, and that constitute how an individual goes about "working" at the profession, policy, which in turn influences daily professional practice, is itself the product of political and bureaucratic processing (Nagel, 1990). These processes can be viewed in terms of cycles in policy change by the time periods of the 1910s, 1930s, 1960s, and 1980s. Within each of these periods the focus is on economic, education, social, urban-regional planning, science, and political issues that eventually emerge into established policies. Because this book emphasizes the issues affecting community counseling

practice, a brief discussion will be given of the history of social policy.

Social policy has targeted the areas of poverty, racial discrimination, criminal justice, and mental and physical disability problems. In Chapters 1 and 2 of this book, attention is given to the history of counseling and community counseling. Part of this history was shaped by legislation attempting to improve the quality of life of those with mental illness. Since 1920 federal laws have provided policies on the employment rights of those with physical and mental disabilities, laws that emerged from such indicators as the high unemployment rates of persons with disabilities, a national mood to extend basic human rights to all citizens, and the need to give the opportunity to as many individuals as possible to earn a living wage and not depend completely on entitlement funds.

The war on poverty received considerable attention in the 1960s and Nagel (1990) believed that its greatest gains were in the form of judicial precedents, including: (a) welfare recipients were entitled to at least minimum due process before their benefits could be terminated; (b) delinquent, illegitimate or neglected children were entitled to a hearing with due process; and (c) tenants could withhold rent if landlords failed to satisfy minimum implied warranties of habitability. Work incentive programs were also begun during this period. Concerning racial discrimination, the gains have been mainly at the Supreme Court and congressional levels during the 1960s in such areas as voting rights, criminal justice, education, and housing (Nagel, 1990).

The social policy that emerged in the 1960s also focused on criminal justice, particularly emphasizing bail reform; the minimum rights for people on parole, probation, or in prison; and attempts at reducing delay in the criminal and civil justice process. These directives have continued since the '60's; and because of such political forces as change in the administration and national mood toward speedy sentencing and lengthy incarceration for many crimes, these issues will maintain an important place on the policy agenda.

An understanding of the history of social policy has many implications for the community counselor. Counselors should be concerned about the rights of their clients, and social policies have as their substantive focus the provision of many of these basic rights. Also, many policies only respond to part of the problem resolution. More policies relevant to an important issue need to be developed, and this is especially true with disability policy. Historically, it appears that different legislation has only attended on a piecemeal basis to a segment of the client's overall life functioning. Established policy can be an invitation to further advocacy efforts and eventually lead to a more developed policy to meet the living and working needs of all those with disabilities. Finally, since history involves a process or an evolution of events that may culminate in a satisfactory response to an important problem, community counselors can learn, from how policy has evolved, what represented effective or noneffective components of the process. As history of social policy provides an invitation to increased advocacy, it also invites the counselor to become a player in policy development.

## THE PLAYERS IN POLICY DEVELOPMENT

Whether the policies are designed to arrange the distribution of community resources, to protect the public interests, to transfer resources from one group to another, or to remedy different societal problems through the allocation of resources and specific legislation, there are many players in policy making. Policy development is actually a complex activity which could escape a rational explanation (West, 1988). The actors in the unfolding drama of policy development will depend on the nature of the policy, the target population affected by the particular policy, and who is specifically responsible for the decision-making process and eventual policy adoption. Legislation or policy enacted by the U.S. government, for example, will involve members of Congress, interest groups, subcommittees responsible for the initial development of a particular policy, members of the executive branch, and perhaps federal and local courts. All of these groups constitute the policy environment and will have a role in the process of policy formation, a process that demands persistence, strategy, timing, compromise, and occasionally, pure chance (Davidson & Olezek, 1985). Bargaining is often at the heart of a particular policy development process, when there could be an exchange of goals or resources.

For the community counselor, mental health legislation, family policies, professional and organizational mandates, such as ethics, and legislation that affects the daily living of those with physical or mental disabilities and other at-risk populations, are the policies having perhaps the greatest impact on the professional practice of the counselor. Whether these policies are developed at the neighborhood, county, state, or national level will determine who will be involved in policy formulation. Regardless of the type of policy, however, certain constituencies will be involved in any policy.

### Interest Groups

Interest groups are organized groups seeking to influence policy making, and can range from very small to very large, from one local organization to a coalition of hundreds of organizations united to support or to deter a specific piece of legislation (West, 1988).

These groups may initiate or monitor policy agenda, and can play either dominant or subordinant roles throughout the policy process. Many policies that involve community mental health, persons with physical or mental disabilities, and families have been initiated by selected interest groups.

## Personnel Responsible for Policy Making

These individuals, as stated earlier, can vary according to the "level" at which the policy will be developed and adopted. The personnel can range from members of Congress, the executive branch of federal, state, and local governments, to administrative personnel in a specific professional organization. Within each one group there is a distribution of power, with the mutual goal of enacting legislation. These groups cannot be represented only as components of a policy environment, but can also be described as policy communities. These communities may be tightly knit, such as with administrative personnel, particular professional organizations, or local or county governments. Within these groups there is usually a division of labor and concomitant specialization.

The community counselor's function as one of the players in policy formation depends on the counselor's professional responsibilities, level of competence, interest, and opportunity to become involved. Community counselors should be interested in societal problems that affect their clients, and with opportunity and appropriate competence to handle problem identification and development issues, they can make a difference both in client functioning and the environment in which the client lives, learns, and works.

To achieve this difference in policy development and implementation, a number of recommendations can be considered, many of which are suggested by the Center on Human Policy, Syracuse University (1992), and adapted here for community counselors:

**1.** Examine one's own personal assumptions, especially in regard to how they affect policy and practice for one's clients. This self-exploration should be a continuing process, for even your basic assumptions about your client's rights to access to services, educational training, and different careers may reflect gender, cultural, or class stereotypes and biases.

**2.** Examine the beliefs, values, and assumptions held in a human service agency about men, women, poor people, people with disabilities, and people of races and cultures other than those represented by the majority of agency employees. In other words, what is the agency culture, and how well does it accommodate diversity? This examination can include, when appropriate, whether pressure is placed on clients and their family members to conform to what is favored in the agency culture.

**3.** Identify existing policies that affect one's clients, especially legislation, regulations, and practices that affect both the counselor's and the agency's ability to provide flexible, client-centered services. Too great an emphasis on accountability and measurable outcomes, for example, may cause administrators to feel that they must approach the delivery of services conservatively and from a stance in which they attempt to exert control over client decisions (Center on Human Policy, 1992).

**4.** If the community counselor is working for an agency, attempt to establish a climate that facilitates respect, listening to and understanding of clients and their families. Training and staff meeting experiences can be developed to establish this type of climate.

**5.** Inform local, regional, or national policy makers of problems that have not received policy attention, or perhaps enacted policy requirements that pose problems due to class, gender, or cultural insensitivity.

While these five recommendations suggest how the community counselor can become a vital player in policy development, there is an additional issue embedded in understanding policy and its implementation, namely, understanding the ingredients of policy design. Though problem definition, agenda setting, policy formulation, policy adoption, and attention to the players in policy development are all essential components of policy design as discussed earlier in this chapter, Kingdom (1984) and Nagel (1990) believe there are other design factors, and identify the following:

**1.** The target population, namely, for whom the policy should be designed. Designers frequently have several choices of target groups, and outcomes will vary depending on which targets are selected. Within the same policy there may be many target populations. Counselor certification and licensure policies are an example. Policy directives may affect not only counselors themselves, but also their clients and different agencies that sponsor them. Therefore if there is a problem to be solved, it is useful to begin the analysis by determining who the target population might be, and then determining why they are not already engaged in the behavior that would solve or ameliorate the problem (Nagel, 1990).

**2.** Policy participation, namely, is there willing participation from the target population that may facilitate or deter the achievement of policy goals? This participation implies a clarification of participant expectations and a specification of the rules, actions, or decisions that are required, prohibited, or permitted during policy development. For a policy to have desirable results, a large number of people in different situations may have to make decisions and take action in harmony with planned policy objectives. Such partici-

pation implies the availability of personnel, as well as an understanding of their values, their knowledge of the problem, and even their risk estimates.

**3.** Support, namely, encouragement or endorsement from policy makers in order that progress can be made to develop a policy response to the identified problem. Many policies related to counselor certification or licensure, for example, may not directly affect specific constituencies, such as social workers or psychologists, but for the policy to eventually receive legislative approval, support from these professional groups may be necessary.

**4.** Knowledge, namely, the quality of the information upon which a policy is based influences policy development and implementation. For a policy to address a problem effectively, facts need to be carefully gathered about the nature, impact, and negative outcomes of a particular problem. Statistical information that identifies the number affected by the concern, as well as alternative approaches for problem solution, should be considered.

**5.** A decision-making approach that weighs different solutions for problem remediation is an important factor during policy development. A particular issue may suggest multiple solutions, and policy makers should be able to utilize a decision-making approach that will result in the best possible choice. Values of policymakers not only play a central role in policy outcomes, but need close scrutiny when different choices are considered for policy direction.

An awareness of the many facets of policy design assists the counselor to gain a perspective on what constitutes the success or failure of policy. Policy failure is fundamentally a problem of policy design (Nagel, 1990). Successful policies are the products of policy designs that are dynamic and responsive to change, reflect current knowledge, involve participation by all interested parties, and embody purposes and goals in harmony with public values. All of these characterisitics challenge the community counselor to take the responsibility to understand the underlying dynamics of those policies affecting their professional practice and the welfare of their clients. An added responsibility, which is central to the counselor's participation in policy development, is advocacy, which will be discussed in the next section.

## ADVOCACY

In this book, we have continually emphasized two basic premises of community counseling: (1) that it is a growth-oriented, developmental process; and (2) that it focuses on the interaction between the client and his or her environment. In other chapters, we have discussed principles of client development. It is equally important for the community counselor to know about and to employ the principles of community (environmental) development. Dunham (1963) indicated that to be effective, a community development program must:

a. be based on actual needs of the community
b. allow the community maximum freedom and self-determination
c. be carefully planned and well organized
d. be dynamic and flexible
e. involve voluntary cooperation and self-help
f. involve all groups in the community
g. engender attitudes of self-direction and cooperation
h. be run democratically
i. enlist broad citizen participation

The role of the professional is to use professional skills to enable the members of the community to achieve their objectives and to increase their capacity for initiative, integration, and resourcefulness. To effectively

achieve these goals, Selig (1977) indicated that the community counselor must:

a. "thoroughly understand the attitudes, sentiments, values and perceptions of consumers,"
b. "meet the needs as seen by the consumers,"
c. utilize "indigenous people, especially leaders,"
d. possess a persistent and ultimately infectious commitment to the process of making things happen," and
e. make sure that "the program... fit(s) into existing structures in the community" (pp. 49–50).

At the same time, Selig (1977) summarized a number of criticisms that have been leveled at community development/community organization approaches. These include the observations that these approaches:

a. often focus more on process than on concrete tasks or goals
b. place disproportionate emphasis on psychological and cultural aspects but ignore economic considerations
c. focus on changing values and attitudes, rather than on changing behaviors
d. intervene at only one level of a complex social system that is affected by other levels
e. often take a long time to show their effects
f. aim for consensus, which may limit their scope to superficial matters rather than to more important, more conflict-arousing issues

Recognizing these hazards, the community counselor should try to develop community interventions that avoid or minimize them. Advocacy is one important intervention that can be utilized by counselors in their efforts for community development.

Advocacy has played a significant role in shaping social policy and in influencing the policy community concerning counseling issues. Many interest groups have been formed with the goal of advocating both for the rights of those who could not advocate for their own rights and for vital concerns related to the professional practice of counselors such as certification and licensure. Legislation has authorized and expanded programs to advocate for consumers, both from within the service providing system and external to the service-providing system (e.g., the Protection and Advocacy for Mentally Ill Persons Act of 1983) (West, 1988).

Although many counselors may have a strong professional identification with advocacy, the literature on the activity is sparse and scattered. There was a surge of articles in the late 1960s and early 1970s, but only occasional comments have appeared since that time (Sosin & Caulum, 1983). Relatively little is known about advocacy styles and strategies and almost nothing is known about what methods are most effective (Sosin & Caulum, 1983).

Advocacy involves directed activity on behalf of individuals or organizations in relation to mandated or proposed services; it is ultimately designed to assist in the protection of rights. Since the 1970s, the emergence of human rights has been a focus for advocacy (Harries-Jones, 1991). Generically, advocacy means to plead the cause of another individual and to follow through with action in support of that cause (Tesolowski, Rosenberg, & Stein, 1983). The advocacy of social movements is bound up with a lengthy process of political empowerment, and is distinct from the usual forms of "pleading" in the courts. Harries-Jones (1991) believed that "the most striking feature of advocacy through empowerment is 'advocacy with' the group challenging dominant values, rather than 'advocacy for' a client

or class of clients" (p. 5). Advocacy through a process of political empowerment attempts to raise social issues to the level where a large group of people, or community, is given the capacity to act (Harries-Jones, 1991). One goal for advocacy efforts, consequently, is social change, a change defined as an innovation in technology, culture, values, or in the distribution of wealth and power, which can transform the structure of the society in which it occurs (Hall, Clark, & Creedon, 1987).

For a community counselor assuming the role of advocate, this role includes acting as the client's supporter, advisor, champion, and if need be, the client's representative in dealings with the court, the police, the social agency, and other organizations. But either the counselor or the client can adopt the role of self-advocate. In this role one speaks or acts on behalf of oneself. For clients, especially those who are mentally ill, advocacy may mean pursuing their own interests, being aware of their rights, and taking responsibility for tackling infringements of those rights (Williams & Shoultz, 1984). Yet lengthy training and preparation of those with mental or physical disabilities is required for true self-advocacy, since individuals must learn to respect themselves and to be self-confident, to recognize their rights and needs, and "the most appropriate ways of meeting them, and the most effective channels for seeking help in doing so" (Williams & Shoultz, 1984, p. 88).

Sosin and Caulum (1983) believed that the focus of an advocacy definition should be on the activities involved in advocacy, not on the overall role. Therefore, the advocate is simply defined as on who, at a given moment in time, is carrying out an advocacy attempt. Sosin and Caulum (1983) described advocacy as:

*An attempt, having a greater than zero probability of success by an individual or group to influence another individual or group to make a decision that would not have been made otherwise and that con-*

*cerns the welfare or interests of a third party who is in a less powerful status than the decision maker. (p. 13)*

This definition, although implying that the advocacy activity is not necessarily appropriate for all situations in which a specific decision or problem is being considered, includes everything from political advocacy to child advocacy. Advocacy is an attempt, in other words, to influence a decision maker using such techniques as persuasion or coercion. An essential part of advocacy, consequently, is to make the public understand the worth of an alternative framework of an argument (Harries-Jones, 1991).

During the past 20 years, several categories of advocates have been identified. Some of these categories have been referred to as surrogate parents, profesional advocates, ethical review boards, and intracommunity action networks (Tesolowski et al., 1983). Each advocacy category has its own functions and goals and utilizes its own methods to accomplish its objectives.

Surrogate parents, for example, might include those persons who, when parents or guardians are unavailable, are appointed by a local education agency or a court to represent personally a handicapped child in the educational process through proper identification, evaluation. and placement. Professional advocates usually focus on the protection of client rights and generally work in a direct-care human service profession. Citizen advocates are volunteers who may be matched with such a population as handicapped persons. The ethical review board developed by an agency can be established as a safeguard against inhumane treatment and the violation of human and civil right of individuals (Tesolowski et al., 1983). This review board can operate as a screening mechanism at two levels: (1) for the review and modification of all proposed individual and general service programs, and (2) for consideration of institutional policies.

Finally, an intracommunity action network is a resource through which local government services and private sector merchants are integrated to assist a specific needy population.

Similar forms of advocacy have been identified as case advocacy or policy advocacy. In the former, the community counselor is an advocate for the client and his or her welfare. In the latter, the counselor works as an advocate of societal change or changes in agency policy. Nulman (1983) maintained that in policy advocacy the professional plays essentially a disruptive role. The task is to remedy, to change, whereas institutions generally operate to minimize change. To accomplish this change the counselor has to work to shape, to select, and to influence policy. Many claim that case advocacy is the best technique (Sosin & Caulum, 1983).

Another important issue concerning advocacy is the appropriate level of intervention. Advocacy can occur at the individual level, the administrative level, or the policy level. Each level of advocacy represents an attempt to influence a different type of decision (Sosin & Caulum, 1983). At the individual level, advocacy focuses on the manner in which a specific client or group is dealt with in a single, concrete situation. A question concerning the acceptance of a client for services is an example of advocacy at the individual level. Administrative-level advocacy attempts to convince decision makers to change agency regulations—such as the verification procedures used in public welfare. It necessitates working with individuals and groups who determine policy rather than administrative personnel who carry out policy (Woodside & Legg, 1990). Policy-level advocacy attempts to convince decision makers to alter basic rules or laws, such as the overall nature of the criteria relating to national social welfare eligibility (Sosin & Caulum, 1983). The policy advocate engages in a dialogue with those in power in the institution "in an attempt to persuade them to adjust, refine, enforce, or change policy for the benefit of the clients in the system" (Woodside & Legg, 1990, p. 41). Persons with blindness and deafness have been the first to establish national advocacy organizations, resulting from the realization that if appropriate legal rights and assistance were to be provided to these groups, then a national organization focusing on advocacy would be necessary. These groups of persons with disabilities have proved effective, since laws have been passed that offer special financial assistance and promote self-reliance. Also, the emergence of parents of children with disabilities as advocates has changed the course of disability policy in the years following World War II (Shapiro, 1993).

The issue of the appropriate strategy is a significant one in advocacy. Gamson (1968) identified three strategies: coercive, utilitarian, and normative. Coercive strategies rely on conflict, dissension, and complaint. Utilitarian strategies rely on bargaining and negotiation. Normative strategies rely on moral arguments and the mobilization of common values. Sosin and Caulum (1983) believed that normative strategies are best used in an alliance situation, namely, when the two parties share a basic understanding about advocacy and perhaps about the needs of clients. The role of the advocate is "thus to mobilize these widely shared, normative sentiments" (Sosin & Caulum, 1983, p. 16). An adversarial context often calls for coercive strategies. In the absence of the willingness to listen to shared understandings, it might be difficult to use normative procedures to get the attention of the decision maker.

If a community counselor is to utilize advocacy skills, how should they be implemented, and what are the components of these skills? There are many and include:

1. *Avoidance of conflict of interest.* Such avoidance is particularly important for self-advocacy efforts. If a community counselor, for example, develops a self-advocacy group among his/her clients at an agency where the clients are receiving services and the counselor is employed, then there are obvious limitations to the extent to which the counselor can encourage concern and protest about the agency, its operation, its management, the type of opportunity available, and so on, without facing serious and probably irresolvable conflicts of interest (Williams & Shoultz, 1984).

2. *Timing.* The helping process can be a difficult one beset with an incredible number of stumbling blocks, hurdles, and pitfalls. The counselor should be aware when a decision maker is most attuned to listen to an advocacy position. On a legislative level to introduce legislation to change policy, it has been suggested that introducing a bill early in a governmental session increases the chances of favorable consideration (Dear & Pati 1981).

3. *Support.* It is advisable for the community counselor to gather as much support as possible. The value of multiple support tends to be enhanced even further when at least one of the supportive people has a distinct position of authority or credibility on the particular issue. A counselor, for example, who may be advocating for services for a particular child will enhance his/her efforts when support is gained from such professionals as a school psychologist, when it is warranted, and the child's teacher. Multiple supports are likely to make the advocacy more visible and they multiply the power that can be applied to push the issue past crucial obstacles. On a policy level, the advocate of social legislation should seek to obtain the support or sponsorship of the majority party.

4. *Knowledge.* If an advocate is to be successful, an understanding both of the appropriate laws or policy and how the human delivery system works is essential. Many advocacy attempts have failed because the counselor has not taken the time to become familiar with the intricacies of the "system,"

and with determining who are the influential people within that system who make the important decisions. Included in the knowledge is an awareness of the vital interests of the decision maker. When an issue touches on the keen concerns of decision makers, support for the steps to change can more readily follow.

**5.** *Compromise.* When appropriate, successful advocacy is based on compromise, gaining support, and nullifying opposition (Dear & Patti, 1981). When advocating for a particular issue, negotiations may be necessary. In other words, without serious harm to the client, a community counselor may have to modify somewhat her/his position in order to gain needed support. This is especially true on the legislative level. There is "probably nothing more axiomatic in the legislative process than the notion that successful action requires an accomodation to diverse and sometimes conflicting interests" (Dear & Patti, 1981, p. 294).

**6.** *Communication.* The ability to listen, to present one's posititiion cogently, to understand the needs of the other person, and to confront in a facilitative manner are not only counseling skills, but also advocacy skills. These counseling skills help to establish a better relaticnship with the other party. They engender more receptivity for one's position.

**7.** *Persistence and patience.* Advocacy efforts can be frustrating, especially when the community counselor must consider many ccnstituencies when attempting to change an existing situation for the better. Such persistence and patience have been especially true for counselors' strategies that advocate for certificatior and licensure laws. In the United States gaining the necessary support for this legislation has required learning from experience, focusing on the opposition, and persistence at lobbying different political groups. It has been a long journey, but counselors have realized the important role that advocacy plays in licensure (Morrissey, 1995).

Since advocacy implies earnest efforts for change, Watz lawick, Weakland, and Fisch (1974) believed that there are usually four procedural steps to produce any change. Though these authors refer more to the management and change of human problems, their suggested steps are also quite applicable to advocacy attempts directed also to social institutions:

1. A clear definition of the problem in concrete terms
2. An investigation of the solutions attempted so far
3. A clear definition of the concrete change to be achieved
4. The formulation and implementation of a plan to produce this change

These skills, as well as the advocacy process itself, can be illustrated in the advocacy for those with mental health problems. Counseling practitioners have always held that (a) their primary duty is to help the client, and (b) no one is usually more qualified than they to know what assistance the client needs (Willetts, 1980). For years, moreover, the plight of mental patients was ignored. The perceptions of the outside world combined with the atmosphere of the hospital or institution tend to make the patient feel dependent and to take away initiative. Clients need advocates to speak for them if abuses occur. The client is often poor, uninformed about the human service delivery process, and intimidated by what is going on either in the institution or with the helping professional.

A basic issue regarding advocacy for clients with mental health problems is who the advocate should be. Lawyers are expensive, for example, and it is debatable whether social resources should be used to pay lawyers for case advocacy (Willetts, 1980). Many complaints of clients can be satisfactorily resolved simply by talking things over among all parties. In the selection of the advocate, attention should be given to whether an in-house advocate is more effective than one from outside the institution or agency. The problem of conflict of interest arises, an issue discussed earlier in this chapter, and perhaps one way to lessen the possibility of conflicts of interest is for the advocate to be an employee of a separate but related mental health program, such as a state employee working in a locally funded program (Willetts, 1980).

Another alternative is self-advocacy, a role that was also identified earlier in this chapter. Through educational programs persons with mental illness may be trained to stand up for their rights. Such an effort demands the development of skills and knowledge, which involve the skills of assertive communication; problem-solving; general communication skills which include effective, verbal expression, eye contact, body posture and facial expression; and program planning. The knowledge components of training include an understanding of one's own needs and values, an awareness of important human rights as well as legal and civil rights, the limitations of rights, and knowledge of the policy-making process (Williams Shoultz, 1984).

Once the question of who is to be the advocate for the client is resolved, then additional advocacy steps might include investigating complaints, talking with the client, showing a commitment for the client's rights through an interest in learning about the client's needs and how the "situation" could be better, writing a report or verbally presenting the issue to relevant parties, and following up on any decisions that are made. The communication of the relevant issues for the client imply timing, the gaining of needed support, a knowledge of the policies and "system," and the ability to compromise, when necessary, while still responding to the basic complaint.

State-mandated advocacy programs are spreading throughout the United States (Willetts, 1980). Although each state may design its own program, the responsibility for representing the rights of clients often falls on the community counselor. With more formerly institutionalized persons living in the community and receiving outpatient care, for example, the need for counselors as advocates will increase. While advocacy requires a sustained immersion in social equality endeavors (Tesolowski et al.,1983), human service programs must facilitate the development of their professionals as advocates.

## EXERCISE

On an individual level advocacy is demonstrated in the following case example.

### Case Study

Barry, a community counselor, is notified that one of his clients with whom he has been working at a career counseling agency, has been seen in the emergency room for severe bruises and lacerations. The client, Mrs. W., explains to the counselor that she has been beaten by one of the mental health aides at the clinic where she has been receiving mental health services for six months. The beating occurred outside the clinic, just after a change in the working shift, and Mrs. W. states that the assailant claims that she was constantly harassing him during the time of group counseling. Mrs. W. believes this is not so, and that other clients have reported that they were physically or emotionally abused at different times by members of the staff, explaining that because they are poor and disadvantaged they are easy targets for any abuse.

After documenting her claim of abuse, the counselor discusses the situation with the supervisors and other administrative personnel at his client's agency. Following this discussion, the counselor wishes to become an advocate for those reporting the abuse.

1. What are the advocacy steps that should be used by the counselor in this particular situation?

2. What do you believe would be an appropriate course of action by the agency's staff?

## REFERENCES

Anderson, J. E. (1982). *Cases in public policy-making,* (2nd ed.). New York: Holt, Rinehart & Winston.

Baumheier, E. C., & Schorr, A. L. (1977). *Social policy* In J. B. Turner, R. Mortis, M. N. Ozawa, B. Phillips, B. Schreiber, & B. K. Simon (Eds.), *Encyclopedia of social work* pp. 1453–1463 Washington, DC: National Association of Social Workers.

Brubaker, E, & Brubaker, T. H. (1995). Critical policy issues. In G.Smith, S. Tobin, E. Robertson-Tchabo, & P. Power (Eds.), *Strengthening aging families* pp. 235–247 Thousand Oaks, CA: Sage Publications.

Center on Human Policy, *Research and Training Center,* School of Education, Syracuse University. (1972). *Disability and family Policy.* Policy Bulletin No. 2., Spring.

Cobb, R. W., & Elder, C. D. (1982). Issue creation and agenda building. In J. Anderson (Ed.), *Cases in public policy-making* (2nd ed. pp. 3–11). New York: Holt, Rinehart & Winston.

Davidson, R. H., & Olezek, W. J. (1985). *Congress and its members* (2nd ed.) Washington, DC: Congressional Quarterly Press.

Dear, R. B., & Pati, R. J. (1981). Legislative advocacy: Seven effective tactics. *Social Work, 26,* 289–296.

Dunham, A. (1963). Some principles of community development. *International Review of Community Development, 11,* 141–151.

Gamson, W. (1968). *Power and discontent.* Homewood, IL: Dorsey Press.

Hahn, H. (1988). Politics of physical differences: Disability and dissemination. *Journal of Social Issues, 44,* 39–47.

Hall, G. W., Clark, G. C. & Creedon, M.A. (1987). *Advocacy in America.* Lanham, MD: University Press of America.

Harries-Jones, P. (Ed.). (1991). *Making knowledge count. Advocacy and social science.* Montreal, Canada: McGill-Queen's University Press.

Jones, C. O. (1984). *An introduction to the study of public policy* (3rd ed.). Monterey, CA: Brooks/Cole.

Kingdom, J. W. (1984). *Agendas, alternatives, and public policies.* New York: Harper Collins.

May, J. V., & Wildavsky, A. B. (1978). Introduction. In J. V. May and A. B. Wildavsky (Eds.), *The policy cycle* (pp. 10–14). Beverly Hills, CA: Sage Publications.

Morrissey, M. (1995, March). Persistence and patience named as keys to achieving licensure. *Counseling Today,* 16–19.

Nagel, S. S. (Ed.). (1990) . *Policy theory and evaluation.* Westport, CT: Greenwood Press.

Nulman, E. (1983, January–Febuary). Family therapy and advocacy: Directions for the future. *Social Work,* 12–17.

Selig, A. L. (1977). *Making things happen in communities: Alternatives to traditional mental health services.* San Francisco: R & E Research Associates.

Shapiro, J. P. (1993). *No pity.* New York: Random House.

Sosin, M. & Caulum, S. (1983, January–Febuary). Advocacy: A conceptualization for social work practice. *Social Work* (January–February), pp. 12-17.

Tesolowski, D. E., Rosenberg, H., & Stein, R. J. (1983 July–September). Advocacy intervention: A responsibility of human service professionals. *Journal of Rehabilitation,* 35–39.

Walker, J. L. (1977). Setting the agenda in the U.S. Senate: A theory of problem selection. *British Journal of Political Science, 7,* 423–445.

Watzlawick, P., Weakland, J., & Fisch, R. (1974) . *Change. Principles of problem formation and problem resolution.* New York: W. W. Norton.

Weimer, D. L., & Vining, A. R. (1992) . *Policy analysis—concepts and practice* (2nd ed.). Englewood Cliffs, NJ: Prentice Hall.

Wergin, J. G. (1973). *A model for the evaluation of policy in organizations.* Doctoral dissertation, University of Nebraska, 1973. Dissertation Abstracts International. (University Microfilms No. DDJ74–13030.)

West, J. A. (1988). *The handicapped children's protection act of 1986: A case study of policy formation.* Unpublished doctoral dissertation, University of Maryland, College Park, MD.

Willetts, R. (1980, September). Advocacy and the mentally ill. *Social Work,* 372–377.

Williams, P., & Shoultz, B. (1984). *We can speak for ourselves. Self-advocacy by mentally handicapped people.* Bloomington, IN: Indiana University Press.

Woodside, M. R., & Legg, B. H. (1990). Patient advocacy: A mental health perspective. *Journal of Mental Health Counseling, 12,* 38–40.

Zimmerman, S. L. (1988) . *Understanding family policy.* Newbury Park, CA: Sage Publications.

# 15

# EVALUATION OF SERVICES

The credibility of counseling and related professions is a continuing issue for both consumers and legislators. The evaluation of services provided by community mental health centers, for example, has emerged as an important topic since 1980 (Lebow, 1982). Wheeler (1980) stated, "Backed by recent judicial decisions establishing standards of clinical care, fostered by the disillusionment of the general public, and mandated by legislative action, mental health evaluation has become a critical component of program operations" (p. 88). Though the Spring 1984 issue of the *Community Mental Health Journal* was devoted to a description of selected statewide outcome evaluations in the mental health field, outcome evaluation was still not flourishing on a statewide level (Berren, 1984). Most human service organizations evaluated policies and programs only periodically, if at all (Schulberg, 1981).

Another factor that has contributed to the creation of an evaluation climate within the counseling profession is the Community Mental Health Center Amendments of 1975 (PL 94–63). This legislation requires mental health centers to establish ongoing quality assurance programs and provides an emphasis on research with local application. Administrators must think in terms of evaluating the

techniques and programs used in their centers (Anderson, 1981). The importance of evaluating social programs emerges from the continuing challenge of developing ways to remedy the serious deficiencies in the quality of human life and the vital need to identify the barriers to successful implementation of social programs (Rossi & Freeman, 1989).

This chapter will discuss the different aspects of program evaluation. It will not only explain the varied meanings of evaluation and its history, but will also highlight such important considerations as the settings and roles of the community counselor when performing program evaluation activities and the difference between evaluation and research. Further, the different "types" of program evaluation and characteristics of good evaluations will be identified.

## DEFINITIONS, PURPOSES, AND HISTORY OF PROGRAM EVALUATION

Unfortunately, the term "program evaluation" does not have a standardized and commonly accepted meaning. Though a popular term, evaluation is an elastic word and does not only imply measurement and data collection. An evaluation can cover processes ranging from simple score-card tallies to elaborate number-crunching systems (Burgrabbe & Swift, 1984). It can be based on facts or on unfounded assumptions, or express a label that is applied loosely to a number of methods for gathering and analyzing data. Program evaluation is a key concern of management, and its distinctive feature is that it is concerned with the program. It addresses questions about both the implementation of the program's activities and their resulting outcomes (Rutman & Mowbray, 1983). It is a way to compare program components, activities, or outcomes to standards of desirability and a way to see how closely a program meets its goals and objectives.

Consequently, there are widely different interpretations of the term "program evaluation," but one accepted meaning is the process of identifying the decision areas of concern, selecting appropriate information, and collecting and analyzing information in order to report summary data useful to decision makers in selecting among alternatives (Franklin & Thrasher, 1976). It is a systematic effort to describe, understand, and judge the status of an organization and the effects of its operations and to recommend and implement suggestions for enhancing programs toward and achievement of the goals of a particular program. This definition implies that an evaluation should make specific statements for actions that should be taken by decision makers. With its emphases both on decision-making functions and the determination of program effectiveness, program evaluation is seen as an aid to policy analysis. It explores such possible program characteristics as the efficient acquisition of resources, the transformation of program inputs into outputs, and the extent to which a program achieves its goals or produces certain effects.

In summary, the main purposes of program evaluation include: (a) determining effectiveness of programs, (b) determining success in achieving objectives, (c) placing a value on objectives, (d) valuing effectiveness, (e) assessing desirable and undesirable outcomes, (f) acting as a tool of management, (g) focusing on decision making, (h) structuring feedback of evaluation results, (i) judging evaluations, and (j) recommending alternatives to decision makers.

There is another perspective however, for understanding the purposes of program evaluation. Rossi, Freeman, and Wright (1979) explained that there are four sets of questions with which one is concerned in doing evaluation.

1. Program planning questions

    **a.** What is the extent and distributions, for example, of the population needing counseling services?

2. Program monitoring questions

    **a.** Is the program reaching the persons, community, or other target units to which it is addressed?

    **b.** Is the program providing the services or other benefits that were intended in the project design?

3. Impact assessment questions

    **a.** Is the program effective in achieving its intended goals?

    **b.** Can the results of the program be explained by some alternative process that does not include the program?

4. Economic efficiency questions

    **a.** What are the costs to deliver services and benefits to program participants?

    **b.** Is the program an efficient use of resources compared with alternative uses of the resources?

Although the basic purposes of evaluation are to provide objective estimates of achievement and to provide guidance for the conduct of program activities, achieving these purposes can generate many evaluation activities. Neigher and Schulberg (1982) pinpointed four such activities.

## Generating Better Information for Decision Makers

Frequently, the evaluation process begins after the decision has been made to implement an education, training, or social-action program. But a needs assessment, or estimates of cost and operation feasibility, or projections of demand and support, are all important precursors to decisions about whether to actually start a program. It is important to determine if there is a need for a program before one seriously considers installing it. A program, for example, requiring large financial expenditures may be developed in a counseling center before an assessment is made whether a particular population will use the service. Likewise, training programs for community counselors may be offered without determining whether organizational barriers will make it possible for the trainees to apply their newly acquired skills.

Information further extends to seeking facts about program objectives, namely, whether the objectives are valid and useful for attacking the needs the program is designed to serve, and, is the content relevant to the program objectives and does it cover those objectives adequately? If either the objectives or the content are not relevant, then evaluation can contribute to decisions about program modification.

## Determining Accountability

Accountability can take many forms, and includes public data disclosure and citizen participation in the evaluation process. A funding source may want to know whether a program has been effective in meeting specific population needs. Effectiveness may be judged in comparison with the performance of another group or with earlier performance by the same group. Also, effectiveness may be viewed as either short- or long-term, and this depends on the nature of the program and the needs it serves. Moreover, assessment of actual costs can fall under the term accountability, and this assessment can be related to the effects or benefits the program appeared to achieve: "Have we spent $5.00 on a 50-cent program?" Much of the discussion of accountability in the counseling field assumes as an underlying premise that improved information and delivery structure can contribute to the productivity and efficiency of resource use. In other words, can greater benefits or effects be obtained at the same cost?

## Performing Advocacy

This considers program evaluation as a strategy used by organizations to advance their interest when vying for resources. This activity has many implications for policy makers. Frequently, a program needs support in order that it may continue. For example, evaluation in the areas of community counseling may indicate that recidivism rates have been reduced, or, in contrast to institutionalized care, services delivered in a community setting are 50 percent more cost-effective. When this information is communicated to those responsible for making decisions, then the program or particular service may be viewed in a much more favorable light.

## Conducting Evaluation Research

This activity applies scientific methods to establish causal linkages between intervention and their outcomes. These linkages can be explored either by isolating dependent variables and manipulating independent ones, or by maximizing the influence of independent variables while minimizing sources of variance. Yet, Neigher and Schulberg (1982) indicated that key requirements of the evaluation research model often cannot be met in evaluating human service programs. "It is seldom possible to randomly assign subjects among experimental and control groups; intervention technique anticipated outcome may have only tenuous theoretic linkages, and many programs simultaneously employ multiple interventions" (p. 735). Mental health programs are not like laboratory experiments. They seldom start and end at specific predetermined points. Baselines and final measurements cannot be clear-cut.

## HISTORY

The definitions and purposes of program evaluation show a wide array of activities. It has not always been so. In fact, until the mid-1960s there were relatively few attempts to evaluate the delivery of human services, especially mental health programs. The history of program evaluation is unfortunately brief, and most writers agree that it has emerged as a specialized function largely in the period since post–World War II (Franklin & Thrasher, 1976).

Rossi et al. (1979) explained that the immediate Post–World War II period saw massive inputs of resources to remedy unattended problems and unmet needs for urban development and housing, technological and cultural education, occupational training, and preventive health activities. They further stated that this was the initial period of major commitments to international programs of family planning, health and nutrition, and rural community development. Resource expenditures were huge, and these commitments were accompanied by continual cries for "knowledge of results." This was a boom period for evaluation research; and by the end of the 1950s, large-scale evaluation programs were commonplace (Rossi & Freeman, 1989). Throughout the world projects were begun that included evaluation components.

Prior to the mid-1950s, however, there were few reported studies of program evaluation in human service agencies. In 1939, the Cambridge-Somerville Youth Study was begun to evaluate the effectiveness of therapeutic interventions. It explored the efficacy of using "big brother" counseling to reduce antisocial behavior among teenage predelinquent males (Rutman & Mowbray, 1983). It was completed and published in 1951. In the mid-1950s, an experiment was designed to test the effectiveness of a preventive social work service to schoolgirls defined as potentially delinquent (Meyer, Borgatta, & Jones, 1965). About the same time, a study entitled "The Chemung County Evaluation of Casework Service to Multi-Problem Families" was reported (Rutman & Mowbray, 1983). The focus of this study was on the effectiveness of intensive case work with multiproblem families.

By the 1960s, during the "Period of the Great Society," a program transition occurred from one of expansion to one of accountability. Evaluations of penal rehabilitation projects, public housing programs, delinquency prevention programs, and psychotherapeutic and psychopharmacological treatments were being undertaken in the United States. Knowledge of the methods of social research, including the art of the social survey and the technology of computer-assisted statistical analysis, became widespread (Rossi et al., 1979). Yet, initially, accountability entailed little more than documenting the program efforts that were expended, that is, the numbers of clients receiving various types of services. More objective evidence on program effectiveness was being requested by funding bodies, legislators, and the general public. This accountability change must also be viewed within the context of reforms that were taking place in public administration, such as zero-base budgeting, management by objectives, and cost-benefit analysis.

The growth of publications, national and international conferences, and special sessions on evaluation studies at the meetings of academic and practitioner groups are testimony to the continuing development of the field. Rossi & Freeman (1989) believed, however, that "social progam activities and consequently the evaluation enterprise clearly are shaped by the changing moods of the times" (P. 35). They have a pendulum swing quality. Disenchantment with program outcomes and the curtailment of domestic federal expenditures can affect the new implementation of social programs and their consequent evaluation activities. But new social problems emerge, and the 1990s has seen the rise of homelessness and the increased incidence of AIDS. Programs are being developed to respond to these concerns, which in turn stimulates further growth of activity in the evaluation research field (Rossi & Freeman, (1989). Consequently, program evaluation is currently more than the application of methods. It is a political and managerial activity in which "there will continue to be resource restraints that require choosing which social problem areas to concentrate on and which social programs should be given priority" (Rossi & Freeman, 1989, p. 38).

## EVALUATION OPPORTUNITIES FOR THE COMMUNITY COUNSELOR

Though evaluation is a major tool of management, as well as an aid to policy analysis (Spaniol, 1975), evaluators generally come out of the academic research tradition (Weiss, 1972). There has been an academic orientation to program evaluation in which the activities have mainly comprised conducting studies and analyzing the data. Yet academic researchers usually have been hesitant to make practical recommendations based on the data analysis. Because they often are unfamiliar with agency politics and internal management issues, academicians have not taken the responsibility for translating and interpreting evaluation results. But if program evaluation is to have any relevance for agency decision making, recommendations must be made and actions taken that are in harmony with an agency's philosophy.

Such relevance demands participation both in the implementation of the evaluation results and the research process itself.

This participation is what Kurt Lewin called "action research" (Weiss, 1972). It involves self-study procedures and requires that an evaluator identify agency difficulties, collect information, help make necessary changes, and after the changes have been effected, evaluate their effectiveness. All of these activities are, with training, within the capabilities of the community counselor. Although counselors usually wear many hats in the performance of their varied tasks, there are many evaluation opportunities that can be understood easily and can be carried out by persons of modest expertise and experience. When these tasks are accomplished, practitioners have a better understanding not only of whether their job activities are in harmony with agency goals, but also of how to improve work performance and how much impact their work efforts have had on positive client outcome.

Another opportunity for community counselors to perform evaluation activities is when they act as consultants for agencies. A consultant role has many dimensions. Frequently, the role implies that the consultant advises an agency on what is wrong with the delivery of services or becomes actively involved in finding solutions to an agency's current difficulties with clients. Agency consultation itself came about as a result of the passage of the Community Mental Health Act in 1963 (Werner, 1978). Prevention was emphasized, with special attention to primary prevention, namely, a reduction in the incidences of mental disorders. Werner (1978) suggested that one example of assisting an agency in its primary prevention efforts is to help an agency deal more effectively with specific parts of a mental health program.

In order for the community counselor to implement the role of a program evaluator, specific knowledge and skills are required. These are many and include:

1. A knowledge of the different operations of an agency, as well as an understanding of its goals and the needs of the population that the agency is attempting to meet.

2. An understanding of the different ways to collect reliable information or data that are related to the purpose of the evaluation.

3. A knowledge of how to utilize available resources for statistical analysis.

4. Interpersonal skills to communicate with the different managers or supervisors of an agency. An evaluator can face considerable problems of rapport and resistance both to evaluation procedures and, later, to changes in a program that may be suggested by evaluation results.

5. The skill to determine among the many issues or problems of an agency what particular issue is evaluable.

6. The skill to organize evaluation activities.

7. Advocacy skills to promote evaluation results.

8. A knowledge of the different methods of program evaluation, methods that have been developed to respond to varied evaluation needs of an agency.

With an awareness of the purposes, activities, and history of program evaluation, as well as a knowledge of selected opportunities for performing evaluation, an understanding is needed both of whether a program is evaluable and of the differences between research and evaluation. Much confusion over the differences of the two terms has been generated. Though research and evaluation may overlap, there are decided differences. Whereas basic research puts the emphasis on the production of knowledge and leaves its use to the natural processes of dissemination and application, program evaluation starts out with use in mind (Weiss, 1972). Evaluation also usually takes place in an action setting, where the most important thing that is going on is the pro-

gram. A research activity has relevance to the extent that it relates to one hypothesis or theory. Research methods are limited and emphasize "hard" data obtained through tightly controlled experimental procedures. But program evaluation methods may include a full range of activities and utilize both "hard" and "soft" data (Wheeler & Loesch, 1981).

Table 15–1 illustrates the further differences between program evaluation and basic research. However, as Weiss (1972) indicated, there are important similarities between evaluation and other types of research. She explained that like other research, "evaluation attempts to describe, to understand the relationships between variables, and to trace out the causal sequel" (p. 8). Also, program evaluators use a broad array of research methods to collect information—interviews, questionnaires, tests of knowledge and skill, attitude inventories, observation, content analyses of documents, records, and examination of physical evidence.

An important ingredient for an effective evaluation is when an agency has clearly defined goals or objectives. Such clarity facilitates "evaluability" of a program. Many "opportunity-type" programs, namely, those activities that attempt to increase an agency's capabilities or opportunities to bring about a positive change in a client's capacity to earn or to adjust to life circumstances, have often been elusive and difficult to sort out and measure. Most of the innovative antipoverty and other programs of the 1960s were designed to provide "opportunities" for people and their goals were vaguely formulated.

There are many criteria for determining whether a program is evaluable. The main ones are: a well-defined program, plausible causal linkages, and purpose.

## A Well-Defined Program

One of the essential ingredients of a well-defined program is clearly specified goals and

**TABLE 15–1   DIFFERENCES BETWEEN PROGRAM EVALUATION AND BASIC RESEARCH**

| Program Evaluation | Research |
|---|---|
| Basic management function | Not a basic management function |
| Broad concept—includes "hard" research as one of its potential components | More narrow concept |
| Broad approach to "ways" of knowing | Necessary adherence to experimental standard |
| Management decision focus | Focus on new knowledge or causes |
| Emphasis on applicability to agency concerns and priorities | Emphasis on more general concerns and priorities that may not have immediate applicability |
| Concerned with understanding relationship of events to established goals and objectives | Concerned with explaining and predicting |
| Frequent use of personal judgment | Emphasis on the objective and rigorous |
| Descriptive, intuitive, qualitative, and quantitative | Tends more toward quantitative |
| Least generalizability "scientifically" | More generalizability "scientifically" |

effects. Goals are the end results that programs claim to pursue and for which they can be held accountable. If an evaluator is to provide feedback for improving a program, then information should be obtained linking the program's activities to goal attainment. When goals are clearly specified, moreover, the question can then be answered: "Is the program adequately meeting the purposes for which it was funded?"

Frequently, a program is simply a statement on paper of what the planners in an agency hoped to accomplish (Hyman & Wright, 1971; Rossi & Freeman, 1989). It may never have been fully translated into action by the field staff. Consequently, a program is often merely a sketch that has to be completed.

Unfortunately, program goals are often vaguely stated. Examples of nebulous goals are "attain individual adjustment," "fulfill individual capacities" 'or "improve the quality of life." Though it may be necessary to tolerate a certain amount of vagueness for funding or legislative purposes, clear goals should be specified that are in harmony with the mission of the agency. For example, a community mental health center that seeks to reduce the recidivism rate of deinstitutionalized patients should specify, upon implemen-

tation of a program for this purpose, what is meant by "reducing the recidivism rate." When there is a clear specification of program outcomes, this can serve as the basis for an effective evaluation exercise. Similarly, a counseling center that aims to reduce the incidence of substance abuse should accurately define what is meant by "reduce."

## Plausible Causal Linkages

For program evaluations to be effective, it means that the program being examined has a realistic chance of reaching its specified goals and effects. In other words, cause and effect relationships between program activities and the effects should be identified. If a job-finding program, for example, has been developed and implemented in an agency working with those who have emotional problems, then the relationship must be explored between this program and such effects as increased awareness of employment opportunities, interviewing skills, and the actual attainment of a job. Yet often the causal assumptions linking a program to some of its goals or effects are weak. Many "counseling interventions" are illustrative of these weak linkages. Such interventions are developed with the assumption that with proper counseling more people will find jobs or will lead satisfying lives. This could be true, but a more definite link between "counseling" and a "more satisfying life" should be established.

## Purpose

This is an important factor because the purpose for conducting a program evaluation can also establish the criteria used to judge the value of a particular evaluative activity. An evaluation could be used as an attempt to justify a weak or bad program by deliberately selecting only those aspects that "look good" on the surface. If that is the purpose, then the standard for a good evaluation might be simply the number of people who request services from a particular agency, and not the quality of services that are delivered. Also, an evaluation might be done to "whitewash" a program, namely, to cover up a program's failure by utilizing a subjective approach in the evaluation. Thus, an evaluator may be asked by agency administrators to overlook "hard data" or statistics identifying a large number of "unsuccessful" cases in preference for information generated from the impressions of staff on what the agency should be accomplishing.

Generally, evaluations may be undertaken for management and administrative purposes, to identify ways to improve the delivery of interventions, to evaluate the appropriateness of program changes, to decide whether to expand or curtail programs, to test innovative ideas on how to deal with community programs, and to support advocacy of one program as opposed to another (Rossi & Freeman, 1989).

Although there may be additional realities that could be considered when planning a useful evaluation, such as methodology, cost, and the implementation of the program evaluation design, the factors of a well-defined program, plausible causal linkages, and the purpose must be initially explored when developing a plan for a program evaluation. An appreciation of these issues establishes a basis, therefore, for understanding the different types of program evaluations. Once a determination is made that a program is evaluable, then the next decision can be considered: "What kind of an evaluation should be conducted?"

## APPROACHES AND MODELS OF PROGRAM EVALUATION

The many approaches to performing program evaluation studies reflect different agency needs. One agency may be looking for information to establish a program relevant to a specific population. Another may be seeking an answer to whether their program is really making a difference in the lives of the consumers of services. Still another agency may be asking how to improve existing services. Whatever the agency's need, there are a variety of ways that correspond to the many agency needs for program evaluation. There is no one theory of evaluation per se. Most of the approaches to program assessment are outgrowths of established bodies of knowledge (Franklin Thrasher, 1976).

Burck and Peterson (1975) identified six common evaluation strategies, but explain them with a tinge of tongue-in-cheek cynicism. They feel they also exemplify common ills in program evaluation. The approaches are:

**1.** *The Sample-of-One method.* The evaluator uses a restricted sampling of opinion, often discussing a program with one or two others and then offering an opinion as if a comprehensive survey had been taken.

**2.** *Brand A versus Brand X method.* Many evaluators feel that a valid program evaluation effort must include a comparison group. In the attempt to compare the outcomes of one program, perhaps an experimental one, to a traditional program, the outcomes of nonequivalent groups are often compared because of practical limitations. The results are consequently inconclusive, if not misleading.

**3.** *The Sunshine method.* This method assumes that elaborate program exposure is evidence of a good program. Administrators may judge programs, for example, on how they appear, and questions of quality and impact are seldom raised.

**4.** *The Goodness-to-Fit method.* The credibility of a program is sometimes judged by the degree to which it can fit into established procedures. But a service program requiring special scheduling or temporary adjustments in staffing assignments may be considered frivolous and a nuisance. Seldom does anyone raise the issue of whether clients may benefit from the program.

**5.** *The Committee method.* This approach implies that to evaluate effectiveness, simply bring together a group of congenial people who have been associated with the program and who are willing to discuss its effectiveness. After the group process runs its predictable course, the committee arrives at a seemingly spontaneous consensus.

**6.** *The Shot-in-the-Dark method.* This method of evaluation is used when well-intended program activities are conducted without a clearly established set of program objectives. Because there is no clear direction or standard, an evaluation randomly searches for any outcome measure that demonstrates the fact that the program has made an impact. (Burck & Peterson, 1975)

Lebow (1982) has identified five models or approaches to program evaluation of mental health services, which comprise:

**1.** *The Organizational model.* This approach evaluates the appropriateness and viability of the organizational structures, the scope of the operation, the efficiency of management, the quantity of services provided, and the relation of services to community need and demand. This model examines the quantity of services offered; the productivity of staff, programs, and facilities; and the movement patterns of clients within the care system. The information generated from this evaluation describes only quantity, not quality; how the agency's structure is conducive to offering treatment and not how good the treatment is that is offered.

**2.** *The Care-Process model.* In this approach the quality of service is compared with some standard of practice. As Lebow (1982) stated, "This model focuses on appropriate assignment of clients to services and the effectiveness of service delivery" (P. 101). It evaluates the actual behavior of the agency staff, for the "quality" of a facility can be measured by the services offered by the practitioners.

**3.** *The Consumer-Evaluation model.* This model focuses on the consumer's opinion about services offered. These consumers may either be clients who assess services they have received, or residents of the community who evaluate the service system as a whole.

**4.** *The Efficacy model.* This approach evaluates the community mental health center's (CMHC's) performance in changing clients and consultees. Questionnaires may be used to collect information, and data may be gathered from clients, the counselor, and significant others, that is, family members or close friends. Outcomes are the goals in this model, but many factors that affect outcome may be well beyond the control of the counselor (Lebow, 1982).

**5.** *The Community-Impact model.* This model assesses the CMHC's influence on the community as a whole. Measures of community impact include the community's knowledge of services and the mental health of the community. But the community's mental health is even harder to measure than that of clients.

According to Lebow (1982), each model has a distinct focus and intent, and a place in community mental health center evaluation. Each approach offers unique and valuable data. The best approach to CMHC assessment will combine information from several models.

Underlying the preceding specific models for conducting program evaluation within agencies are more comprehensive approaches to agency assessment. The evaluator should be familiar, however, with these approaches, and when guided by this knowledge, be able to make a timely decision about what particular evaluation would be the most feasible. For example, many evaluations are conducted around the question: "Is our program effective?" when a more appropriate evaluation might focus on how the program was developed and whether or not program activities are in harmony with the agency's mission. Each evaluation direction demands a specific methodology. In this chapter, three kinds of program evaluations will be discussed. They represent the most frequently used approaches for program assessment. Another approach that is often associated with program evaluation, namely, needs assessment, is discussed in Chapter 7.

## FORMATIVE EVALUATION

Often agency or program administrators want to know how a program can be improved, or how it can become more efficient or effective. The appropriate label for this kind of evaluation is "formative evaluation," and it encompasses the multitude of jobs connected with helping the staff to get the program running smoothly (Fink & Kosecoff, 1978). It is a form of organizational assessment that takes place during the early stages of a program. In order to improve a program, it will be necessary to understand how well the program is moving toward its objectives so that changes can be made in the program's components. It is a time-consuming form of evaluation

because it requires becoming familiar with many aspects of a program and then providing personnel with information and insights to help them improve it (Morris & Fitz-Gibbon, 1978; Rossi & Freeman, 1989). But before beginning a formative evaluation, the evaluator should make sure that there really is a chance of making changes for improvement. Consequently, such questions will need to be asked as:

**1.** What problems are there and how can they be solved?

**2.** What are the program's most important characteristics—materials, activities, administrative arrangements?

**3.** How are the program activities supposed to lead to attainment of the objectives?

**4.** Are the program's important characteristics being implemented?

**5.** Are they leading to achievement of the objectives?

As a result of the formative evaluation, revisions are made in the materials, activities, and organization of the program. These adjustments are made throughout the formative evaluation period. Morris and Fitz-Gibbon (1978) identified steps that should be followed in conducting a formative evaluation.

**1.** Find out as much as possible about the program. Written documents describing the program should be read, and people should be asked what the program is supposed to be and do.

**2.** Estimate how much the evaluation will cost.

**3.** Focus the evaluation. Visualize what components of the program appear to provide the key to whether it succeeds or fails: Where is the program too poorly planned to merit success, and what effects might the program have that its planners have not anticipated?

**4.** Negotiate your own role as an evaluator. The evaluator and the program staff should agree about the basic outline of the evaluation, which includes the approaches to measure program implementation. It also means coming to an agreement about services and responsibilities.

**5.** Prepare a program statement, which entails holding a meeting with agency/program administrators to specify the program's goals and developing and examining a program rationale, namely, why each activity, for example, is expected to lead directly or indirectly to the achievement of the program objectives.

**6.** Write the program statement. This is an in-house report describing what the evaluator has learned about the major goals of the program as well as why and when the implemented program is expected to achieve them.

**7.** Monitor program implementation and the achievement of program objectives. This step involves making sure one is asking the right questions, identifying what courses of action will result from the information that the evaluator provides, and designing a monitoring system that could include the construction or purchasing of instruments. If instruments are to be administered, a design for their implementation and most effective use will have to be developed. Following their administration, the data will be analyzed with an eye toward program improvement.

**8.** Report and confer with planner and staff. This is the last step, and includes deciding what the evaluator wants to say and choosing a method of presentation. Presenting the report is an important aspect of evaluation. Priorities for program improvement must be carefully considered, and changes that are more likely to be implemented could be suggested.

Ideally, the planning of a program and the development of its evaluation plan should be done concurrently. If the counselor is involved in program development, then he/she should be aware within an evaluative perspective whether the program responds to client needs and whether the planned activities are actually feasible and relevant.

The varied steps in the formative evaluation process can be illustrated by briefly examining a transitional care services program in a community mental health center. Developed for chronically and severely disabled patients, the treatment was built on behavioral theory. Though strongly supported by staff, it does not seem to be doing an efficient and effective job. The administration is exploring replacing this approach with a treatment based upon psychoanalytic and therapeutic milieu principles, but the exploration is becoming controversial. A change of programs could be seen as a direct criticism of the staff's theoretical orientation.

In approaching this evaluation task, the evaluator would want to find out as much as possible about the behavioral program and the proposed new approach. After talking with people, including clients served by the existing program, the evaluator would begin to identify his/her own evaluation role and come to an agreement about services and responsibilities. A meeting would then be held to specify the program's goals, and a program statement would be developed which would include the outcome objectives, the persons responsible for program implementation, the specific activities, the materials used, the duration of the activities, and the progress expected. A plan would be developed to monitor the program implementation and the achievement of the program's objectives. This may include the use of measuring instruments, such as paper and pencil tests. When the monitoring time is completed, the data will be analyzed to assess whether the program is meeting the designated objectives, and if not, why.

## SUMMATIVE EVALUATION

This is the most popular approach in conducting a program evaluation. It answers such questions as: "How effective is Progam Y? Is it worth continuing or expanding?" The goal of this evaluation is to collect and present information needed for summary statements and judgments of the program and its value. Summative evaluation can also be called impact assessment. There are problems when conducting this type of evaluation. Rossi and Freeman (1989) believed that "establishing impact essentially amounts to establishing causality" (p. 230). The concept of causality generally implies that conditions are such that $A$ is a cause of $B$, and that if $A$ is introduced, $B$ is more likely to result. If one develops a program to teach job interviewing skills to a population of middle-aged women who are returning to the work force after many years of homemaking, then it is assumed that the acquisition of such skills will facilitate the securing of employment. But there may be other factors that can lead to obtaining a job. Consequently, the critical issue in summative evaluation is whether or not a program produces effects different from what would have occurred either without the intervention or with an alternative intervention (Rossi & Freeman, 1989).

An evaluator, when attempting this kind of assessment, should provide a basis against which to compare the program's accomplishments. It is a good idea to contrast the program's effects and costs with those produced by an alternative program that aims toward the same goals. Summative evaluations, moreover, result in recommendations to continue or discontinue the program and to expand or cut it back.

There are five distinct phases of a summative evaluation according to Morris and Fitz-Gibbon (1978). They are:

Phase 1.    Focusing the evaluation. This phase includes deciding what needs to be known, and by whom. It comprises finding out as much as one can about the program, identifying a similar program and describing these programs precisely.

Phase 2.    Selecting appropriate measures. After deciding what should be measured, one's evaluation concerns would be consolidated into a few instruments, data analysis should be planned, and a sampling strategy for administering the instruments will be chosen.

Phase 3.    The collection of data. This will include establishing the evaluation design, such as, for example, a control group design with a pretest; administering the instruments, scoring them; and recording the data.

Phase 4.    Analyzing the data.

Phase 5.    Preparing an evaluation report.

These phases may be better understood from the following example. A youth-service bureau that provides services to youths age 8 to 18 who are having personal, family, and legal problems wants to determine if their program is effective. The agency is funded by the state juvenile services administration and matching funds are provided by the county. Additional funding consists of individual and corporate donations. The services offered include individual, family, and group counseling; information and referral; crisis intervention; and informal and drop-in counseling. Services that are considered optional include tutoring, education, and youth advocacy. The goal of the agency is to deter youth who have been identified by the juvenile justice system from further delinquent activity. Voluntary referrals are accepted from other social service agencies, police, courts, families, schools, and the state's juvenile services administration.

In beginning the evaluation, one would consult with program administrators for the meaning of "effective" and to learn as much as possible about the agency. Let us assume that the staff responded by explaining, "significantly reducing the number of youth who have been referred to us for delinquent acts from any further contact with the juvenile services administration." Of particular importance in this evaluation is determining also what the state juvenile services administration means by "effective". Following an understanding of the agency and its objectives, the evaluator would then locate another, similar agency, perhaps in a different county of the same state, with similar activities that promote a reduction of further delinquent activity. The evaluator may then decide that a brief questionnaire, to be given to all the recipients of services of both agencies, would be the most appropriate instrument to collect needed information. The questionnaire is then sent to the "consumer," and necessary steps are followed to ensure the maximum return rate. Also, a form of the questionnaire should be sent to the juvenile service administration to solicit feedback on information from their records on any delinquent activity by the consumers that received attention from the agency. Questionnaire results are then analyzed. Finally, a report would be prepared that described the evaluation, identifies its results, and makes recommendation on whether the program was "effective."

When conducting a summative evaluation, consequently, the evaluator should identify one, or if necessary, several outcome measures that represent the objectives of the program. These objectives should be operationalized as much as possible. If behaviors are to be increased, for example, then the specific behavior and the amount of change desired should be defined. Also, when using behavior data, many evaluators follow the practice of collecting the data three to six months after program completion. Questionnaires are usu-

ally utilized when collecting this data. If one wishes to measure learning acquisition following program completion, then the evaluator should consider collecting data immediately after a program, using pre-post program questionnaires, simulations, and interviews. The same time framework and measurement methods could be employed when gathering information after a program focusing on attitude or feeling change. A basic theme running through all summative evaluation efforts is the measurability of results.

## THE SYSTEMS APPROACH

In contrast to the summative model of evaluation, which is concerned with the degree of success in reaching a specific objective, the systems model establishes the degree to which an organization realizes its goals under a given set of conditions (Rossi & Freeman, 1989; Schulberg & Baker, 1971). It is concerned with establishing a working model of an organization that is capable of achieving a goal. This approach is appropriate to a large counseling center that has many functions or activities. The systems model would focus upon the effective coordination of the agency's many activities, the acquisition and maintenance of necessary resources, and the adaptation of the organization to the environment and to its own internal demands. This approach will ask the question, for example, "How close does the organizational allocation of resources approach an optimum distribution?" (Etzioni, 1960).

This model of evaluation is a more demanding and expensive one for the evaluator (Schulberg & Baker, 1971). It requires that one determine the highly effective allocation of means. This demands considerable knowledge of the way in which an organization functions. Yet one advantage of this approach is that the evaluator can include in the data collection much more information than is possible in classical research design. For example, if an evaluator is addressing the effectiveness of an agency that has a transitional program that assists ex-mental patients to find and maintain paid employment, one might discover that the success rate is very low. The evaluation results could suggest that the program be dropped. Yet if the evaluator shifts to a system model of evaluation and considered the data within the context of all the functions of the agency, which might include, for example, the promotion of better attitudes toward hiring the mentally disabled, the development of everyday living skills, and the enhancement of the client's low self-concept, then the objective of hiring the mentally handicapped would be viewed within the context of other, but related functions. From this perspective, the evaluator would be able both to develop many hypotheses explaining the failure of the job-finding effort and to suggest possible concrete avenues for bringing about future change.

Schulberg and Baker (1971) have done extensive work in utilizing the systems approach for evaluating the mental hospital. They view the hospital as an open system exchanging inputs and outputs with its environment. They examined the intraorganizational processes of the hospital, the exchanges and transactions between the hospital and its environment, and the processes and structures through which parts of the environment are related to one another. A change in community attitudes towards the function of the mental hospital, for example, could influence the types of hospital activities that prepare the patient for a return to the community. A systems evaluation approach, consequently, would examine the many linkages, and recommendations would be suggested that offer different options for program improvement (Rossi & Freeman, 1989).

These three approaches to conducting a program evaluation within varied counseling settings respond to different questions or demands that agencies generate when delivering services. As an example, for some career counseling centers it may be important to appraise their overall impact and the consistency with which they produce certain outcomes. Requested usually by the program's sponsors or by other administrative personnel, several types of evaluation information would be collected. A summative evaluation, and occasionally a systems approach, will then be used for evaluating the program's impact. However, other programs may be more concerned with identifying the changing needs of a specific client population in order to develop new activities or improve existing agency objectives. A needs assessment approach may then be utilized.

Whatever the approach, the evaluation itself may be done well or poorly. But good evaluations have certain characteristics that can be used as guidelines to determine whether or not a specific program evaluation will be credible. These characteristics are:

**1.** *Conceptual clarity.* This refers to whether the evaluator shows a clear understanding of the particular evaluation he/she is proposing. Is an effectiveness evaluation being planned, or will the evaluation be directed to improve the program?

**2.** *Precise information needs and sources.* Good evaluation cannot depend on randomly collecting information, gathering "a little here, a little there." An adequate evaluation plan specifies at the onset the information to be collected. If the evaluation is a needs assessment, the evaluation plan will specify what information is important to obtain in order to identify needs of the client population.

**3.** *Description of the object of evaluation.* No evaluation is complete unless it includes a thorough, detailed description of the program or system being evaluated, including the identification of outcomes that are formulated in measurable terms. If a mental health center has been modifying a well-known treatment approach because of its own client needs, then the approach and its modifications should be described accurately. Otherwise, judgments may be made about an activity that doesn't really exist.

**4.** *Representation of legitimate audiences.* An evaluation is adequate only if it includes input from all the legitimate audiences for the evaluation. An evaluation of a counseling center that answers only the questions of the center's staff and ignores questions of clients and community groups is a bad evaluation. Obviously, some audiences will be more important than others and some weighting of their input may be necessary.

**5.** *Technical adequacy.* Good evaluations are dependent on construction or selection of adequate instruments, the development of adequate sampling plans, and the correct choice and application of techniques for data reduction and analysis.

**6.** *Consideration of costs.* Costs are not irrelevant, and it is important for the evaluator to know how much a certain program will accomplish and at what cost. This is particularly important when the evaluator is writing an evaluation report that examines other alternatives that range in both cost and effectiveness.

**7.** *Explicit standards/criteria.* Criteria or standards used to determine whether objectives have been met, or if a program was a success or failure, should be identified when performing a program evaluation. The information taken in an evaluation cannot be translated into judgments or worth without the application of standards or criteria.

**8.** *Recommendations.* An evaluator's responsibility does not end with the collection, analysis, and reporting of data. Recommendations must be provided that imply, for example, whether a program or agency is effective or ineffective. These recommendations must also be tailored to the audience for whom the evaluation was contracted.

**9.** *Sensitivity to political problems in evaluation.* Evaluation itself has a political stance (Weiss, 1973). The evaluator needs to recognize that different value systems are operating in any evaluation scheme. The evaluator should consider the values of the agency under evaluation, the sponsoring authority, the subjects of the evaluation, and the evaluator's own values. Because evaluation is usually undertaken to recommend stability/ survival and growth/change, its results enter the political area. These results often suggest such political issues as the problematic nature of some programs and the unchallengeability of others (Weiss, 1973).

The programs with which an evaluator deals in many areas of mental health or career counseling have developed from the conflict of political opposition, support, and bargaining. Attached to these political realities are the reputations of legislative sponsors, the careers of administrators, and the jobs of program staff. As Weiss (1973) stated, social programs are the creatures of legislative and bureaucratic politics. The evaluator is faced with the tasks of understanding these issues, for being aware of political sensitivities helps the evaluator formulate an evaluation design that will be both effective and appropriate to the realistic needs of the agency. Often, for example, inflated promises are made in the guise of program goals. As an illustration, an agency that provides independent living skills for deinstitutionalized patients may also promise the procurement of employment for these clients. The goals of independent living may be real; the employment goals may be the program's "window dressing." The evaluator must sift the real from the unreal, the important from the unimportant. The program evaluation itself is most likely to affect decisions when the evaluator considers the values, assumptions, and even the covert goals that may set the direction of a program.

# CONCLUSION

Federal and state policies relevant to social programs usually require that such programs establish ongoing evaluation procedures. Techniques used in these programs should be evaluated for their effectiveness and possibility of improvement. There are now a wide range of opportunities for acceptable approaches in program evaluation. The number of community counselors who are concerned about evaluation is growing.

At the same time, many counselors perceive themselves as not being adequately prepared in program evaluation methods and skills (Wheeler, 1980). Though the majority of community counselors may be well versed in basic scientific research and statistical procedures, there is a lack of training in the specific methods of program evaluation. The increased public and private expenditures of the past decade may have improved the social order, but new problems with the mentally ill, drug abusers, and unemployed have emerged. Social change efforts will necessarily continue and grow. Program evaluation, emphasizing the adequate assessment of existing and innovative programs, can have a major impact on social problems.

Systematic evaluations of social programs are a relatively recent development (Rossi et al., 1979; Rossi & Freeman, 1989). Program evaluation is an important area of activity devoted to collecting, analyzing, and interpreting information on the need, implementation, and impact of intervention efforts to improve social conditions and community life. The ability to conduct meaningful program evaluation is rapidly becoming a survival skill for counselors as they become increasingly dependent on external sources of funding for programs (Wheeler, 1980). Accountability demands have intensified and this trend is likely to continue. This chapter is intended to help the reader to conceptualize and to understand the purposes of evaluation and the methods by which it obtains information and generates conclusions.

## EXERCISE

The following case example illustrates a few of the difficulties in conducting program evaluation, and is an invitation to the reader to apply the chapter material to an important situation.

## Case Study

Opportunity Inc. is a youth services agency located in the suburbs of a major, eastern U. S. city. It provides services to youths age 8 to 18 who are having personal, family, and legal problems. The agency's catchment area consists of several counties, and all services are provided to youths in the catchment area at no charge.

Opportunity Inc. is funded by the State Juvenile Services Administration and its activities are monitored by that administration. The agency also receives additional funding from county administrations. Other funding consists of individual and corporate donations raised by several service-related organizations in the catchment area.

The services provided to youths by the agency are outlined in regulations set forth by the Juvenile Services Administration. Mandated services include individual, family, and group counseling; information and referral; crisis intervention; and informal or drop-in counseling. Services which are considered optional by the Juvenile Services Administration and are not currently being offered by Opportunity Inc. include tutoring; leisure time/special activities; community development, consultation, education, resource mobilization, and youth advocacy. The agency has recently begun to provide psychological evaluation and testing for those clients in need of such services.

The mission of Opportunity Inc. is to prevent juvenile delinquency in its catchment area. The written goals of the agency are:

1. To identify conditions of the physical and social environment that provide opportunities for or precipitate delinquent acts and attempt to alter these conditions so that delinquent acts are less likely to occur.

2. To deter those youth who have been identified by the juvenile justice system from further contact with the Juvenile Services Administration.

3. To deter those youth who have not been identified by the juvenile justice system from delinquent activity.

4. To maximize the potential of youth who participate in services for responsible, productive, and gratifying participation in society.

Voluntary referrals are accepted from other social service agencies, police, courts, families, schools, and the Juvenile Services Administration. Opportunity Inc. also provides services to those youths who are required to receive counseling services after being adjudicated by the Juvenile Services Administration or being classified as a child in need of supervision. Currently, approximately 50 percent of this agency's clients have had some form of contact with the Juvenile Services Administration; of these, approximately 36 percent have been adjudicated. The majority of the remaining 50 percent have been referred from other sources; very few clients are self-referred.

Opportunity Inc. is located in a lower-level four-bedroom apartment in a large apartment complex. The apartment has been structually modified to provide five separate offices and a large waiting room. The agency is staffed by a full-time director, four full-time counselors, one volunteer, a part-time consulting psychologist, and a receptionist.

The standard procedures for the delivery of services by Opportunity Inc. are as follows: Most requests for counseling services are received over the telephone. At that time the agency director or a staff counselor will attempt to obtain some basic information about the individual, the nature of the problem, and the referral source. Unless it is a crisis situation and there is a need for an immediate session, the client is scheduled for an intake interview with the first available counselor. Depending on the size of the waiting list, this may take several weeks or more (the current waiting list time is approximately six to eight weeks). The counselor will briefly explain the intake procedure to the caller and will ask that the client's entire family attend the intake.

At the time of the intake, the counselor will first meet with the family to further explain the procedure and obtain some basic information. The counselor then meets with the client alone to obtain his or her perception of the problem. The counselor then meets with the parents to obtain their perceptions of the problem and additional information, such as family history. The counselor will then meet with the entire family to observe their interaction and to formulate treatment goals.

The case is then presented at the next weekly staff meeting, which is attended by the entire staff and the consulting psychologist. At that time the staff decides which counselor would be best suited to work with the case, based on the needs of the client and the skills of the counselor. Also, a basic treatment plan is developed based on the goals formulated by the counselor and the client. The staff also determines whether clients will be seen as a family or whether individual counseling would be more appropriate.

Counselors generally see their clients on a weekly basis for one-hour sessions. If a counselor is experiencing any difficulties in working with a client, these issues are discussed at the weekly staff meeting; suggestions are solicited from other staff members and from the consulting psychologist. The decision to successfully terminate treatment is made when the counselor and the client feel that enough progress has been made toward attaining treatment goals. Although the focus of Opportunity Inc. is short-term treatment, there are no limits imposed on the number of contacts a client may have with the agency.

You have been asked by this agency to conduct an evaluation focusing on the question, "Do our services make any difference?" With this question, how would you proceed with this evaluation? What are some of the initial difficulties that you may encounter, considering what was explained in the material in this chapter?

## REFERENCES

Anderson, W. (1981, April) . How to do research in community mental health agencies. *Personnel and Guidance Journal, 59,* 517–522.

Berren, M. (1984) . Statewide outcome evaluation: An introduction to the special issue. *Community Community Mental Health Journal, 20,* 4–13.

Burck, H. D., & Peterson, G. (1975). Needed: More evaluation, not research. *Personnel and Guidance Journal, 53,* 563–569.

Burgrabbe, J., & Swift, J. (1984, March/April) Evaluating your EAP: A practical approach. *EAP Digest,* 12–34.

Etzioni, A. (1960). Two approaches to organizational analysis: A critique and a suggestion. *Administration Science Quarterly, 5,* 257–278.

Fink, A., & Kosecoff, J. (1978). *An evaluation primer.* Beverly Hills, CA: Sage Publications,

Franklin, J., & Thrasher, J. (1976). *An introduction to program evaluation.* New York: John Wiley.

Hyman, H., & Wright, C. (1971). Evaluating social action programs. In F. Caro (Ed.), *Readings in evaluation research.* New York: Russell Sage.

Keppler-Seid, H., Windle, C., & Woy, J. (1980). Performance measures for mental health programs. *Community Mental Health Journal, 16,* 217–234.

Lebow, J. (1982). Models for evaluating services at community mental health centers. *Hospital and community psychiatry, 33,* 1010–1014.

Meyer, H., Borgatta, E., & Jones, W. (1965). *Girls at vocational high.* New York: Russell Sage.

Morris, L., & Fitz-Gibbon, C. (1978). *Evaluator's handbook.* Beverly Hills, CA: Sage.

Neigher, W., & Schulberg, H. (1982). Evaluating the outcomes of human service programs. *Evaluation Review, 6,* 731–752.

Peterson, G., & Burck, H. (1982). A competency approach to accountability in human service programs. *Personnel and Guidance Journal, 60,* 491–495.

Rossi, P., & Freeman, H. (1989). *Evaluation—A systematic approach* (4th ed.). Newbury Park, CA: Sage.

Rossi, P., Freeman, H., & Wright, S. (1979). *Evaluation: A systematic approach.* Beverly Hills, CA: Sage.

Rutman, V., & Mowbray, G. (1983) . *Understanding program evaluation.* Beverly Hills, CA: Sage.

Schulberg, H. C. (1981). Outcome evaluations in the mental health fields. *Community Mental Health Journal, 17,* 132–143.

Schulberg, H. C., & Baker, F. (1971). Program evolution models and the implementation of research findings. In F. Cara (Ed.), *Readings in evaluation research.* New York: Russell Sage.

Spaniol, L. (1975). *A model for program evaluation in rehabilitation.* Madison, WI: University of Wisconsin, Regional Rehabilitation Research Institute (Monograph XIX, Series 3).

Weiss, C. H. (1972) . *Evaluating action programs.* Boston: Allyn & Bacon.

Weiss, C. H. (1973). Where politics and evaluation research meet. *Evaluation, 1,* 4–13.

Werner, J. (1978) . Community mental health consultation with Agenus. *Personnel and Guidance Journal, 56,* 364–368.

Wheeler, P. T. (1980). Mental health practitioners' perceptions of their preparation in program evaluation. *American Mental Health Counselors Association Journal, 2,* 88–96.

Wheeler, P. T., & Loesch, L. (1981, May). Program evaluation and counseling: Yesterday, today, and tomorrow. *Personnel and Guidance Journal, 59,* 573–581.

# EPILOGUE

# 16

# FUTURE DIRECTIONS FOR COMMUNITY COUNSELING

This book appears at a time of intense reconsideration of the existing health care, welfare, and human services delivery systems in our country. It is impossible to prophesy the future of community counseling without knowing the changes that will result from this reevaluation. Nonetheless, there are a number of presently operating, clearly identifiable trends in our society that will surely have an impact on the future form and function of community counseling. These include:

**1.** Societal trends that will affect the profession, that is, changes in client populations and in settings for practice, consumerism, the growth of technology, and the economics of health care.

**2.** Trends and issues within counseling that will affect the theory and practice of community counseling, that is, a lifespan developmental orientation; the increased emphasis on environment-behavior interaction; the shift from emphasis on removing pathology to emphasis on promoting resources and coping; the shift from theory-based to skill-based practice; the increased emphasis on cost-effective treatments; the movement from an exclusively direct treatment–oriented mission

to one involving a full range of interventions; and a focus on evaluation and research.

**3.** Issues and trends related to the professionalization of community counseling, including professional identity, credentialing, professional education, and international expansion of the field.

Although it is not possible to predict with certainty exactly what changes will result from these trends and issues, we can be sure that they will have an effect on the directions the field of community counseling will take in the future.

## SOCIETAL TRENDS

### Changes in Clientele and Settings

The first societal trend we shall examine is the shift in clientele and in settings. As longevity continues to increase, there will be a markedly increased need for gerontological counselors. The increased number of children being raised in one-parent families may require more services from community counselors. Because of shifts in the ethnic and racial composition of American society through immigration and differential birth rates, community counselors will be working more with populations that have been underrepresented in the provision of services in the past, such as cultural minorities. Thus, counseling approaches that address the needs of African Americans, Hispanics, Asian Americans, Native Americans, and immigrants from around the globe must be developed, researched, and practiced. Counselors, through their professional organization, are currently involved in educating legislators, insurance providers, and society as a whole about their ability to provide effective, economical services to clientele who have been excluded from service or underserved in the past. This, too, will place community counselors in contact with clients who differ socially and culturally from those served in the past, such as those clients who are covered by third-party insurers like Medicare, Medicaid, Civilian Health and Medical Program of the Uniformed Services (CHAMPUS), Blue Cross/ Blue Shield, and other private insurance plans. Finally, as a result of the Americans with Disabilities Act and other legislation providing for equal access to services for persons with disabilities, community counselors will have to learn to work with clients who are deaf, mute, or challenged in other ways that render traditional counseling approaches ineffective.

As the value of counseling has become recognized in the workplace and as the structure of work has been changing to accommodate a broader range of lifestyles, new settings in business and industry—such as employee assistance programs and human resources development offices—will be hiring proportionately more community counselors. Moreover, counselors continue to find increased acceptance of their professional role in hospitals, clinics, community mental health centers, family service agencies, and health maintenance organizations (Forrest & Affemann, 1986). With the increase in the number of older persons in society, we may expect an expanded role for community counselors in nursing homes, senior citizens' centers, and hospices, as well.

## Consumerism

A second societal trend is the growth of consumerism. This has had its effects on counseling in the development of self-help groups as an alternative to seeking help from professionals, in the demand for freedom of choice of services and service providers, and in the dramatic increase in the number of malpractice suits against professionals and institutions. Clients are demanding the right to be informed about the cost and effectiveness of services and to hold professionals, including community counselors, liable for misrepresentations and inept practices. Despite its hazards for the individual counselor, this trend has significant potential to benefit the profession as a whole. Insofar as community counseling can demonstrate superior cost-effectiveness as compared to other service providers, it stands to gain wider acceptance and recognition throughout a society that embraces this value.

## New Technology

The third societal trend affecting the future development of community counseling is the growth of and value placed on technology. This trend has both general effects on the emotional well-being of those living within the society and specific effects on the practice of community counseling. We live in a time and culture in which technology is valued because of its contribution to our material comfort and despite its potential for mass destruction. It is incumbent on the community counselor to assist people to live with both the benefits and the threats of technology. It is also necessary for the counselor to learn to use technologies for the betterment of society.

Living with the constant threat of nuclear war over the past half-century certainly has had its impact on the quality of life, and advances in other technological fields will unquestionably also have implications for community counseling. Genetic engineering may change the types and incidence of problems faced by future generations. The emotional effects of living with a transplanted organ have yet to be evaluated. What will be the emotional effects of the relative isolation, disorientation, and weightlessness experienced in space travel? Nearer at hand, community counseling must become prepared to assist people to deal with the emotional effects of job obsolescence resulting from advances in computer technology and in robotics. The latter may represent a particularly severe problem, because the majority of those displaced by robotics will have the lowest level of compensatory skills and, often, the fewest developed resources to cope with their displacement.

The other aspect of this trend is the development of a technology for use in counseling. This technology involves the areas of electronics (audio and video recording), data processing (interactive systems, information storage and retrieval), psychoactive drugs, and behavior modification (biofeedback, relaxation programs, etc.). These devices will increasingly affect the community counselor's role, functions, practices, and effectiveness. Electronic recording technology has changed the nature of counseling supervision and also allows replay to clients as part of the counseling process. The gathering and providing of information can now be done on a computer, thereby freeing the counselor's time to work with the client on solving problems. These technologies do, however, raise issues concerning client confidentiality, such as limiting access to electronically stored records. Also, counselors must take care that the use of this technology does not interpose a barrier between the counselor and the client, depersonalizing the counseling process. Psychoactive medication administered by physicians allows counselors to work with clients formerly too withdrawn, agitated, or confused to benefit from counsel-

ing. The negative side of this development, of course, is the criminal misuse of psychoactive drugs by addicts and thrill-seekers, presenting a major problem for counselors and other health and human services professionals to address. Behavioral technology is already well established within counseling practice and will certainly be even more broadly applied to the future. Relaxation techniques can be used to help eliminate phobias, reduce physical complaints, and otherwise contribute to positive health. Similarly, biofeedback may be used to treat physical (blood pressure, headaches, etc.) and emotional (anxiety) symptoms. The potential benefits of behavioral technology are great; but in the past, these techniques have too often been applied by overzealous advocates to populations who had no choice in their use—schoolchildren, prisoners, persons in mental institutions, and mentally retarded individuals. Thus, all of the technological developments applicable in counseling present both potential benefits and potential risks, and the community counselor must be aware of both aspects in determining their appropriate use.

## Economic Considerations

The final societal trend to be considered is the effect of economic considerations on the development of community counseling. Inevitably, economic factors are used to justify the political decisions to support or to cut back on publicly funded human services at the local, state, and national levels (Fein, 1958; Rubin, 1978). In the views of many policy analysts (e.g., Boulding, 1967), economic considerations outweigh the social ones in political decision making, even on social issues such as mental health. Therefore, it is important for the community counselor to be aware of trends in the economics of health care and of human services delivery. This involves such issues as: (a) the cost of providing services, (b) the cost of not providing those services, (c) the cost-benefit ratio that is acceptable to society, (d) the relative costs of different service delivery alternatives, and (e) who pays for the services that are rendered. In purely economic terms, divorced of any social or moral considerations (although economists do take these factors into account), the question becomes: What is the least society needs to pay in order to attain a level of well-being that it finds acceptable? This question, of course, can never lead to a single, permanent answer, because poorer societies are forced to accept lower levels than richer ones, and richer ones are forced to accept lower levels in periods of recession than in periods of prosperity.

Figuring the costs of mental health problems and services is an extremely complex process, requiring that one make certain assumptions that can significantly affect the final figure. Rubin (1978) cited certain categories of direct costs, including: (a) direct care (e.g., public and private hospitals; community mental health facilities; general medical services, nursing homes, and rehabilitation facilities; private practice by relevant professionals; children's programs; and psychoactive medication); (b) research on problems; (c) training of personnel; (d) construction and development of facilities; and (e) management of programs. The indirect costs of mental health problems include the loss to society of the productive capacity of those with problems, including those in long-term institutions, those who experience short-term work absences, and those who work at less than their full potential as a result of their problems. One can, if one chooses, add complexities such as how to figure in the cost of disability payments to persons with problems, whether to figure in the cost of food for those in institutions, and whether to figure the differences in productive output by those now engaged in providing services as compared with their output if available for employment elsewhere in the economy. As one can see, by including or by excluding certain considerations, one can raise or lower the stated costs of problems and the costs of services to treat them (Fein, 1958). In general, political liberals try to maximize the stated costs of problems and minimize the stated costs of services, in order to justify providing more services. Conservatives, on the other hand, seek to minimize the stated cost of problems and maximize the cost of services as a justification for cutting back on services.

Another economic consideration is who is to pay for these services—the federal government, the state, the local community, the person's employer, or the individual? Again, the pendulum has swung back and forth among these levels, depending on the contemporary social and legal views of what responsibilities should be assigned to what level. One factor that frequently enters into the consideration of this matter is who can best insure against the loss. As such, the insurance companies have, through profit motive or social pressure, moved into providing third-party payment for mental health services. As the costs of health care have risen at a much more rapid rate than is accounted for by general inflation, providing coverage for services has no longer proved profitable; and insurers have sought to limit or to stop coverage for these services. This, in turn, has become a major political issue, in part reflecting differences of political opinion as to the responsibilities and rights of insurance companies.

Finally, no matter who pays, that party will have the same economic concern: Am I getting the most effective use of my money? Could I receive equal (or better) services for less cost? This becomes a marketplace issue among the providers of services, each trying to convince the public (both the ones who pay and the ones who legislate as to who can provide services) that their service is better or cheaper than that offered by the other possible providers. This has led to the growth of cost-controlled practice groups such as HMOs, many of which will look to community counselors as cost-effective service providers.

## TRENDS AND ISSUES AFFECTING THEORY AND PRACTICE

Seven trends and issues within counseling that will affect future theory and practice in community counseling will be examined in this section. These include the emphasis on lifespan development; on environment-behavior interaction; on mobilizing client resources and coping skills; on skill-based practice; on cost-effective treatment approaches; on primary and tertiary, as well as secondary, prevention; and on evaluation and research.

### Lifespan Development

Counseling's acceptance of lifespan development as its fundamental science is particularly appropriate today, as the increases in longevity noted in the prior section of this chapter have expanded the meaning of lifespan. Along with this change has come the recognition that development is a life-long process and not just a process that ends with the attainment of maturity, as earlier conceptualizations held. Thus, the years after middle age are now seen to have potential for positive growth, not merely for decline. Two counseling approaches offer particularly useful tools to community counselors in assisting clients with lifespan development. One is Schlossberg's (1984) concept of coping with transitions, with its analysis of the characteristics of the particular transition (the type, the context, and the impact), of the individual (personal and demographic characteristics, psychological resources, and coping responses), and of the environment (social support systems, options) and its consequent use of problem solving, coping skills, and support systems to assist the client through the transition. Transitions are an inevitable part of living; and the longer one lives, the more of them one will experience. Schlossberg's model is particularly relevant to counseling concerning how one can cope with these transitions. The other concept of particular use in lifespan developmental counseling is Super's (1980) life-career rainbow. This model provides a systematic framework for charting the range and intensity of the various life roles that one may play at different ages and life stages. For example, one's roles as child, student, worker, parent, citizen, leisurite, homemaker, volunteer, congregant, etc. may wax and wane in importance at different times in one's life. By suggesting a way to chart the course of one's involvement in these life roles, Super has provided a useful tool for lifespan developmental counseling. An approach to charting life roles suggested by Super's model is shown in Figure 16–1. In this illustration, the life roles of a 70-year-old man are plotted. A large X indicates major involvement in that role at that time, and a small x indicates minor involvement. Blank space indicates no involvement.

In this illustration, the man's parents died when he was in his early 30s. After college, he

**FIGURE** 16–1  Life roles of a 70-year-old man

| | Ages | | | | | | | | | | | | | | |
|---|---|---|---|---|---|---|---|---|---|---|---|---|---|---|---|
| **Life Roles** | Birth | 5 | 10 | 15 | 20 | 25 | 30 | 35 | 40 | 45 | 50 | 55 | 60 | 65 | 70 |
| Child | X | X | X | X | x | x | x | | | | | | | | |
| Student | | X | X | X | X | x | | x | | | x | x | | X | x |
| Worker | | | | x | x | X | X | X | X | X | X | X | X | x | |
| Citizen | | | | x | x | x | x | x | x | X | X | x | x | x | x |
| Volunteer | | | | | | | | x | x | x | x | x | x | X | X |
| Parent | | | | | | X | X | X | X | X | x | x | x | x | x |
| Hobbyist | | | x | x | | | | | | | x | x | x | x | |

took some continuing education courses that were required by his job; and at the time of his partial retirement, he went back to school to complete a master's degree. He worked part-time while in high school and college and was employed as an accountant throughout his working years. He had an interest in politics throughout his adolescence and adulthood, and in his middle 40s and early 50s, held elective office on the county board of aldermen. He had, from his mid–30s on, volunteered regularly at his church's outreach center, becoming particularly active in this role in his retirement. He was the parent of two children, whom he supported through college. In his youth, he collected stamps, and in his 50s and 60s, he dabbled in photography as a hobby. Thus, the lifespan developmental counselor now has tools to conceptualize both continuity (life roles) and change (transitions). This should move lifespan development from the realm of theory to the realm of practice in community counseling.

## Environment-Behavior Interaction

The second trend affecting the theory and practice of community counseling is an increased focus on environment-behavior interaction. As early as 1936, Kurt Lewin defined the principle that behavior is a function of the person and that person's environment; that is, that one can only understand a person's behavior when considering it within its environmental context. This principle, however, is only beginning to find its way systematically into the doctrine of the mental health fields, even though it is doubtful that one could find a professional in these fields who would dispute its validity or its relevance to practice.

Thus, counselors view behavior contextually, rather than in isolation. This has fostered an emphasis on community-oriented preventive measures and has promoted an advocacy role for counselors. Changing client behavior is now generally recognized as an ineffective

goal unless the new behavior is adaptive to and supported by the setting in which it will be practiced. The importance of behavior-environment interaction is also an underlying principle in the development of cross-cultural counseling, with its recognition that behavior that might be appropriate in one cultural context may be viewed as grossly inappropriate in another. For example, one of the authors recalls seeing an unemployed Puerto Rican client fly into a murderous rage when asked at an intake interview whether he helped his working wife with the housework. In this client's cultural context, that apparently innocent question was seen by the client as an aspersion on his masculinity, which is a central value for men in his culture.

The importance of attending to the effects of the environment in counseling has been operationalized by Super (1993), who suggested that counseling is done along a continuum, the two poles of which are situational and personal. "[S]ituational counseling… focus[es] on different types of situations (career, family, etc.) and personal counseling …focus[es]…on individuals whose problems are based primarily in their own approach to and coping with situations, not on factors in the situations they encounter" (Super, 1993, p. 135). Thus, the person and the environment, in some combination, interact to form the problem and must both be involved in the solution to that problem.

## Resources and Skills

The principal unique contribution of counseling to the mental health field is counseling's focus on mobilizing client resources and skills as the essential strategy for promoting growth and coping. This strategy avoids the long-standing, unresolved debate as to whether mental health problems are biological, learned, psychodynamic, or socially imposed in origin. Clients cannot wait for the resolution of this issue (if it will ever be resolved) to get on with the tasks of life. Even in the unlikely event that eventually all mental health problems are found to be biochemical in etiology and curable by psychoactive drugs, all persons will still encounter problems of living that will require them to use their resources and skills in order to cope. It is, therefore, safe to say that community counseling is well advised to pursue this approach and to develop further its methods for identifying and mobilizing client resources and skills. For counselors, this requires the development of two sets of skills: (1) the skills needed for living and coping with life situations, and (2) the skills needed to help clients to recognize, develop, and apply these life skills.

## Skill-Based Practice

A fourth trend affecting theory and practice is the shift from theory-based to skill-based counseling practice. The defining of specific counselor competencies and the demonstration of these as determinants of fitness to practice is a major change in the field. Rigidly following the techniques dictated by a single theoretical model, regardless of the nature of the client or the problem, is no longer professionally acceptable. Community counselors now not only must possess a range of skills derived from a variety of theoretical approaches, but also must know when to apply each of them and how to combine them into a multimodal approach. This shift moves the counselor from being a technician to being a true professional.

## Cost-Effective Treatments

The fifth trend, which is largely driven by the public's and the insurers' reactions to the exceptionally high rate of increase in health care costs, is toward cost-effective treatments. This includes brief, focused, time-limited individual counseling (for example, Janis,

1983; Peake, Borduin, & Archer, 1988; Wells, 1994), crisis counseling, group counseling (as discussed in Chapter 10), programming (as discussed in Chapter 11), and other techniques that provide maximum service to the maximum number of clients in the minimum amount of time, at minimum per client cost. These techniques are in many cases at least as effective as longer, more expensive individual approaches and may offer additional benefits, such as peer feedback, group support, and the realization that one is not alone in having to deal with a particular problem. Thus, counseling approaches that assist clients to gain problem-solving skills and coping capacities as rapidly but as effectively as possible are the approaches that are most likely to survive in the field, given the current societal pressures.

## Full Range of Interventions

The sixth trend affecting community counseling theory and practice is the shift from an exclusive emphasis on individual treatment for specific problems to a recognition that the aims of the field can only be accomplished if the full range of services, including preventive and rehabilitative services, are brought to bear in promoting coping. This change reflects the shift from the medical, treatment of individual illness model to the public health, promotion of community health model. This is consistent with counseling's posture as a profession that seeks to promote health, rather than to cure illness. Medicine has long had the task of treating persons who are ill, which is unquestionably a much needed, full-time job. The allied field of public health has defined its role as preventing illness, rather than curing it after it has occurred. Consequently, public health has defined three types of prevention: primary prevention, or preventing a disease from occurring; secondary prevention, or preventing the disease from further damaging the patient, once it has occurred (that is, the traditional medical treatment role); and tertiary prevention, or preventing the effects of the disease, once they have been contained, from further incapacitating the patient (that is, the traditional rehabilitative role). Thus, a complete health-oriented approach requires all three types of activities: preventive efforts, direct service treatment, and rehabilitation for those treated (i.e., primary, secondary, and tertiary prevention, respectively). Counseling, as a health-oriented discipline, has adopted this model in defining its role.

We have, throughout this book, looked at community counseling's efforts in prevention (education, programming, consultation, etc.), treatment, and rehabilitation. Unquestionably, counseling will continue to develop and improve its methods in all three areas, but a special comment is warranted concerning preventive services. Certainly, there is much truth to the old adage that an ounce of prevention is worth a pound of cure. It is part of the doctrine of the mental health field that this adage is applicable to its domain. For example, Albee (1985) has pointed out that we will never have enough mental health professionals to treat all those in need of such services, so that we had better devote efforts to preventing problems rather than to the hopeless task of producing enough professionals to help people deal with these problems. To date, however, no really adequate technology of preventive services has been developed. This has not been a result of overlooking this issue (for example, Buckner, Trickett, & Corse, 1985), but rather reflects the pressure society has put on these fields to deal with the high numbers of those in immediate need of services. Moreover, it is frequently difficult to demonstrate effective prevention, because it requires proving that something did not occur as a direct consequence of a particular intervention. Most funding bodies are more ready to support a campaign to fight an existing dramatic crisis than to support e forts to prevent a potential crisis that may not occur. Finally, there must be agreement on the cause of a phenomenon if

one is to figure out a way to prevent it, and no such agreement exists in the mental health field. Nonetheless, given the prevalence of mental health problems, there is good reason to devote greater attention to efforts at prevention, and one may expect proportionately more emphasis on prevention in the future.

## Evaluation and Research

The final trend affecting theory and practice to be mentioned here is the increased emphasis on evaluation and research in counseling. The quality of counseling is now measured by its effectiveness and economy, rather than by its artistry or conformity to a theoretical model. This trend moves counseling into the category of scientifically based endeavors, which both increases its validity and justifies its existence according to the values prevalent in our society. Through rigorous evaluation of its techniques, processes, and outcomes, the parameters of the field can be carefully defined and the necessary competencies for practice can be determined.

The line between evaluation and research is, at best, blurred. Research essentially addresses basic, theoretical issues, whereas evaluation assesses the efficacy and cost-efficiency of applied techniques and programs. To remain viable, counseling must pursue both these processes. The ultimate question for counseling is: What *techniques*, applied by what *counselors* working with what *clients* facing what *problems* under what *environmental conditions*, produce what *outcomes*? Obviously, it is impossible at the present stage of development of the field to answer all of that question at once. We assume, however, that by answering parts of the question we will eventually be able to build a full answer. Thus, we may now test whether reflection works better with dependent or independent clients in increasing feelings of self-worth, or whether hearing-impaired clients resolve conflicts more rapidly working with counselors who use sign language or by using an interpreter with nonsigning counselors. Until thousands of such bits of information are accumulated, we cannot put them together to answer the general question. We can, however, use research to determine the validity of some basic theoretical issues, such as whether repression exists as a phenomenon, and if so, under what conditions it leads to hostility, passivity, or other behaviors. If, for example, we were to find that repression does not exist, there is no need to develop or evaluate techniques to deal with it.

## ISSUES AND TRENDS RELATED TO PROFESSIONALIZATION

In addition to the issues of theory and practice, community counseling faces issues related to its existence as a profession. In this section four such issues will be explored: professional identity, professional credentialing, professional education, and the worldwide scope and potential for this field.

### Professional Identity

As was noted in Chapter 2, community counseling is in the anomalous position of having more accredited training programs than any other counseling specialization except for school counseling, but being the only specialization accredited by CACREP that has neither a division to represent it within the American Counseling Association nor a specialized professional journal. Clearly, if community counseling is to remain viable, these deficits must be remedied.

Before these structures can be put in place, several basic issues must be resolved in the field of counseling. The first of these issues is whether community counseling is a generalist field or a targeted specialization within counseling. If it is the former, then why identify it by the adjective *community*, thereby making it sound parallel to school counseling, career counseling, mental health counseling, and the

other counseling specializations? If, on the other hand, it is a targeted specialization like all the others, what is its unique target? How does it differ from mental health counseling, career counseling, or gerontological counseling? According to the counseling code of ethics, discussed in Chapter 4, a counselor may only provide services in areas in which he/she is knowledgeable, experienced, and competent. What is the scope of community counseling, given the fact that no one can be equally competent in all areas? Should a community counselor undertake career counseling with a client when a career counselor, who has greater expertise in this area, is available? Should a community counselor address a client's issues with his/her family when family counselors are available? Until these issues are resolved, the structural supports for community counseling cannot be put in place, and groups outside the field of counseling (such as legislatures that approve licensure laws, third-party payers, and the general public) will continue to question the professional credibility of a field that has not yet resolved these issues. Therefore, the swift resolution of these issues is of highest priority to community counseling and to counseling as a whole.

### Credentialing

Another trend, related to the issues of consumerism, evaluation, and professional identity discussed earlier in this chapter, is that of professional credentialing. Counselor licensing and certification and the accreditation of counselor education programs are, in good measure, responses to consumer demands for an indication of competence. Counselor certification is also a possible basis for determining who will qualify to receive third-party payment. To be credible, these processes must be functionally related to the trend toward evaluation; otherwise, the credentials will merely appear to be self-serving. That is, the credentials must be based on the counselor's demonstrating that he/she is able to select and use those professional skills that have been shown through research to be effective in working with clients like the one being served. Moreover, credentials must be used to attest to competence rather than to limit competition among service providers. As discussed in Chapter 2, general certification as a counselor is available to community counselors through the National Board for Certified Counselors (designation: national certified counselor, abbreviated as NCC following the counselor's name and academic degrees), although specialized certification in community counseling (such as exists in school counseling, career counseling, mental health counseling, and gerontological counseling) is not yet available. In addition to professional certification, the majority of states now license counselors, based on their professional education, experience, and ability to pass a licensing examination (Glosoff, 1994).

As is the case with most professions, counselors must participate in continuing education in their field in order to maintain their certification and/or license. This helps counselors keep up to date with advances in their field.

As has been suggested, certification and licensure are intended to protect the public from unqualified individuals offering services. To the extent that these processes are used for this purpose, they are valid and should be enthusiastically supported. They should not, however, be allowed to become mechanisms for excluding competent practitioners in order to control the marketplace for services.

## Education of Community Counselors

The third issue is that of professional education. No profession can exist without established patterns of training for its practitioners. As indicated in Chapter 2, entry-level education for community counselors, as defined by the professional organizations in the field (National Board for Certified Counselors;

Council for Accreditation of Counseling and Related Educational Programs), consists of two years of full-time graduate study that includes courses in counseling theory, human development, social and cultural aspects of behavior, counseling and consultation techniques, appraisal of clients, group processes, career and lifestyle development, professional ethics and practices, research and evaluation methods, and some specifics of community counseling practice. Supervised practicum and internship experiences are also included in the educational requirements. This is a demanding and wide-ranging set of knowledge and skills, but is it sufficient to produce effective community counselors? What about preventive, educational, or administrative skills? What about knowledge of the effects of drugs or of exercise? As professionals, counselors can never stop learning. Obviously, no member of any profession is fully educated at the time of graduation from professional school. When a physician graduates from medical school, that physician is not immediately qualified as a neurosurgeon. Further specialized learning and experience are required. Similarly, no counselor fresh out of a graduate program is an expert advocate, consultant, or counselor. Lengthening the period of formal training might resolve this problem; but then the cost of fully trained personnel might become prohibitive, and even more persons in need of services would remain unattended. Therefore, part of the solution is in continuing education for counselors educated up to a reasonable entry level in programs of minimal feasible length. Over the years, that minimum length has increased from one to two full academic years, but any lengthier preservice educational programs for community counselors will need to be thoroughly justified relative to the cost of longer time in school before professional entry.

Another issue confronting community counselor education is that different professional roles require different mixes of knowledge and skills. Thus, a line counselor (i.e., a direct service provider) must be more proficient at individual client appraisal than an agency administrator, whereas the administrator must be more proficient at management techniques. Most agency administrators, however, start out their careers as line counselors. Should the education of line counselors, therefore, place weight on the learning of management techniques when that means that less time can be devoted to teaching basic counseling skills? Perhaps a better model is the shortest feasible education required to become competent to provide direct client services (two years), followed later in one's career by further education in supervisory or management techniques, as one's career path dictates.

## International Aspects

The final issue of professionalization to be touched upon is the international potential of this field. For many historical, economic, and social reasons, community counseling has been primarily an American phenomenon. Foremost among these reasons are the prior existence of counseling as a recognized occupation in American society, sufficient affluence in the society to support this occupational role, and America's awareness of and concern with its mental health needs. Nonetheless, problems of living are not confined to people who live in the United States. Indeed, the environmental causes of many such problems—starvation, unemployment, disease, the threat of attack—are infinitely more severe in many other countries.

Although the model of the community counselor—the effective professional educated in the essential knowledge and skills in the minimum necessary period of time—is highly appropriate to meet the needs and resources of these countries, we must be careful that the content of professional education is appropriate to the local culture. An American model, based on an assumption of freedom of choice and self-determination of one's destiny, does not fit the prevailing ethos in many other countries. Therefore, much of the field's knowledge base and skills training must be adapted to local conditions. Nonetheless, the ultimate aim of assisting people to use their resources and skills to cope with the problems of living that confront them appears valid across cultures.

Many countries, particularly those that are relatively better off economically (e.g., Belgium, Britain, Denmark, France, Japan, Sweden), already have settings in which community counselors could function, such as clinics and community agencies (Jansen, 1986). In other cultures, perhaps different modes of service delivery would prove more effective. Thus, Third World countries might utilize native healers, supervised by community counseling professionals, to assist their citizens to mobilize their resources and to develop ways to cope with rapid cultural change. That a similar arrangement could work effectively was demonstrated by a pilot project in social psychiatry in Colombia, South America (Argandoña & Kiev, 1972). Only by careful attention to the consideration of cultural relevance can community counseling become the worldwide accepted approach it has the potential to be.

## CONCLUSION

This book has attempted to present an overview of the evolving field of community counseling. By the very fact of its recency, community counseling has been able to benefit from the contributions and limitations of the longer-established human service professions, incorporating their effective elements while discarding those ideas and techniques that have proved to be outmoded or ineffective. Additionally, arising from the discipline of counseling, community counseling has contributed its own unique elements to the process of helping clients to cope with problems of living. Foremost among these elements are the emphases on coping skills, on mobilizing environmental supports, and on promoting healthy development.

It is the belief of the authors that the community counseling approach offers great potential for helping clients—be they individuals, families, groups, organizations, or communities—to attain optimal functioning, both in the United States and across other cultures. As a field dedicated to the principles of human growth, development, and potential for change, community counseling will remain open to change and development within itself in the future. Therefore, this book has presented a still photograph of a moving object; but the only real constants that can characterize community counseling are continual growth, increasing professionalism, and improving service to its clients.

## REFERENCES

Albee, G. W. (1985). The answer is prevention. *Psychology Today, 19*(2), 60–64.

Argandoña, M., & Kiev, A. (1972). *Mental health in the developing world: A case study in Latin America.* New York: Free Press.

Boulding, K. E. (1967). The boundaries of social policy. *Social Work, 12,* 3–11.

Buckner, J. C., Trickett, E. J., & Corse, S. J. (1985). *Primary prevention in mental health: An annotated bibliography.* Rockville, MD: National Institute of Mental Health.

Fein, R. (1958). *Economics of mental illness.* New York: Basic Books.

Forrest, D. V., & Affemann, M. (1986). The future of mental health counselors in health maintenance organizations. *AMHCA Journal, 8,* 65–72.

Glosoff, H. L. (1994). *Education, experience, & examination requirements of credentialed counselors as dictated by state statutes.* Alexandria, VA: American Counseling Association.

Janis, I. L. (1983). *Short-term counseling: Guidelines based on recent research.* New Haven, CT: Yale University Press.

Jansen, M. A. (1986). *European mental health policies and practices: Rehabilitation of the chronically mentally ill* (Final Report: International Exchange of Experts and Information in Rehabilitation). New York: World Rehabilitation Fund.

Lewin, K. (1936). *Principles of topological psychology.* New York: McGraw-Hill.

Peake, T. H., Borduin, C. M., & Archer, R. P. (1988). *Brief psychotherapies: Changing frames of mind.* Newbury Park, CA: Sage.

Rubin, J. (1978). *Economics, mental health, and the law.* Lexington, MA: D. C. Heath.

Schlossberg, N. K. (1984). *Counseling adults in transition: Linking practice with theory.* New York: Springer.

Super, D. E. (1980). A life-span, life space approach to career development. *Journal of Vocational Behavior, 16,* 282–298.

Super, D. E. (1993). The two faces of counseling: Or is it three? *Career Development Quarterly, 42,* 132–136.

Wells, R. A. (1994). *Planned short term treatment* (2nd ed.). New York: Free Press.

# *Appendix: Interview Guide*

Name: _____

Address: _____

Phone:  Home_____     Work _____

Referred by: _____

The counselor will follow the interview guide in gathering information about a new client. After each section, a space is available for comments.

## I. INTRODUCTION

*Goals*

Identify why client has come to the interview.
Establish a relationship.
Determine a hierarchy of importance among the client's presenting problems.
Establish how the client perceives the most pressing presenting problem.
Observe readily identifiable client strengths.

*Areas to Explore*

*Client appearance*

appropriately attired
grooming
neatness
facial expressions
gross motor behavior
eye contact

*Personal manner*

nervousness
habits
politeness

*Visible disability*

*Motivation to change*

*Self-expression*

> responsiveness
> verbal skills
> verbal responsiveness
> verbal appropriateness
> verbal ability to communicate
> nonverbal behavior

*Motivation for counseling*

> promptness to interview
> comfort interacting with counselor
> willingness to self-disclose

*QuestionsThat You May Ask*

> What causes you to seek counseling?
> What is going on in your life these days?
> What do you like about yourself?
> What do you dislike about yourself?

*Comments*

## II. WORK/CAREER EXPERIENCES, GOALS AND INTERESTS

*Goals*

> To identify client interest and career goals.
> To assist client to become aware of his/her lifestyle, and in some instances, a career
> direction consistent with client

*Areas to Explore*

> Client's interest in certain occupational and other life role areas
> Matching interests with client abilities
> Different paths to fulfilling interests
> Major accomplishments in previous employment
> Types of decisions made
> Likes/dislikes of work-related tasks
> Avocational interests
> Special areas of interest
> Special areas of competence
> History of career successes or failures
> Situational constraints

*Questions That You May Ask*

> What did you like or dislike about your prior current employment?
> What did you do especially well in that job? other jobs?
> How does your educational level match with the skills demanded in your recent jobs?
> Which job category best fits in with your values?
> Do your leisure interests have any employment possibilities?

What do you consider an ideal job?
Do you have the energy to enter a new career?
What do you feel are your strong points?
What is your relationship with co-workers? supervisors?
What do you feel is your most important success?
Have there been any failures that have troubled you?
How do you spend your leisure time?

*Comments*

# III. EDUCATION/TRAINING

*Goal*

To explore how educational and/or training experiences can suggest skills and knowledge for career or other life transitions

*Areas to Explore*

Last grade completed
College/trade school attendance
Subjects like best/worst
Grades in school by subject area
Special achievements
Extracurricular activities

*Questions That You May Ask*

Was your education satisfactory? Unsatisfactory?
How has your education changed the way you think? feel? behave?
What did you learn in your educational program that you think you can use on the job? in other life roles?
Do you feel further education would prepare you for an employment opportunity or activity in an area you would enjoy?

*Comments*

# IV. VALUES

*Goals*

To explore the influence of values on career and other life transitions
To explore the client's hierarchy of importance of different life roles

*Areas to Explore*

Greatest work/life accomplishments
The most meaningful experience in your life
The most influential lessons in your life
Importance of work, family, leisure, and other major life roles
Dreams/hopes for self and family

Most disturbing life issue
Work, family, neighborhood, state, or national issue that receives your strongest support

*Questions That You May Ask*

What is most important in your life?
Who are the most important people in your life?
If you could be doing anything, what would you do?
How do you feel about your current major activities?

*Comments*

## V. ECONOMIC FACTORS

*Goal*

To explore area of financial support

*Areas to Explore*

Primary source of support
Other sources of support
Medical insurance
Other family members who work
Financial benefits client receives, i.e., SSDI, Medicaid,
Medicare, Workers' Compensation

*Questions That You May Ask*

What are your financial support systems?
What is your attitude toward getting help with your finances?
How concerned are you about your financial situation?
With what level of financial security do you need to fee comfortable?

*Comments*

## VI. DISABILITY FACTORS

*Goal*

When appropriate, explore the nature of the client' disability and its impact on life adjustment or career transition.

*Areas to Explore*

Client's understanding of limitations associated with disability
Client's physical, emotional, and intellectual strengths
Client's ability to face problems associated with a disability
Client's transfer of skills from education to employment task

*Questions That You May Ask*

What do you feel are your strong points?
What have you learned from your work experience?
How did you handle your most difficult problems?
How did you manage a recent stress?
What do you believe are your limitations when you consider future employment?
How are you limited in your other life roles?

*Comments*

# VII. PSYCHOSOCIAL FACTORS

*Goal*

To explore how emotional factors, as well as environmental factors, affect an individual's life transitions

*Areas to Explore*

Client's self-knowledge
Client's ability to handle frustration, deal with difficult situations, pressure, or setbacks
Client's ability to cope with a disability or major life transitions
Client's perceived strengths and weaknesses
Client's struggle with current choices
Client's self-perception
Client's decision-making style and skills

*Questions That You May Ask*

What would you like to change/develop further?
What are some particularly difficult/happy moments in you life?
What ways do you find useful in managing stress?
How do you go about solving your problems?
What recent choice that you made has affected you in positive or negative manner?
How do you go about making decisions on major life issues?

*Comments*

# VIII. SOCIAL FACTORS

*Goal*

To explore the client's understanding of an environment that includes diversity of race and gender

*Areas to Explore*

Client's ability to care about others
Client's viewpoints about living with different cultures and genders
Client's tolerance of living among people with different beliefs and cultural backgrounds
Client's ability to cope with sharing and competitiveness

*Questions That You May Ask*

How do you spend your time each day?
How do you feel when you are in social situations?
Are you willing to take risks to make changes?
When you want something, do you have the patience to delay that need?
How do you react to competitiveness?
How do you feel about people of different cultures? different gender?

*Comments*

## IX. SERVICES NEEDED

*Goal*

When appropriate, ensure availability of services for independent functioning within the client's potentiality.

*Areas to Explore*

Physical therapy/occupational therapy/speech and hearing
Job modification
Counseling
Work placement
Education
Training
Economic support (SSI, food stamps, etc.)

*Questions That You May Ask*

Do you have a need for physical therapy or other rehabilitative services?
Would job or home modifications allow you to perform necessary tasks?
Would counseling help you to attain a smoother employment or other life transition?
Would work placement help your growth and development?
With further education/training would you be more employable?
Do you need economic support? For what purposes?

*Comments*

## X. FAMILY

*Goal*

To determine the role of the family in supporting a client in transition.

*Areas to Explore*

Expectations from family members for client's life transition
Family member's knowledge of transition factors
Family resources to cope with a transition
Family roles affecting the client's transition
Family's acceptance of client's transition or potential change

*Questions That You May Ask*

What do you feel are your strengths as a family?
When they found out about your desire for a transition, what did you as a family do?
How do you perceive your family as a source of support? as a barrier?
What duties or activities do you expect your disabled family member to perform around the house?
Has life in your family been better for you since the occurrence of the transition?
How supportive is your family with your pursuit of your chosen life goals?

*Comments*

# XI. ENVIRONMENT

*Goals*

To determine the role of the physical environment in supporting a client in transition
To determine the role of the social environment in supporting a client in transition.

*Areas to Explore*

Physical environment
Social environment

*Questions That You May Ask*

How would you describe your immediate environment? size? power distribution? community? work? school?
What do you like about where you live? work? go to school? seek entertainment?
What do you dislike about where you live? work? go to school? seek entertainment?
How many friends do you have?

*Comments*

# Author Index

# Subject Index

Accreditation, of academic programs, 33
Achievement tests, goal of, 130
Action groups, work of, 219
Action for Mental Health report, 10
Actualization, as aim of counseling, 111
Adjustment, as aim of counseling, 111
Advocacy, 289–294
  administrative-level advocacy, 291
  alternatives to, 293–294
  basic premises of, 289
  case advocacy, 291
  and community counselor, 289–290, 292–294
  criticisms for community level, 289
  definition of, 290–291
  and interests groups, 290
  intervention levels, 291
  policy advocacy, 291
  and program evaluation, 299
  role of advocate, 290
  self-advocacy, 294
  skills related to, 292–293
  strategies for, 291
  surrogate parents, 291
Age, and problems of living, 109–110
Alcohol, Drug Abuse, and Mental Health
    Administration, 12
Alcoholics Anonymous, 8, 176, 210
  as basis for employee assistance programs, 52
Altruism, and group treatment, 208–209
American Association for Counseling and
    Development, 16
American Counseling Association (ACA), 16, 31,
    33, 71
American Counseling Association Code of Ethics
    and Standards of Practice, 62, 75–94
American Mental Health Counselors Association,
    22, 71
American Personnel and Guidance Association
    (APGA), 16
Anal stage, 96
Antianxiety drugs, 177
  categories of, 177
Antidepressants, 177
  categories of, 177
Antipsychotic drugs, 177

indications for, 177
Anxiety, medications for, 177
APTICOM, 131
Aptitude assessment, 130–131
  APTICOM, 131
  Armed Services Vocational Aptitude Battery,
    131
  Differential Aptitude Tests, 131
  General Aptitude Test Battery, 131
  goal of, 130
  interviews, 131
  limitations of, 131
  paper and pencil tests, 130–131
  performance tests, 131
  SAGE, 131
  work samples, 131
Armed Services Vocational Aptitude Battery, 131
Assertion training, 220–221
Assessment. *See* Client assessment
Association for Counselor Education and
    Supervision, 21–22
Association for Specialists in Group Work,
    205–206
Attitudes
  cause of attitudes and intervention, 153–154
  definition of, 153
  elements in formation of, 154
  relationship to behavior, 153
Attitudes assessment, 153–155
  Attitudes Toward Disabled Persons Scale,
    155
  Attitudes Toward Feminism and the Women's
    Movement Scale, 155
  Attitudes Toward Women Scale, 155
  Sex-Role Egalitarian Scale, 155
Attitudes Toward Disabled Persons Scale, 155
Attitudes Toward Feminism and the Women's
    Movement Scale, 155
Autonomy, in Erikson's theory, 99

Behavioral assessment, aspects of, 131
Behavioral technology, types of, 319
Behavioral theory
  of human development, 96
  problems with approach, 110–111